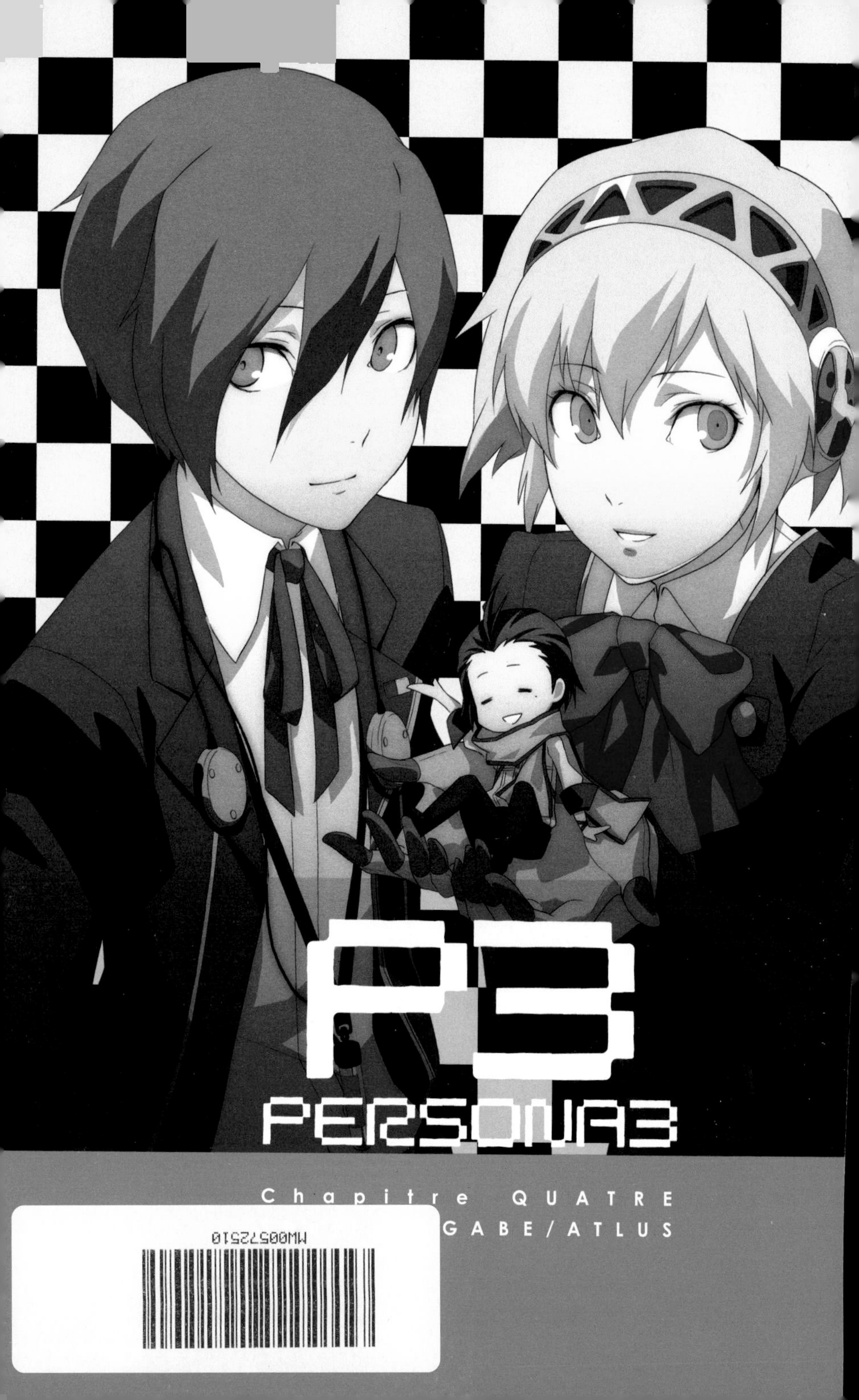

P3 PERSONA3

Chapitre QUATRE

GABE/ATLUS

story

While the actual series of events began ten years ago, it was eight years ago that Mitsuru first summoned her Persona. As of July 2009, the members of S.E.E.S. were continuing their fight against the Shadows while pursuing the truth behind it all.

The members of S.E.E.S. were treated to a generous serving of the truth courtesy of Mitsuru's father when they all visited the Kirijo family's cottage. This led to Yukari watching a video message recorded by her father ten years ago.

S.E.E.S. managed to defeat the final Greater Shadow in November of 2009, but the Dark Hour continued to cycle in every night. It was only then that Chairman Ikutsuki revealed his true objective, which was in direct contrast to everything the S.E.E.S. members had believed to be true.

Mitsuru and Yukari discovered that both of their fathers had been victimized by the same series of events. Their newfound conviction to follow in their fathers' footsteps allowed both Mitsuru's and Yukari's Personas to evolve.

Co-ed baths are every male's dream.

2008 06~10
COMIC
151/162p
93.2%
monochrome
B6

P3 PERSONA3
#14 Plot:01
Fragments PLOT01

P3 PERSONA3
#15 Plot:02
フラグメンツ パート2
発売前夜祭／制作・アトラス

P3 PERSONA3
#16 Plot:03
願いは延べた手よりも遥か
Fragments Pl:03 To sink or Go far

P3 PERSONA3
#17 Perspective:03
然れど想い は細やかな光
The last Fragment Primal love

P3 PERSONA3
#18 Perspective:03.5
それではみなさんさようなら
作・アトラス

Subtitle logo

Eigh Years go

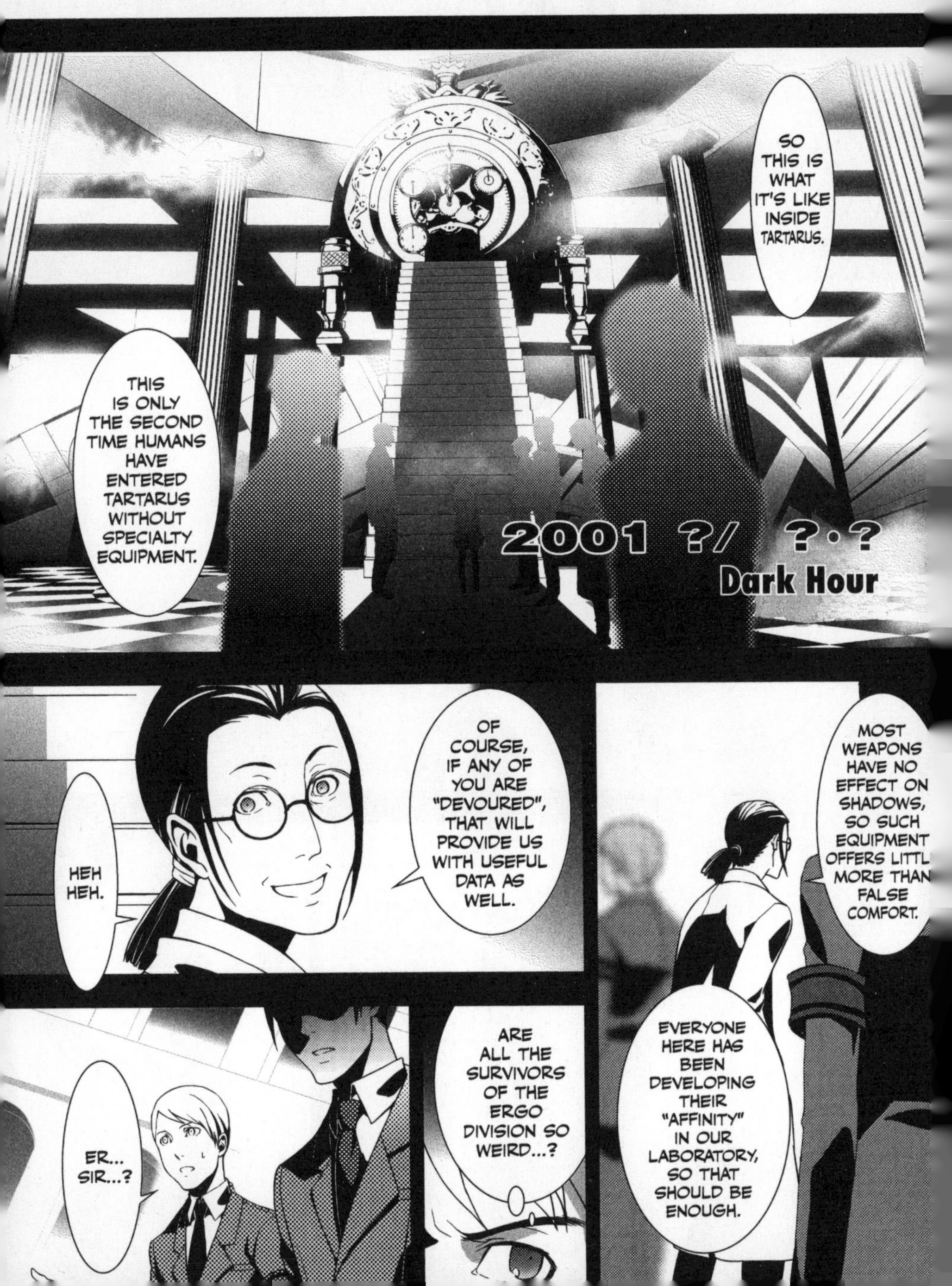
SO THIS IS WHAT IT'S LIKE INSIDE TARTARUS.
2001 ?/ ?·?
Dark Hour
THIS IS ONLY THE SECOND TIME HUMANS HAVE ENTERED TARTARUS WITHOUT SPECIALTY EQUIPMENT.
MOST WEAPONS HAVE NO EFFECT ON SHADOWS, SO SUCH EQUIPMENT OFFERS LITTL MORE THAN FALSE COMFORT.
EVERYONE HERE HAS BEEN DEVELOPING THEIR "AFFINITY" IN OUR LABORATORY, SO THAT SHOULD BE ENOUGH.
OF COURSE, IF ANY OF YOU ARE "DEVOURED", THAT WILL PROVIDE US WITH USEFUL DATA AS WELL.
HEH HEH.
ARE ALL THE SURVIVORS OF THE ERGO DIVISION SO WEIRD...?
ER... SIR...?

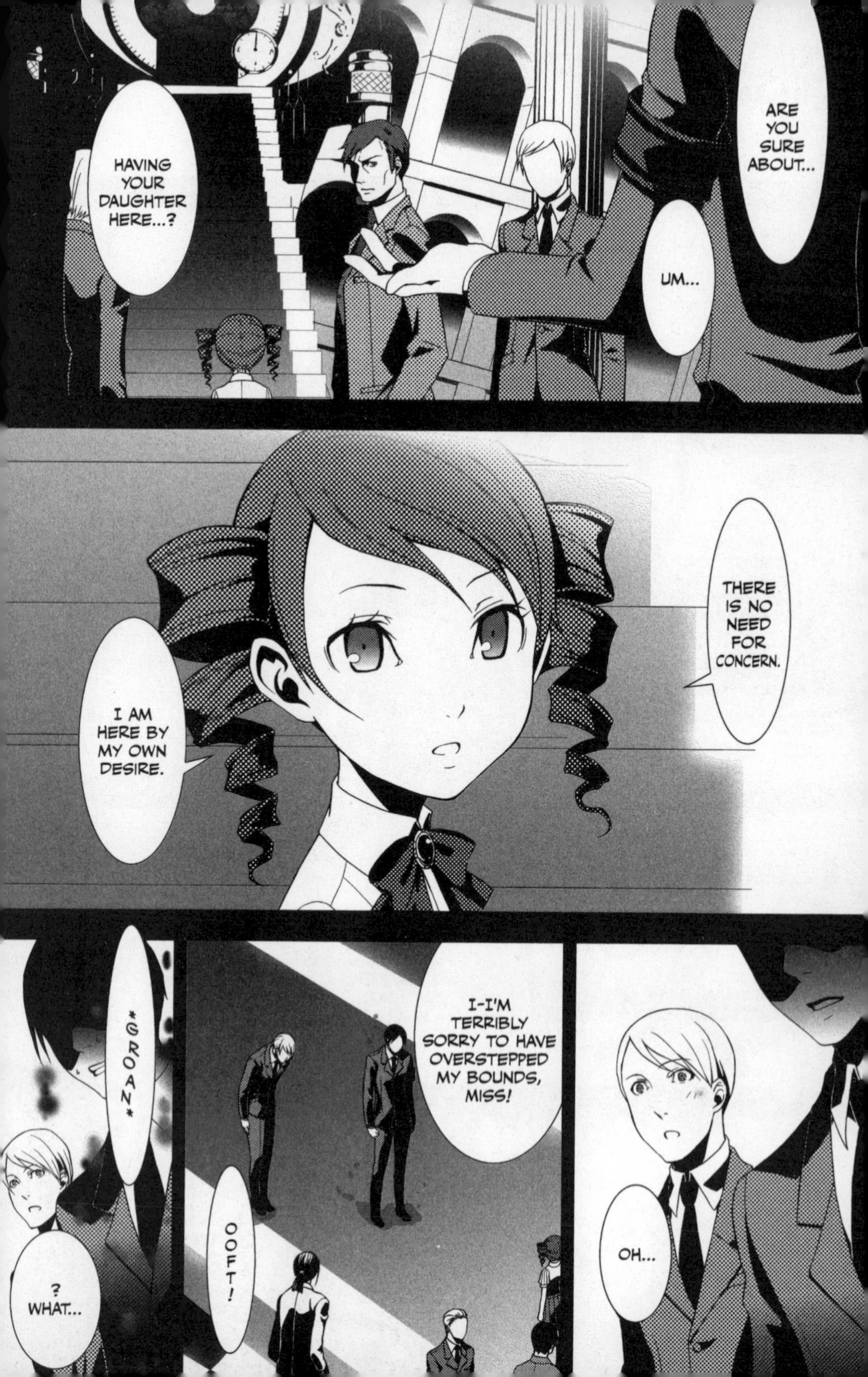
ARE YOU SURE ABOUT...
UM...
HAVING YOUR DAUGHTER HERE...?
THERE IS NO NEED FOR CONCERN.
I AM HERE BY MY OWN DESIRE.
OH...
I-I'M TERRIBLY SORRY TO HAVE OVERSTEPPED MY BOUNDS, MISS!
OOFT!
GROAN
? WHAT...

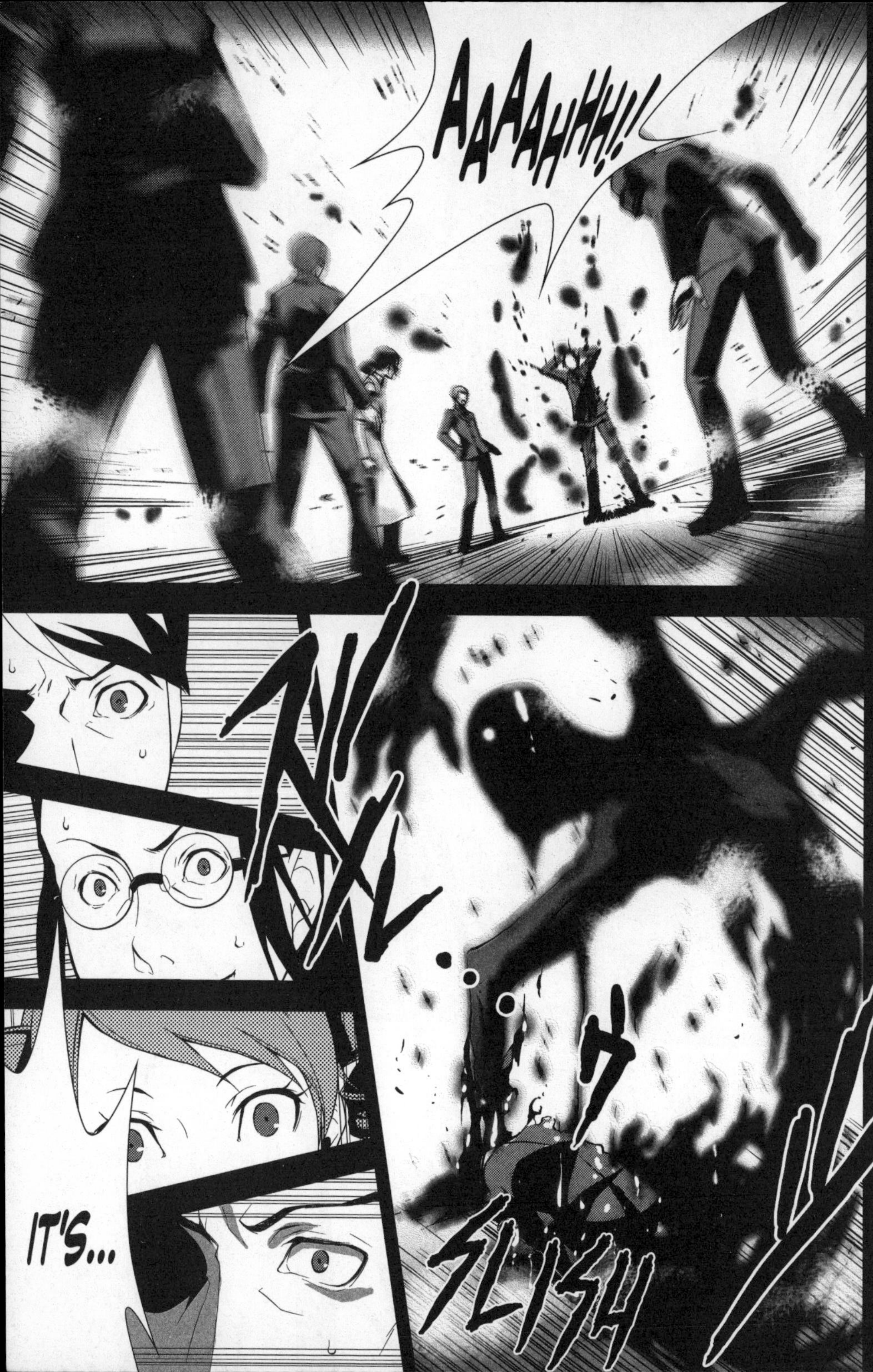
AAAAHHH!!
SLISH
IT'S...

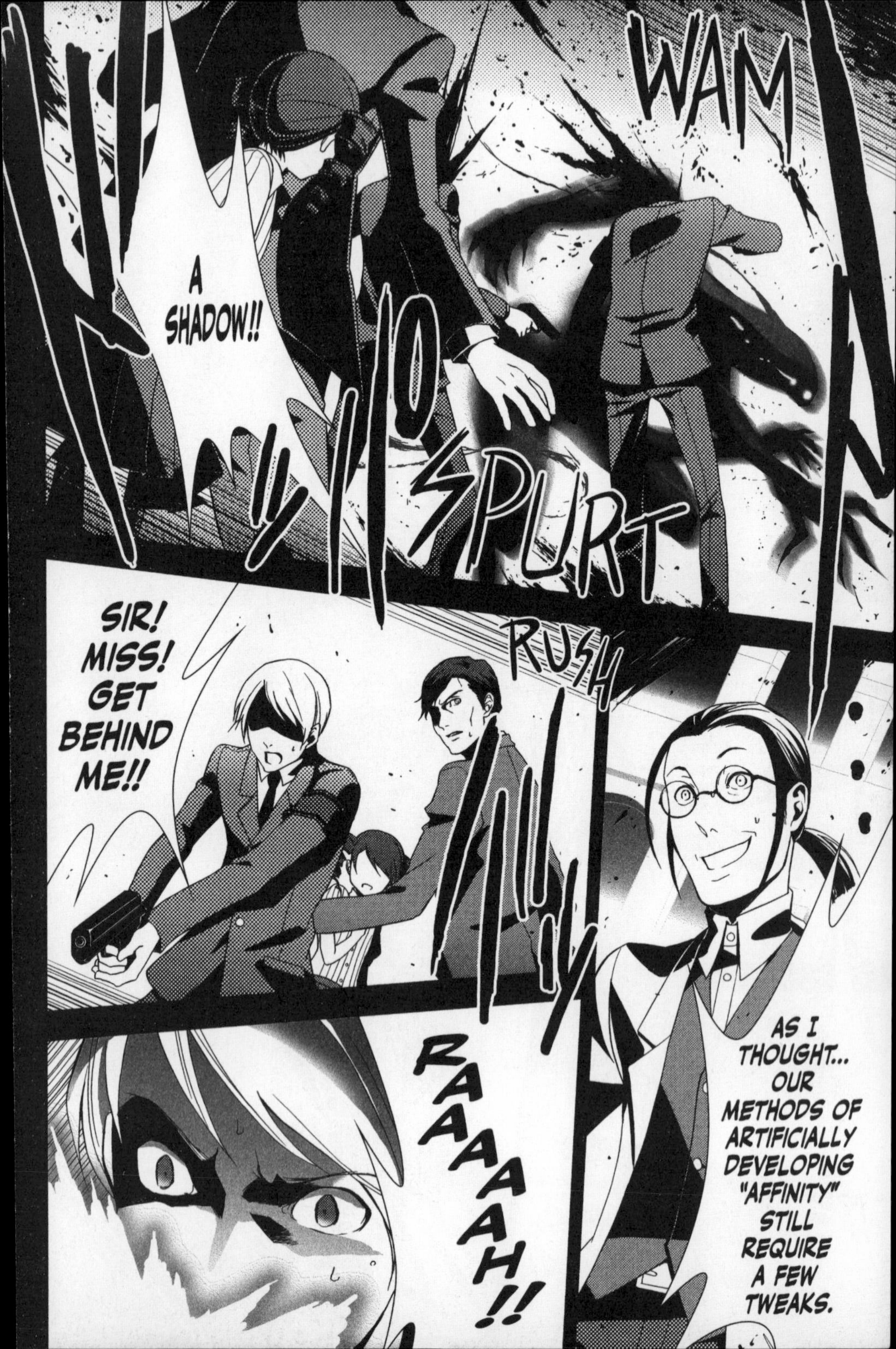
WAM
A SHADOW!!
SPURT
AS I THOUGHT... OUR METHODS OF ARTIFICIALLY DEVELOPING "AFFINITY" STILL REQUIRE A FEW TWEAKS.
RUSH
SIR! MISS! GET BEHIND ME!!
RAAAAAH!!

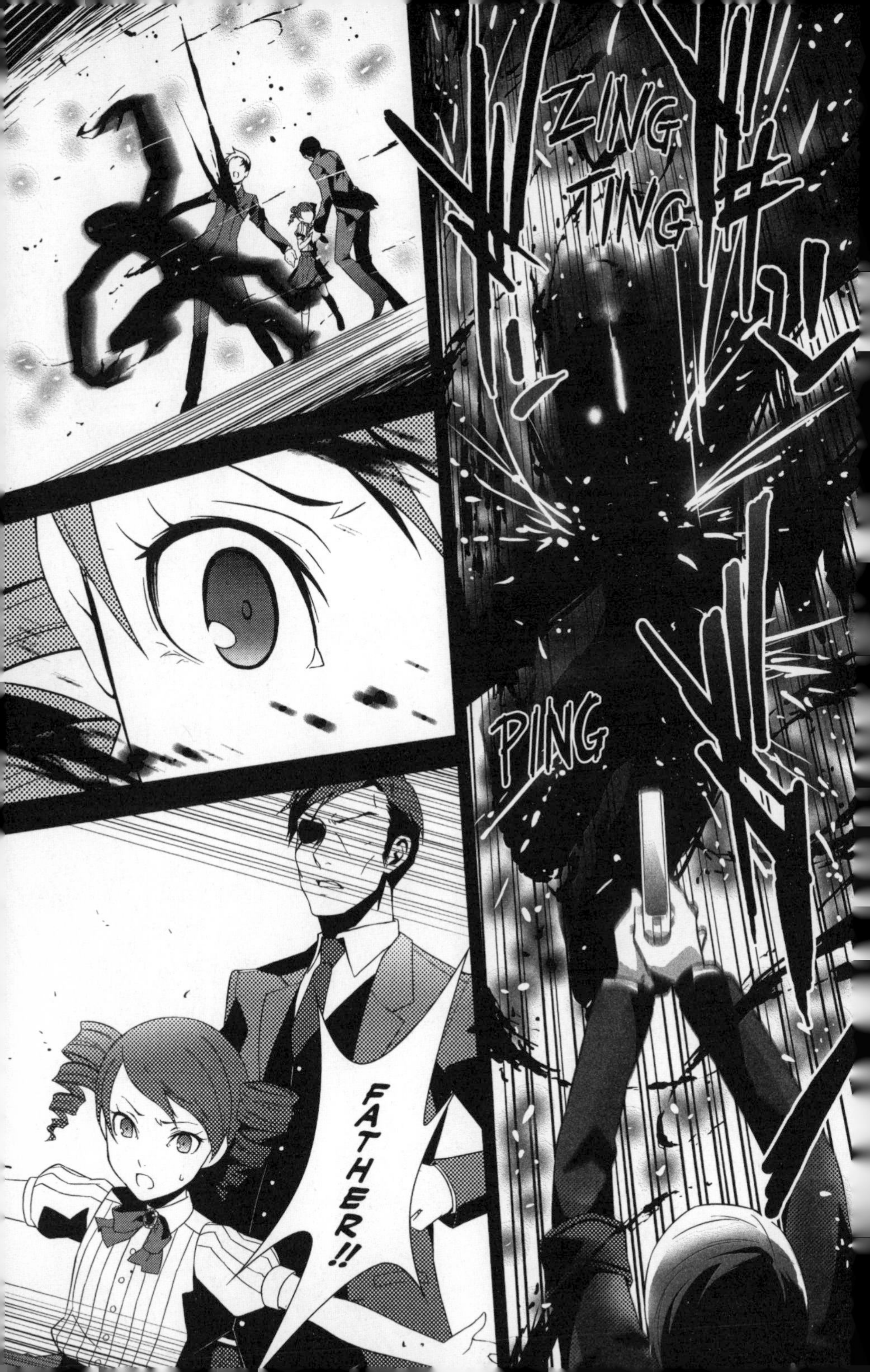
ZING
TING
PING
FATHER!!

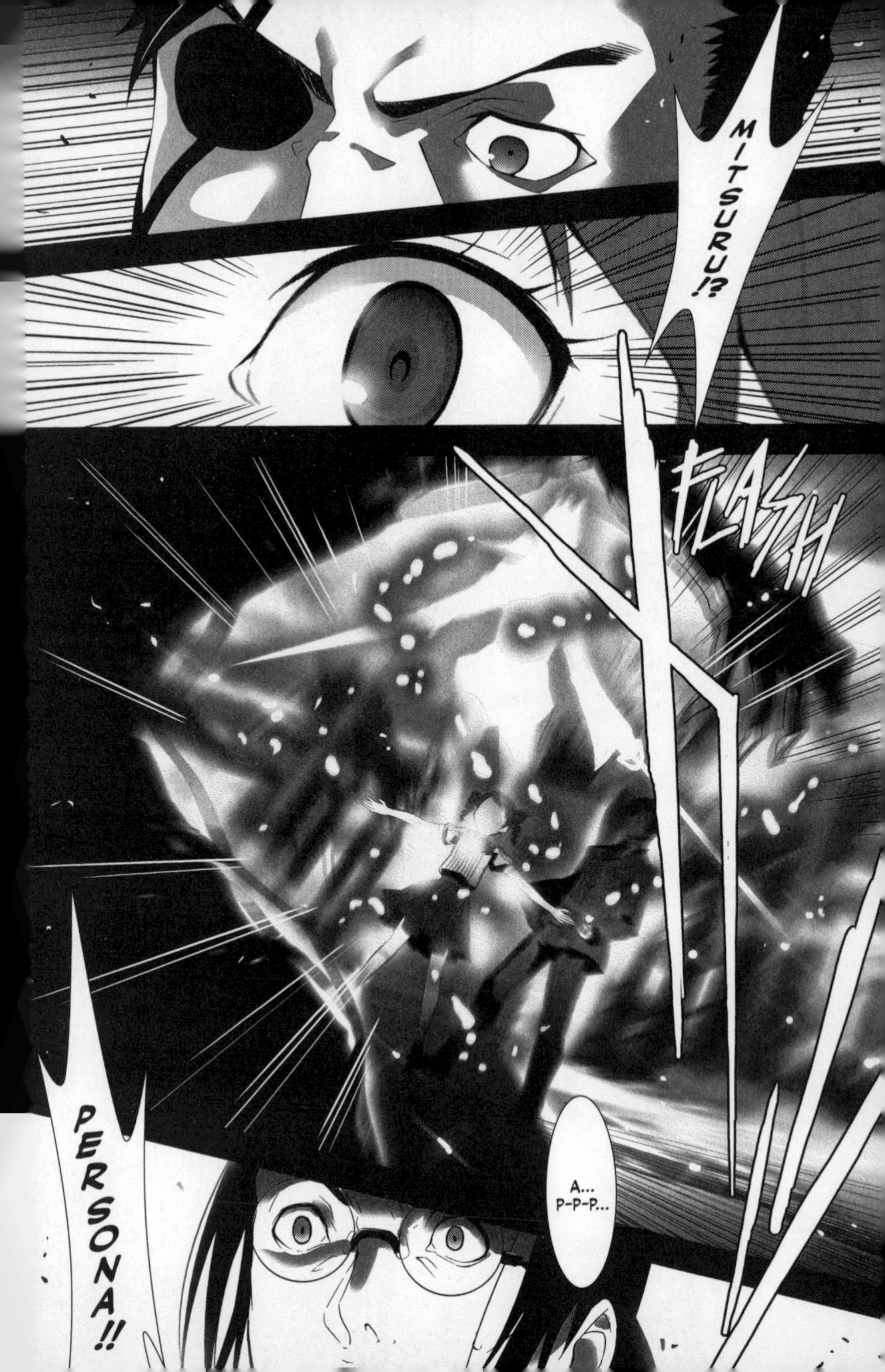
MITSURU!?
FLASH
A... P-P-P...
PERSONA!!

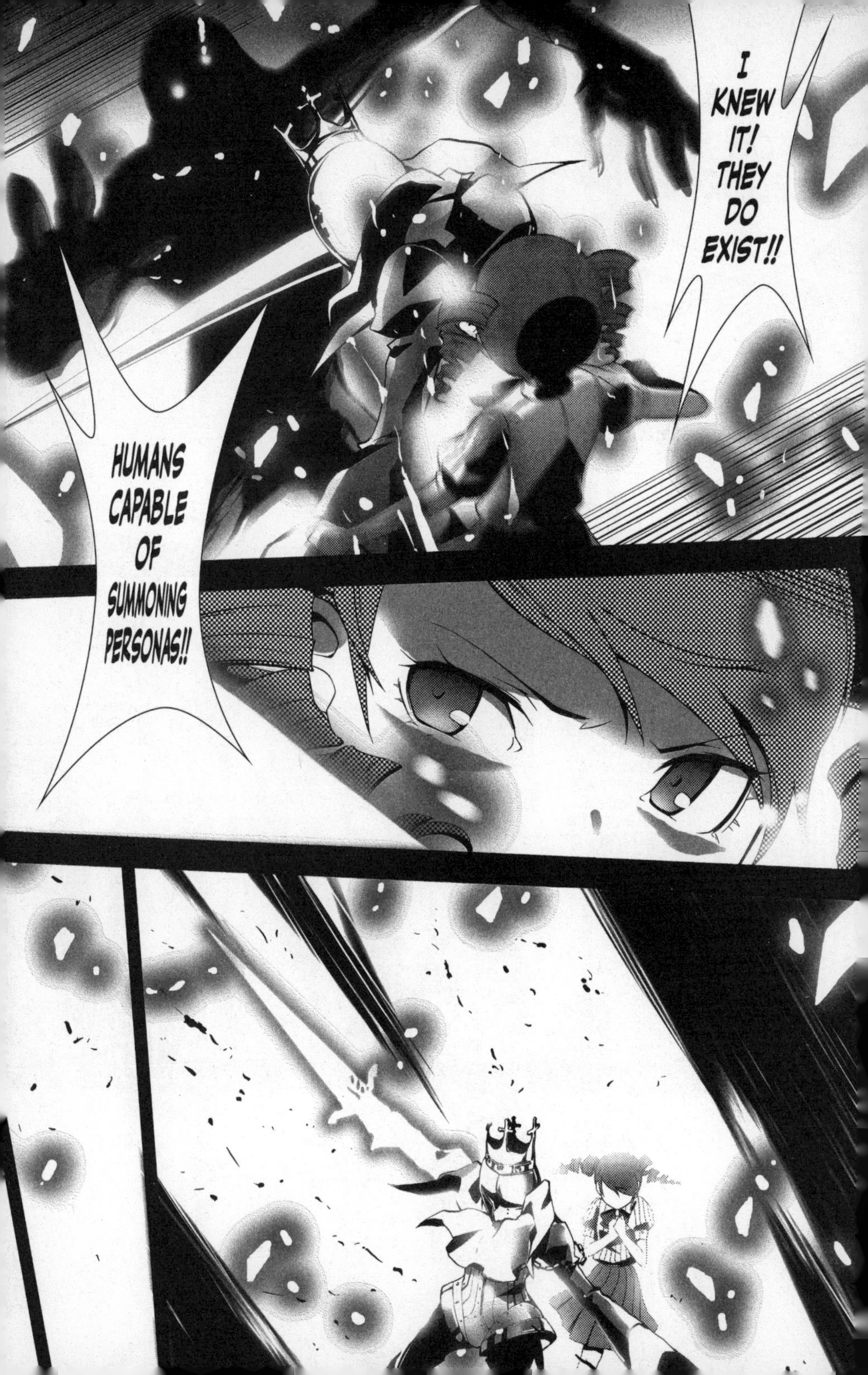

I KNEW IT! THEY DO EXIST!!
HUMANS CAPABLE OF SUMMONING PERSONAS!!

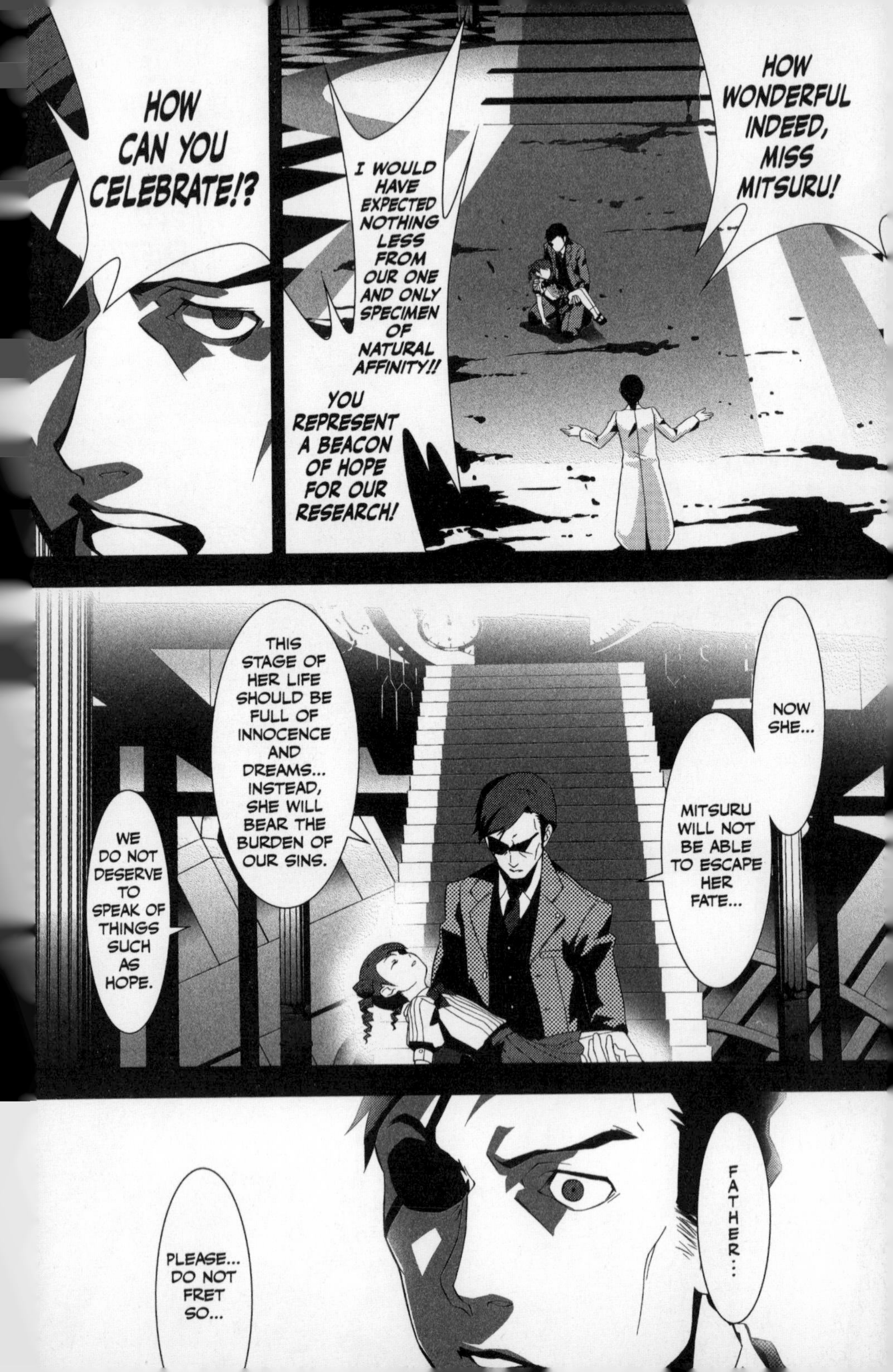
HOW WONDERFUL INDEED, MISS MITSURU!
I WOULD HAVE EXPECTED NOTHING LESS FROM OUR ONE AND ONLY SPECIMEN OF NATURAL AFFINITY!!
YOU REPRESENT A BEACON OF HOPE FOR OUR RESEARCH!
HOW CAN YOU CELEBRATE!?
NOW SHE...
MITSURU WILL NOT BE ABLE TO ESCAPE HER FATE...
THIS STAGE OF HER LIFE SHOULD BE FULL OF INNOCENCE AND DREAMS... INSTEAD, SHE WILL BEAR THE BURDEN OF OUR SINS.
WE DO NOT DESERVE TO SPEAK OF THINGS SUCH AS HOPE.
FATHER...
PLEASE... DO NOT FRET SO...

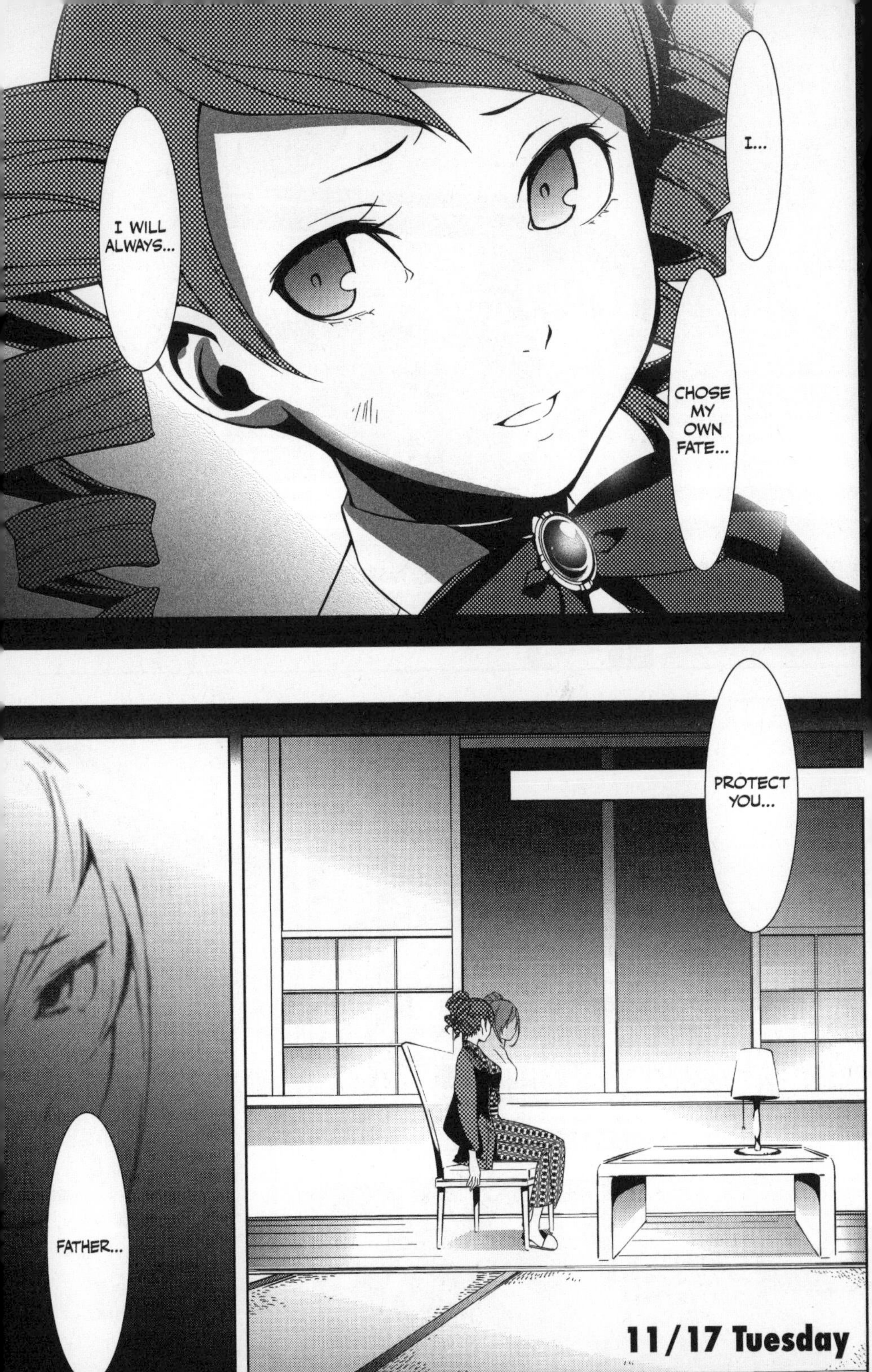
I...
CHOSE MY OWN FATE...
I WILL ALWAYS...
PROTECT YOU...
FATHER...
11/17 Tuesday

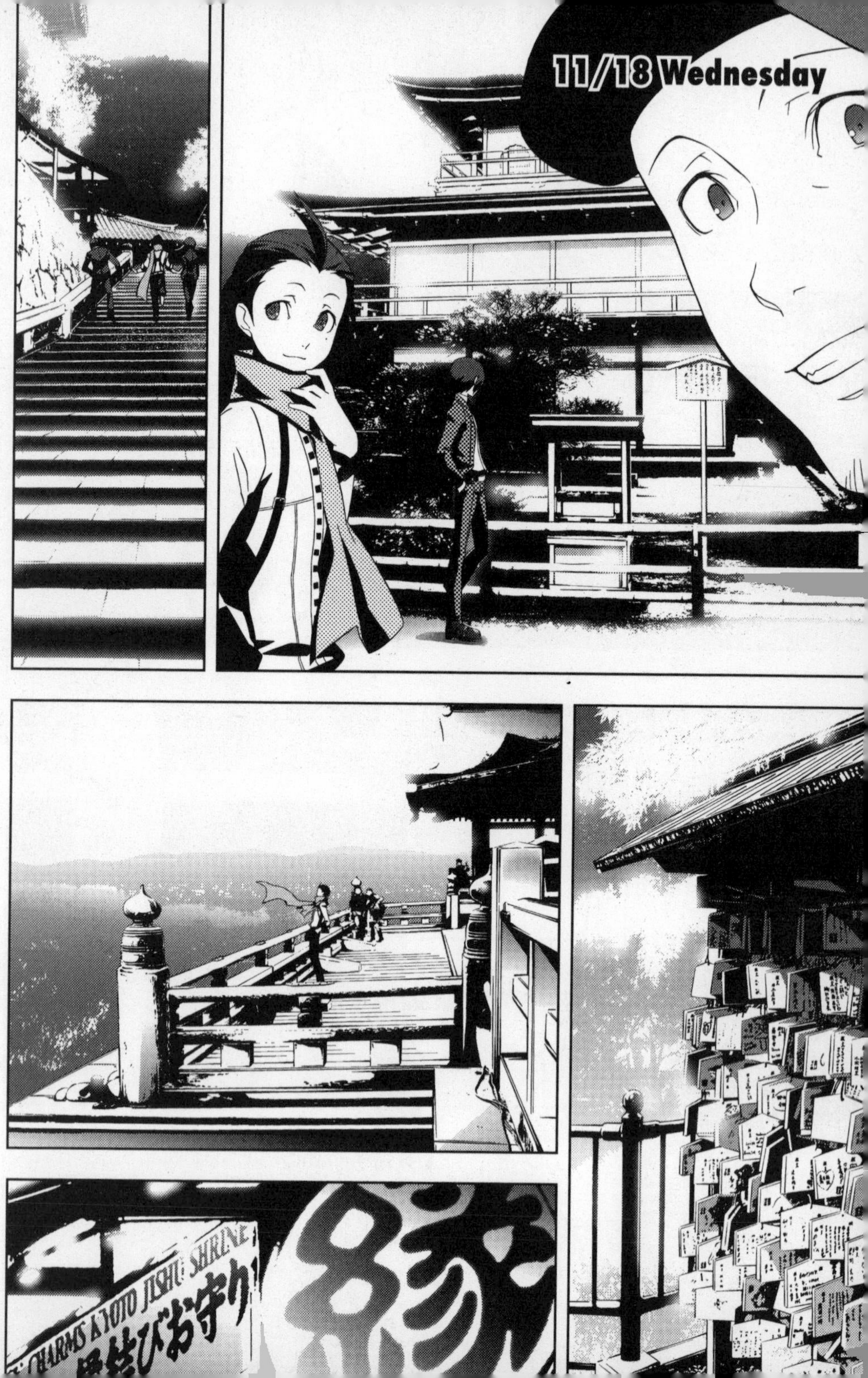

11/18 Wednesday
CHARMS KYOTO JISHU SHRINE
結びお守り

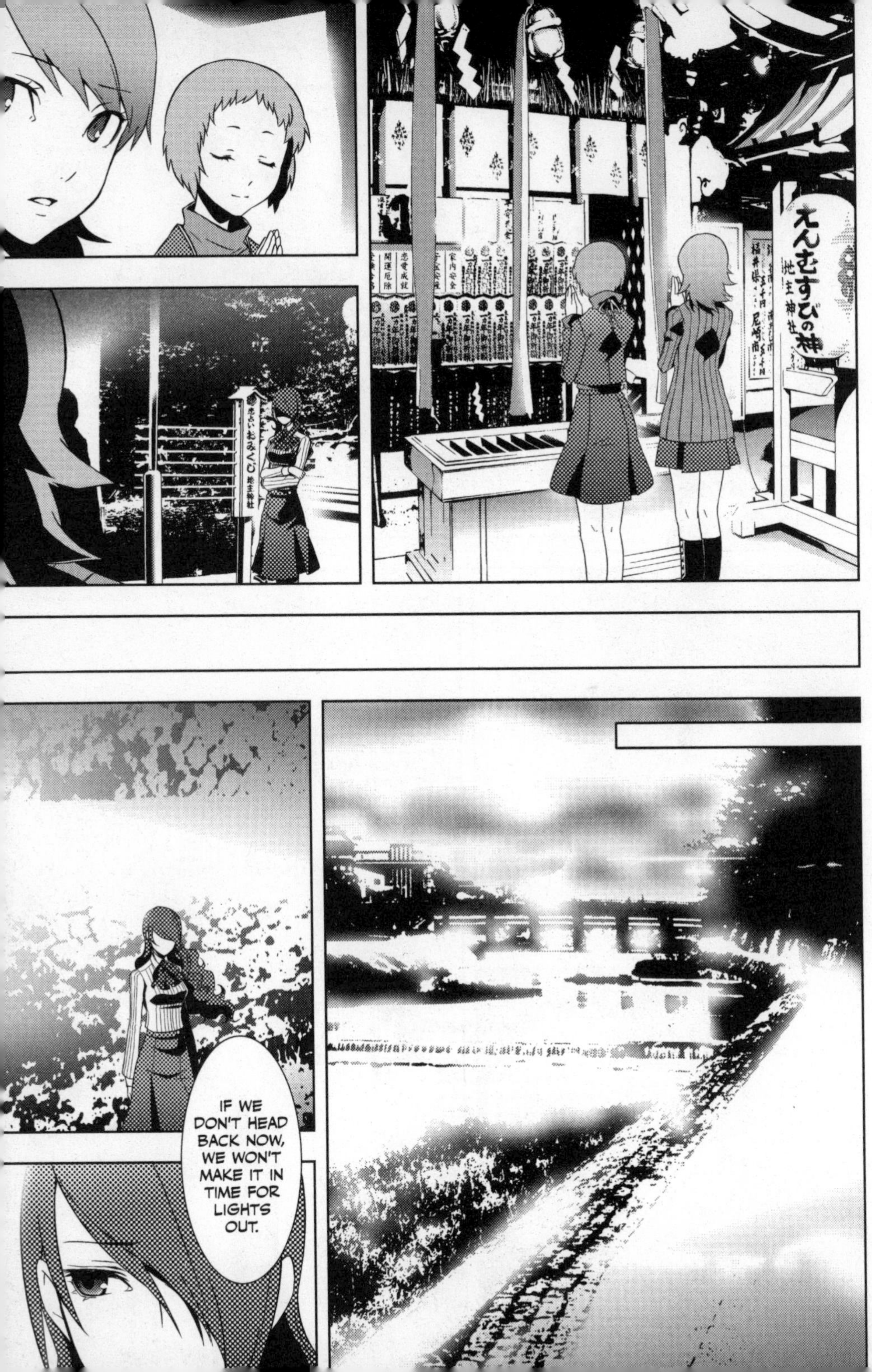
えんむすびの神
地主神社
IF WE DON'T HEAD BACK NOW, WE WON'T MAKE IT IN TIME FOR LIGHTS OUT.

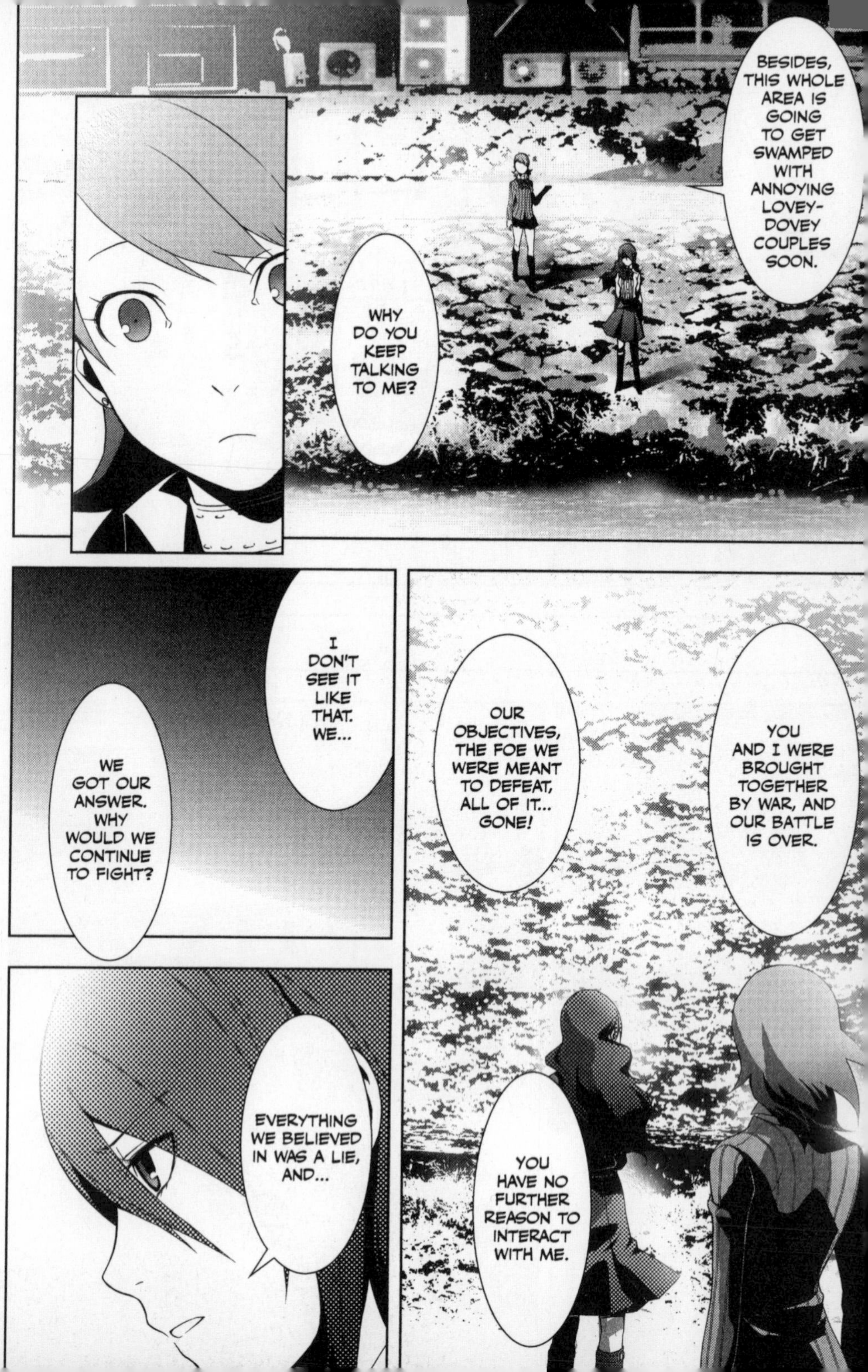
BESIDES, THIS WHOLE AREA IS GOING TO GET SWAMPED WITH ANNOYING LOVEY-DOVEY COUPLES SOON.
WHY DO YOU KEEP TALKING TO ME?
YOU AND I WERE BROUGHT TOGETHER BY WAR, AND OUR BATTLE IS OVER.
OUR OBJECTIVES, THE FOE WE WERE MEANT TO DEFEAT, ALL OF IT... GONE!
YOU HAVE NO FURTHER REASON TO INTERACT WITH ME.
I DON'T SEE IT LIKE THAT. WE...
WE GOT OUR ANSWER. WHY WOULD WE CONTINUE TO FIGHT?
EVERYTHING WE BELIEVED IN WAS A LIE, AND...

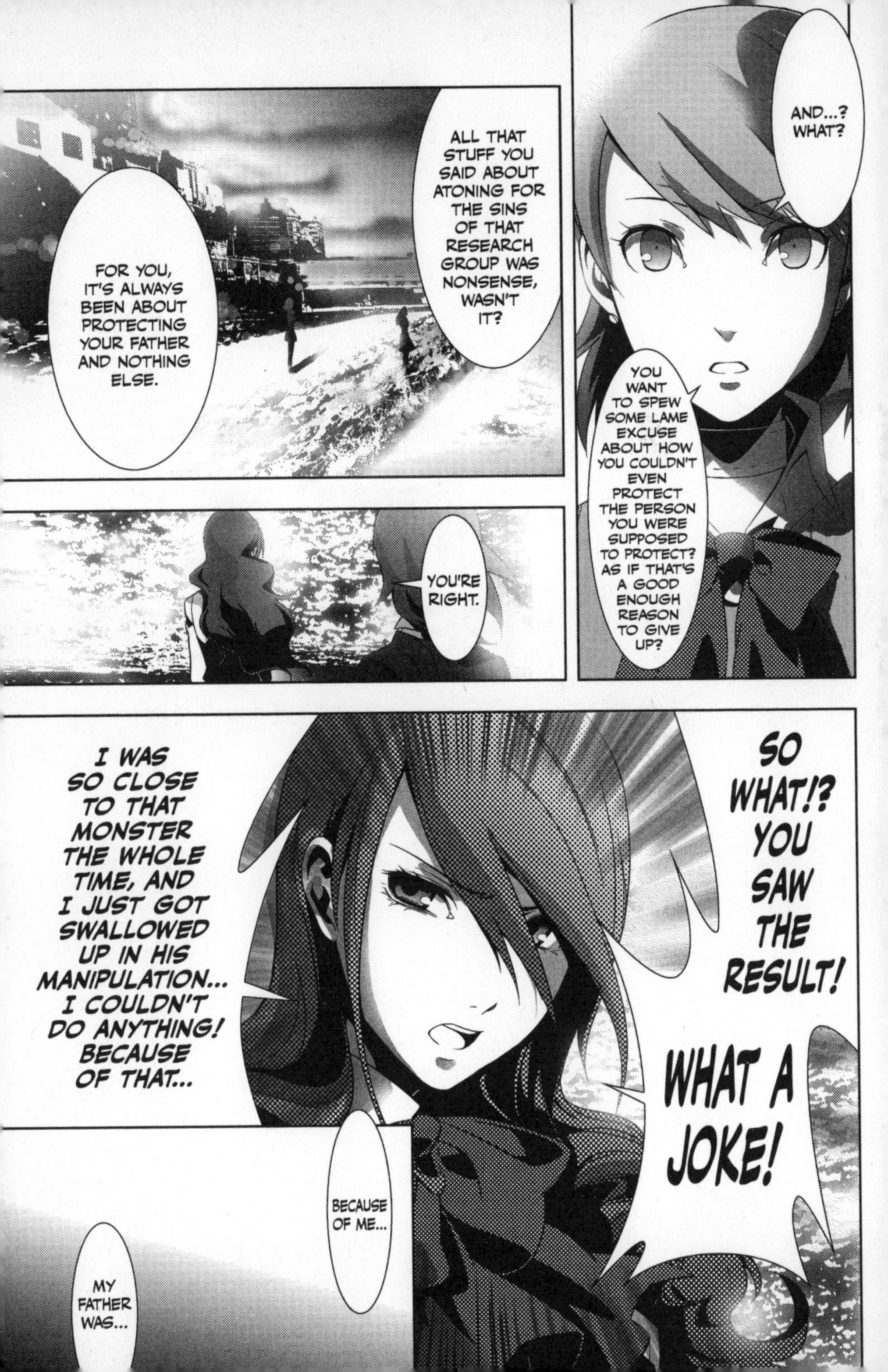
AND...? WHAT?
YOU WANT TO SPEW SOME LAME EXCUSE ABOUT HOW YOU COULDN'T EVEN PROTECT THE PERSON YOU WERE SUPPOSED TO PROTECT? AS IF THAT'S A GOOD ENOUGH REASON TO GIVE UP?
ALL THAT STUFF YOU SAID ABOUT ATONING FOR THE SINS OF THAT RESEARCH GROUP WAS NONSENSE, WASN'T IT?
FOR YOU, IT'S ALWAYS BEEN ABOUT PROTECTING YOUR FATHER AND NOTHING ELSE.
YOU'RE RIGHT.
SO WHAT!? YOU SAW THE RESULT!
WHAT A JOKE!
I WAS SO CLOSE TO THAT MONSTER THE WHOLE TIME, AND I JUST GOT SWALLOWED UP IN HIS MANIPULATION... I COULDN'T DO ANYTHING! BECAUSE OF THAT...
BECAUSE OF ME...
MY FATHER WAS...

P3

PERSONA3

#14 Plot:01

Fragments Pt:01
フラグメンツ　パート1

曽我部修司　原作／アトラス
Design & Finished : Studio Shortcake Screamer

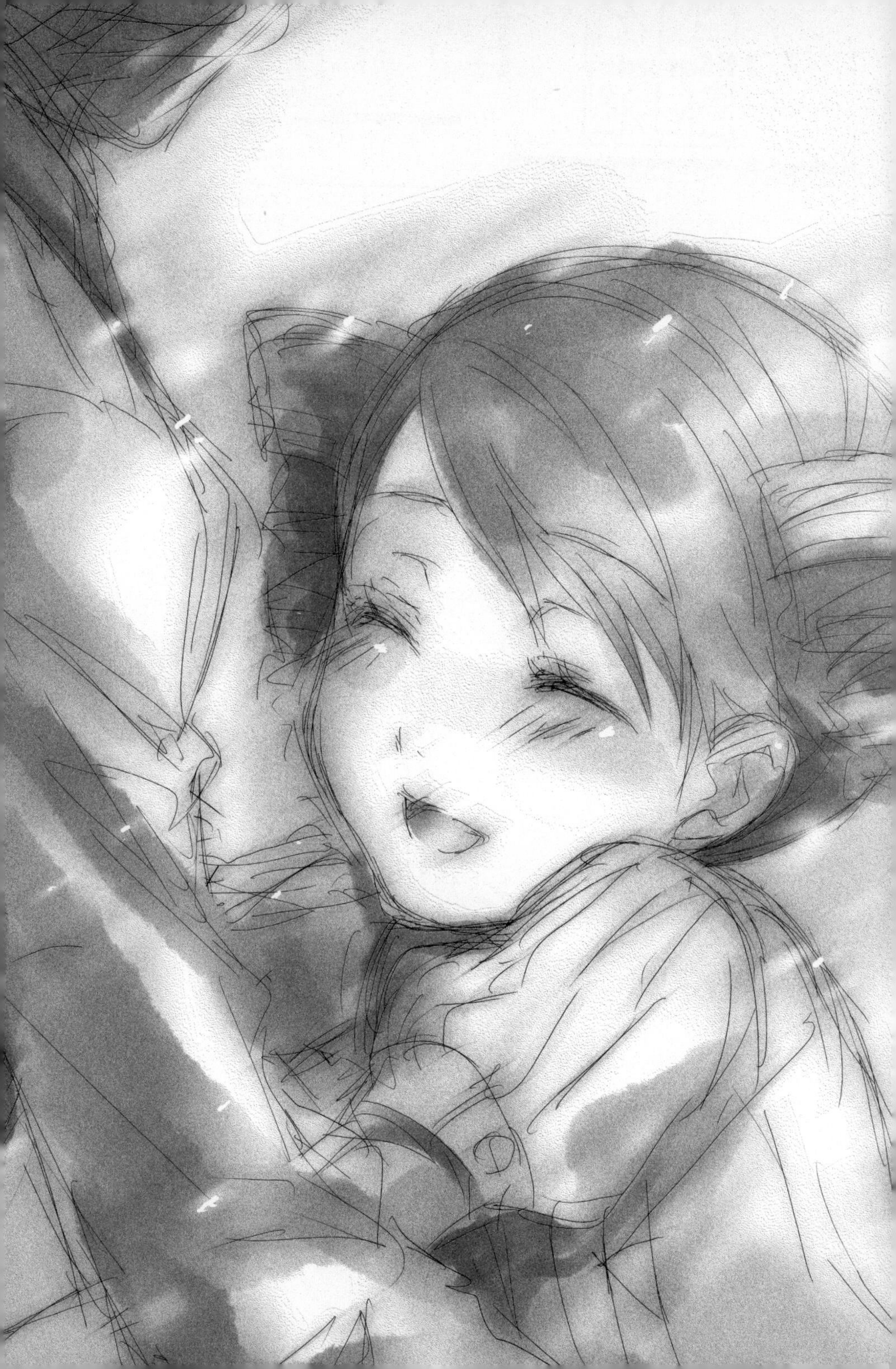

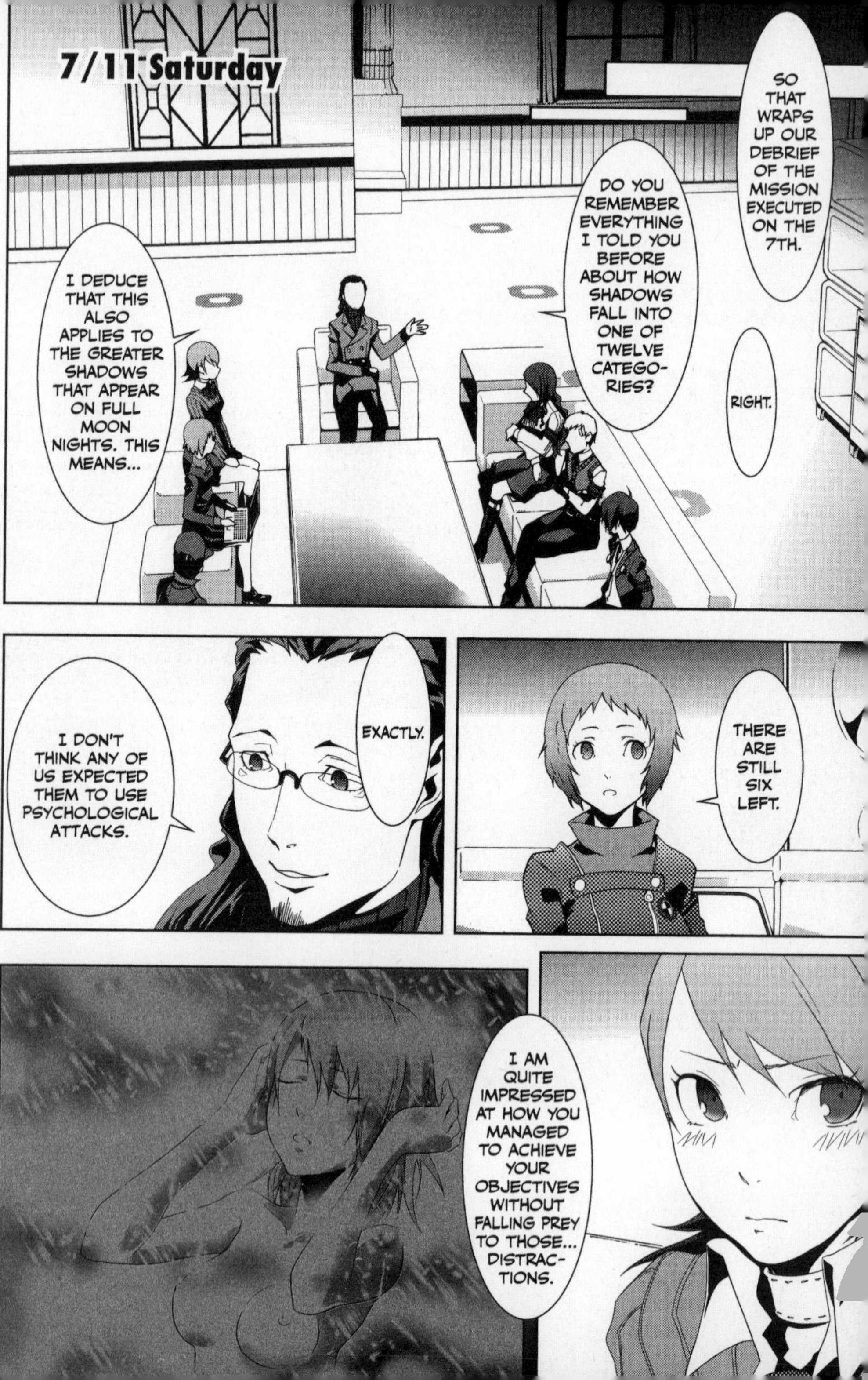
7/11 Saturday
SO THAT WRAPS UP OUR DEBRIEF OF THE MISSION EXECUTED ON THE 7TH.
DO YOU REMEMBER EVERYTHING I TOLD YOU BEFORE ABOUT HOW SHADOWS FALL INTO ONE OF TWELVE CATEGO-RIES?
RIGHT.
I DEDUCE THAT THIS ALSO APPLIES TO THE GREATER SHADOWS THAT APPEAR ON FULL MOON NIGHTS. THIS MEANS...
THERE ARE STILL SIX LEFT.
EXACTLY.
I DON'T THINK ANY OF US EXPECTED THEM TO USE PSYCHOLOGICAL ATTACKS.
I AM QUITE IMPRESSED AT HOW YOU MANAGED TO ACHIEVE YOUR OBJECTIVES WITHOUT FALLING PREY TO THOSE... DISTRAC-TIONS.

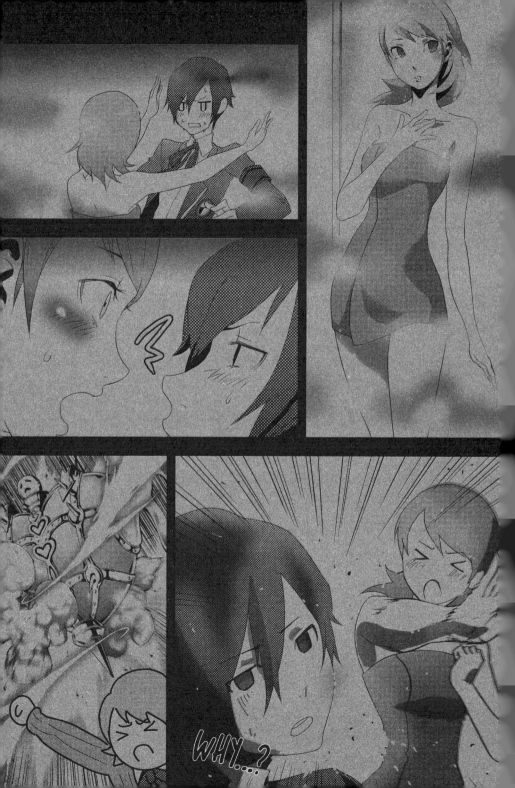

WHY...?

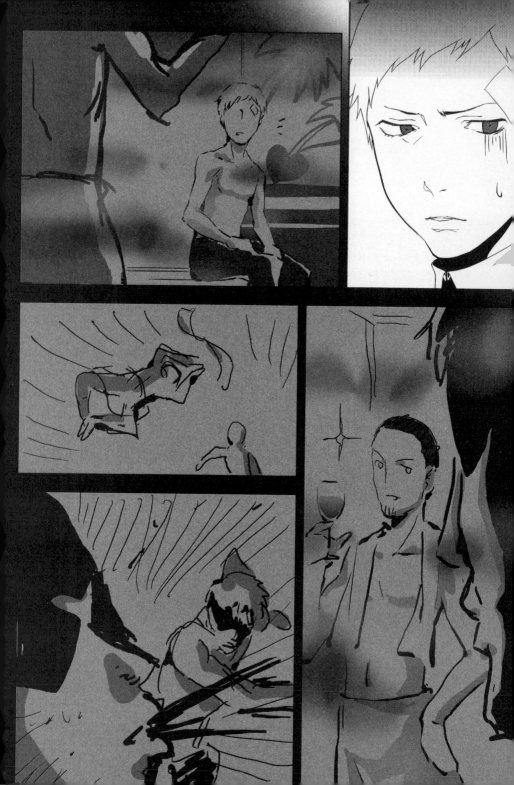

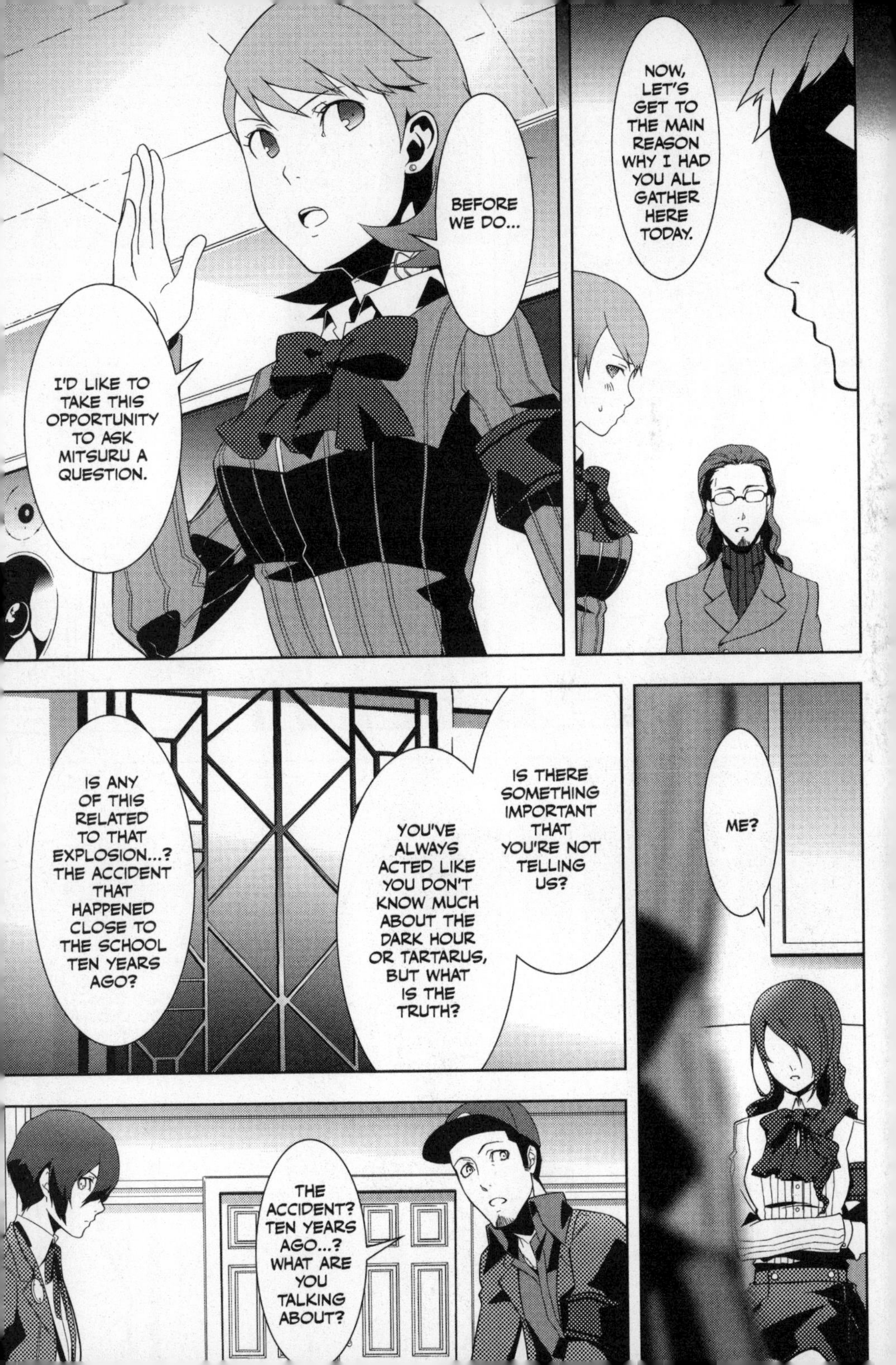
NOW, LET'S GET TO THE MAIN REASON WHY I HAD YOU ALL GATHER HERE TODAY.
BEFORE WE DO...
I'D LIKE TO TAKE THIS OPPORTUNITY TO ASK MITSURU A QUESTION.
ME?
IS THERE SOMETHING IMPORTANT THAT YOU'RE NOT TELLING US?
YOU'VE ALWAYS ACTED LIKE YOU DON'T KNOW MUCH ABOUT THE DARK HOUR OR TARTARUS, BUT WHAT IS THE TRUTH?
IS ANY OF THIS RELATED TO THAT EXPLOSION...? THE ACCIDENT THAT HAPPENED CLOSE TO THE SCHOOL TEN YEARS AGO?
THE ACCIDENT? TEN YEARS AGO...? WHAT ARE YOU TALKING ABOUT?

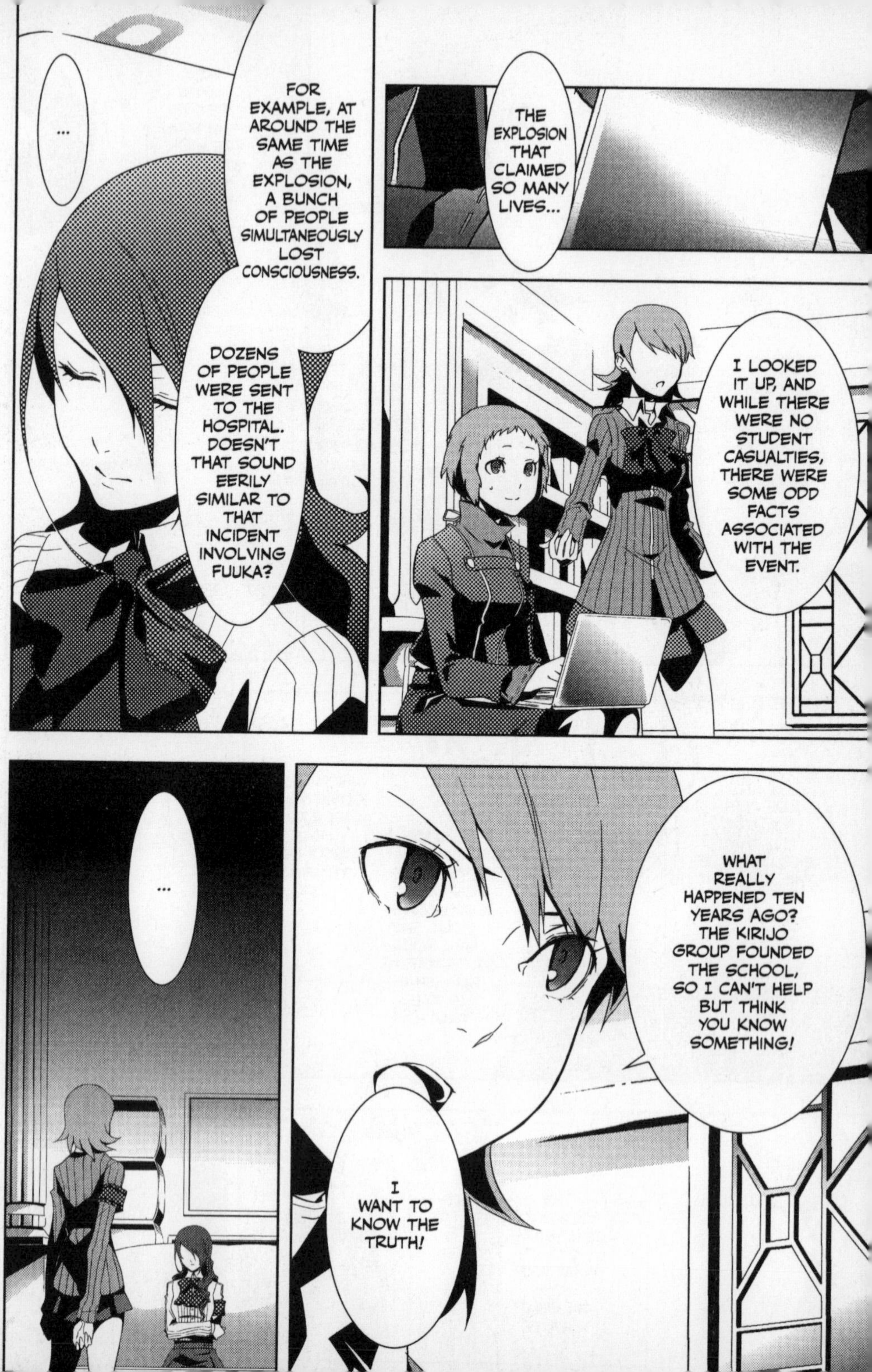
THE EXPLOSION THAT CLAIMED SO MANY LIVES...
I LOOKED IT UP, AND WHILE THERE WERE NO STUDENT CASUALTIES, THERE WERE SOME ODD FACTS ASSOCIATED WITH THE EVENT.
FOR EXAMPLE, AT AROUND THE SAME TIME AS THE EXPLOSION, A BUNCH OF PEOPLE SIMULTANEOUSLY LOST CONSCIOUSNESS.
...
DOZENS OF PEOPLE WERE SENT TO THE HOSPITAL. DOESN'T THAT SOUND EERILY SIMILAR TO THAT INCIDENT INVOLVING FUUKA?
WHAT REALLY HAPPENED TEN YEARS AGO? THE KIRIJO GROUP FOUNDED THE SCHOOL, SO I CAN'T HELP BUT THINK YOU KNOW SOMETHING!
I WANT TO KNOW THE TRUTH!
...

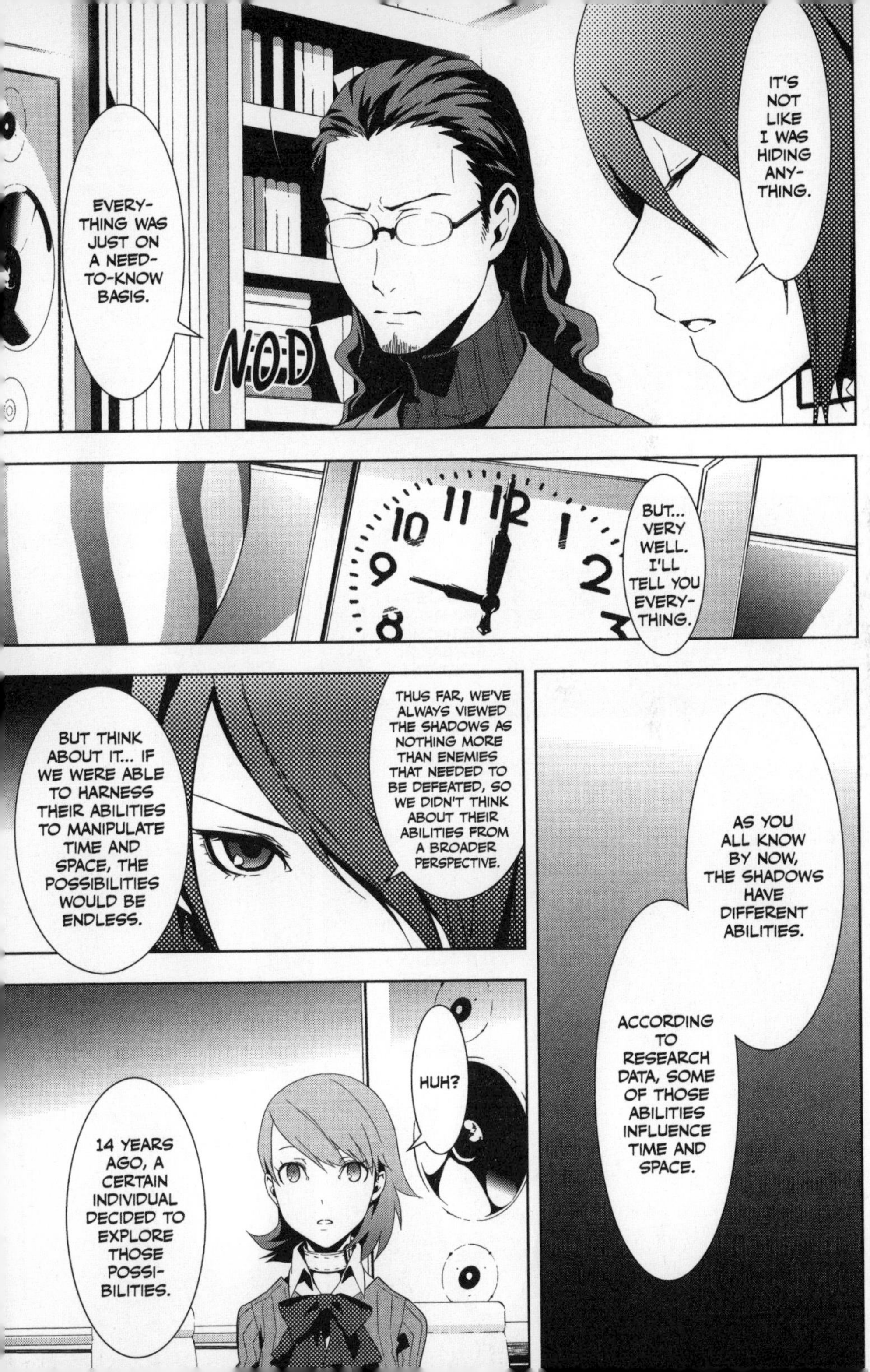

IT'S NOT LIKE I WAS HIDING ANYTHING.
EVERYTHING WAS JUST ON A NEED-TO-KNOW BASIS.
NOD
BUT... VERY WELL. I'LL TELL YOU EVERYTHING.
AS YOU ALL KNOW BY NOW, THE SHADOWS HAVE DIFFERENT ABILITIES.
ACCORDING TO RESEARCH DATA, SOME OF THOSE ABILITIES INFLUENCE TIME AND SPACE.
THUS FAR, WE'VE ALWAYS VIEWED THE SHADOWS AS NOTHING MORE THAN ENEMIES THAT NEEDED TO BE DEFEATED, SO WE DIDN'T THINK ABOUT THEIR ABILITIES FROM A BROADER PERSPECTIVE.
BUT THINK ABOUT IT... IF WE WERE ABLE TO HARNESS THEIR ABILITIES TO MANIPULATE TIME AND SPACE, THE POSSIBILITIES WOULD BE ENDLESS.
HUH?
14 YEARS AGO, A CERTAIN INDIVIDUAL DECIDED TO EXPLORE THOSE POSSIBILITIES.

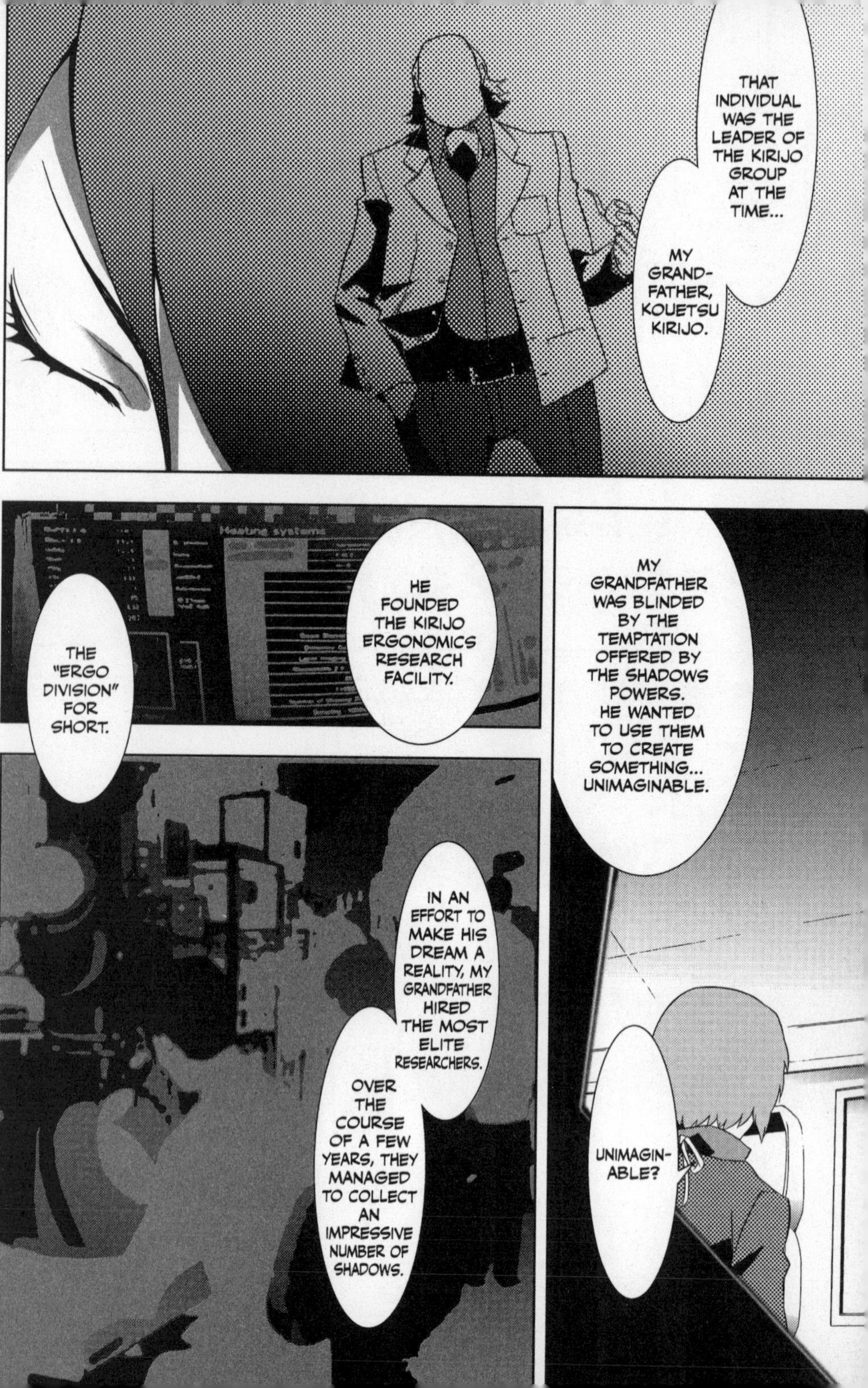

THAT INDIVIDUAL WAS THE LEADER OF THE KIRIJO GROUP AT THE TIME...
MY GRAND-FATHER, KOUETSU KIRIJO.
MY GRANDFATHER WAS BLINDED BY THE TEMPTATION OFFERED BY THE SHADOWS POWERS. HE WANTED TO USE THEM TO CREATE SOMETHING... UNIMAGINABLE.
UNIMAGIN-ABLE?
HE FOUNDED THE KIRIJO ERGONOMICS RESEARCH FACILITY.
THE "ERGO DIVISION" FOR SHORT.
IN AN EFFORT TO MAKE HIS DREAM A REALITY, MY GRANDFATHER HIRED THE MOST ELITE RESEARCHERS.
OVER THE COURSE OF A FEW YEARS, THEY MANAGED TO COLLECT AN IMPRESSIVE NUMBER OF SHADOWS.

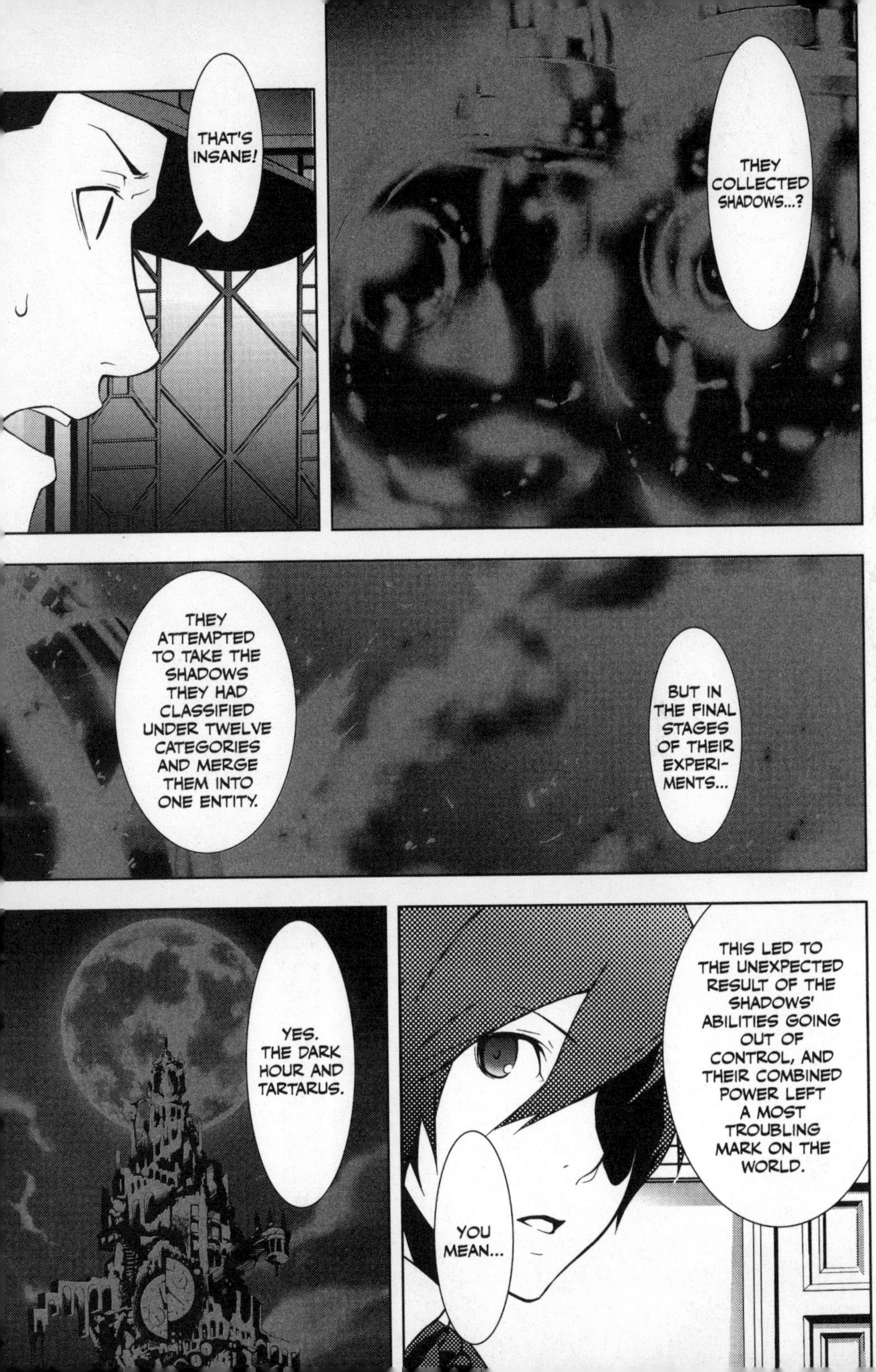
THEY COLLECTED SHADOWS...?
THAT'S INSANE!
THEY ATTEMPTED TO TAKE THE SHADOWS THEY HAD CLASSIFIED UNDER TWELVE CATEGORIES AND MERGE THEM INTO ONE ENTITY.
BUT IN THE FINAL STAGES OF THEIR EXPERIMENTS...
THIS LED TO THE UNEXPECTED RESULT OF THE SHADOWS' ABILITIES GOING OUT OF CONTROL, AND THEIR COMBINED POWER LEFT A MOST TROUBLING MARK ON THE WORLD.
YOU MEAN...
YES. THE DARK HOUR AND TARTARUS.

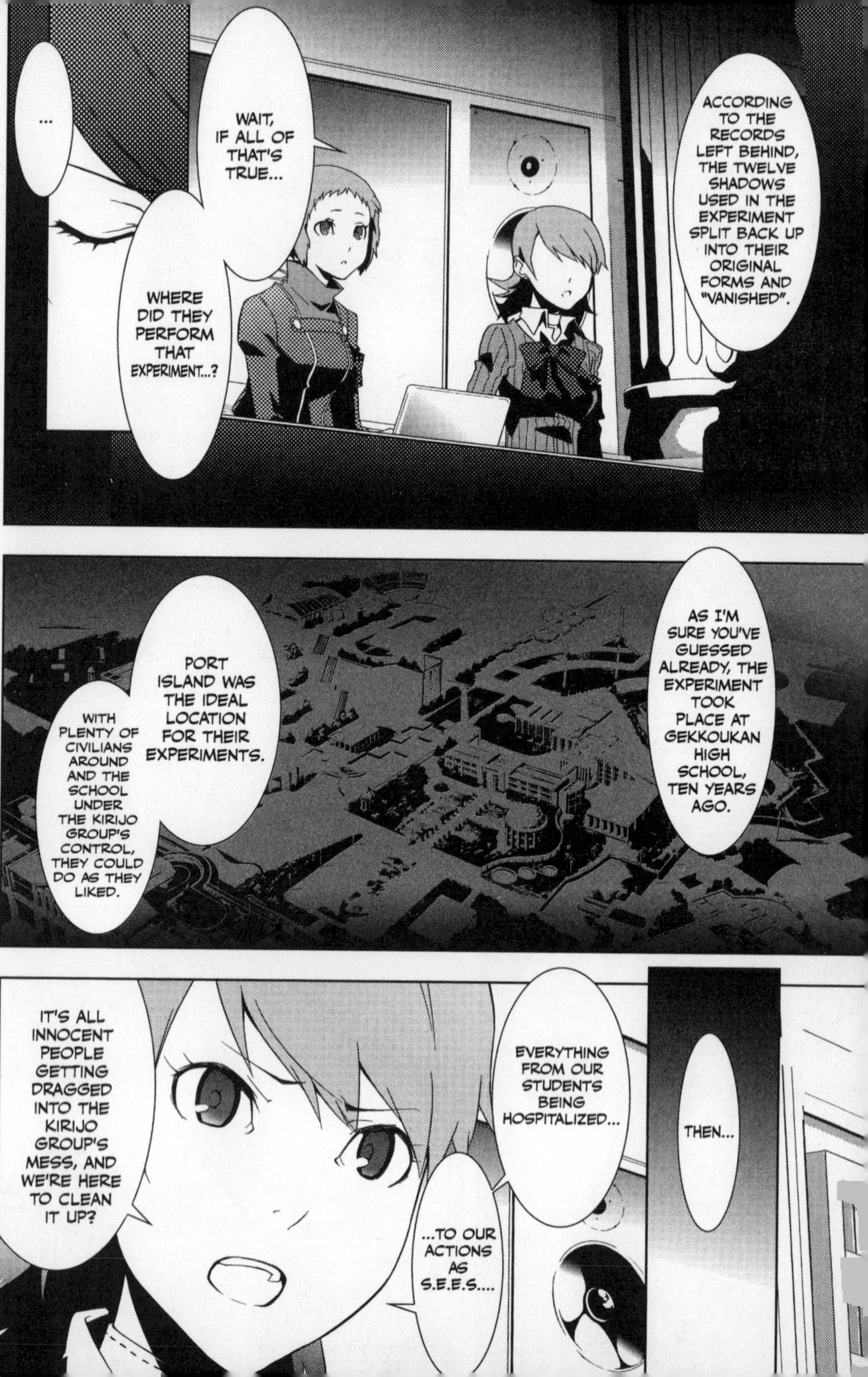

ACCORDING TO THE RECORDS LEFT BEHIND, THE TWELVE SHADOWS USED IN THE EXPERIMENT SPLIT BACK UP INTO THEIR ORIGINAL FORMS AND "VANISHED".
WAIT, IF ALL OF THAT'S TRUE...
WHERE DID THEY PERFORM THAT EXPERIMENT...?
...
AS I'M SURE YOU'VE GUESSED ALREADY, THE EXPERIMENT TOOK PLACE AT GEKKOUKAN HIGH SCHOOL, TEN YEARS AGO.
PORT ISLAND WAS THE IDEAL LOCATION FOR THEIR EXPERIMENTS.
WITH PLENTY OF CIVILIANS AROUND AND THE SCHOOL UNDER THE KIRIJO GROUP'S CONTROL, THEY COULD DO AS THEY LIKED.
THEN...
EVERYTHING FROM OUR STUDENTS BEING HOSPITALIZED...
...TO OUR ACTIONS AS S.E.E.S....
IT'S ALL INNOCENT PEOPLE GETTING DRAGGED INTO THE KIRIJO GROUP'S MESS, AND WE'RE HERE TO CLEAN IT UP?

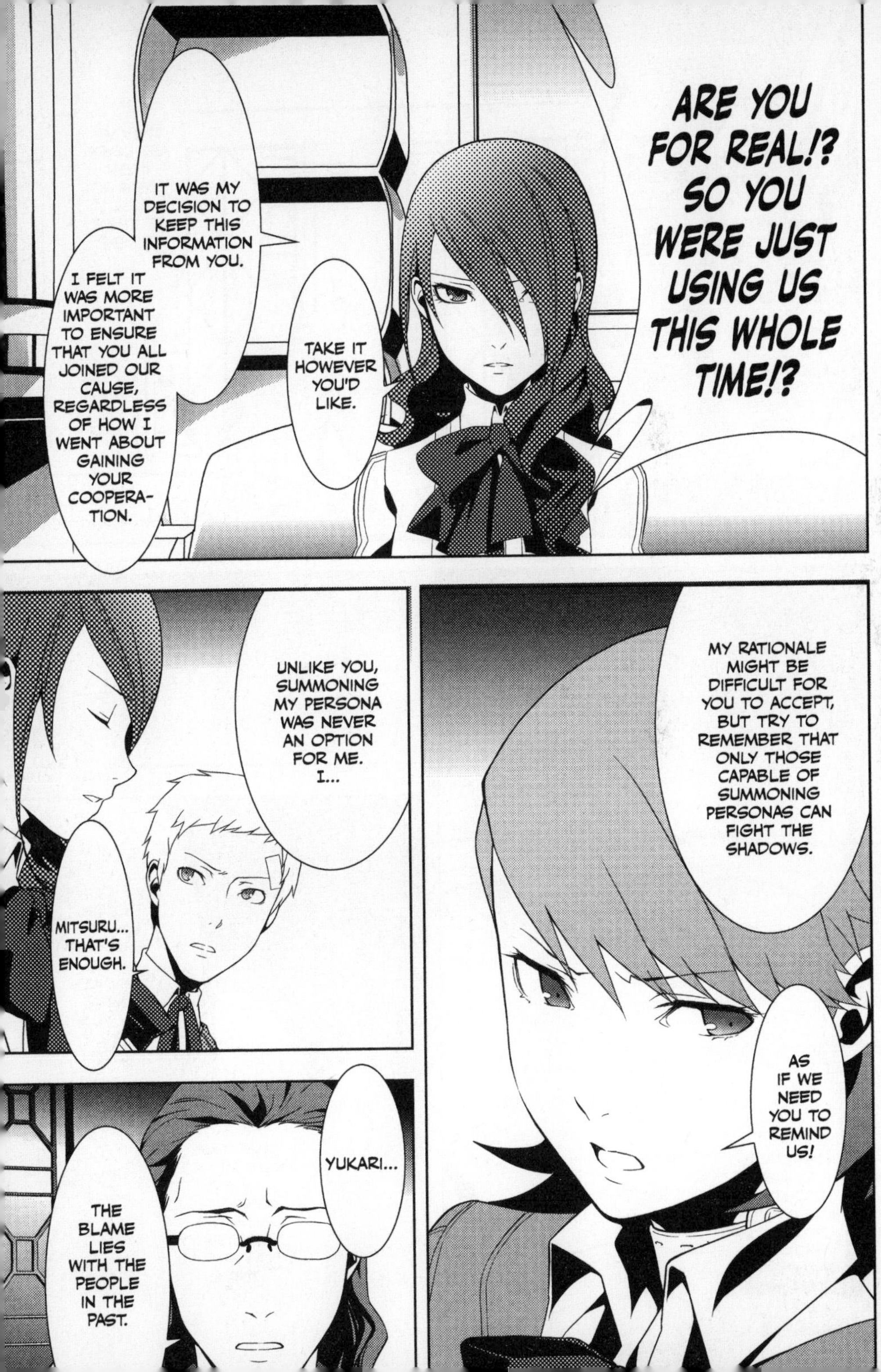
ARE YOU FOR REAL!? SO YOU WERE JUST USING US THIS WHOLE TIME!?
TAKE IT HOWEVER YOU'D LIKE.
IT WAS MY DECISION TO KEEP THIS INFORMATION FROM YOU.
I FELT IT WAS MORE IMPORTANT TO ENSURE THAT YOU ALL JOINED OUR CAUSE, REGARDLESS OF HOW I WENT ABOUT GAINING YOUR COOPERA-TION.
MY RATIONALE MIGHT BE DIFFICULT FOR YOU TO ACCEPT, BUT TRY TO REMEMBER THAT ONLY THOSE CAPABLE OF SUMMONING PERSONAS CAN FIGHT THE SHADOWS.
AS IF WE NEED YOU TO REMIND US!
UNLIKE YOU, SUMMONING MY PERSONA WAS NEVER AN OPTION FOR ME. I...
MITSURU... THAT'S ENOUGH.
YUKARI...
THE BLAME LIES WITH THE PEOPLE IN THE PAST.

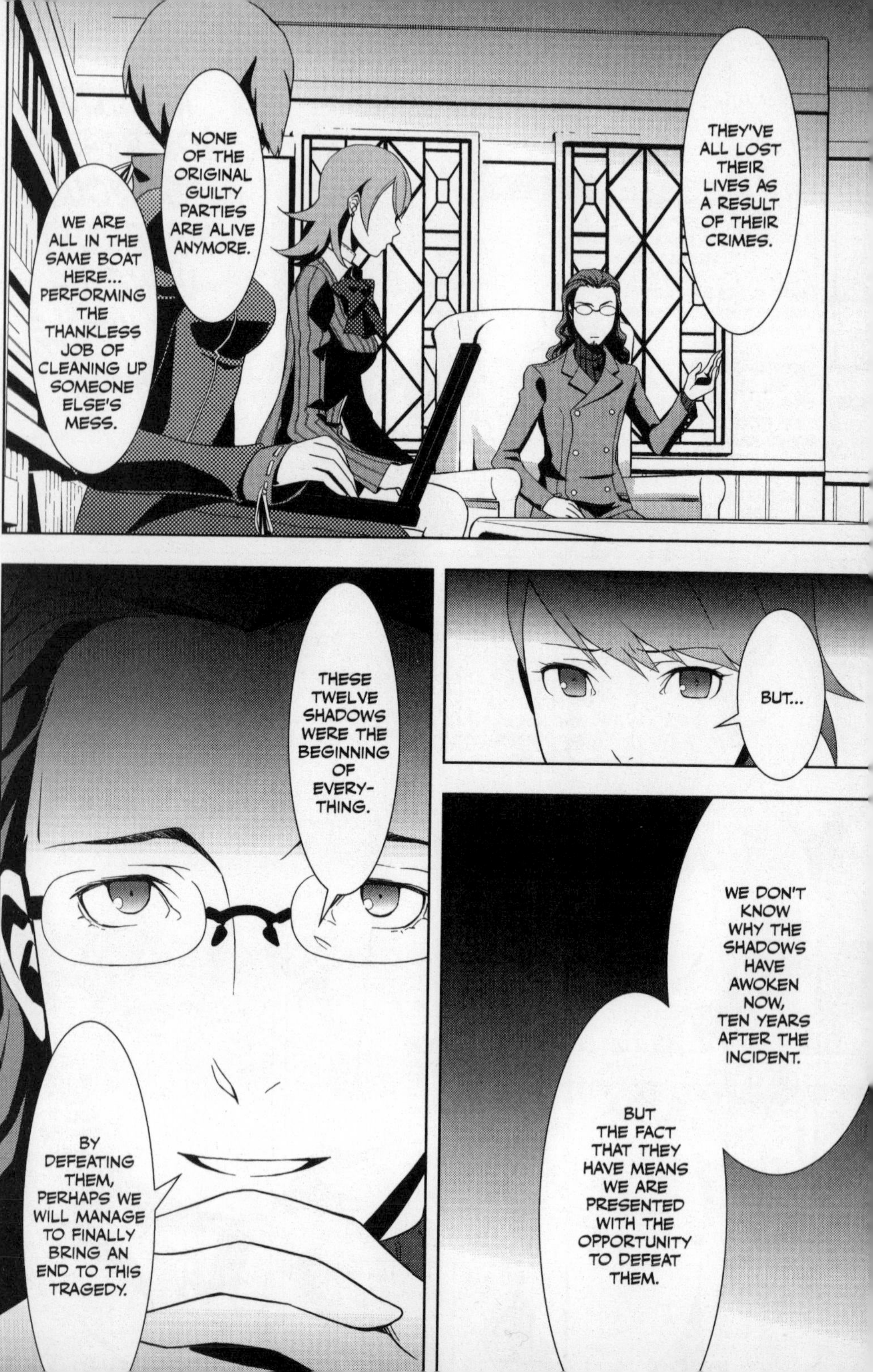
THEY'VE ALL LOST THEIR LIVES AS A RESULT OF THEIR CRIMES.
NONE OF THE ORIGINAL GUILTY PARTIES ARE ALIVE ANYMORE.
WE ARE ALL IN THE SAME BOAT HERE... PERFORMING THE THANKLESS JOB OF CLEANING UP SOMEONE ELSE'S MESS.
BUT...
WE DON'T KNOW WHY THE SHADOWS HAVE AWOKEN NOW, TEN YEARS AFTER THE INCIDENT.
BUT THE FACT THAT THEY HAVE MEANS WE ARE PRESENTED WITH THE OPPORTUNITY TO DEFEAT THEM.
THESE TWELVE SHADOWS WERE THE BEGINNING OF EVERY-THING.
BY DEFEATING THEM, PERHAPS WE WILL MANAGE TO FINALLY BRING AN END TO THIS TRAGEDY.

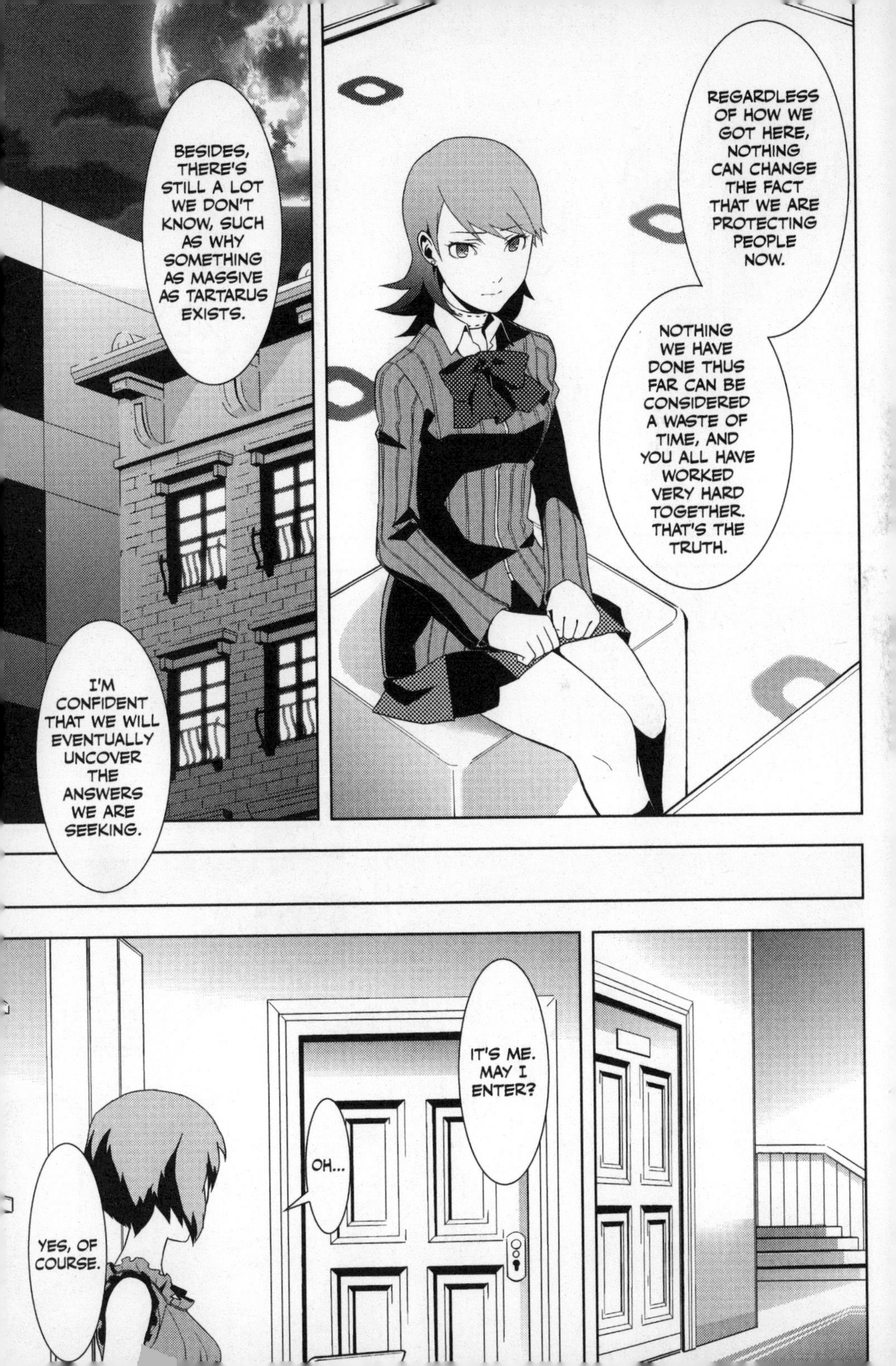
REGARDLESS OF HOW WE GOT HERE, NOTHING CAN CHANGE THE FACT THAT WE ARE PROTECTING PEOPLE NOW.
NOTHING WE HAVE DONE THUS FAR CAN BE CONSIDERED A WASTE OF TIME, AND YOU ALL HAVE WORKED VERY HARD TOGETHER. THAT'S THE TRUTH.
BESIDES, THERE'S STILL A LOT WE DON'T KNOW, SUCH AS WHY SOMETHING AS MASSIVE AS TARTARUS EXISTS.
I'M CONFIDENT THAT WE WILL EVENTUALLY UNCOVER THE ANSWERS WE ARE SEEKING.
IT'S ME. MAY I ENTER?
OH...
YES, OF COURSE.

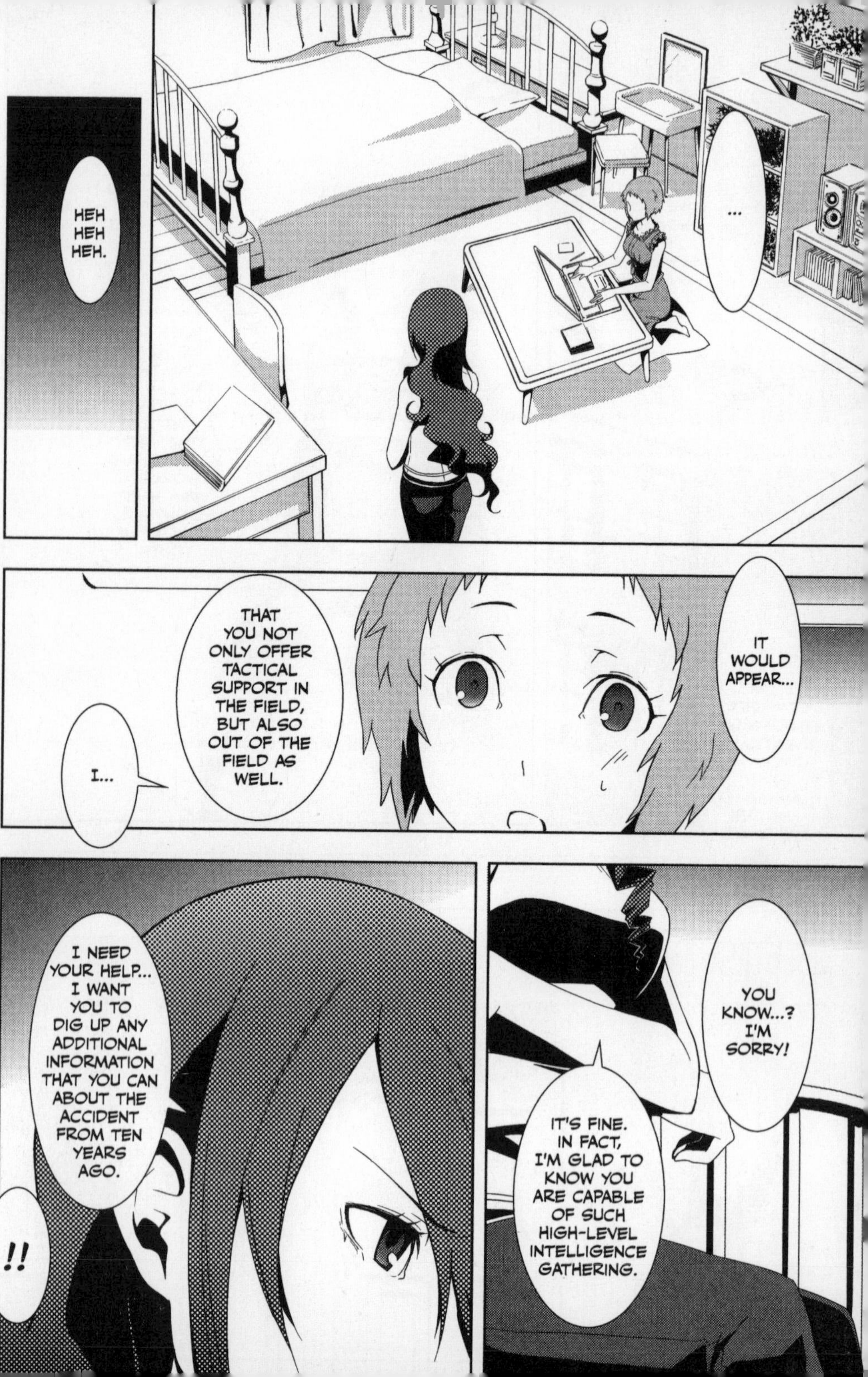
...
HEH HEH HEH.
IT WOULD APPEAR...
THAT YOU NOT ONLY OFFER TACTICAL SUPPORT IN THE FIELD, BUT ALSO OUT OF THE FIELD AS WELL.
I...
YOU KNOW...? I'M SORRY!
IT'S FINE. IN FACT, I'M GLAD TO KNOW YOU ARE CAPABLE OF SUCH HIGH-LEVEL INTELLIGENCE GATHERING.
I NEED YOUR HELP... I WANT YOU TO DIG UP ANY ADDITIONAL INFORMATION THAT YOU CAN ABOUT THE ACCIDENT FROM TEN YEARS AGO.
!!

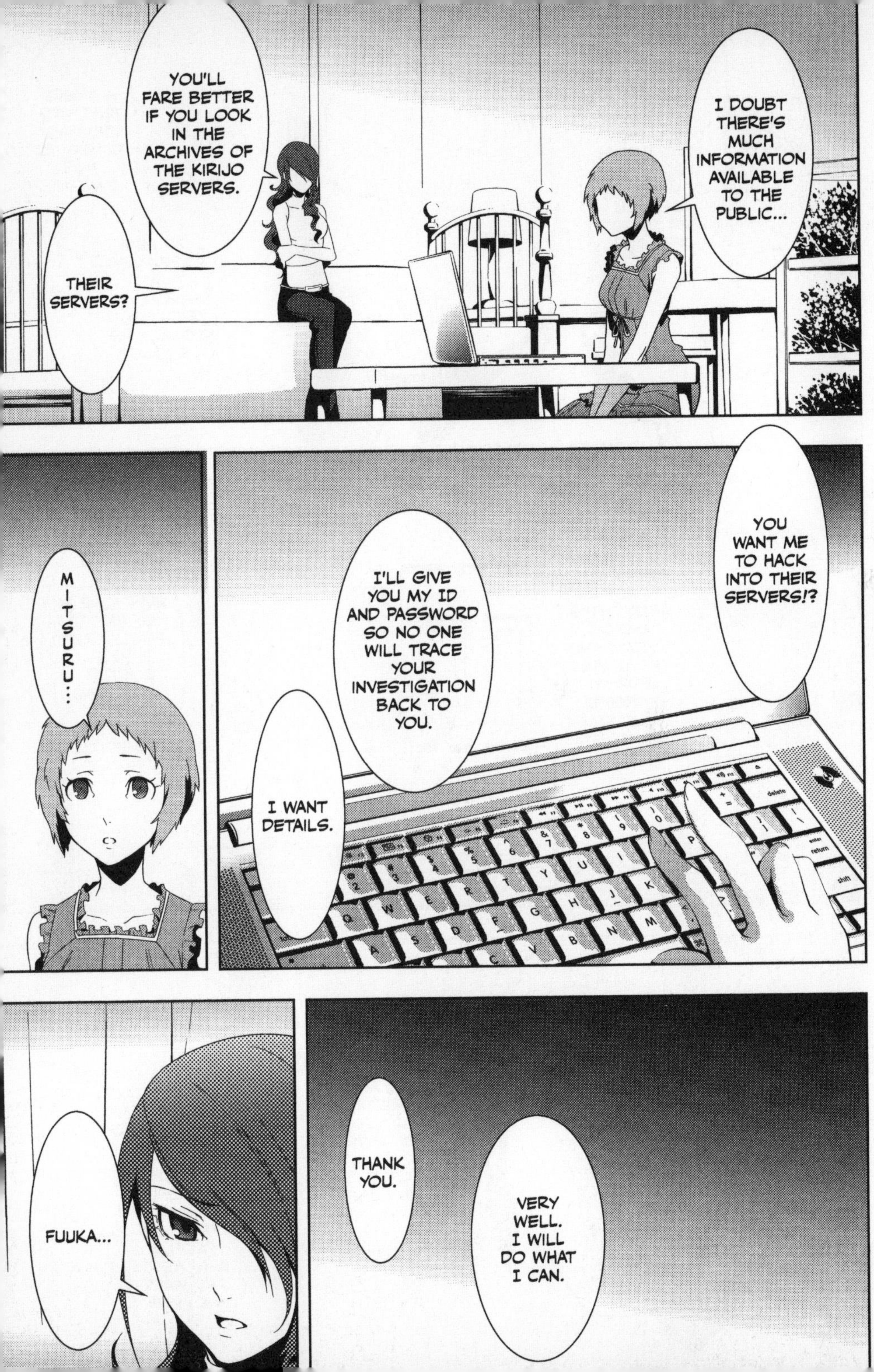
I DOUBT THERE'S MUCH INFORMATION AVAILABLE TO THE PUBLIC...
YOU'LL FARE BETTER IF YOU LOOK IN THE ARCHIVES OF THE KIRIJO SERVERS.
THEIR SERVERS?
YOU WANT ME TO HACK INTO THEIR SERVERS!?
I'LL GIVE YOU MY ID AND PASSWORD SO NO ONE WILL TRACE YOUR INVESTIGATION BACK TO YOU.
I WANT DETAILS.
MITSURU...
VERY WELL. I WILL DO WHAT I CAN.
THANK YOU.
FUUKA...

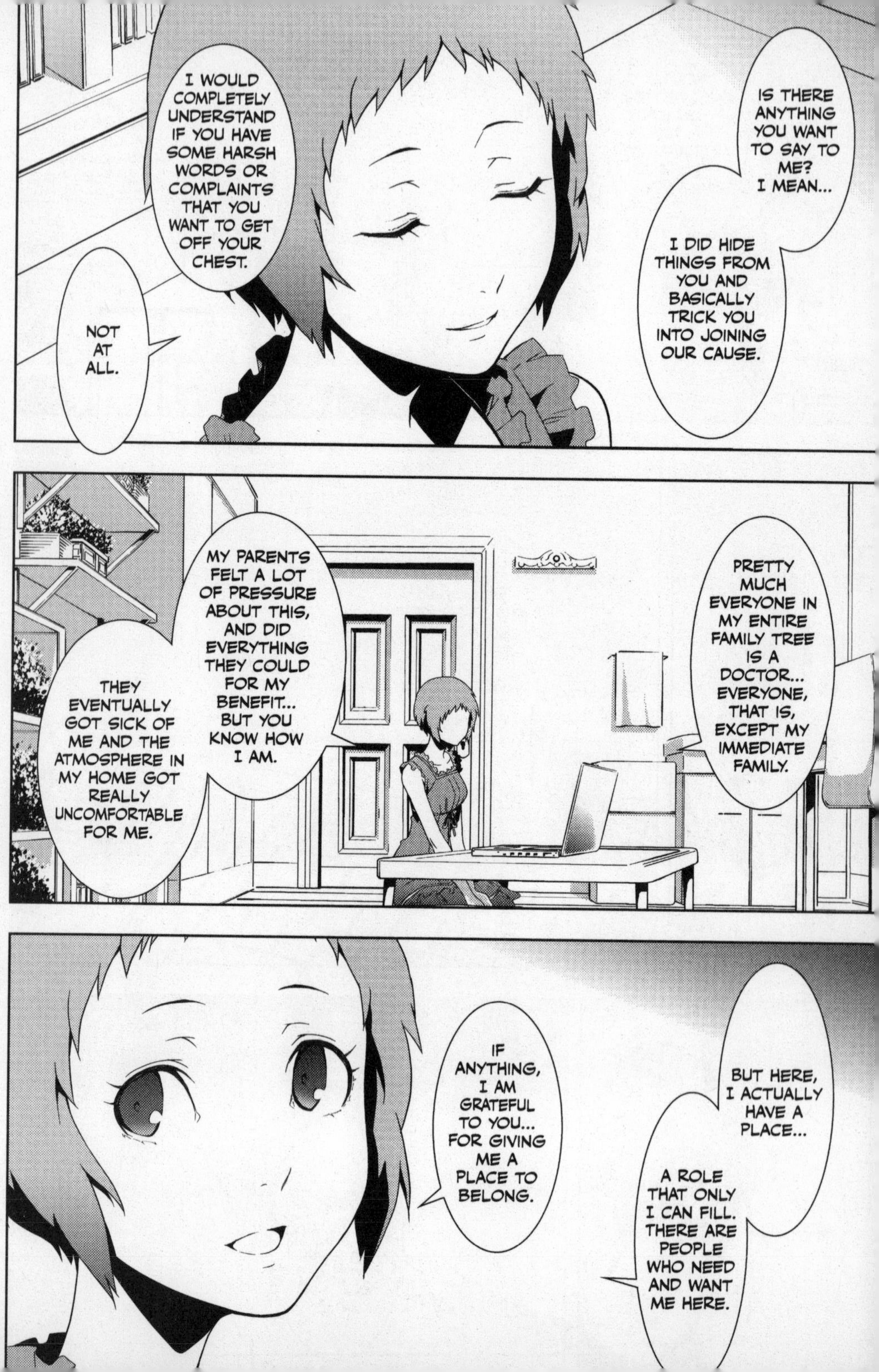
IS THERE ANYTHING YOU WANT TO SAY TO ME? I MEAN...
I DID HIDE THINGS FROM YOU AND BASICALLY TRICK YOU INTO JOINING OUR CAUSE.
I WOULD COMPLETELY UNDERSTAND IF YOU HAVE SOME HARSH WORDS OR COMPLAINTS THAT YOU WANT TO GET OFF YOUR CHEST.
NOT AT ALL.
PRETTY MUCH EVERYONE IN MY ENTIRE FAMILY TREE IS A DOCTOR... EVERYONE, THAT IS, EXCEPT MY IMMEDIATE FAMILY.
MY PARENTS FELT A LOT OF PRESSURE ABOUT THIS, AND DID EVERYTHING THEY COULD FOR MY BENEFIT... BUT YOU KNOW HOW I AM.
THEY EVENTUALLY GOT SICK OF ME AND THE ATMOSPHERE IN MY HOME GOT REALLY UNCOMFORTABLE FOR ME.
BUT HERE, I ACTUALLY HAVE A PLACE...
A ROLE THAT ONLY I CAN FILL. THERE ARE PEOPLE WHO NEED AND WANT ME HERE.
IF ANYTHING, I AM GRATEFUL TO YOU... FOR GIVING ME A PLACE TO BELONG.

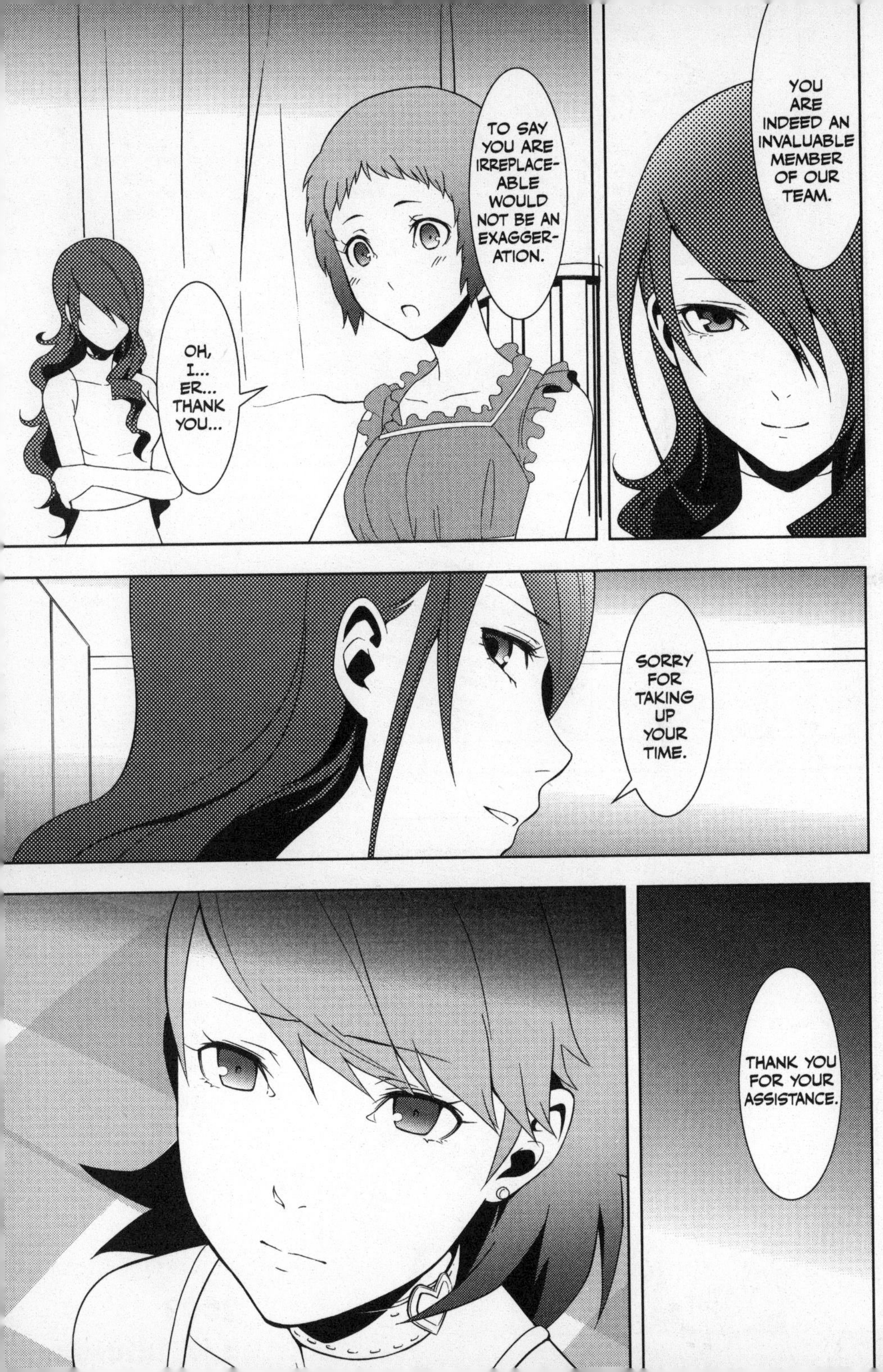
YOU ARE INDEED AN INVALUABLE MEMBER OF OUR TEAM.
TO SAY YOU ARE IRREPLACE-ABLE WOULD NOT BE AN EXAGGER-ATION.
OH, I... ER... THANK YOU...
SORRY FOR TAKING UP YOUR TIME.
THANK YOU FOR YOUR ASSISTANCE.

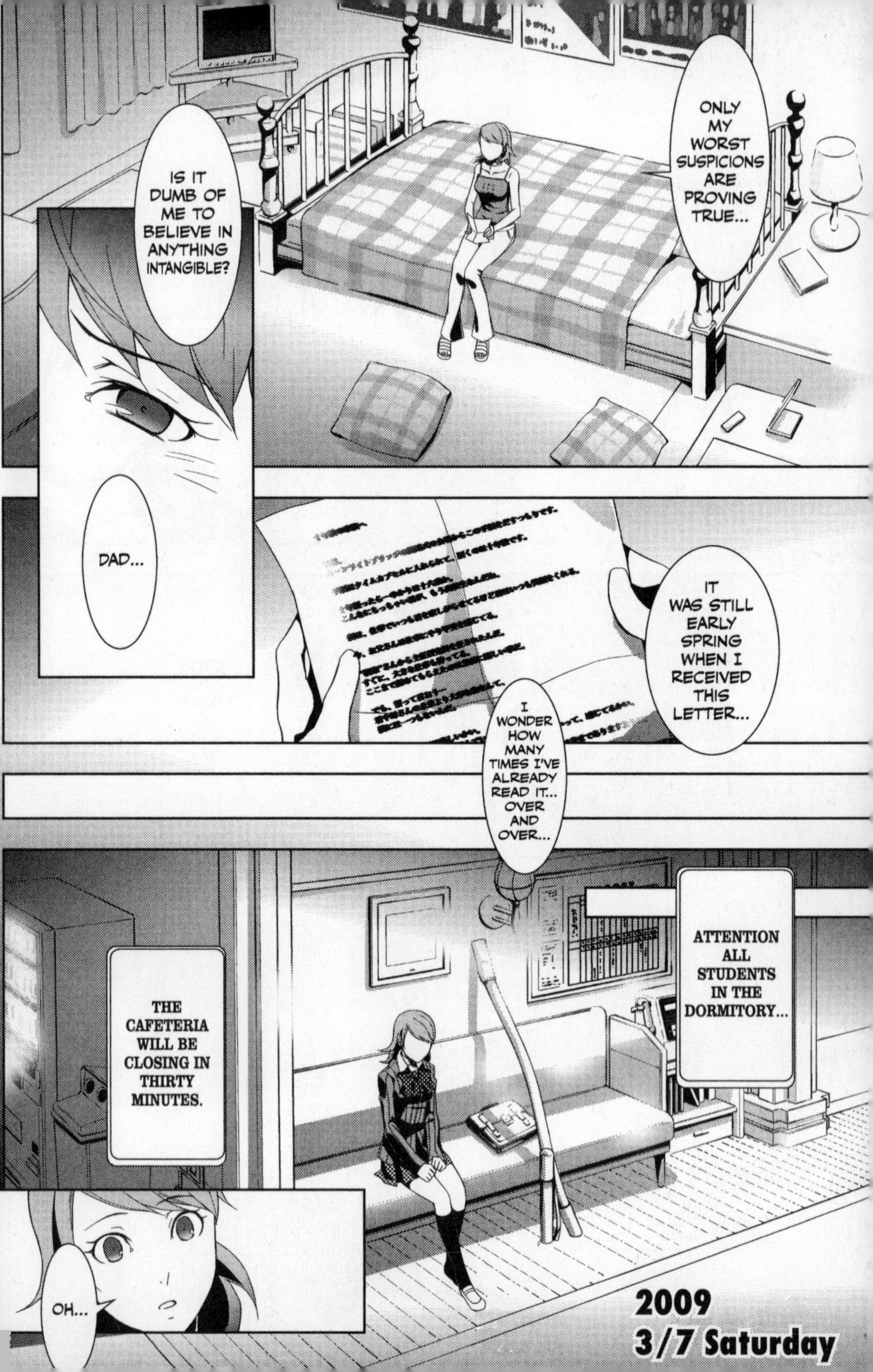
ONLY MY WORST SUSPICIONS ARE PROVING TRUE...
IS IT DUMB OF ME TO BELIEVE IN ANYTHING INTANGIBLE?
IT WAS STILL EARLY SPRING WHEN I RECEIVED THIS LETTER...
I WONDER HOW MANY TIMES I'VE ALREADY READ IT... OVER AND OVER...
DAD...
ATTENTION ALL STUDENTS IN THE DORMITORY...
THE CAFETERIA WILL BE CLOSING IN THIRTY MINUTES.
2009 3/7 Saturday
OH...

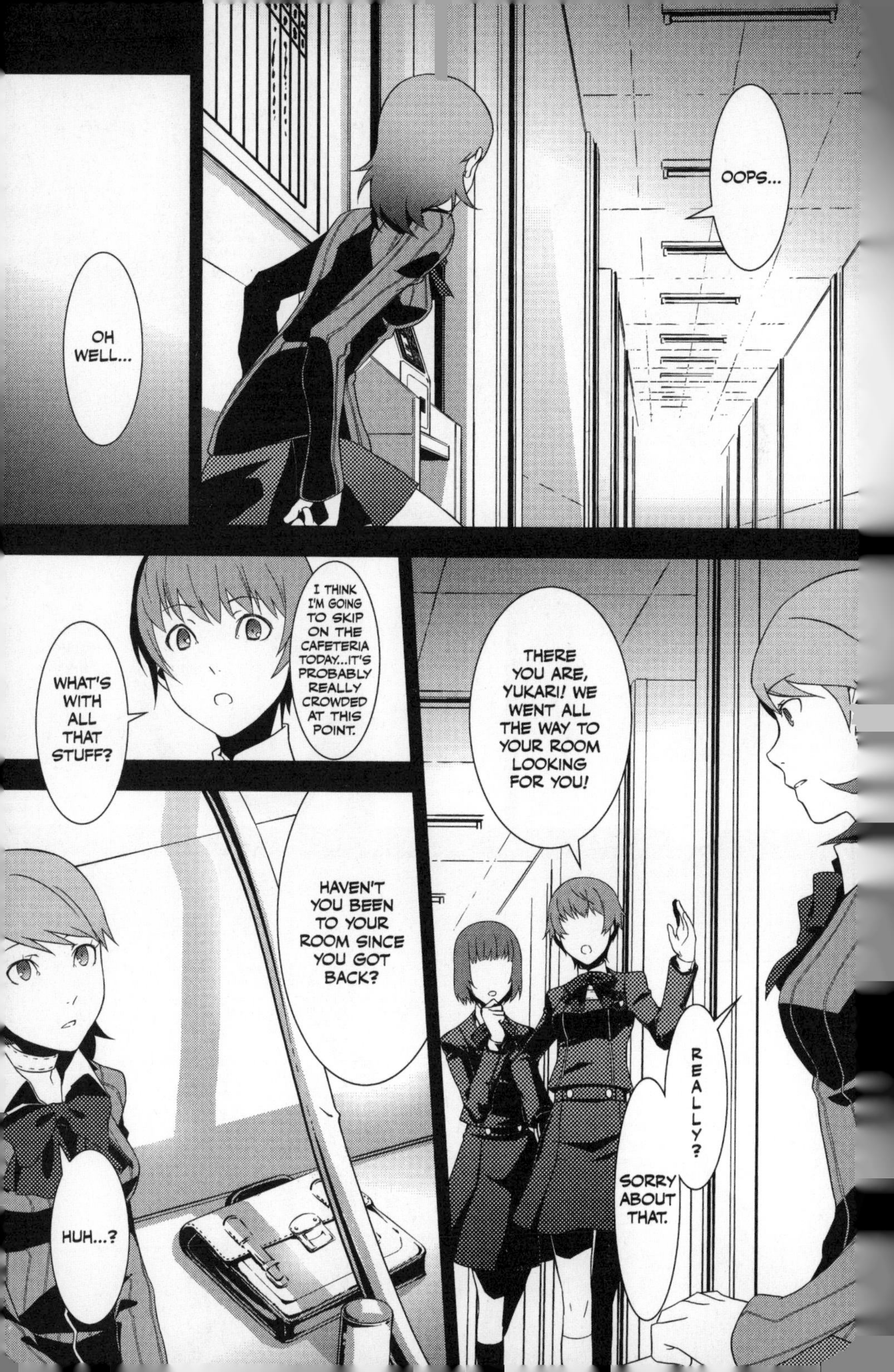
OOPS...
OH WELL...
THERE YOU ARE, YUKARI! WE WENT ALL THE WAY TO YOUR ROOM LOOKING FOR YOU!
REALLY?
SORRY ABOUT THAT.
I THINK I'M GOING TO SKIP ON THE CAFETERIA TODAY...IT'S PROBABLY REALLY CROWDED AT THIS POINT.
WHAT'S WITH ALL THAT STUFF?
HAVEN'T YOU BEEN TO YOUR ROOM SINCE YOU GOT BACK?
HUH...?

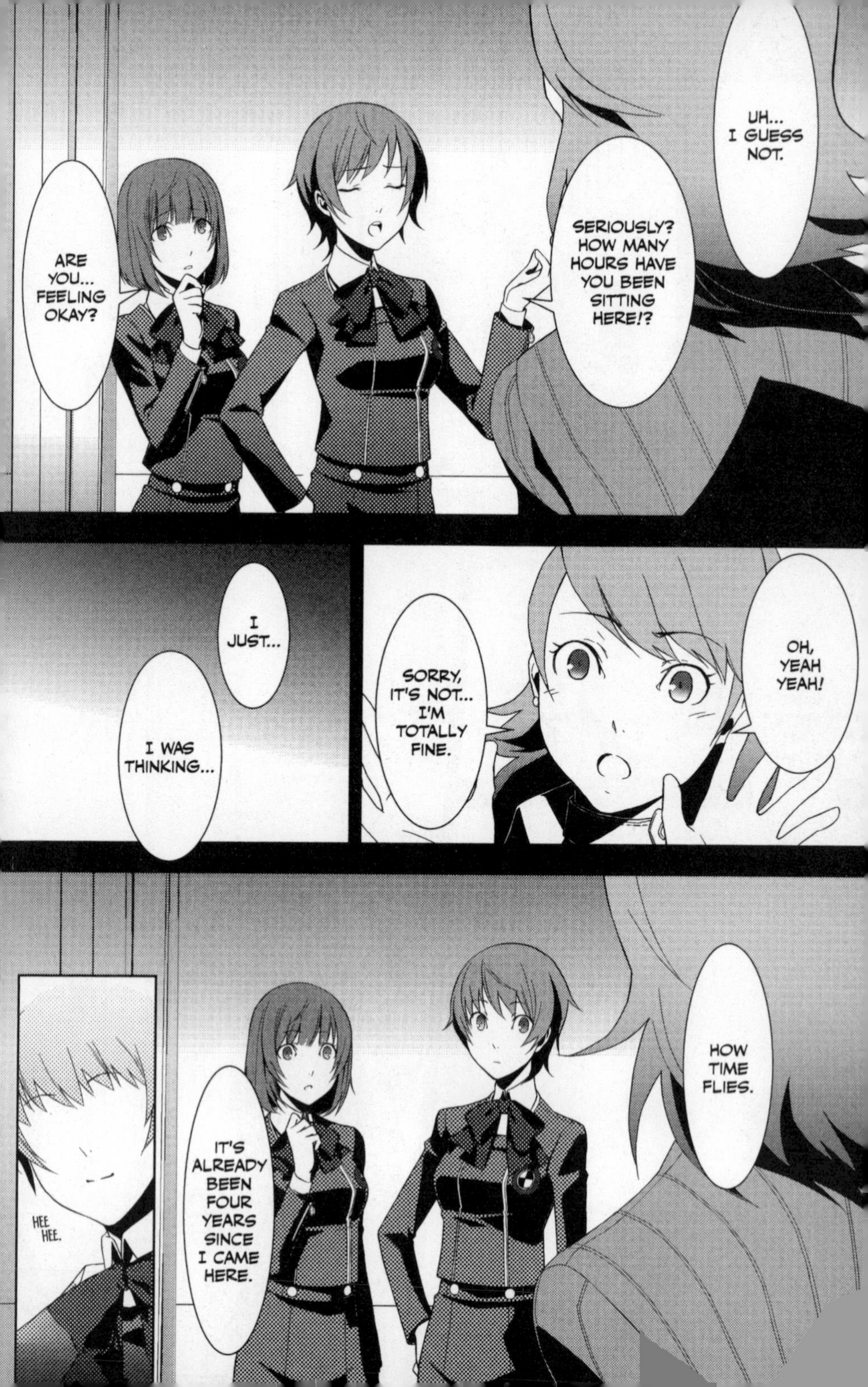
UH... I GUESS NOT.
SERIOUSLY? HOW MANY HOURS HAVE YOU BEEN SITTING HERE!?
ARE YOU... FEELING OKAY?
OH, YEAH YEAH!
SORRY, IT'S NOT... I'M TOTALLY FINE.
I JUST...
I WAS THINKING...
HOW TIME FLIES.
IT'S ALREADY BEEN FOUR YEARS SINCE I CAME HERE.
HEE HEE.

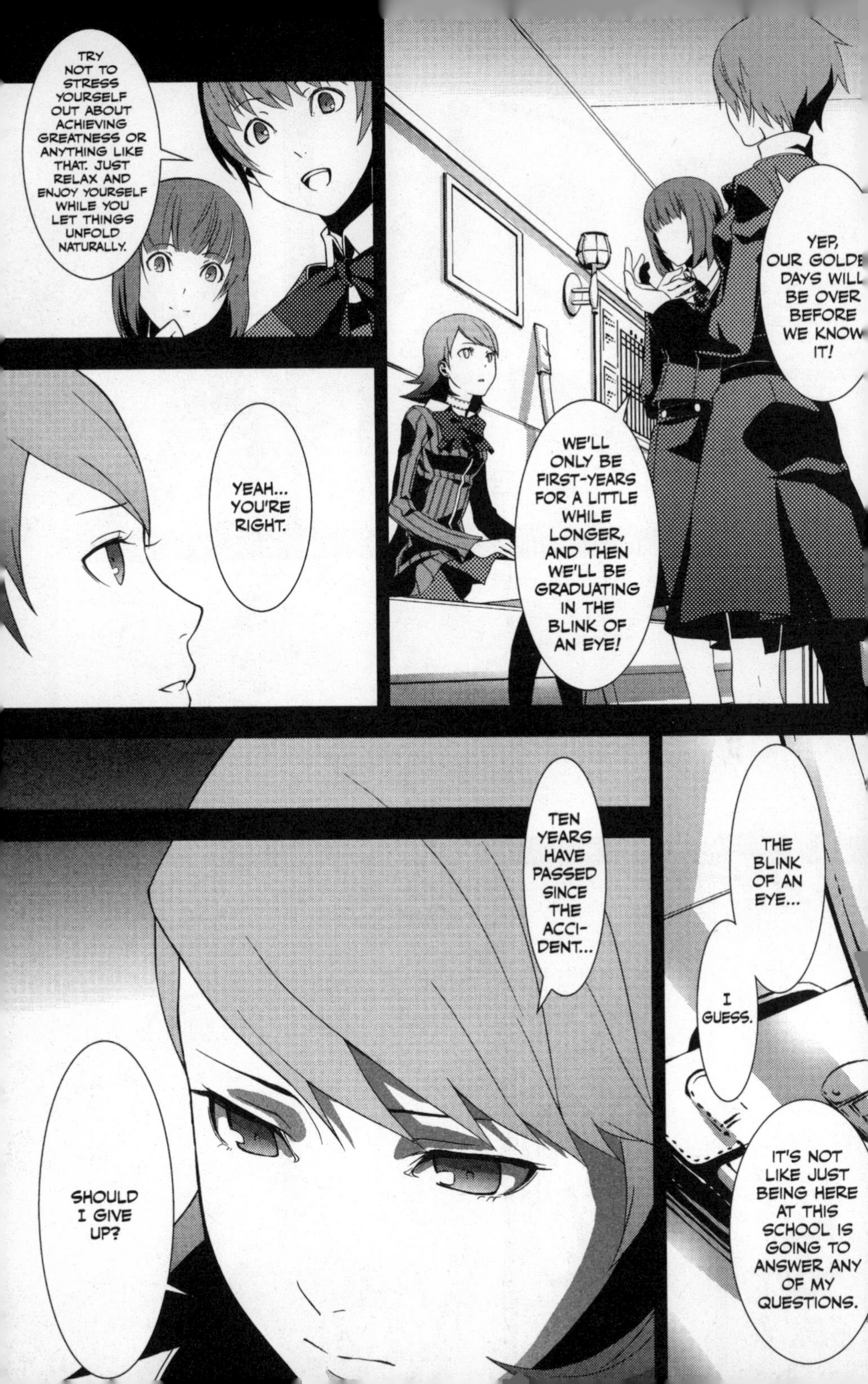
YEP, OUR GOLDE DAYS WILL BE OVER BEFORE WE KNOW IT!
WE'LL ONLY BE FIRST-YEARS FOR A LITTLE WHILE LONGER, AND THEN WE'LL BE GRADUATING IN THE BLINK OF AN EYE!
TRY NOT TO STRESS YOURSELF OUT ABOUT ACHIEVING GREATNESS OR ANYTHING LIKE THAT. JUST RELAX AND ENJOY YOURSELF WHILE YOU LET THINGS UNFOLD NATURALLY.
YEAH... YOU'RE RIGHT.
THE BLINK OF AN EYE...
I GUESS.
IT'S NOT LIKE JUST BEING HERE AT THIS SCHOOL IS GOING TO ANSWER ANY OF MY QUESTIONS.
TEN YEARS HAVE PASSED SINCE THE ACCI-DENT...
SHOULD I GIVE UP?

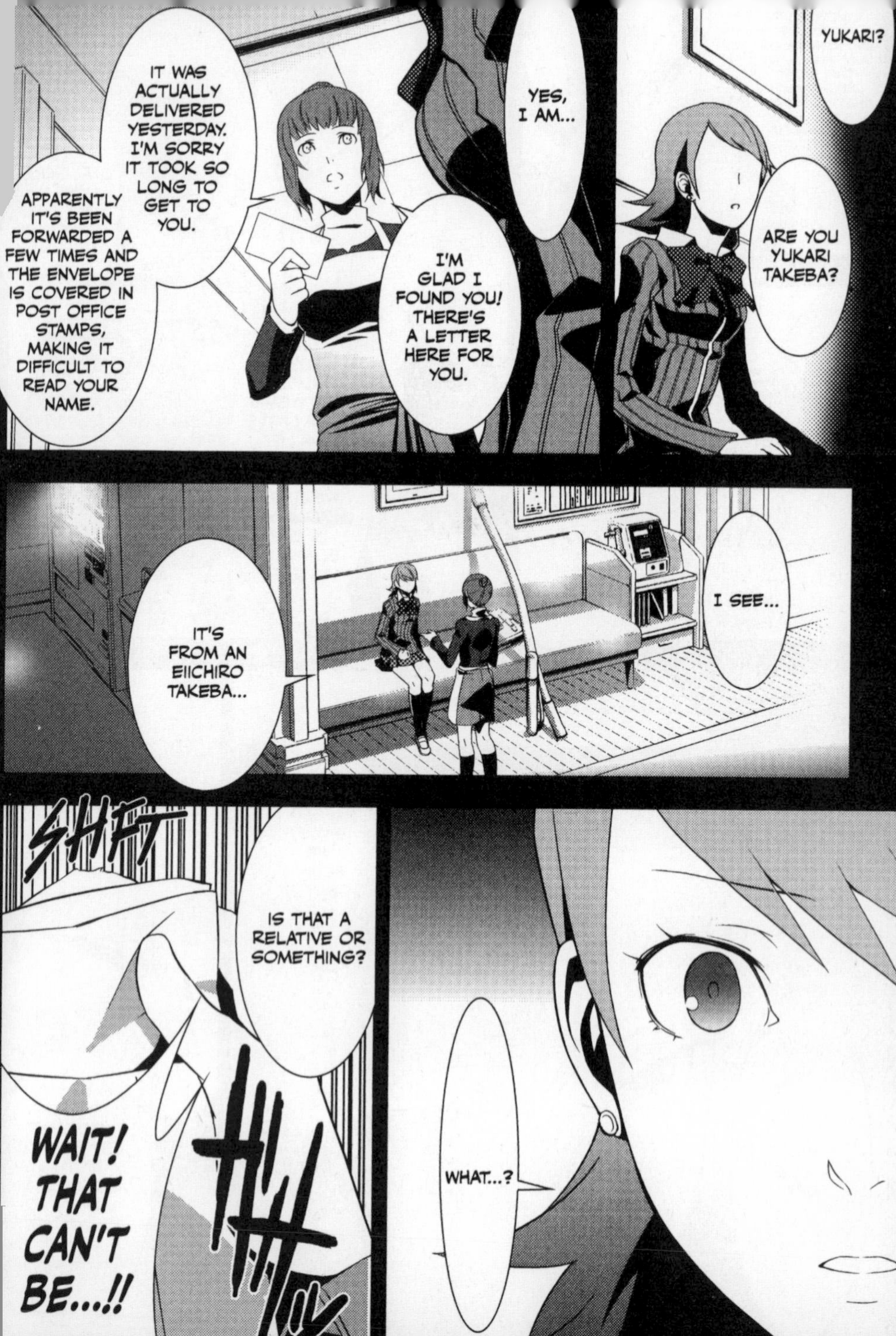
YUKARI?
ARE YOU YUKARI TAKEBA?
YES, I AM...
I'M GLAD I FOUND YOU! THERE'S A LETTER HERE FOR YOU.
IT WAS ACTUALLY DELIVERED YESTERDAY. I'M SORRY IT TOOK SO LONG TO GET TO YOU.
APPARENTLY IT'S BEEN FORWARDED A FEW TIMES AND THE ENVELOPE IS COVERED IN POST OFFICE STAMPS, MAKING IT DIFFICULT TO READ YOUR NAME.
I SEE...
IT'S FROM AN EIICHIRO TAKEBA...
WHAT...?
SHFT
IS THAT A RELATIVE OR SOMETHING?
WAIT! THAT CAN'T BE...!!

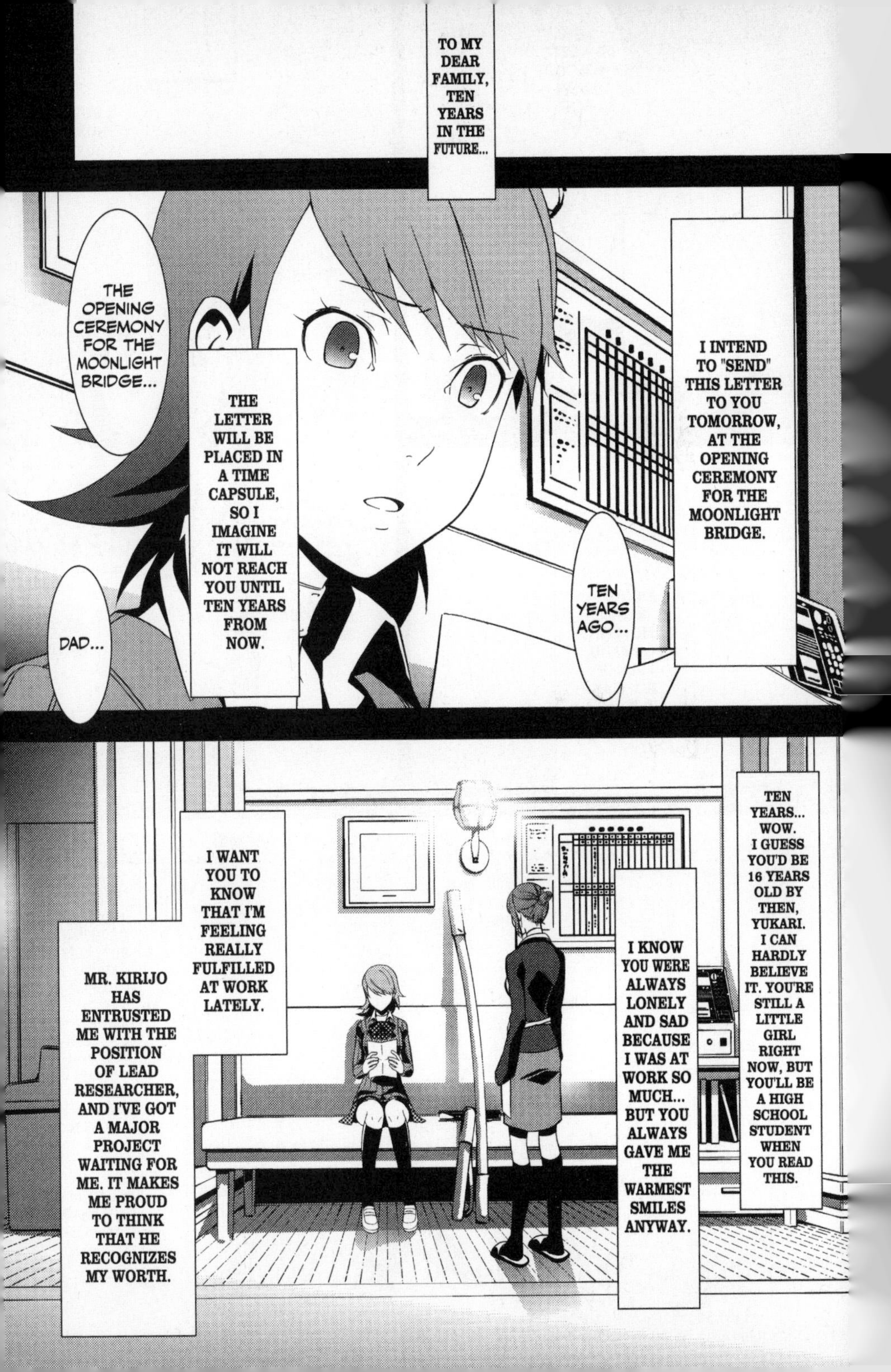
TO MY DEAR FAMILY, TEN YEARS IN THE FUTURE...
I INTEND TO "SEND" THIS LETTER TO YOU TOMORROW, AT THE OPENING CEREMONY FOR THE MOONLIGHT BRIDGE.
TEN YEARS AGO...
THE LETTER WILL BE PLACED IN A TIME CAPSULE, SO I IMAGINE IT WILL NOT REACH YOU UNTIL TEN YEARS FROM NOW.
THE OPENING CEREMONY FOR THE MOONLIGHT BRIDGE...
DAD...
TEN YEARS... WOW. I GUESS YOU'D BE 16 YEARS OLD BY THEN, YUKARI. I CAN HARDLY BELIEVE IT. YOU'RE STILL A LITTLE GIRL RIGHT NOW, BUT YOU'LL BE A HIGH SCHOOL STUDENT WHEN YOU READ THIS.
I KNOW YOU WERE ALWAYS LONELY AND SAD BECAUSE I WAS AT WORK SO MUCH... BUT YOU ALWAYS GAVE ME THE WARMEST SMILES ANYWAY.
I WANT YOU TO KNOW THAT I'M FEELING REALLY FULFILLED AT WORK LATELY.
MR. KIRIJO HAS ENTRUSTED ME WITH THE POSITION OF LEAD RESEARCHER, AND I'VE GOT A MAJOR PROJECT WAITING FOR ME. IT MAKES ME PROUD TO THINK THAT HE RECOGNIZES MY WORTH.

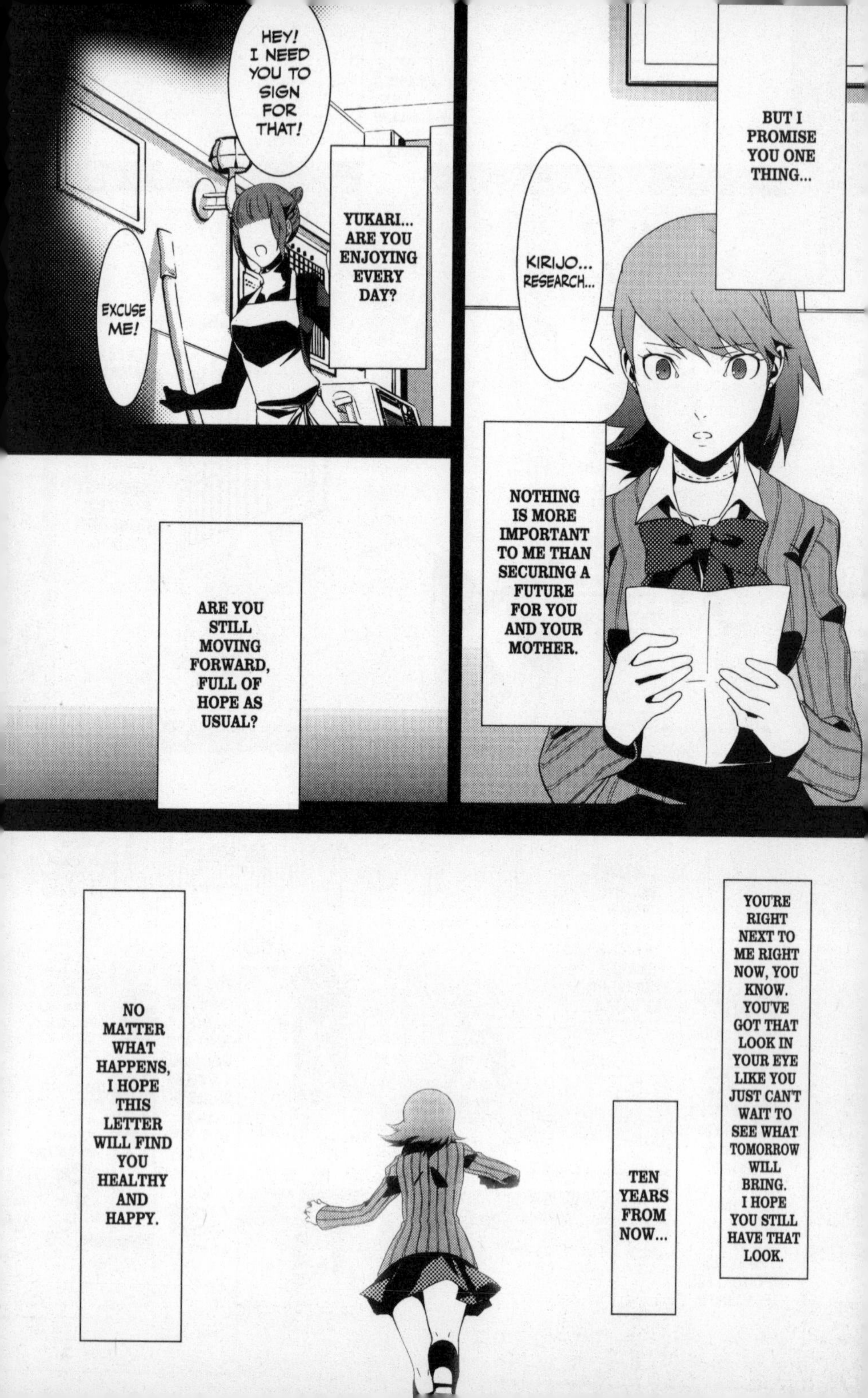
BUT I PROMISE YOU ONE THING...
KIRIJO... RESEARCH...
NOTHING IS MORE IMPORTANT TO ME THAN SECURING A FUTURE FOR YOU AND YOUR MOTHER.
HEY! I NEED YOU TO SIGN FOR THAT!
YUKARI... ARE YOU ENJOYING EVERY DAY?
EXCUSE ME!
ARE YOU STILL MOVING FORWARD, FULL OF HOPE AS USUAL?
YOU'RE RIGHT NEXT TO ME RIGHT NOW, YOU KNOW. YOU'VE GOT THAT LOOK IN YOUR EYE LIKE YOU JUST CAN'T WAIT TO SEE WHAT TOMORROW WILL BRING. I HOPE YOU STILL HAVE THAT LOOK.
TEN YEARS FROM NOW...
NO MATTER WHAT HAPPENS, I HOPE THIS LETTER WILL FIND YOU HEALTHY AND HAPPY.

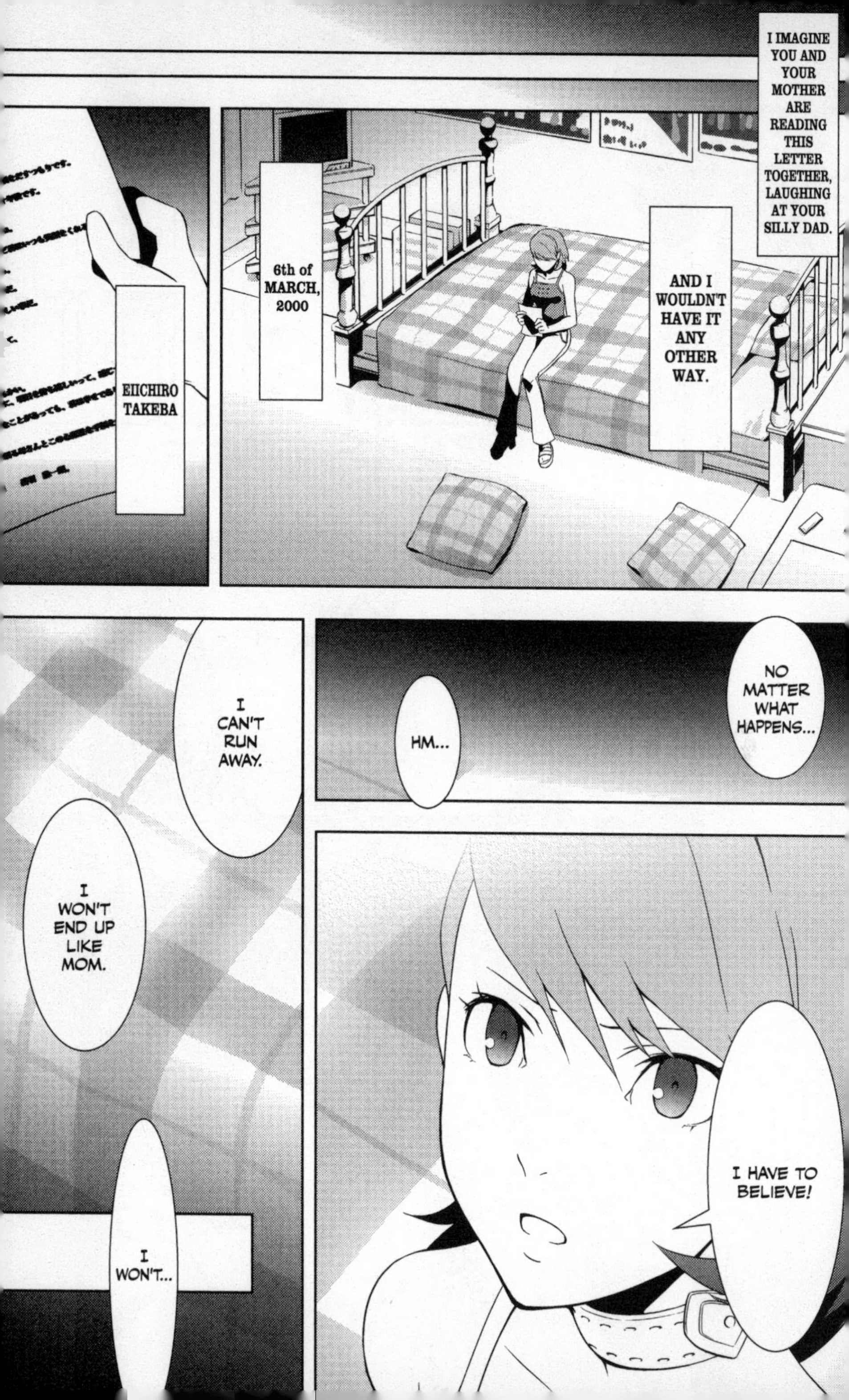
I IMAGINE YOU AND YOUR MOTHER ARE READING THIS LETTER TOGETHER, LAUGHING AT YOUR SILLY DAD.
AND I WOULDN'T HAVE IT ANY OTHER WAY.
6th of MARCH, 2000
EIICHIRO TAKEBA
NO MATTER WHAT HAPPENS...
HM...
I HAVE TO BELIEVE!
I CAN'T RUN AWAY.
I WON'T END UP LIKE MOM.
I WON'T...

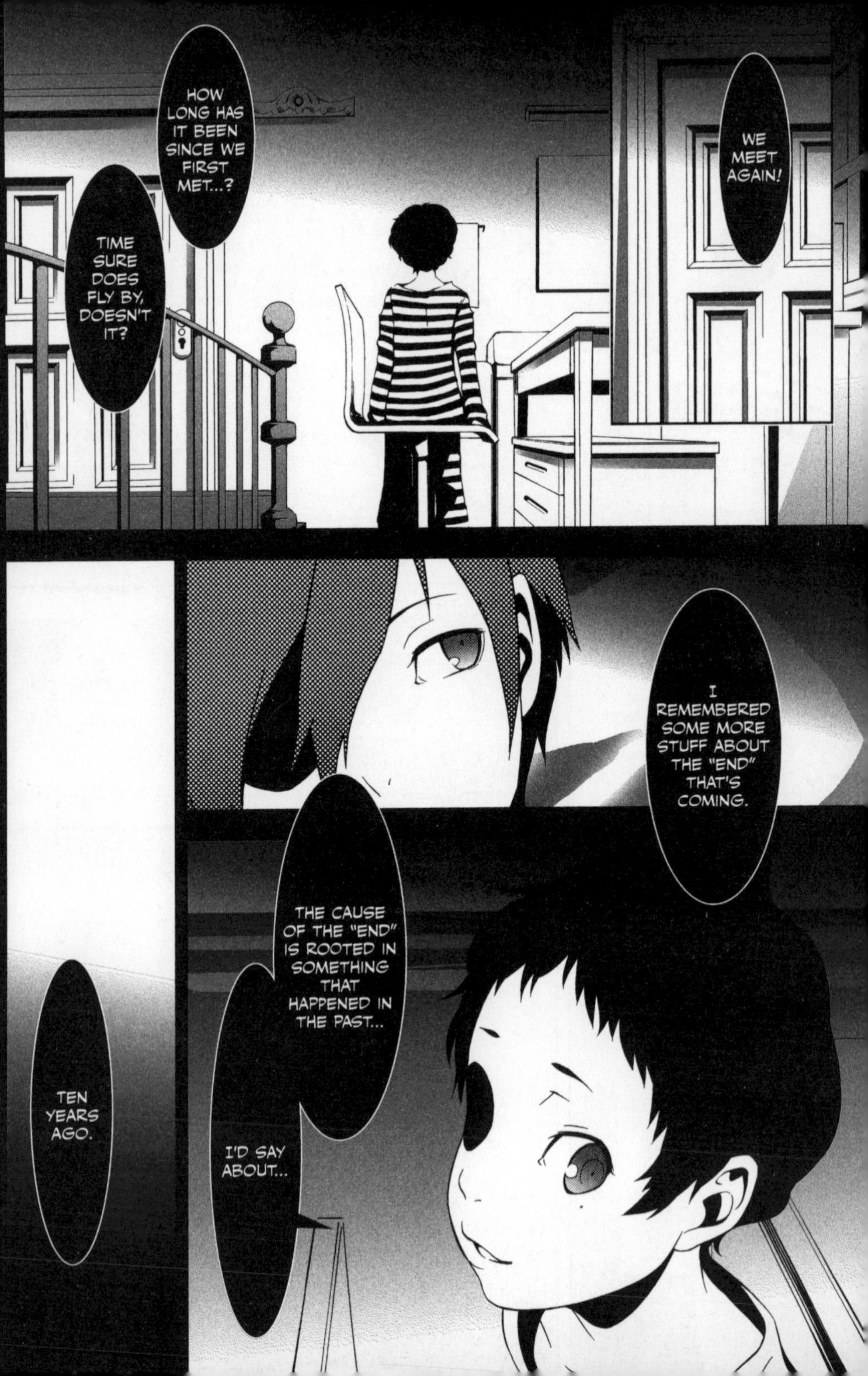
WE MEET AGAIN!
HOW LONG HAS IT BEEN SINCE WE FIRST MET...?
TIME SURE DOES FLY BY, DOESN'T IT?
I REMEMBERED SOME MORE STUFF ABOUT THE "END" THAT'S COMING.
THE CAUSE OF THE "END" IS ROOTED IN SOMETHING THAT HAPPENED IN THE PAST...
I'D SAY ABOUT...
TEN YEARS AGO.

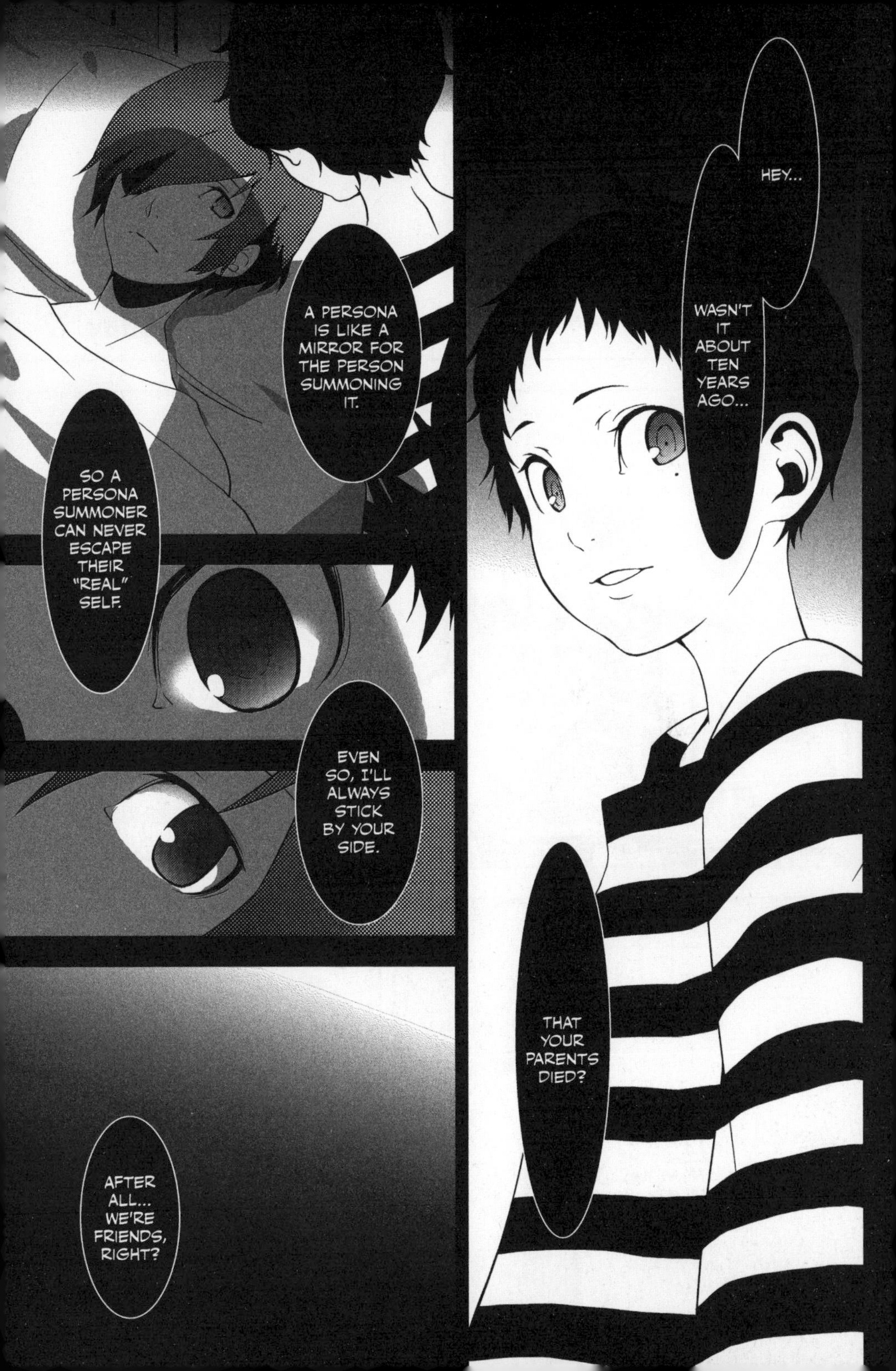
HEY...
WASN'T IT ABOUT TEN YEARS AGO...
THAT YOUR PARENTS DIED?
A PERSONA IS LIKE A MIRROR FOR THE PERSON SUMMONING IT.
SO A PERSONA SUMMONER CAN NEVER ESCAPE THEIR "REAL" SELF.
EVEN SO, I'LL ALWAYS STICK BY YOUR SIDE.
AFTER ALL... WE'RE FRIENDS, RIGHT?

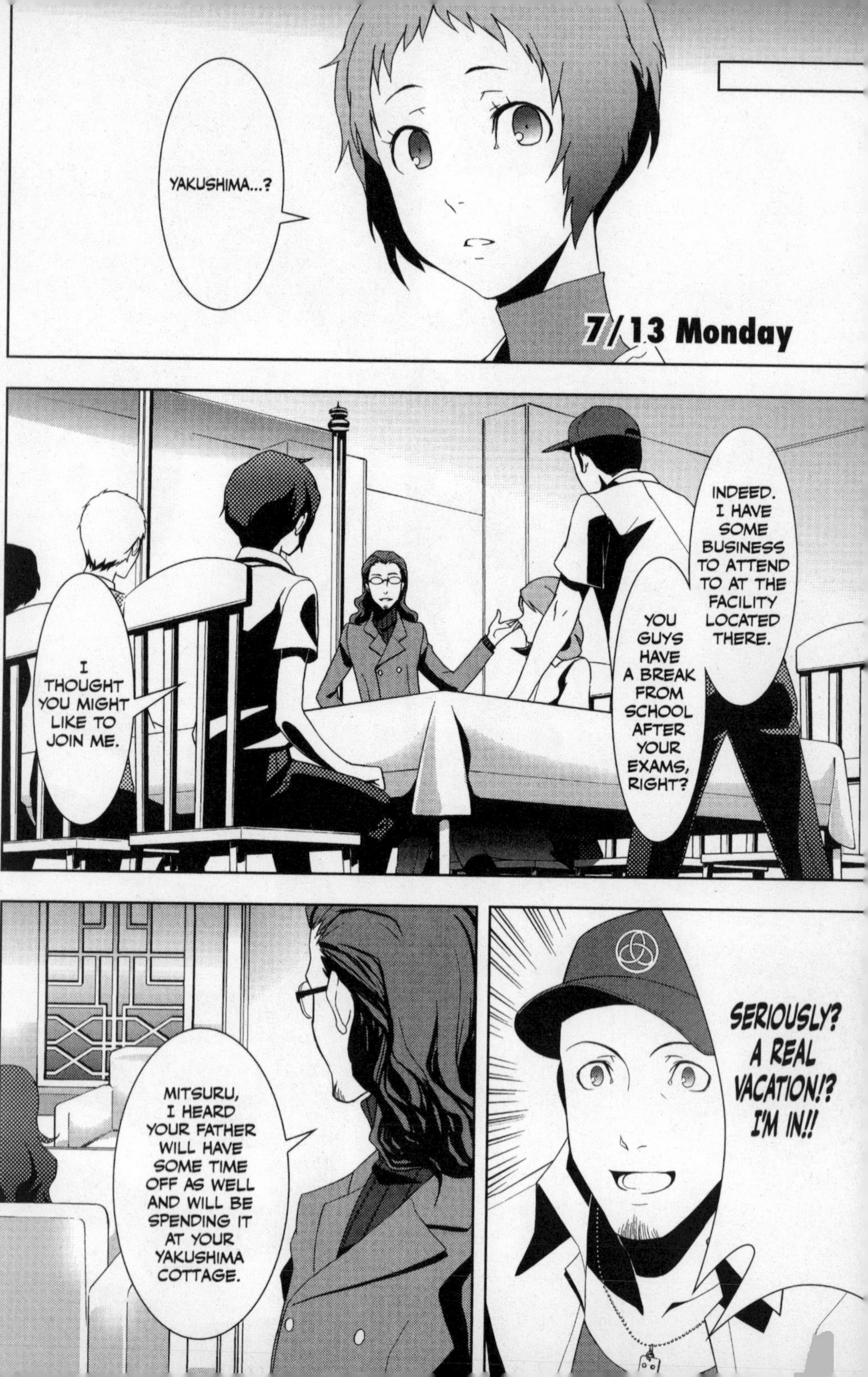
YAKUSHIMA...?
7/13 Monday
INDEED. I HAVE SOME BUSINESS TO ATTEND TO AT THE FACILITY LOCATED THERE.
YOU GUYS HAVE A BREAK FROM SCHOOL AFTER YOUR EXAMS, RIGHT?
I THOUGHT YOU MIGHT LIKE TO JOIN ME.
SERIOUSLY? A REAL VACATION!? I'M IN!!
MITSURU, I HEARD YOUR FATHER WILL HAVE SOME TIME OFF AS WELL AND WILL BE SPENDING IT AT YOUR YAKUSHIMA COTTAGE.

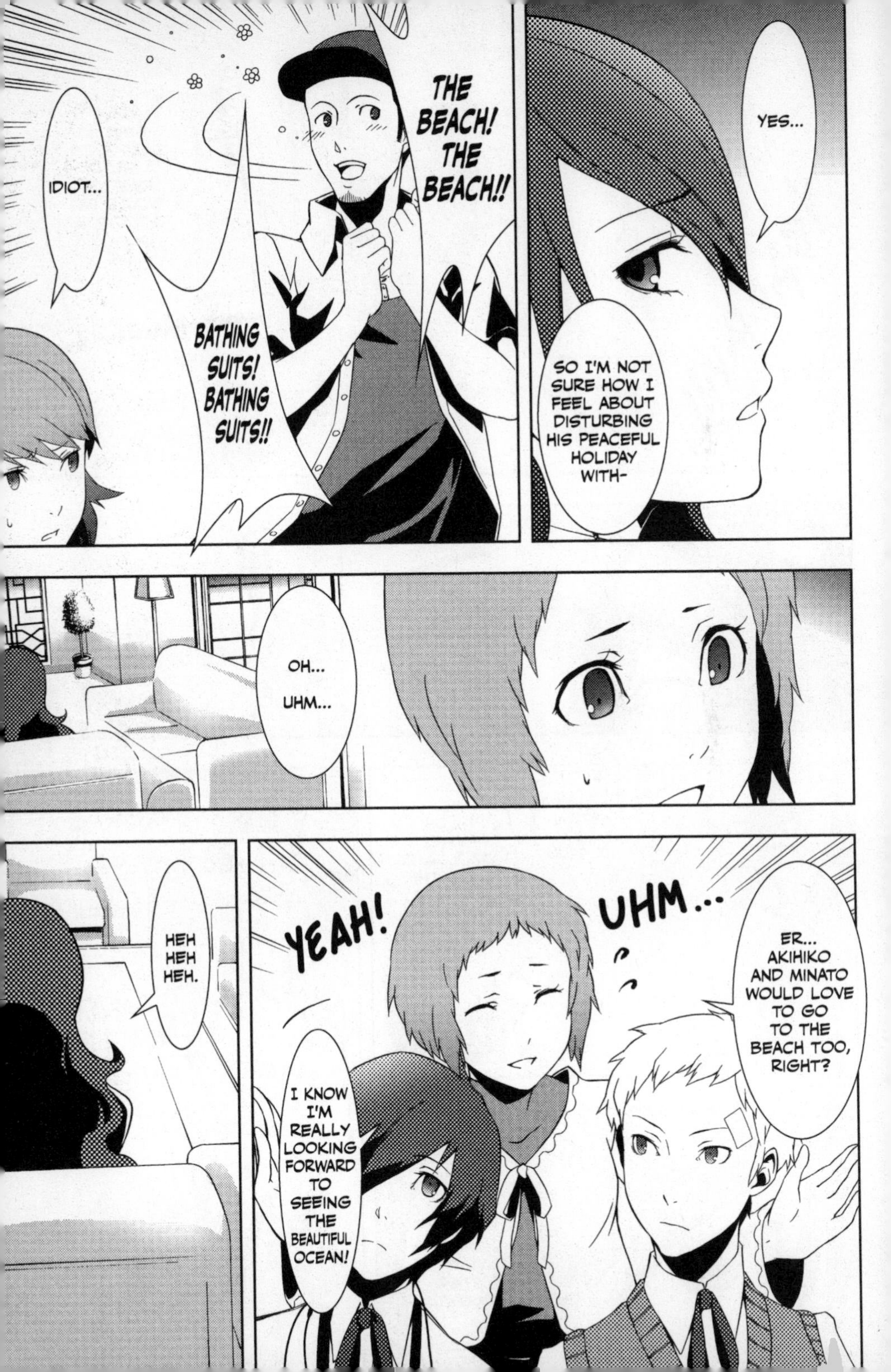
YES...
SO I'M NOT SURE HOW I FEEL ABOUT DISTURBING HIS PEACEFUL HOLIDAY WITH-
THE BEACH! THE BEACH! THE BEACH!!
BATHING SUITS! BATHING SUITS!!
IDIOT...
OH...
UHM...
ER... AKIHIKO AND MINATO WOULD LOVE TO GO TO THE BEACH TOO, RIGHT?
UHM...
YEAH!
I KNOW I'M REALLY LOOKING FORWARD TO SEEING THE BEAUTIFUL OCEAN!
HEH HEH HEH.

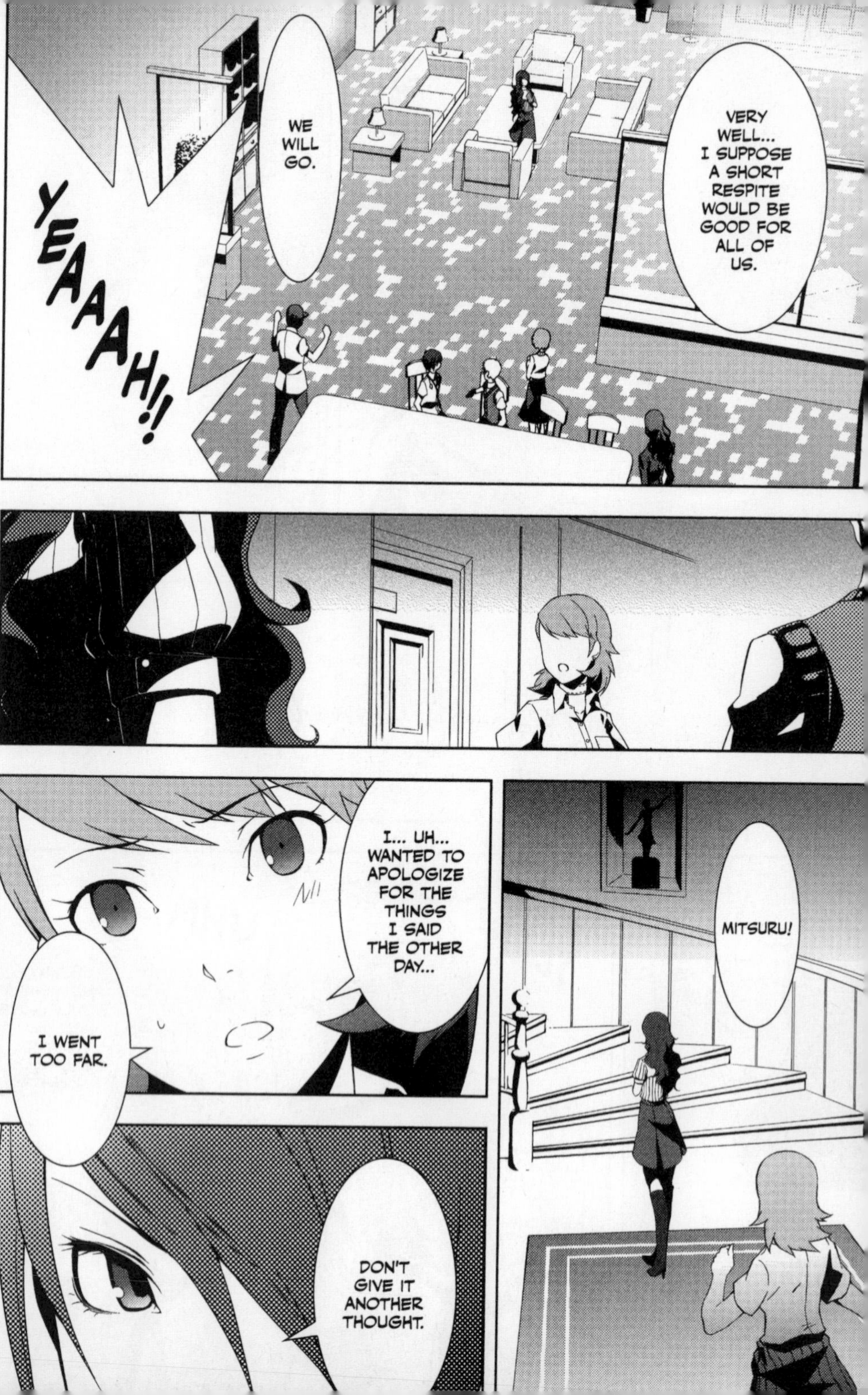
VERY WELL... I SUPPOSE A SHORT RESPITE WOULD BE GOOD FOR ALL OF US.
WE WILL GO.
YEAAAH!!
MITSURU!
I... UH... WANTED TO APOLOGIZE FOR THE THINGS I SAID THE OTHER DAY...
I WENT TOO FAR.
DON'T GIVE IT ANOTHER THOUGHT.

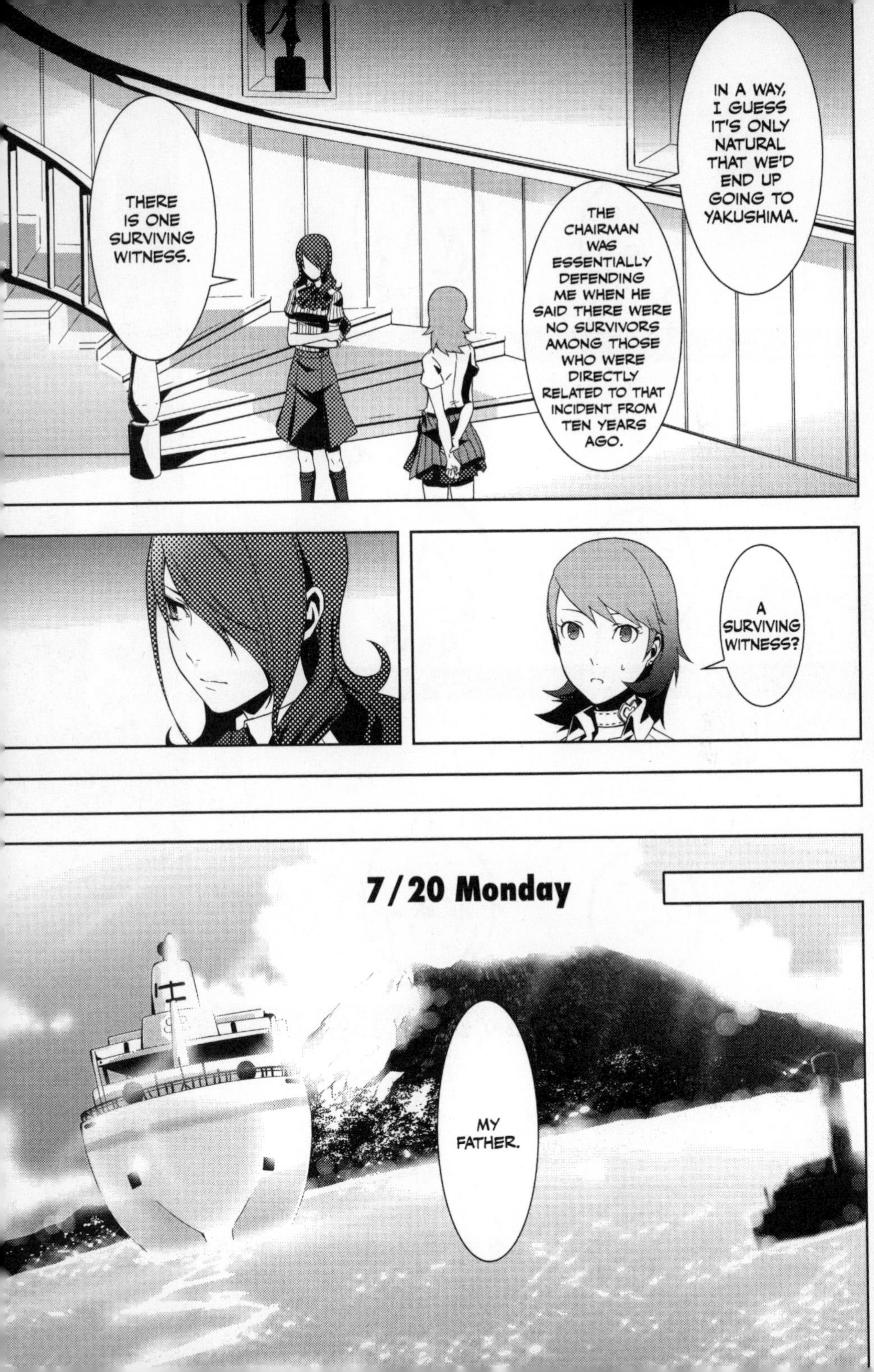
IN A WAY, I GUESS IT'S ONLY NATURAL THAT WE'D END UP GOING TO YAKUSHIMA.
THE CHAIRMAN WAS ESSENTIALLY DEFENDING ME WHEN HE SAID THERE WERE NO SURVIVORS AMONG THOSE WHO WERE DIRECTLY RELATED TO THAT INCIDENT FROM TEN YEARS AGO.
THERE IS ONE SURVIVING WITNESS.
A SURVIVING WITNESS?
7/20 Monday
MY FATHER.

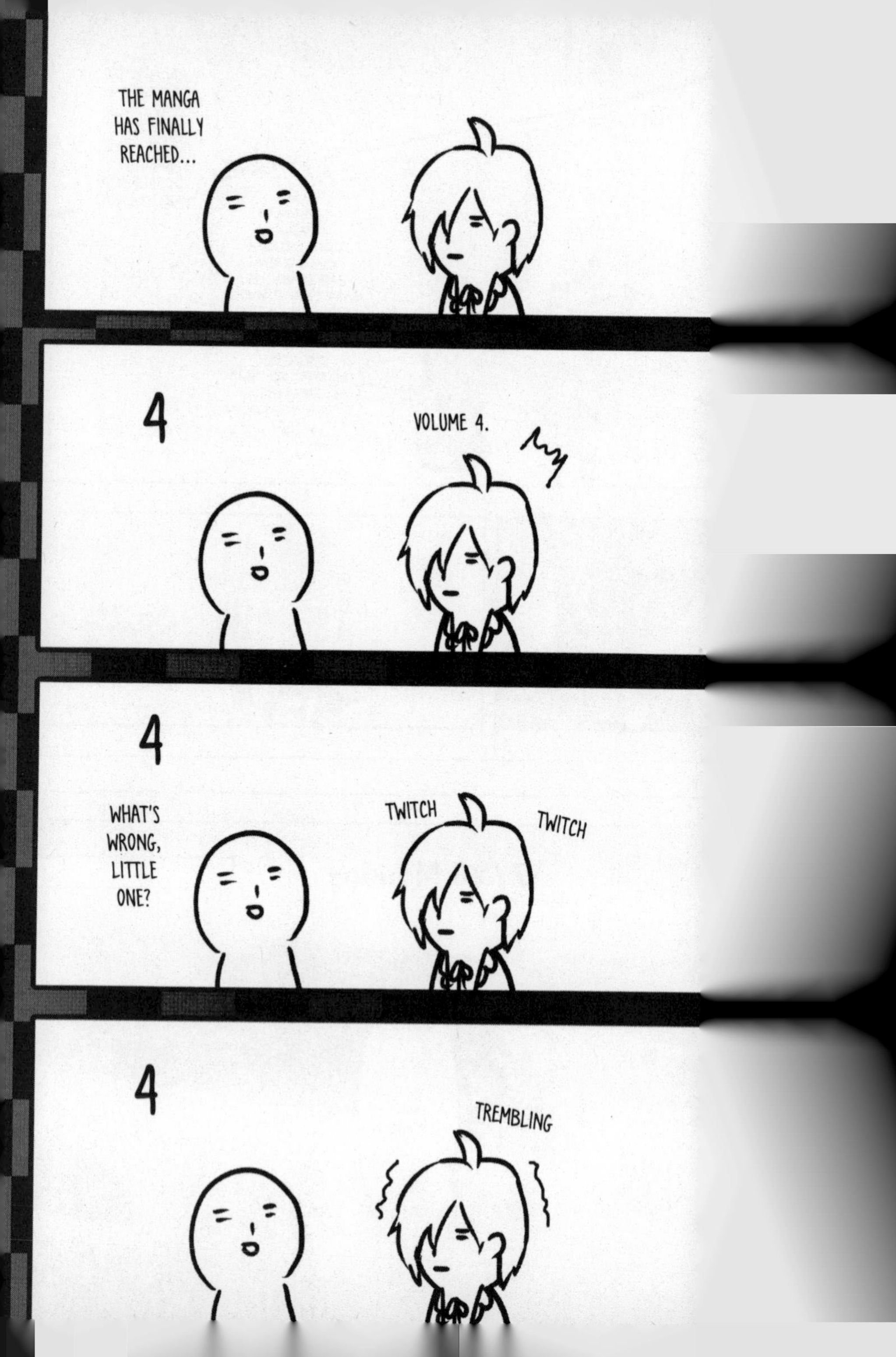
THE MANGA HAS FINALLY REACHED...
VOLUME 4.
4
4
WHAT'S WRONG, LITTLE ONE?
TWITCH
TWITCH
4
TREMBLING

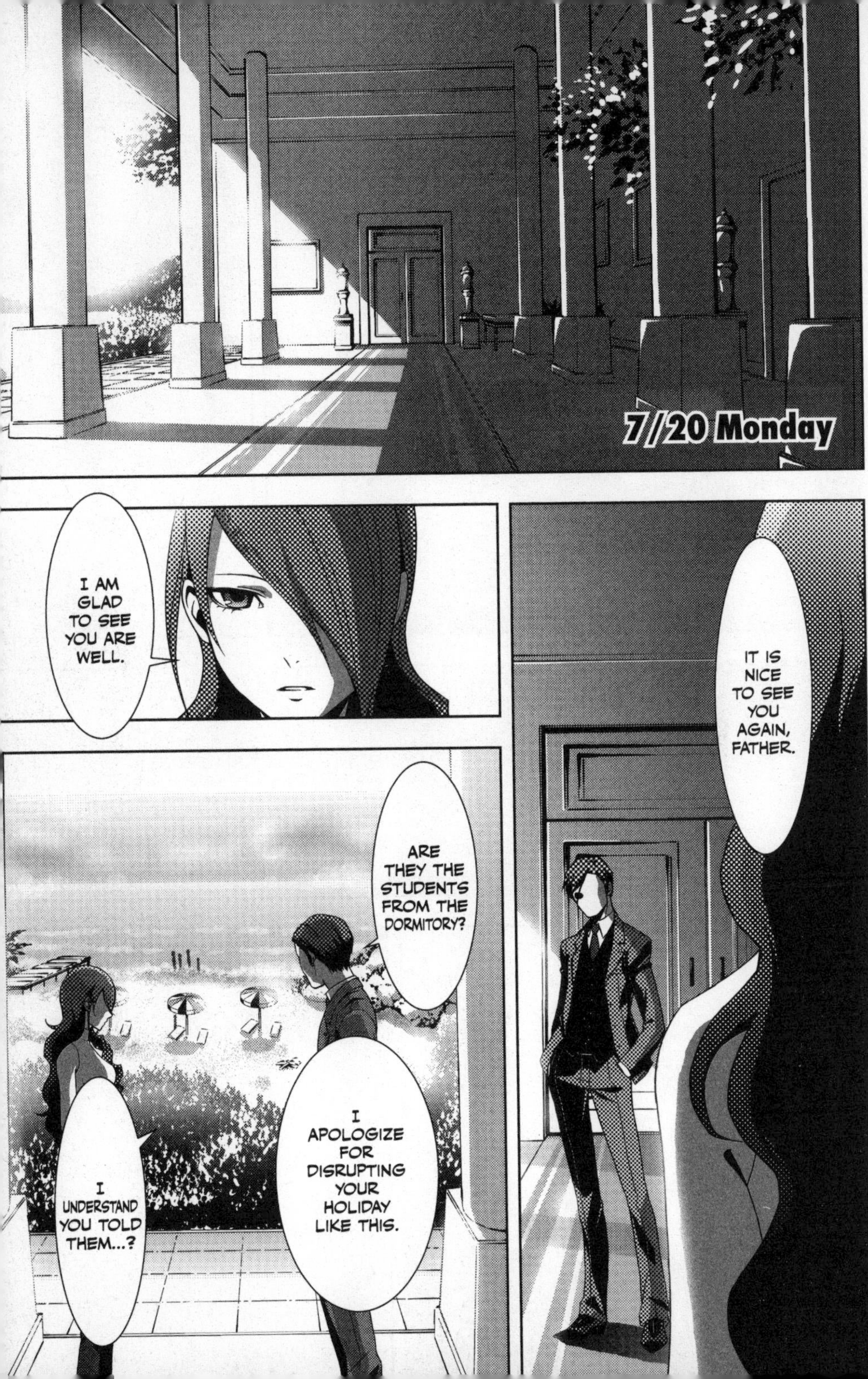
7/20 Monday
IT IS NICE TO SEE YOU AGAIN, FATHER.
I AM GLAD TO SEE YOU ARE WELL.
ARE THEY THE STUDENTS FROM THE DORMITORY?
I APOLOGIZE FOR DISRUPTING YOUR HOLIDAY LIKE THIS.
I UNDERSTAND YOU TOLD THEM...?

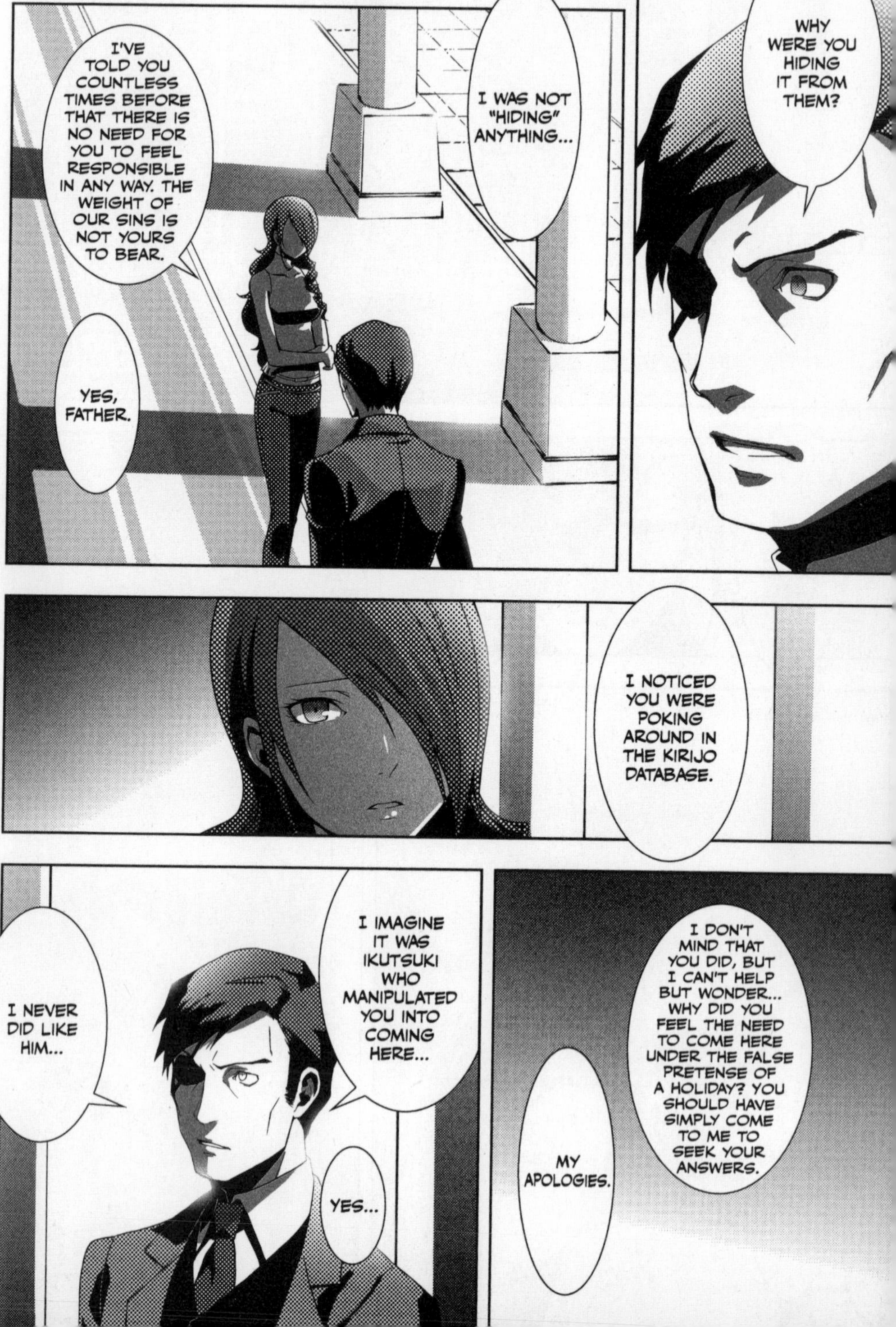
WHY WERE YOU HIDING IT FROM THEM?
I WAS NOT "HIDING" ANYTHING...
I'VE TOLD YOU COUNTLESS TIMES BEFORE THAT THERE IS NO NEED FOR YOU TO FEEL RESPONSIBLE IN ANY WAY. THE WEIGHT OF OUR SINS IS NOT YOURS TO BEAR.
YES, FATHER.
I NOTICED YOU WERE POKING AROUND IN THE KIRIJO DATABASE.
I DON'T MIND THAT YOU DID, BUT I CAN'T HELP BUT WONDER... WHY DID YOU FEEL THE NEED TO COME HERE UNDER THE FALSE PRETENSE OF A HOLIDAY? YOU SHOULD HAVE SIMPLY COME TO ME TO SEEK YOUR ANSWERS.
MY APOLOGIES.
I IMAGINE IT WAS IKUTSUKI WHO MANIPULATED YOU INTO COMING HERE...
I NEVER DID LIKE HIM...
YES...

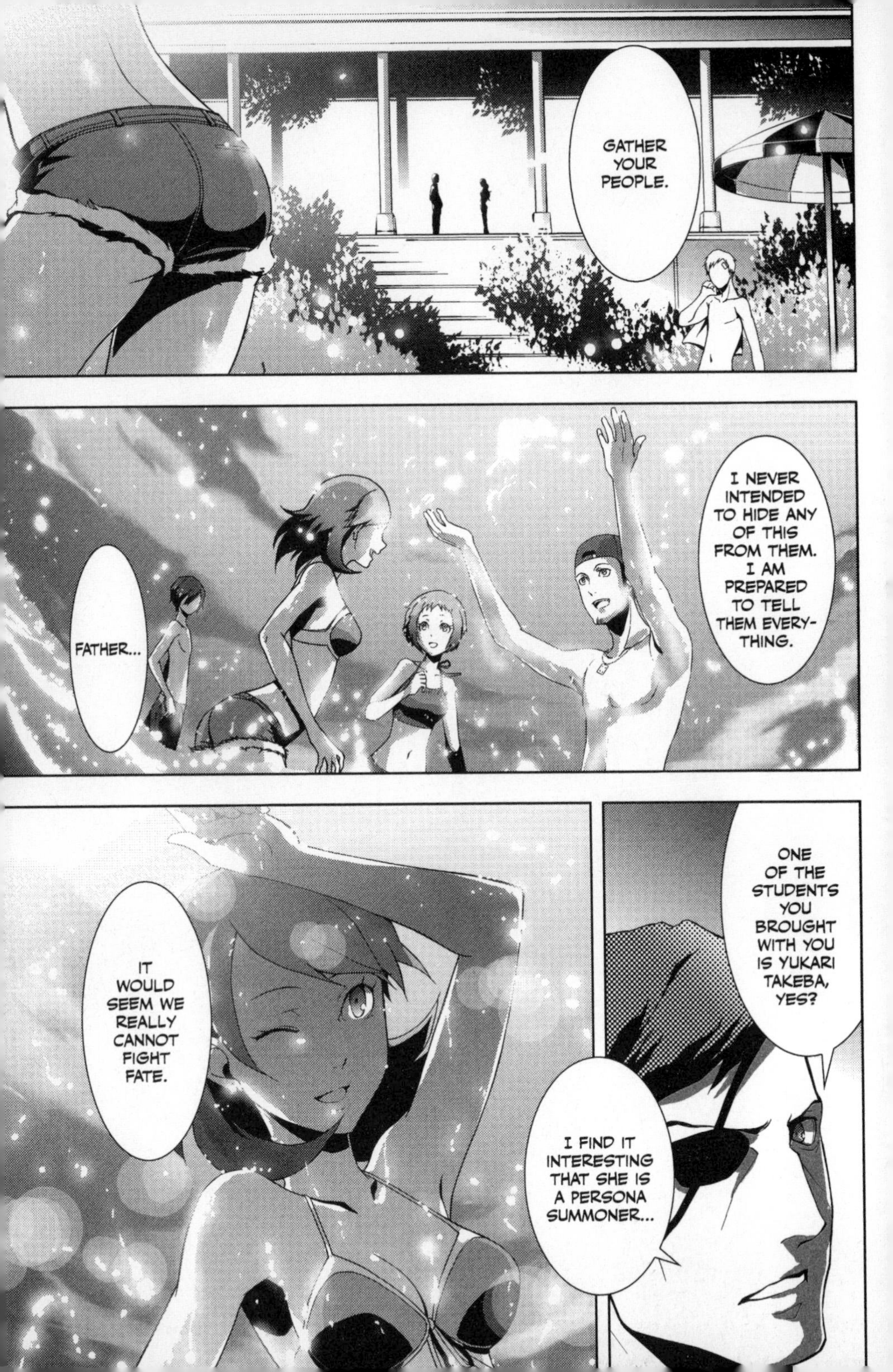
GATHER YOUR PEOPLE.
I NEVER INTENDED TO HIDE ANY OF THIS FROM THEM. I AM PREPARED TO TELL THEM EVERY-THING.
FATHER...
ONE OF THE STUDENTS YOU BROUGHT WITH YOU IS YUKARI TAKEBA, YES?
I FIND IT INTERESTING THAT SHE IS A PERSONA SUMMONER...
IT WOULD SEEM WE REALLY CANNOT FIGHT FATE.

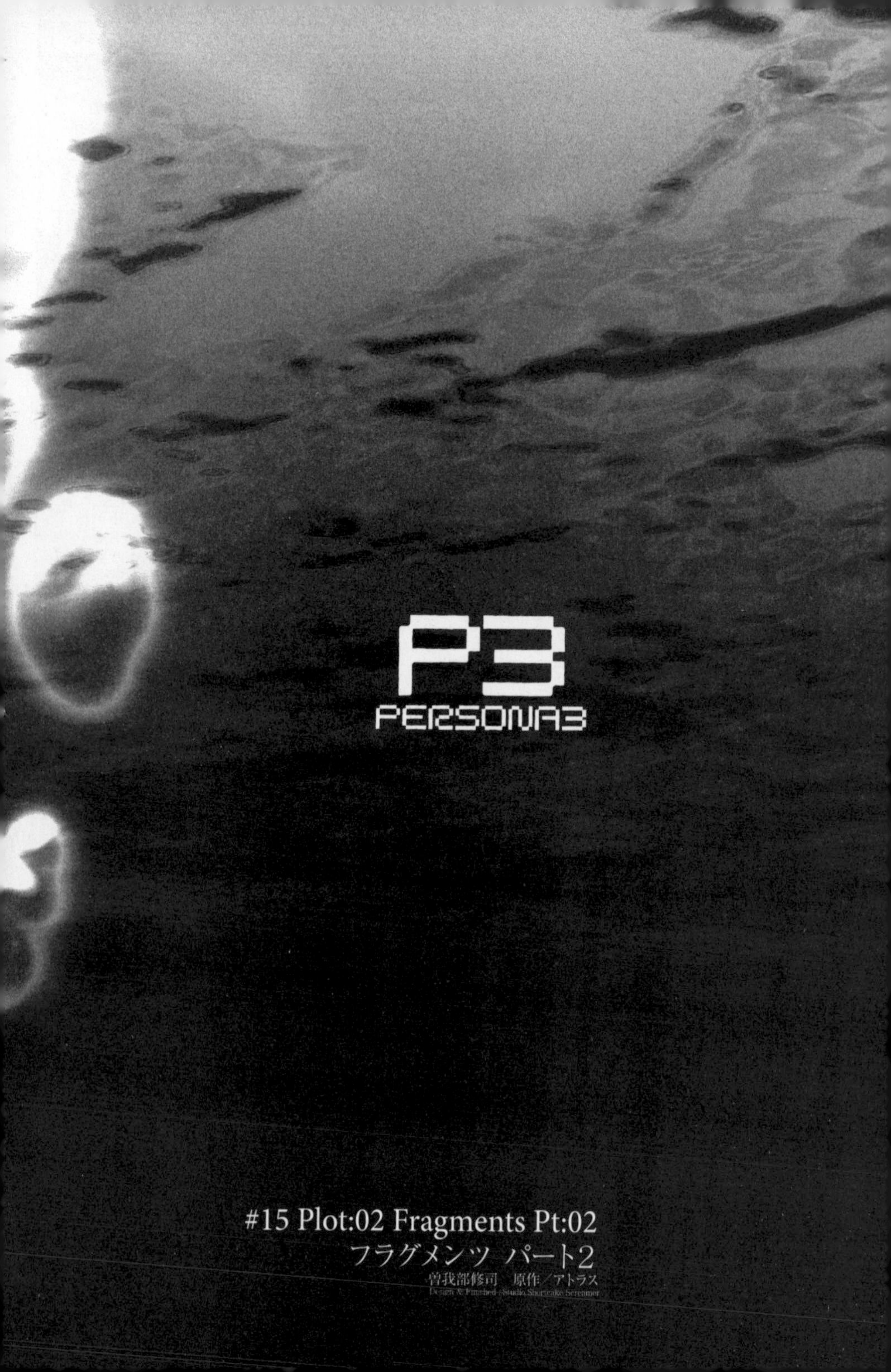

P3
PERSONA3

#15 Plot:02 Fragments Pt:02
フラグメンツ パート2

曽我部修司　原作／アトラス
Design & Finished :Studio Shortcake Screamer

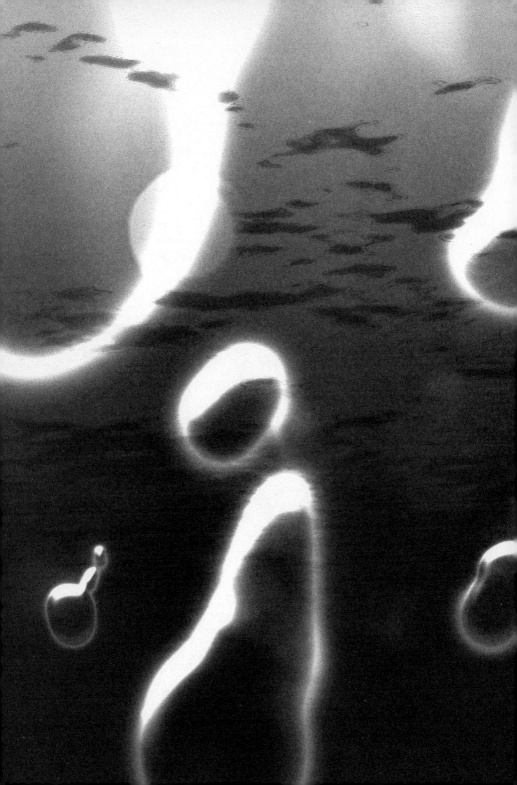

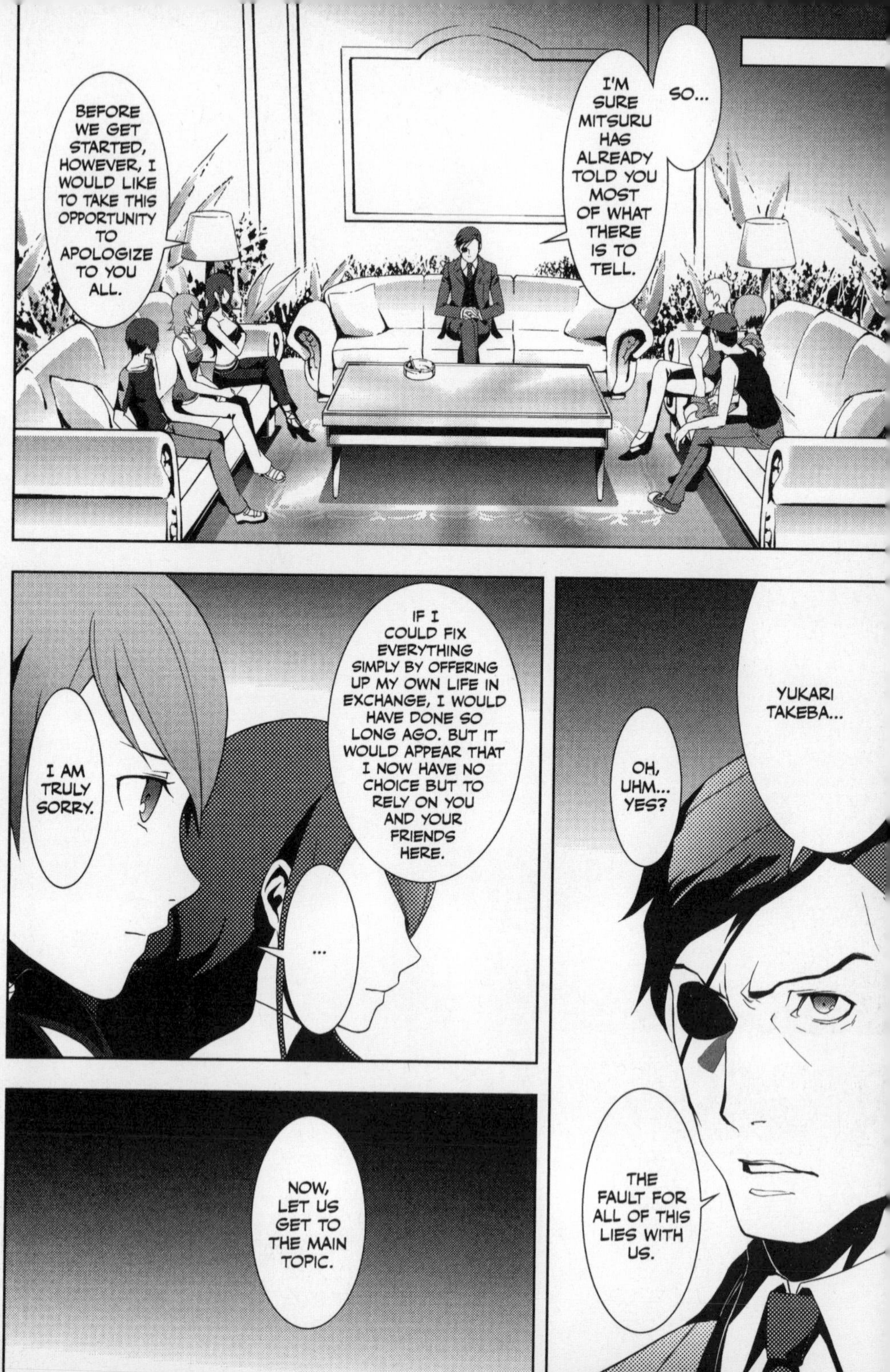
SO...
I'M SURE MITSURU HAS ALREADY TOLD YOU MOST OF WHAT THERE IS TO TELL.
BEFORE WE GET STARTED, HOWEVER, I WOULD LIKE TO TAKE THIS OPPORTUNITY TO APOLOGIZE TO YOU ALL.
YUKARI TAKEBA...
OH, UHM... YES?
THE FAULT FOR ALL OF THIS LIES WITH US.
IF I COULD FIX EVERYTHING SIMPLY BY OFFERING UP MY OWN LIFE IN EXCHANGE, I WOULD HAVE DONE SO LONG AGO. BUT IT WOULD APPEAR THAT I NOW HAVE NO CHOICE BUT TO RELY ON YOU AND YOUR FRIENDS HERE.
I AM TRULY SORRY.
...
NOW, LET US GET TO THE MAIN TOPIC.

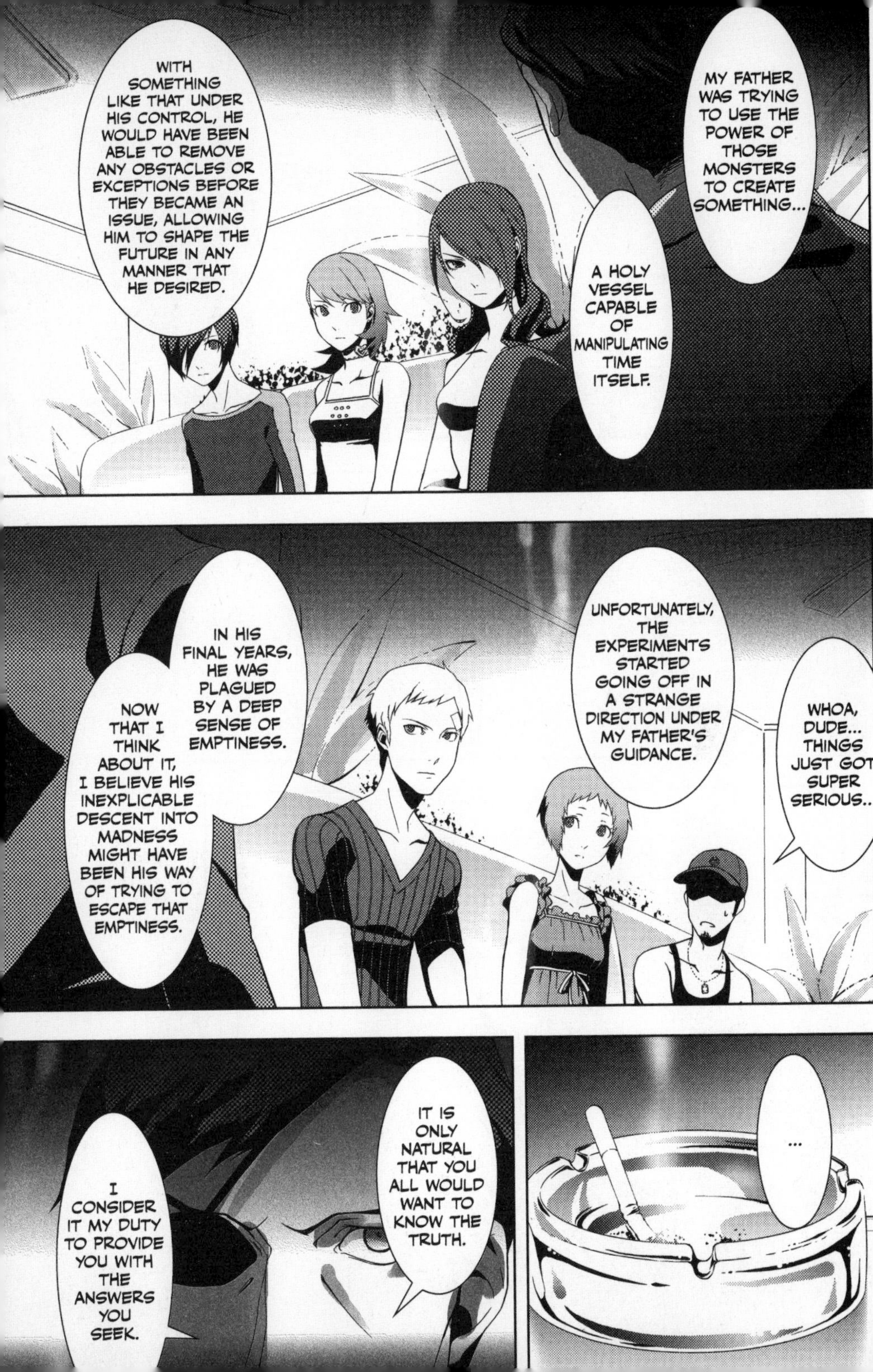
MY FATHER WAS TRYING TO USE THE POWER OF THOSE MONSTERS TO CREATE SOMETHING...
A HOLY VESSEL CAPABLE OF MANIPULATING TIME ITSELF.
WITH SOMETHING LIKE THAT UNDER HIS CONTROL, HE WOULD HAVE BEEN ABLE TO REMOVE ANY OBSTACLES OR EXCEPTIONS BEFORE THEY BECAME AN ISSUE, ALLOWING HIM TO SHAPE THE FUTURE IN ANY MANNER THAT HE DESIRED.
UNFORTUNATELY, THE EXPERIMENTS STARTED GOING OFF IN A STRANGE DIRECTION UNDER MY FATHER'S GUIDANCE.
WHOA, DUDE... THINGS JUST GOT SUPER SERIOUS...
IN HIS FINAL YEARS, HE WAS PLAGUED BY A DEEP SENSE OF EMPTINESS.
NOW THAT I THINK ABOUT IT, I BELIEVE HIS INEXPLICABLE DESCENT INTO MADNESS MIGHT HAVE BEEN HIS WAY OF TRYING TO ESCAPE THAT EMPTINESS.
...
IT IS ONLY NATURAL THAT YOU ALL WOULD WANT TO KNOW THE TRUTH.
I CONSIDER IT MY DUTY TO PROVIDE YOU WITH THE ANSWERS YOU SEEK.

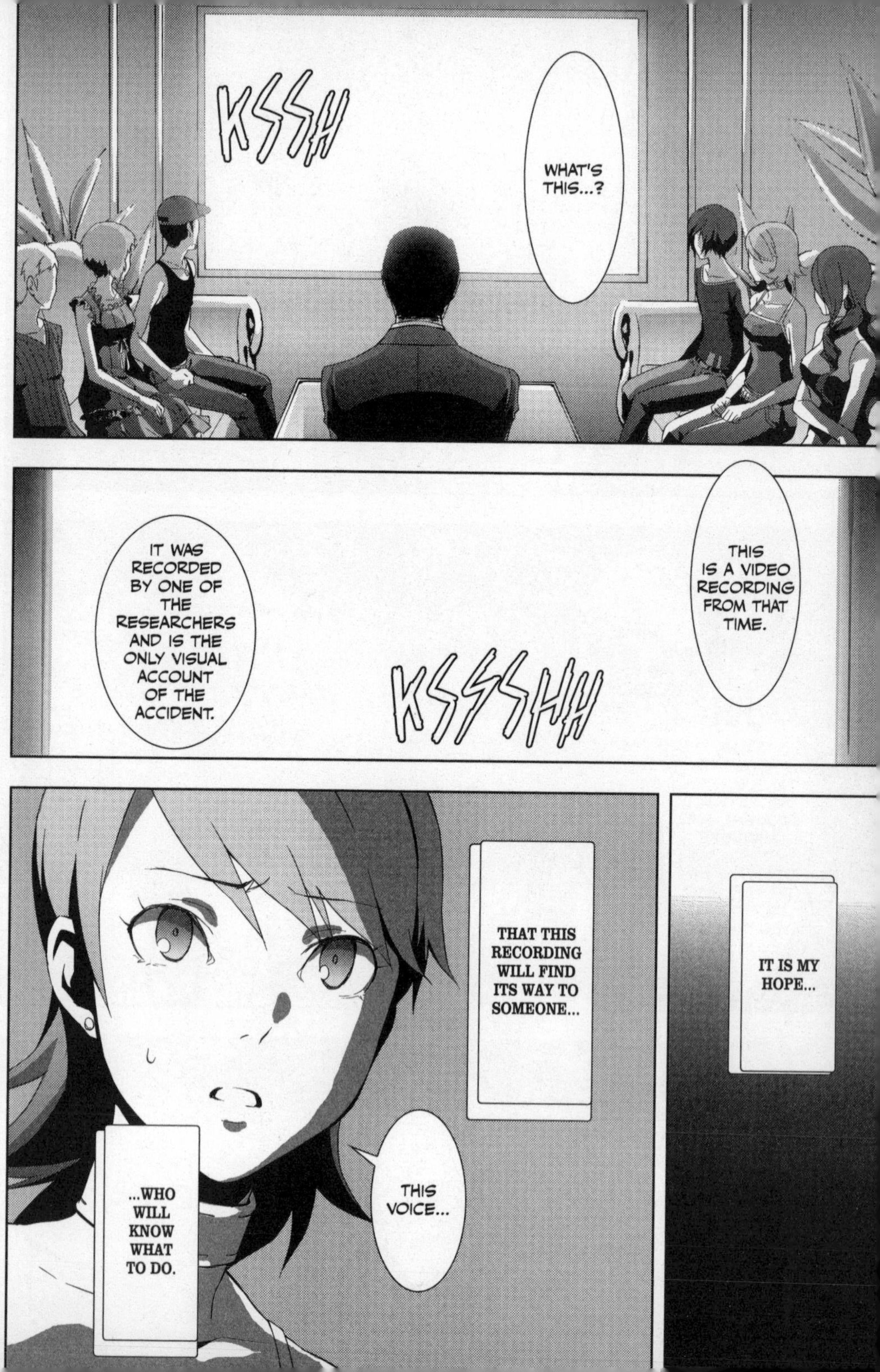
WHAT'S THIS...?
KSSH
THIS IS A VIDEO RECORDING FROM THAT TIME.
KSSSHH
IT WAS RECORDED BY ONE OF THE RESEARCHERS AND IS THE ONLY VISUAL ACCOUNT OF THE ACCIDENT.
IT IS MY HOPE...
THAT THIS RECORDING WILL FIND ITS WAY TO SOMEONE...
THIS VOICE...
...WHO WILL KNOW WHAT TO DO.

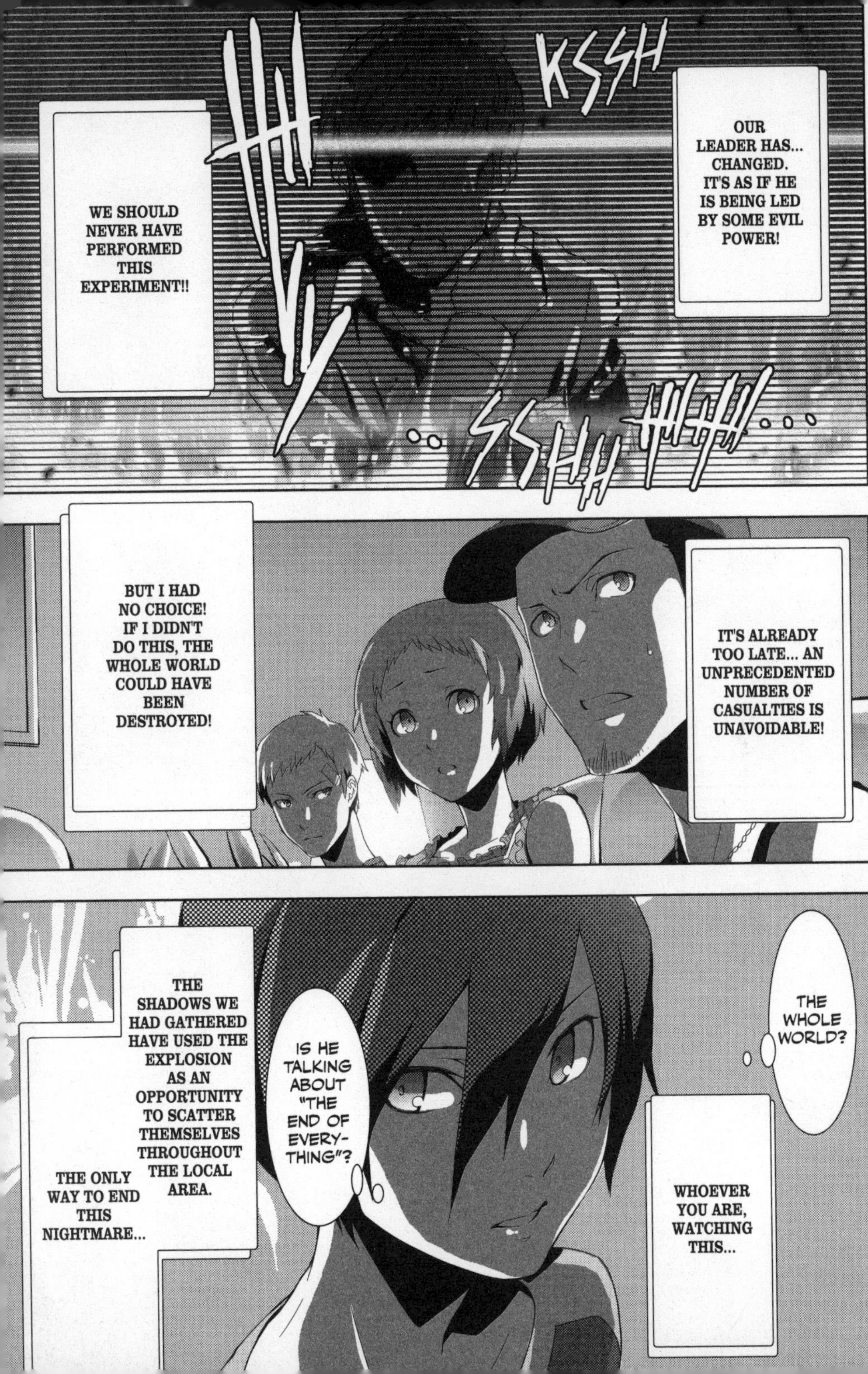
KSSH
OUR LEADER HAS... CHANGED. IT'S AS IF HE IS BEING LED BY SOME EVIL POWER!
WE SHOULD NEVER HAVE PERFORMED THIS EXPERIMENT!!
SSHHHHH...
IT'S ALREADY TOO LATE... AN UNPRECEDENTED NUMBER OF CASUALTIES IS UNAVOIDABLE!
BUT I HAD NO CHOICE! IF I DIDN'T DO THIS, THE WHOLE WORLD COULD HAVE BEEN DESTROYED!
THE WHOLE WORLD?
WHOEVER YOU ARE, WATCHING THIS...
IS HE TALKING ABOUT "THE END OF EVERY-THING"?
THE SHADOWS WE HAD GATHERED HAVE USED THE EXPLOSION AS AN OPPORTUNITY TO SCATTER THEMSELVES THROUGHOUT THE LOCAL AREA.
THE ONLY WAY TO END THIS NIGHTMARE...

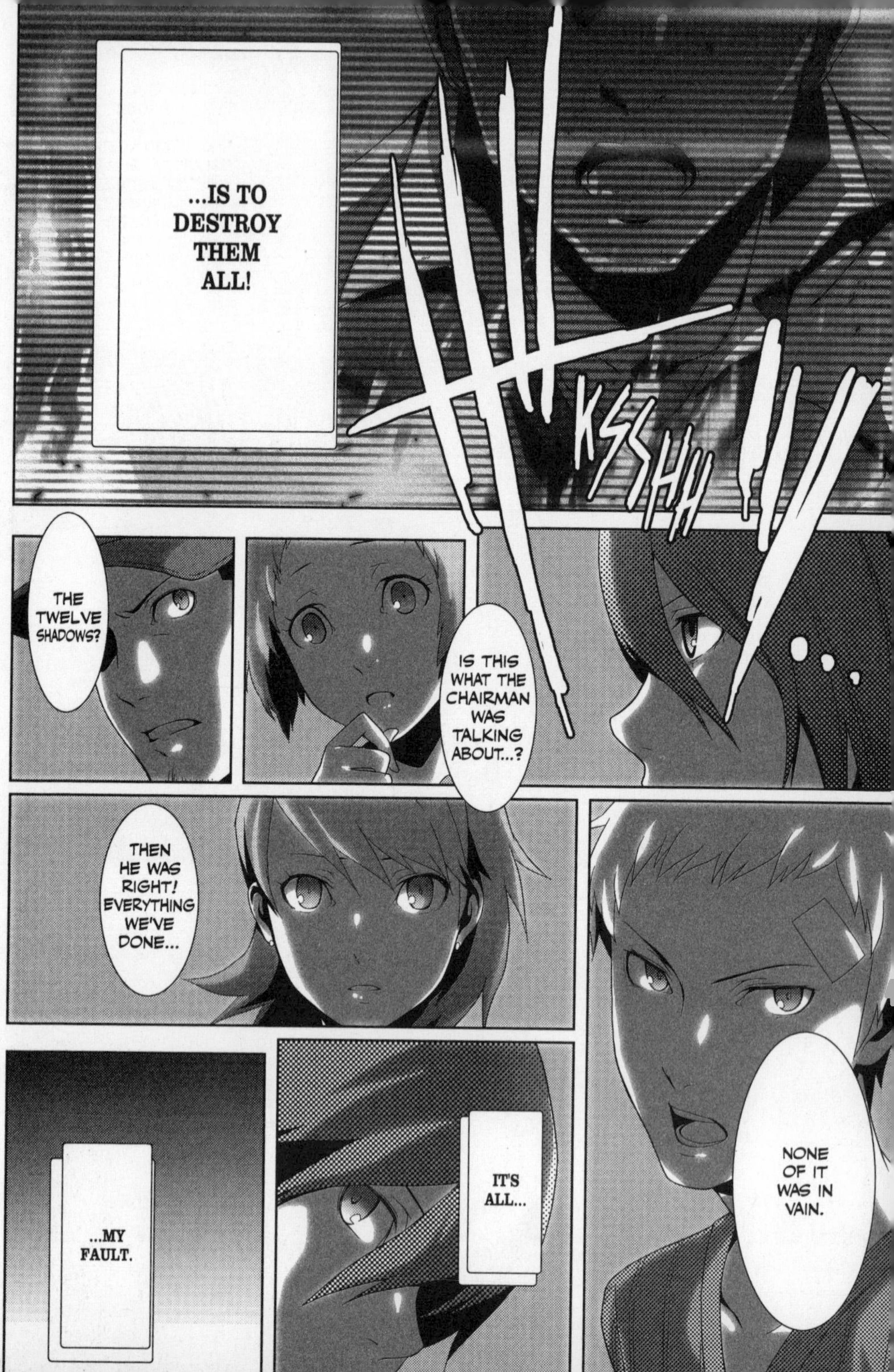
...IS TO DESTROY THEM ALL!
KSSHH
...
IS THIS WHAT THE CHAIRMAN WAS TALKING ABOUT...?
THE TWELVE SHADOWS?
NONE OF IT WAS IN VAIN.
THEN HE WAS RIGHT! EVERYTHING WE'VE DONE...
IT'S ALL...
...MY FAULT.

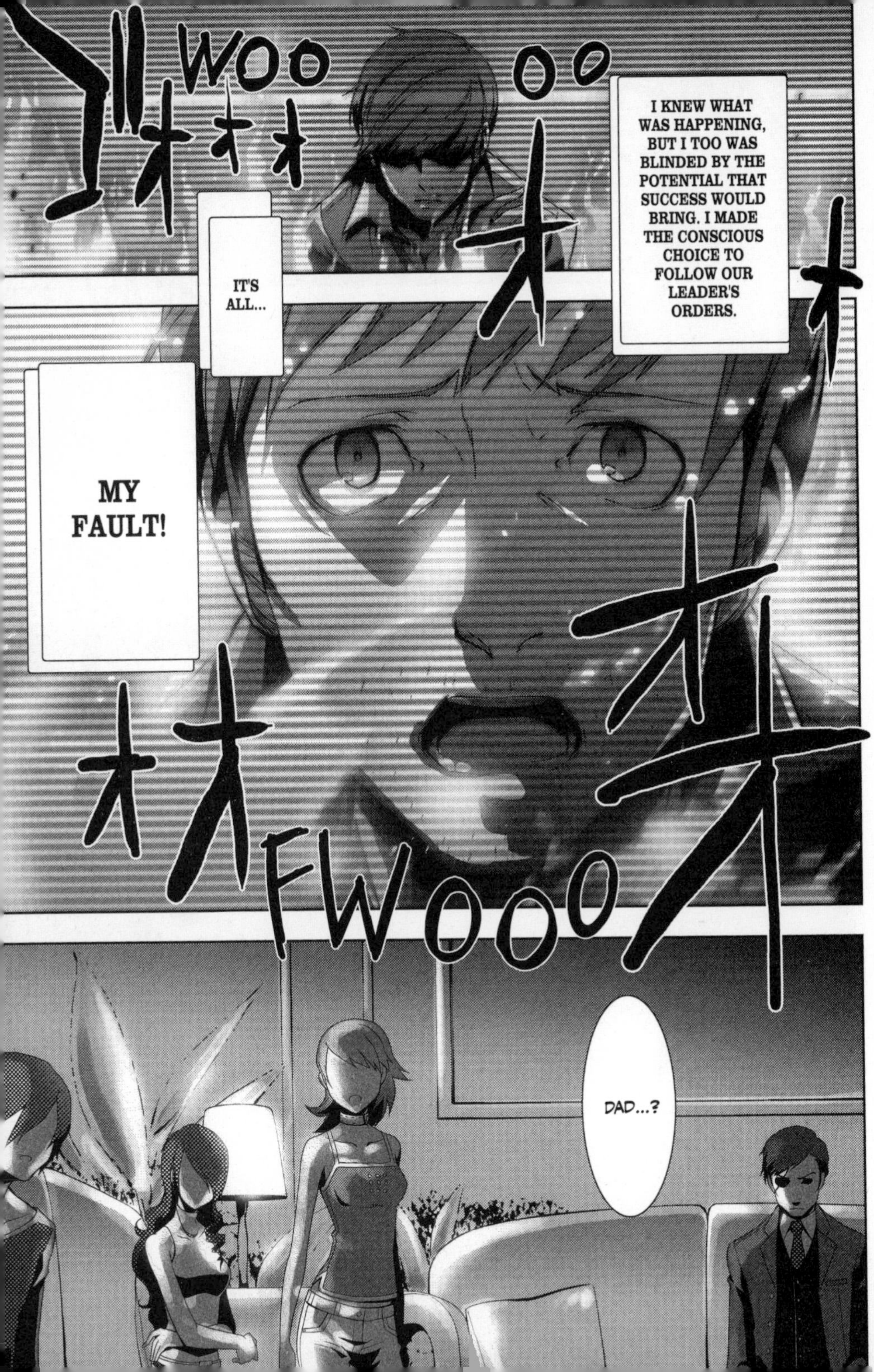

WOOO
I KNEW WHAT WAS HAPPENING, BUT I TOO WAS BLINDED BY THE POTENTIAL THAT SUCCESS WOULD BRING. I MADE THE CONSCIOUS CHOICE TO FOLLOW OUR LEADER'S ORDERS.
IT'S ALL...
MY FAULT!
FWOOO
DAD...?

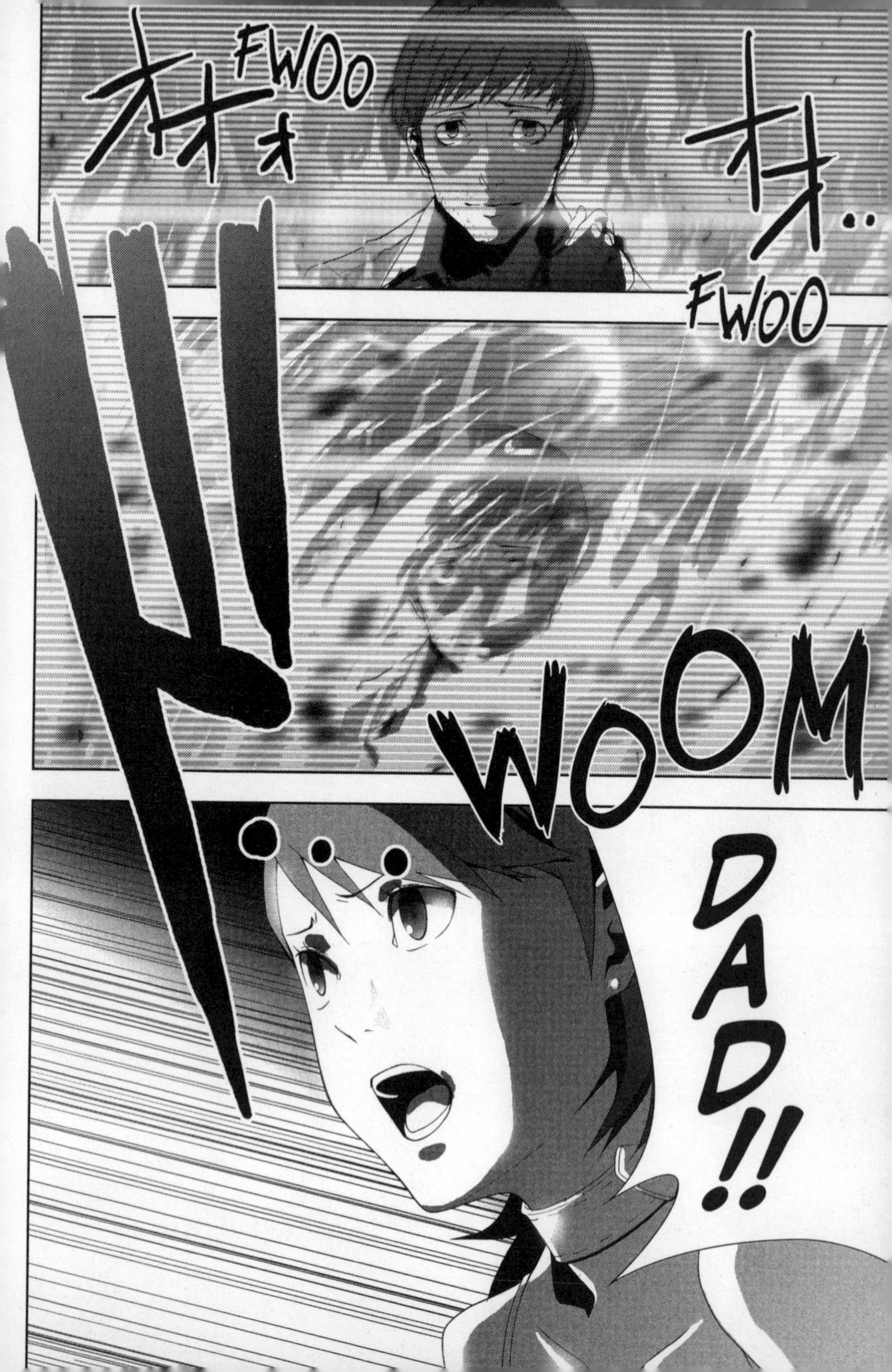
オ..
FWOO
オオォ
FWOO
WOOM
...!!
DAD!!

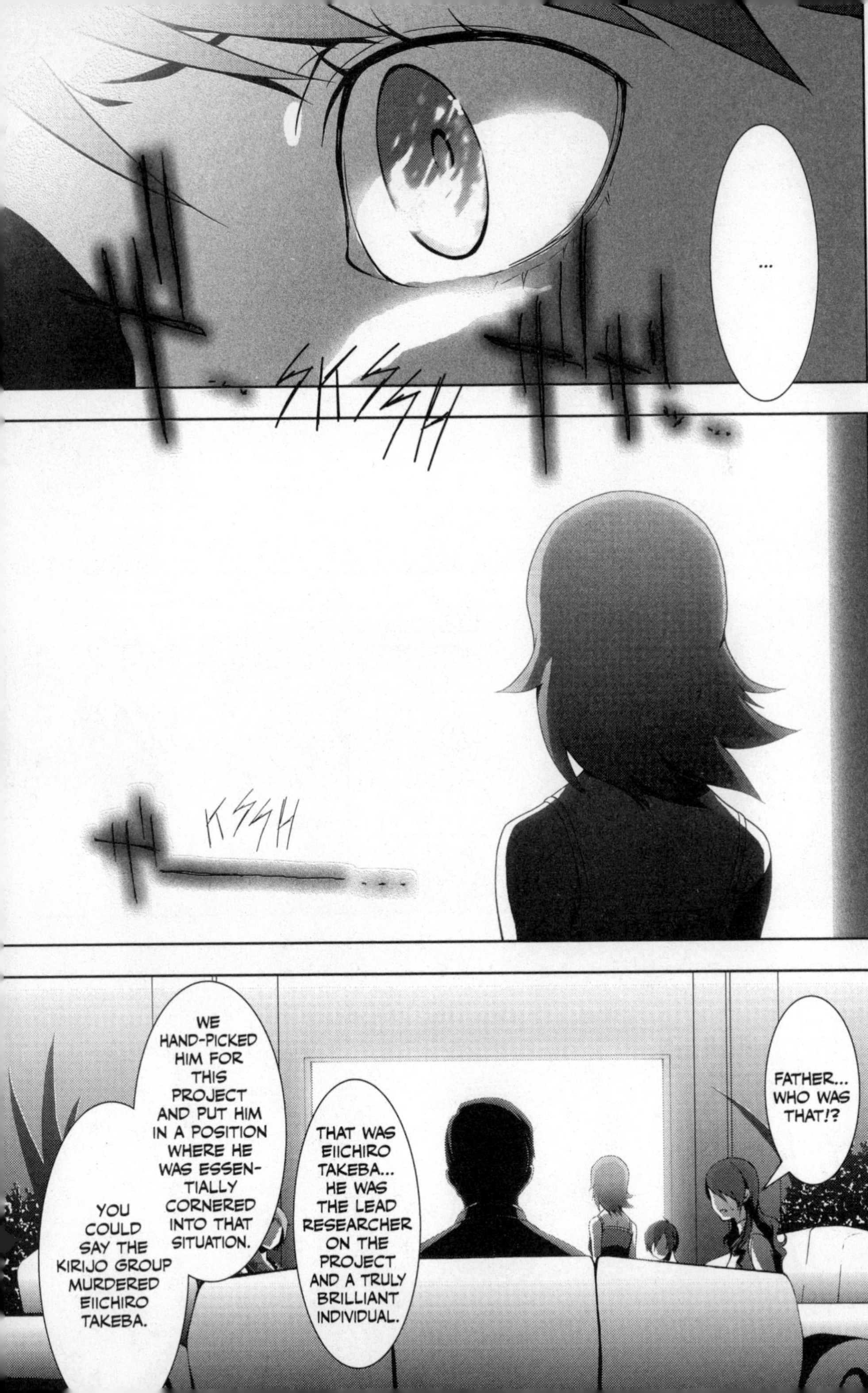
...
SKSSH
KSSH
FATHER... WHO WAS THAT!?
THAT WAS EIICHIRO TAKEBA... HE WAS THE LEAD RESEARCHER ON THE PROJECT AND A TRULY BRILLIANT INDIVIDUAL.
WE HAND-PICKED HIM FOR THIS PROJECT AND PUT HIM IN A POSITION WHERE HE WAS ESSEN-TIALLY CORNERED INTO THAT SITUATION.
YOU COULD SAY THE KIRIJO GROUP MURDERED EIICHIRO TAKEBA.

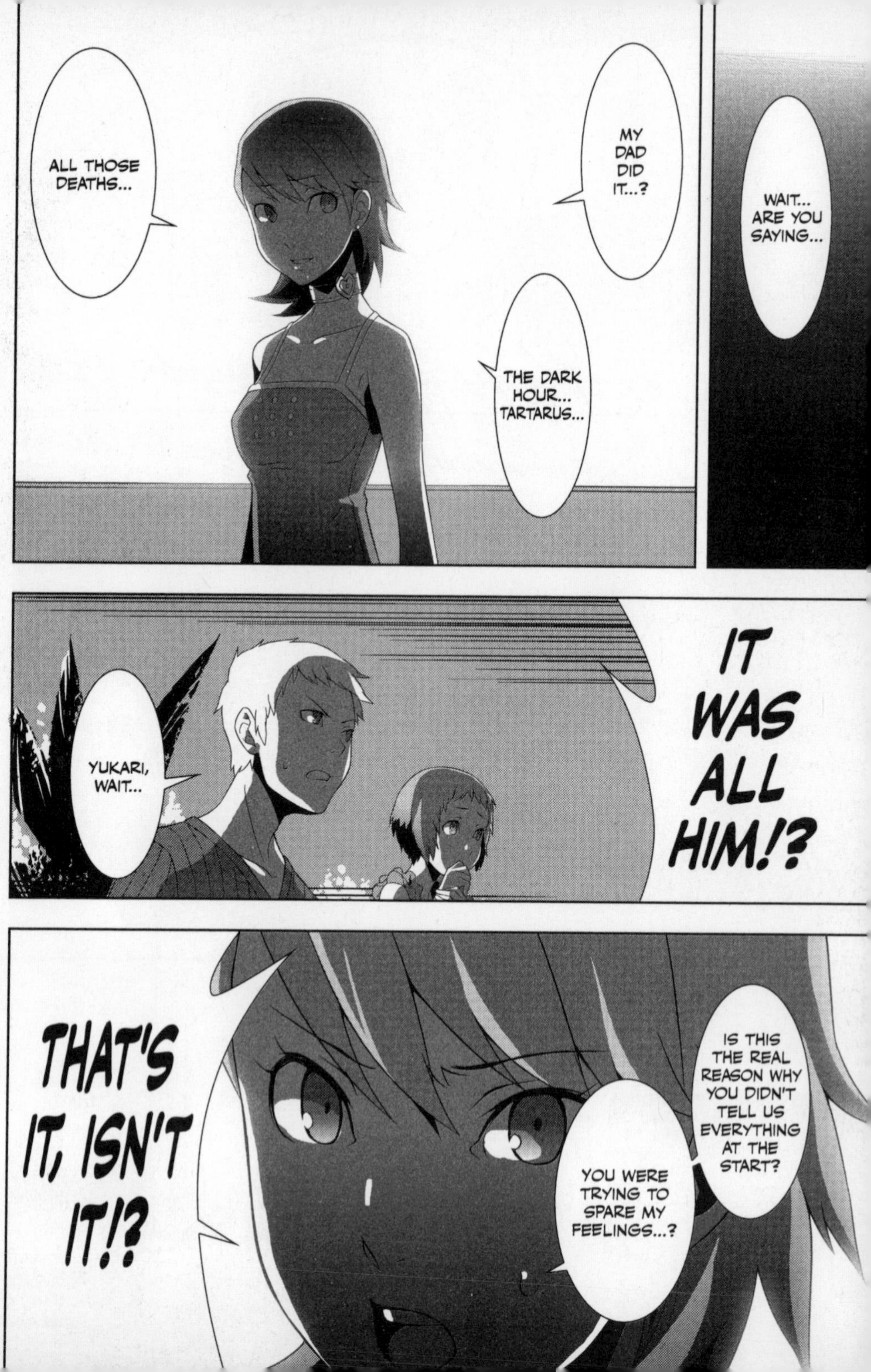

WAIT... ARE YOU SAYING...
MY DAD DID IT...?
THE DARK HOUR... TARTARUS...
ALL THOSE DEATHS...
IT WAS ALL HIM!?
YUKARI, WAIT...
IS THIS THE REAL REASON WHY YOU DIDN'T TELL US EVERYTHING AT THE START?
YOU WERE TRYING TO SPARE MY FEELINGS...?
THAT'S IT, ISN'T IT!?

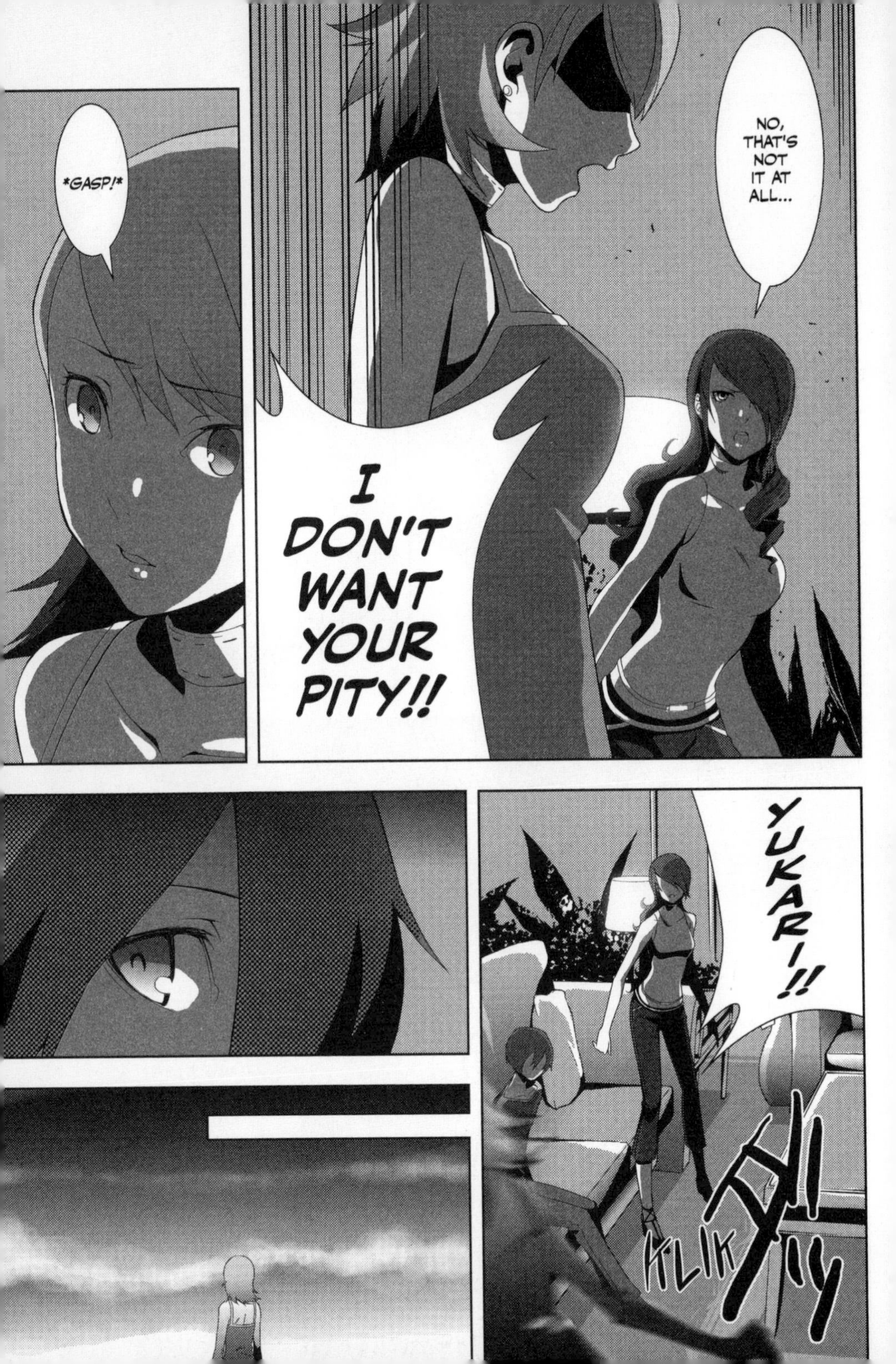
NO, THAT'S NOT IT AT ALL...
I DON'T WANT YOUR PITY!!
GASP!
YUKARI!!
KLIK

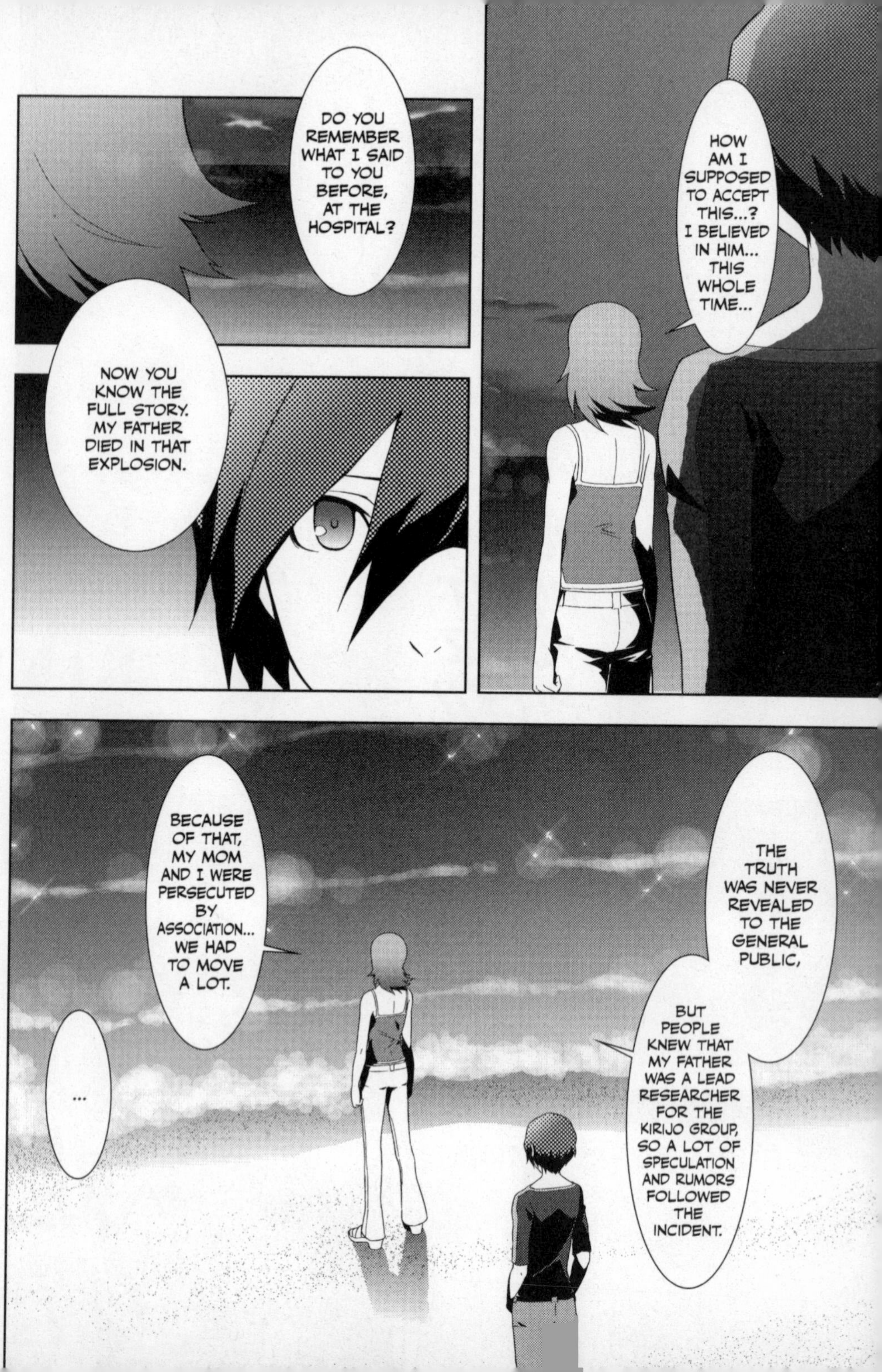
HOW AM I SUPPOSED TO ACCEPT THIS...? I BELIEVED IN HIM... THIS WHOLE TIME...
DO YOU REMEMBER WHAT I SAID TO YOU BEFORE, AT THE HOSPITAL?
NOW YOU KNOW THE FULL STORY. MY FATHER DIED IN THAT EXPLOSION.
THE TRUTH WAS NEVER REVEALED TO THE GENERAL PUBLIC,
BUT PEOPLE KNEW THAT MY FATHER WAS A LEAD RESEARCHER FOR THE KIRIJO GROUP, SO A LOT OF SPECULATION AND RUMORS FOLLOWED THE INCIDENT.
BECAUSE OF THAT, MY MOM AND I WERE PERSECUTED BY ASSOCIATION... WE HAD TO MOVE A LOT.
...

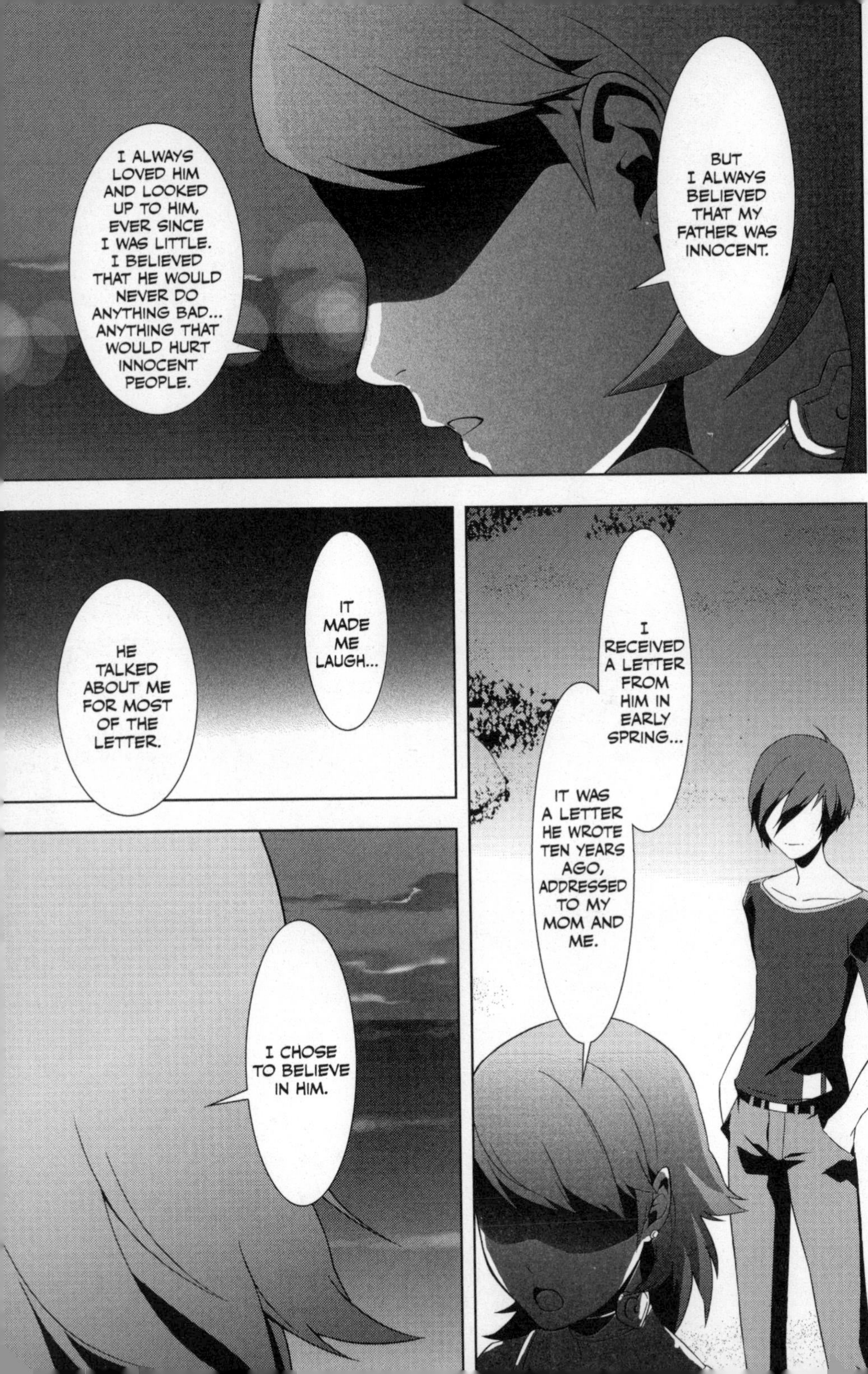
BUT I ALWAYS BELIEVED THAT MY FATHER WAS INNOCENT.
I ALWAYS LOVED HIM AND LOOKED UP TO HIM, EVER SINCE I WAS LITTLE. I BELIEVED THAT HE WOULD NEVER DO ANYTHING BAD... ANYTHING THAT WOULD HURT INNOCENT PEOPLE.
I RECEIVED A LETTER FROM HIM IN EARLY SPRING...
IT WAS A LETTER HE WROTE TEN YEARS AGO, ADDRESSED TO MY MOM AND ME.
IT MADE ME LAUGH...
HE TALKED ABOUT ME FOR MOST OF THE LETTER.
I CHOSE TO BELIEVE IN HIM.

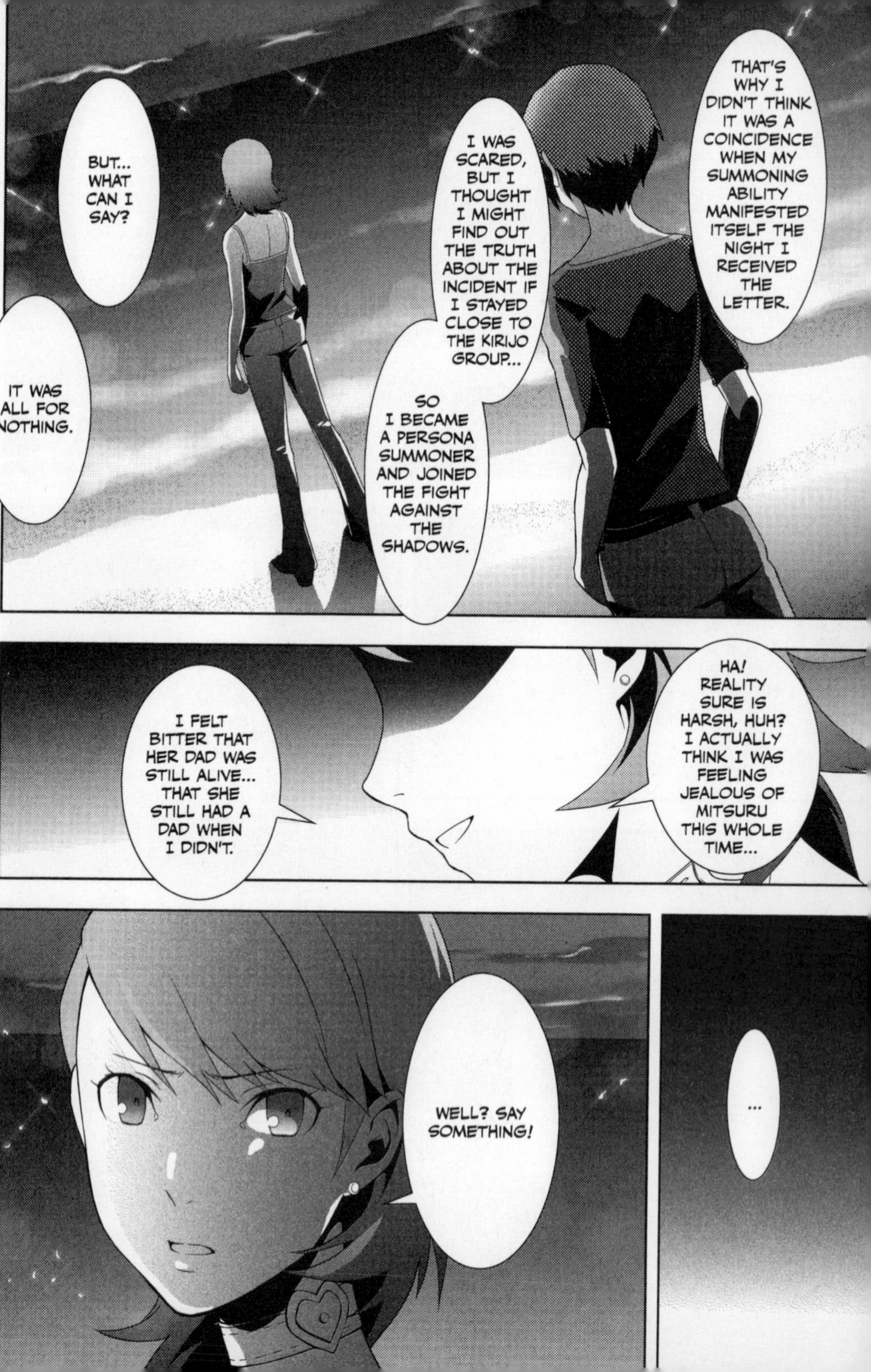
THAT'S WHY I DIDN'T THINK IT WAS A COINCIDENCE WHEN MY SUMMONING ABILITY MANIFESTED ITSELF THE NIGHT I RECEIVED THE LETTER.
I WAS SCARED, BUT I THOUGHT I MIGHT FIND OUT THE TRUTH ABOUT THE INCIDENT IF I STAYED CLOSE TO THE KIRIJO GROUP...
SO I BECAME A PERSONA SUMMONER AND JOINED THE FIGHT AGAINST THE SHADOWS.
BUT... WHAT CAN I SAY?
IT WAS ALL FOR NOTHING.
HA! REALITY SURE IS HARSH, HUH? I ACTUALLY THINK I WAS FEELING JEALOUS OF MITSURU THIS WHOLE TIME...
I FELT BITTER THAT HER DAD WAS STILL ALIVE... THAT SHE STILL HAD A DAD WHEN I DIDN'T.
...
WELL? SAY SOMETHING!

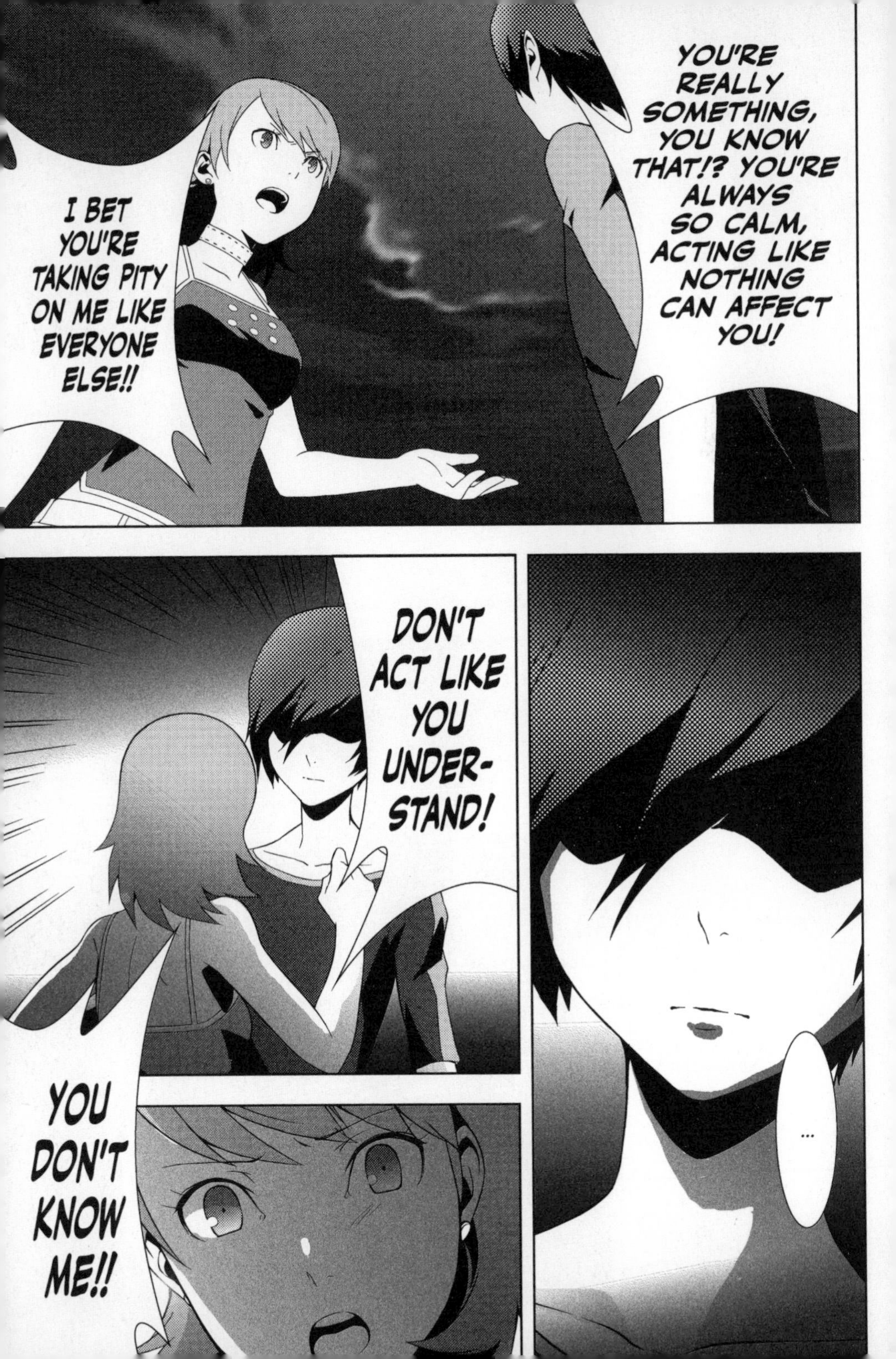
YOU'RE REALLY SOMETHING, YOU KNOW THAT!? YOU'RE ALWAYS SO CALM, ACTING LIKE NOTHING CAN AFFECT YOU!
I BET YOU'RE TAKING PITY ON ME LIKE EVERYONE ELSE!!
...
DON'T ACT LIKE YOU UNDER-STAND!
YOU DON'T KNOW ME!!

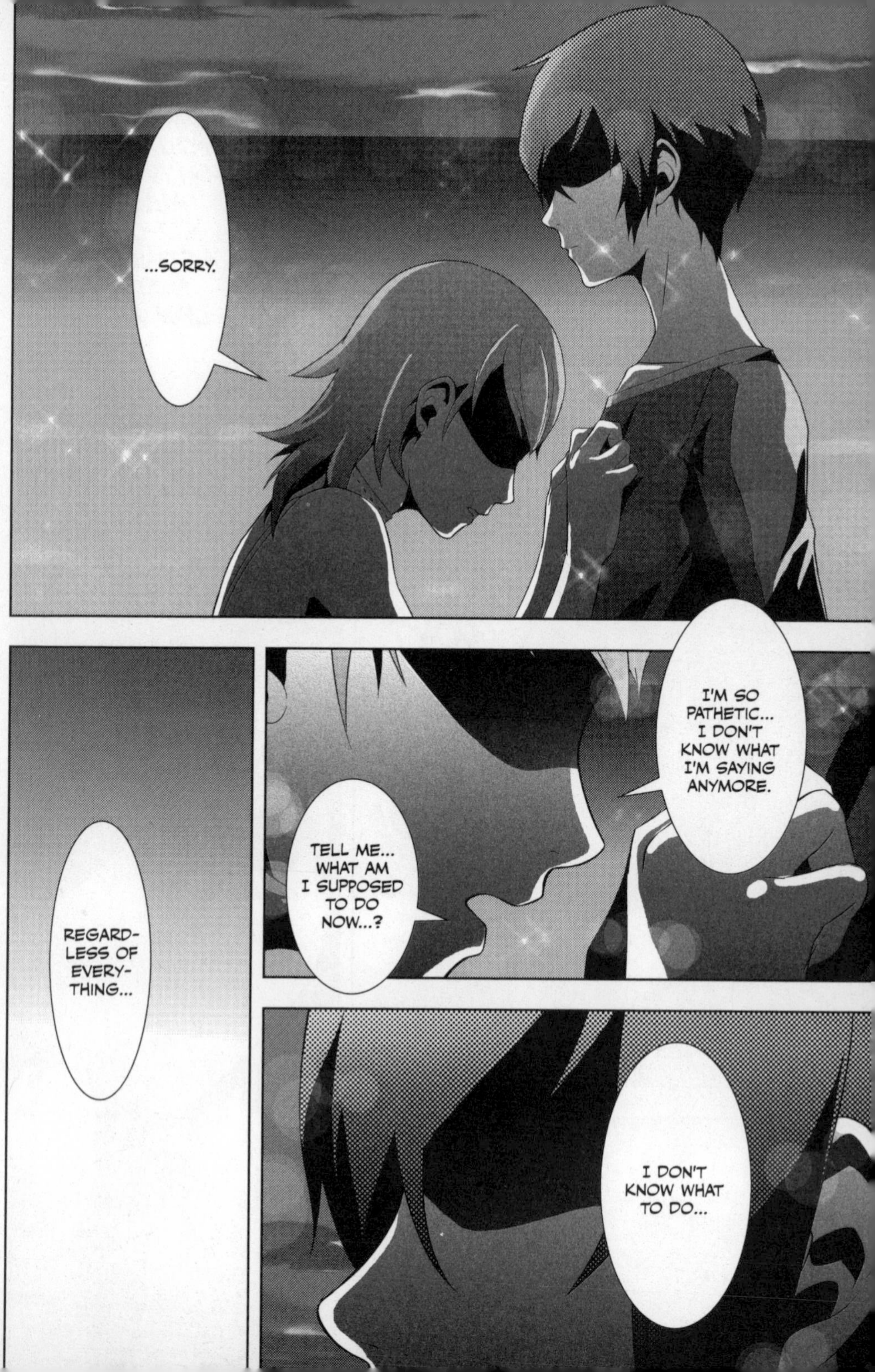
...SORRY.
I'M SO PATHETIC... I DON'T KNOW WHAT I'M SAYING ANYMORE.
TELL ME... WHAT AM I SUPPOSED TO DO NOW...?
I DON'T KNOW WHAT TO DO...
REGARD-LESS OF EVERY-THING...

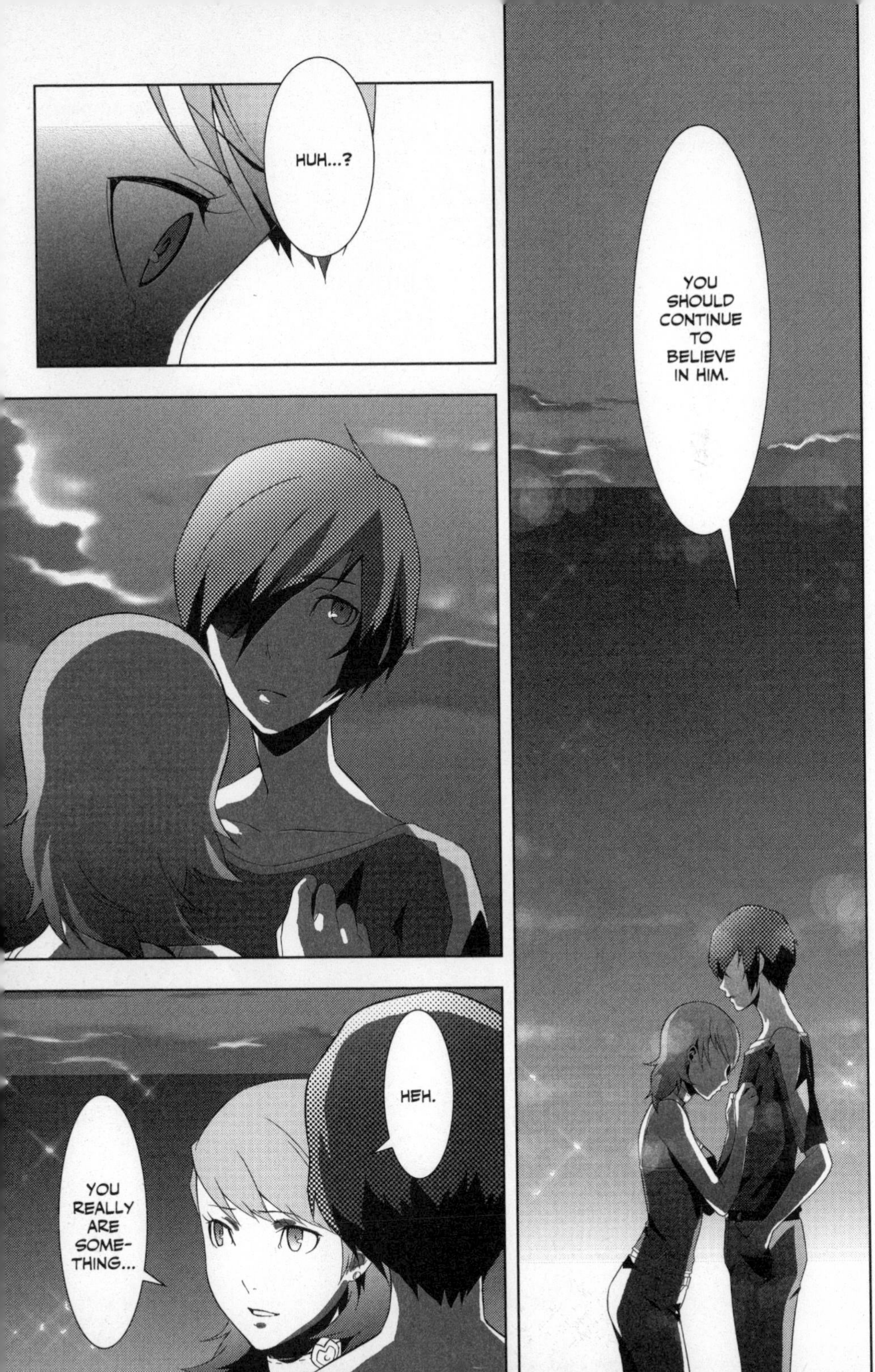
YOU SHOULD CONTINUE TO BELIEVE IN HIM.
HUH...?
HEH.
YOU REALLY ARE SOME-THING...

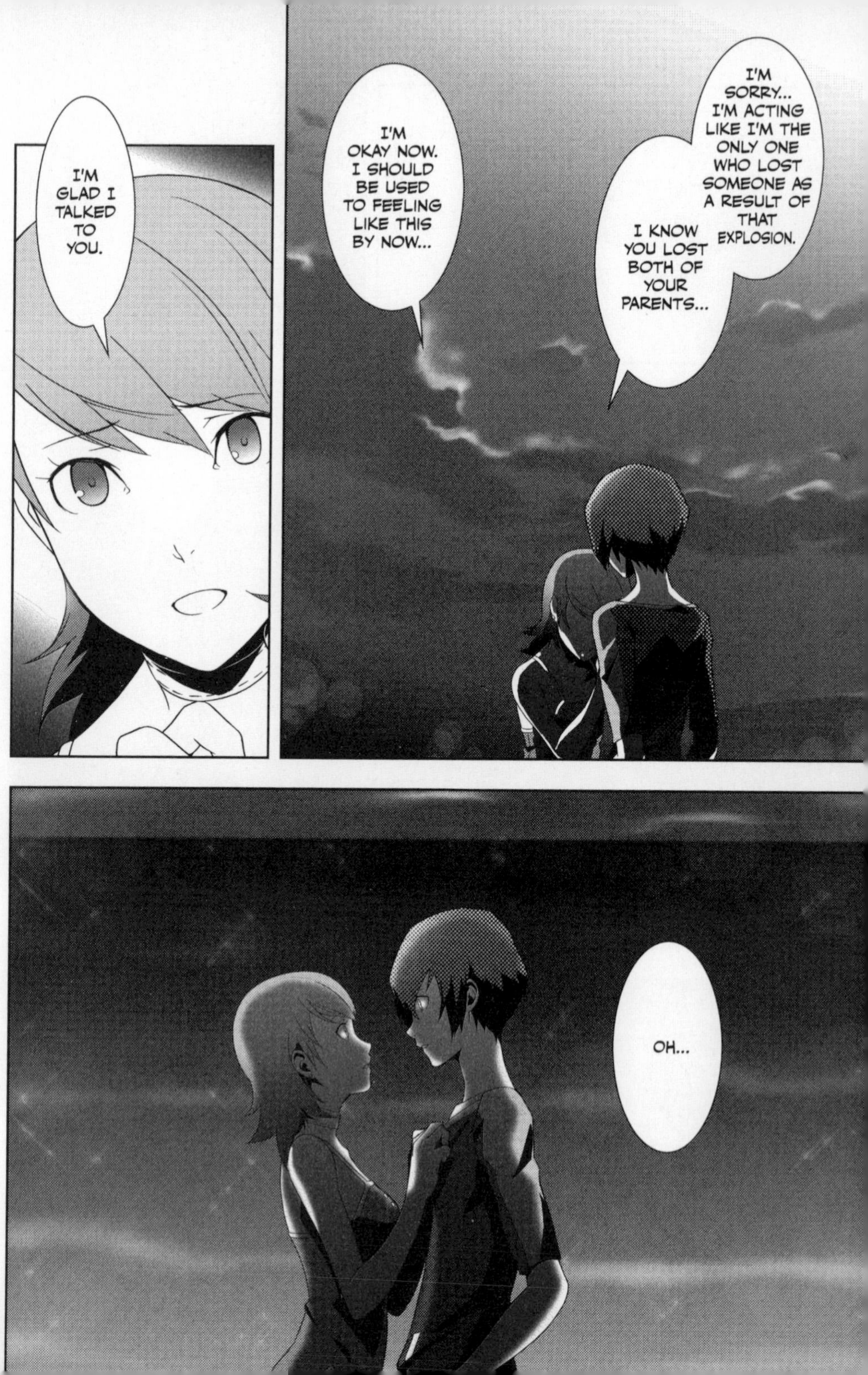
I'M SORRY... I'M ACTING LIKE I'M THE ONLY ONE WHO LOST SOMEONE AS A RESULT OF THAT EXPLOSION.
I KNOW YOU LOST BOTH OF YOUR PARENTS...
I'M OKAY NOW. I SHOULD BE USED TO FEELING LIKE THIS BY NOW...
I'M GLAD I TALKED TO YOU.
OH...

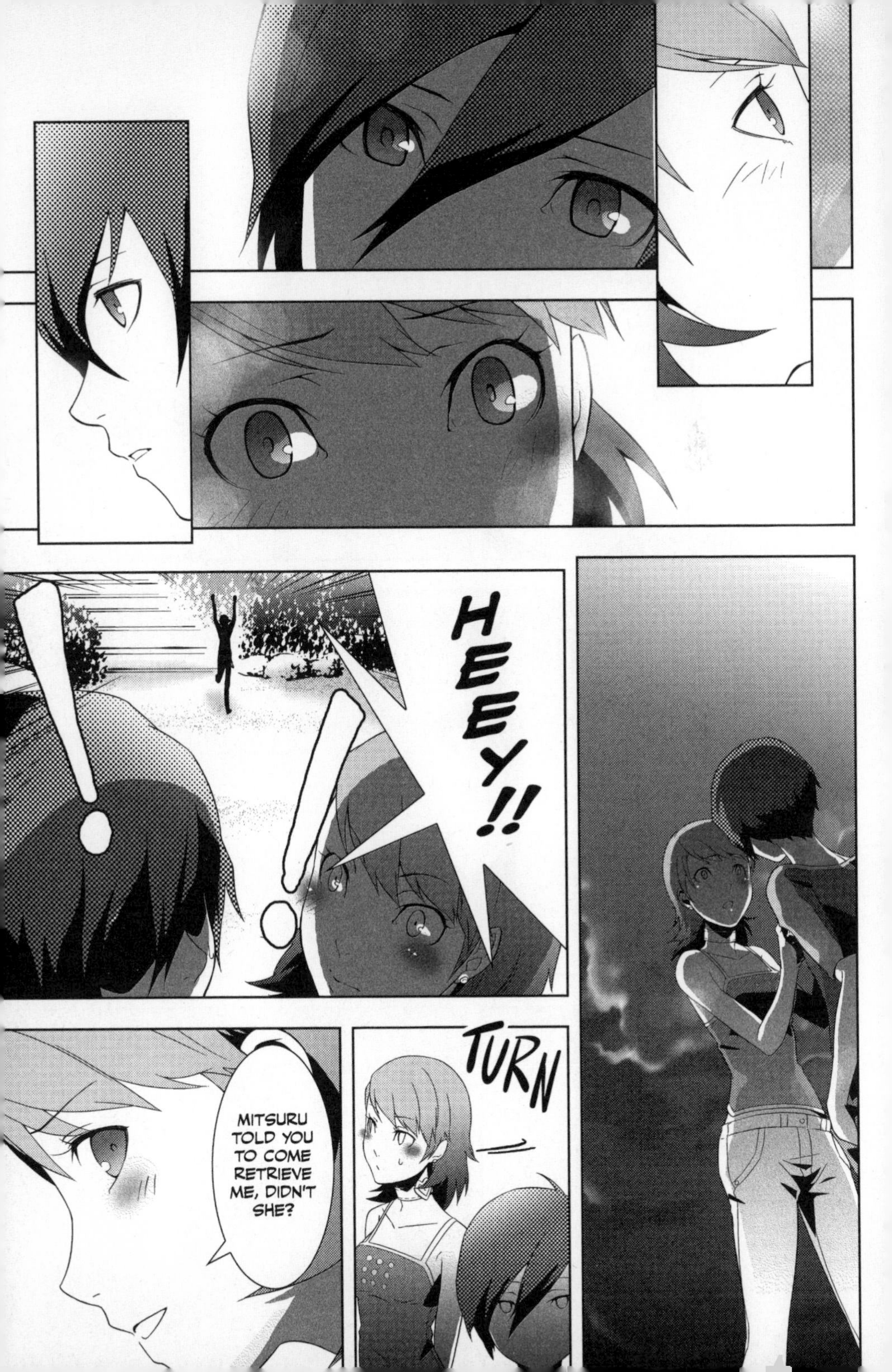
HEEY!!
TURN
MITSURU TOLD YOU TO COME RETRIEVE ME, DIDN'T SHE?

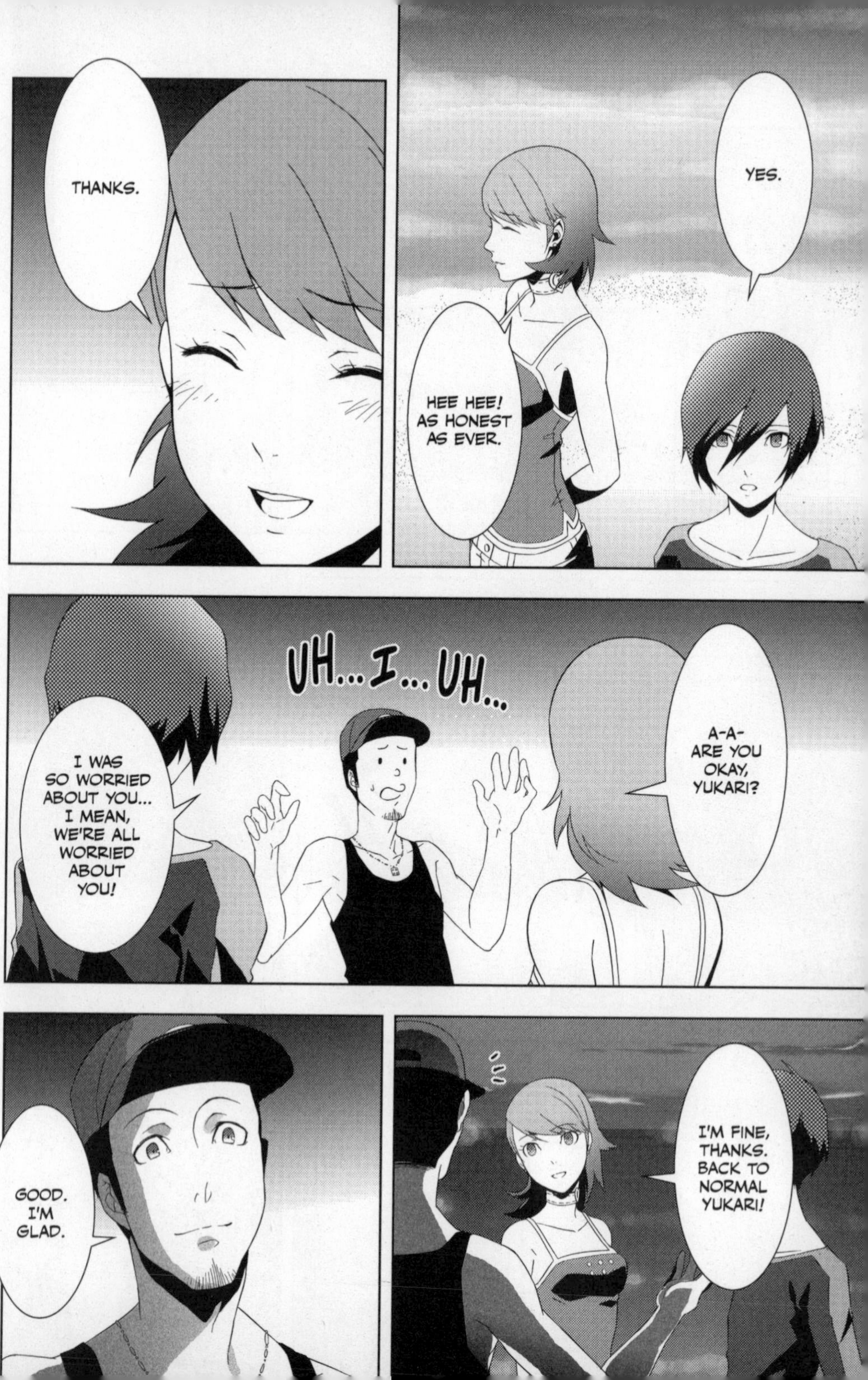
YES.
HEE HEE! AS HONEST AS EVER.
THANKS.
A-A-ARE YOU OKAY, YUKARI?
UH... I... UH...
I WAS SO WORRIED ABOUT YOU... I MEAN, WE'RE ALL WORRIED ABOUT YOU!
I'M FINE, THANKS. BACK TO NORMAL YUKARI!
GOOD. I'M GLAD.

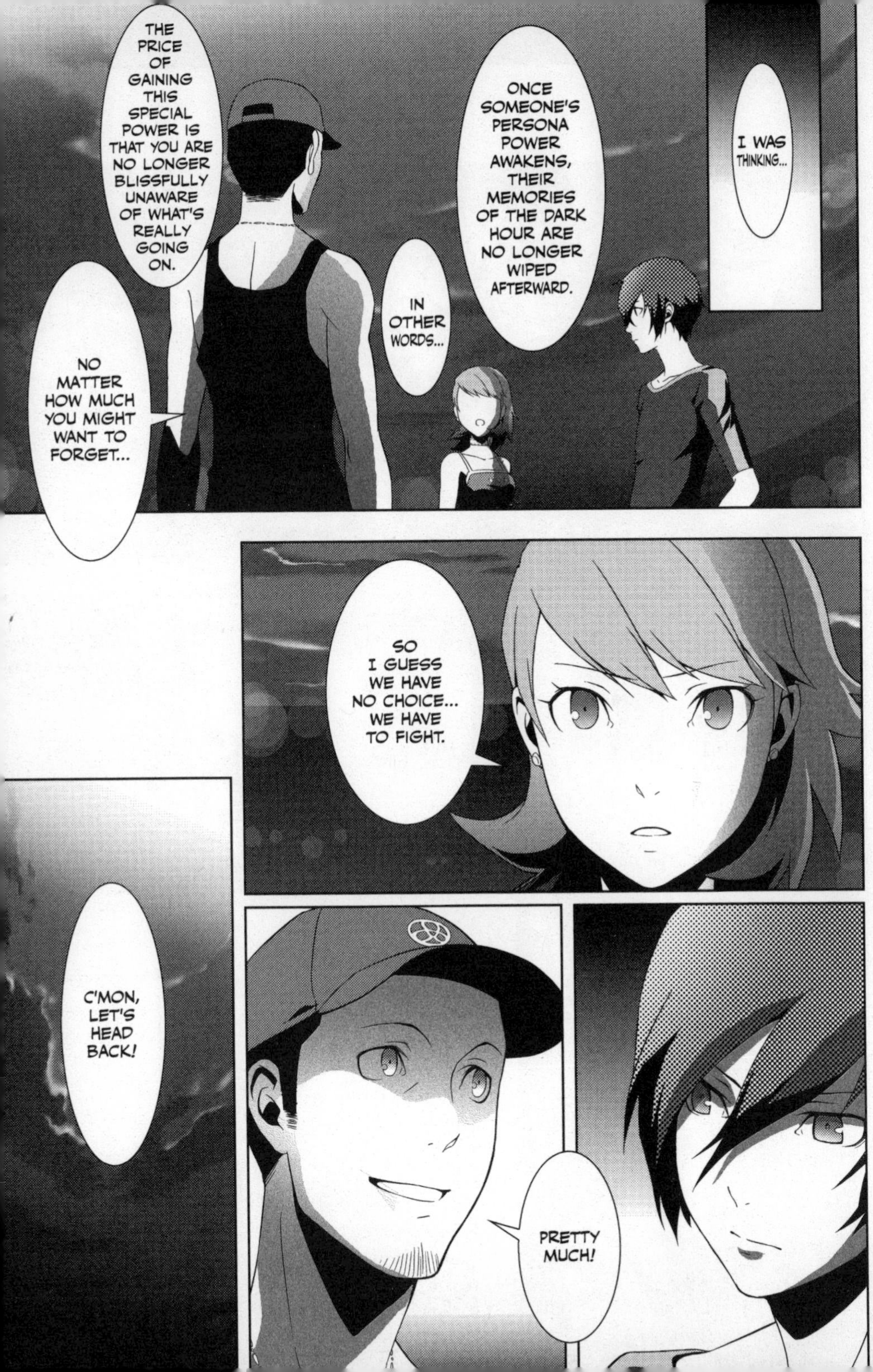
I WAS THINKING...
ONCE SOMEONE'S PERSONA POWER AWAKENS, THEIR MEMORIES OF THE DARK HOUR ARE NO LONGER WIPED AFTERWARD.
THE PRICE OF GAINING THIS SPECIAL POWER IS THAT YOU ARE NO LONGER BLISSFULLY UNAWARE OF WHAT'S REALLY GOING ON.
IN OTHER WORDS...
NO MATTER HOW MUCH YOU MIGHT WANT TO FORGET...
SO I GUESS WE HAVE NO CHOICE... WE HAVE TO FIGHT.
PRETTY MUCH!
C'MON, LET'S HEAD BACK!

Four Months Later

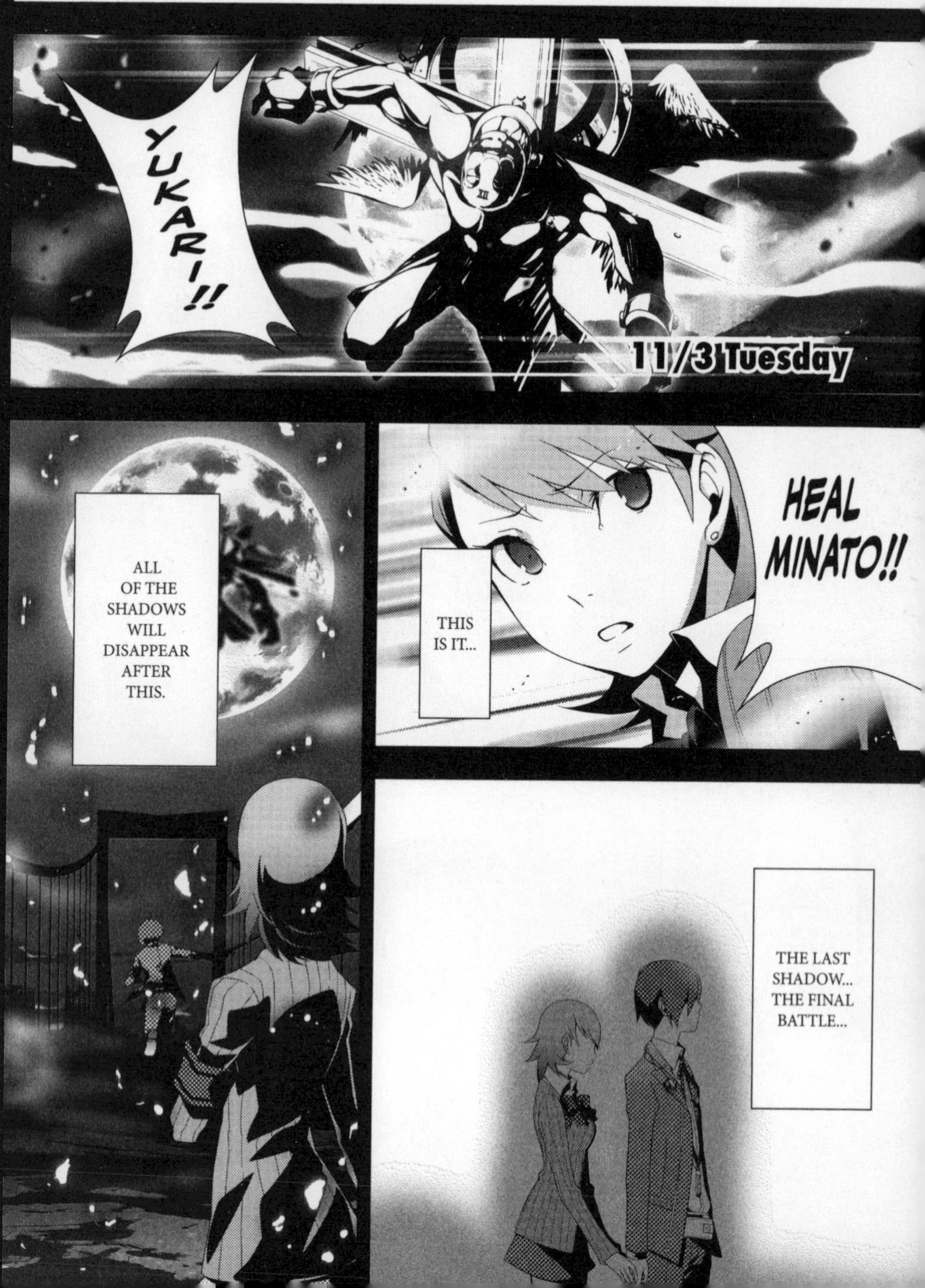

YUKARI!!
11/3 Tuesday
HEAL MINATO!!
THIS IS IT...
THE LAST SHADOW... THE FINAL BATTLE...
ALL OF THE SHADOWS WILL DISAPPEAR AFTER THIS.

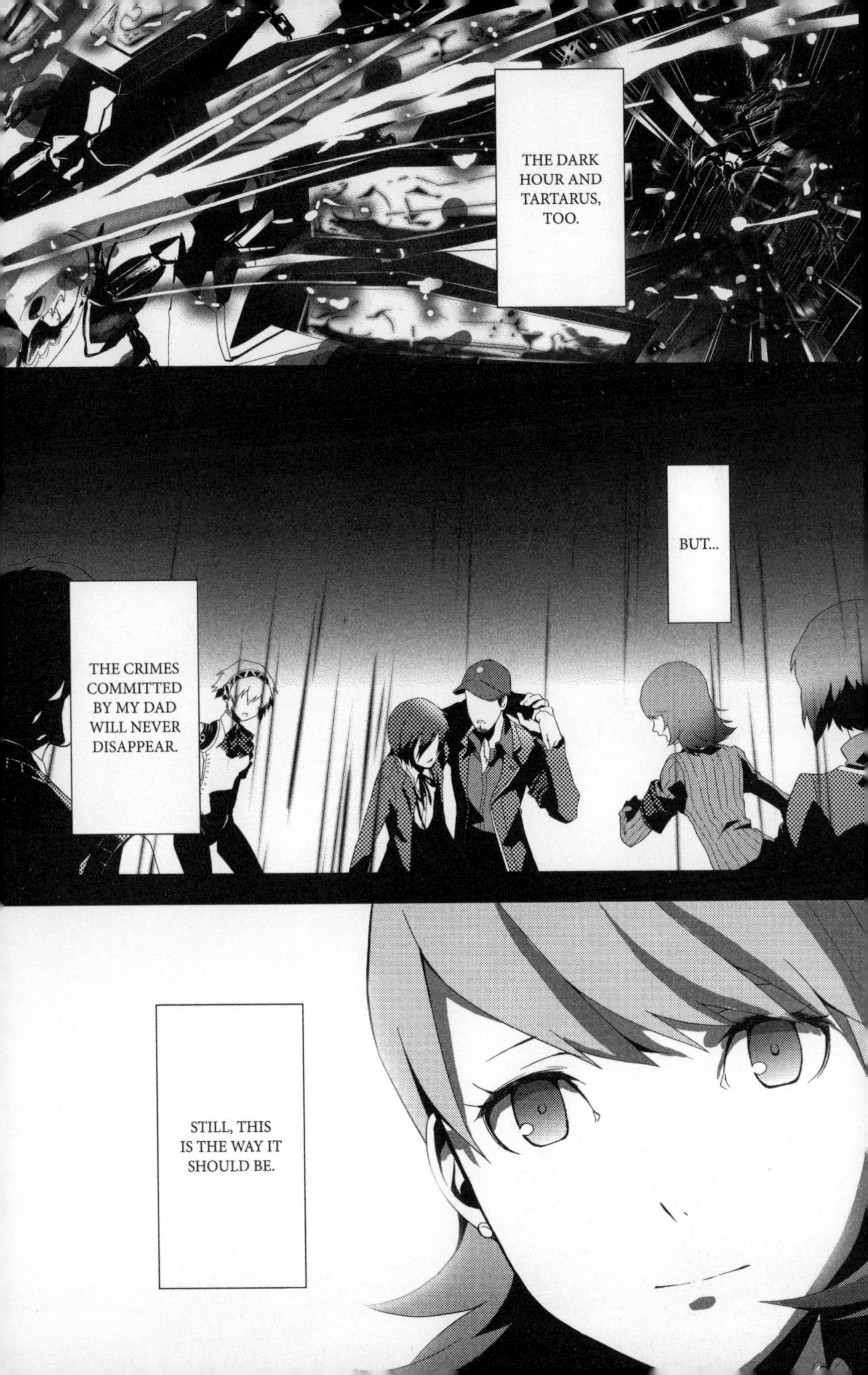
THE DARK HOUR AND TARTARUS, TOO.
BUT...
THE CRIMES COMMITTED BY MY DAD WILL NEVER DISAPPEAR.
STILL, THIS IS THE WAY IT SHOULD BE.

P3 連載プ

TOP SECRET

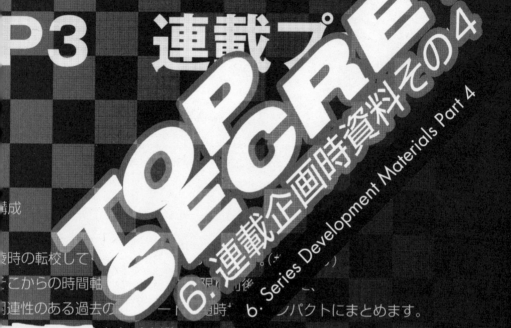

6.連載企画時資料その4

6. Series Development Materials Part 4

構成

…時の転校して…。(…)
…ここからの時間軸…限の前後…、
…関連性のある過去の…ー…時…ンパクトにまとめます。
[redacted]イベント以降は回想の挿入はなるべくせずに、
…ピード感のある感じで一気に進めて行きたいと思います。

…して[redacted]なんですが、
…作では割とそこまでの出番、絡みが少なかったので
…の漫画ではその辺、とくに主人公達との友情的なものを重点的に話の軸として見せ…

…に紙面に表記はしないですが、大まかにこのような順序で進めていきます。

・主人公紹介編	・風花救出編	基本的な世界観や内容
・修学旅行編	・美鶴、ゆかり編	十年前の事件を軸に
・ストレガ編	・真田、天田編	真田、天田、荒垣の因縁と
・順平編		上の二つとほぼ同時進行
[redacted]	[redacted]	最終局面。[redacted]

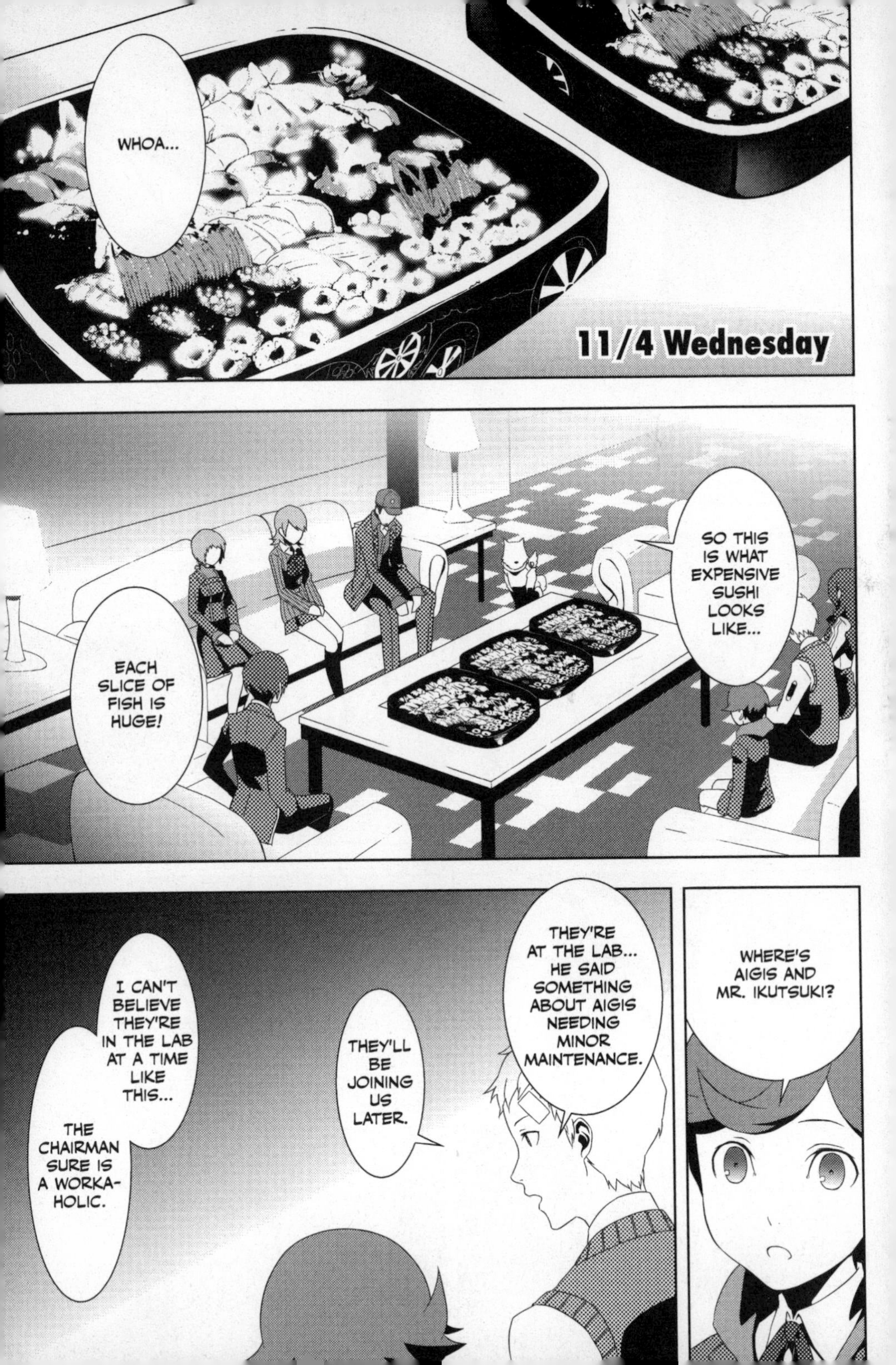
WHOA...
11/4 Wednesday
SO THIS IS WHAT EXPENSIVE SUSHI LOOKS LIKE...
EACH SLICE OF FISH IS HUGE!
WHERE'S AIGIS AND MR. IKUTSUKI?
THEY'RE AT THE LAB... HE SAID SOMETHING ABOUT AIGIS NEEDING MINOR MAINTENANCE.
THEY'LL BE JOINING US LATER.
I CAN'T BELIEVE THEY'RE IN THE LAB AT A TIME LIKE THIS...
THE CHAIRMAN SURE IS A WORKA-HOLIC.

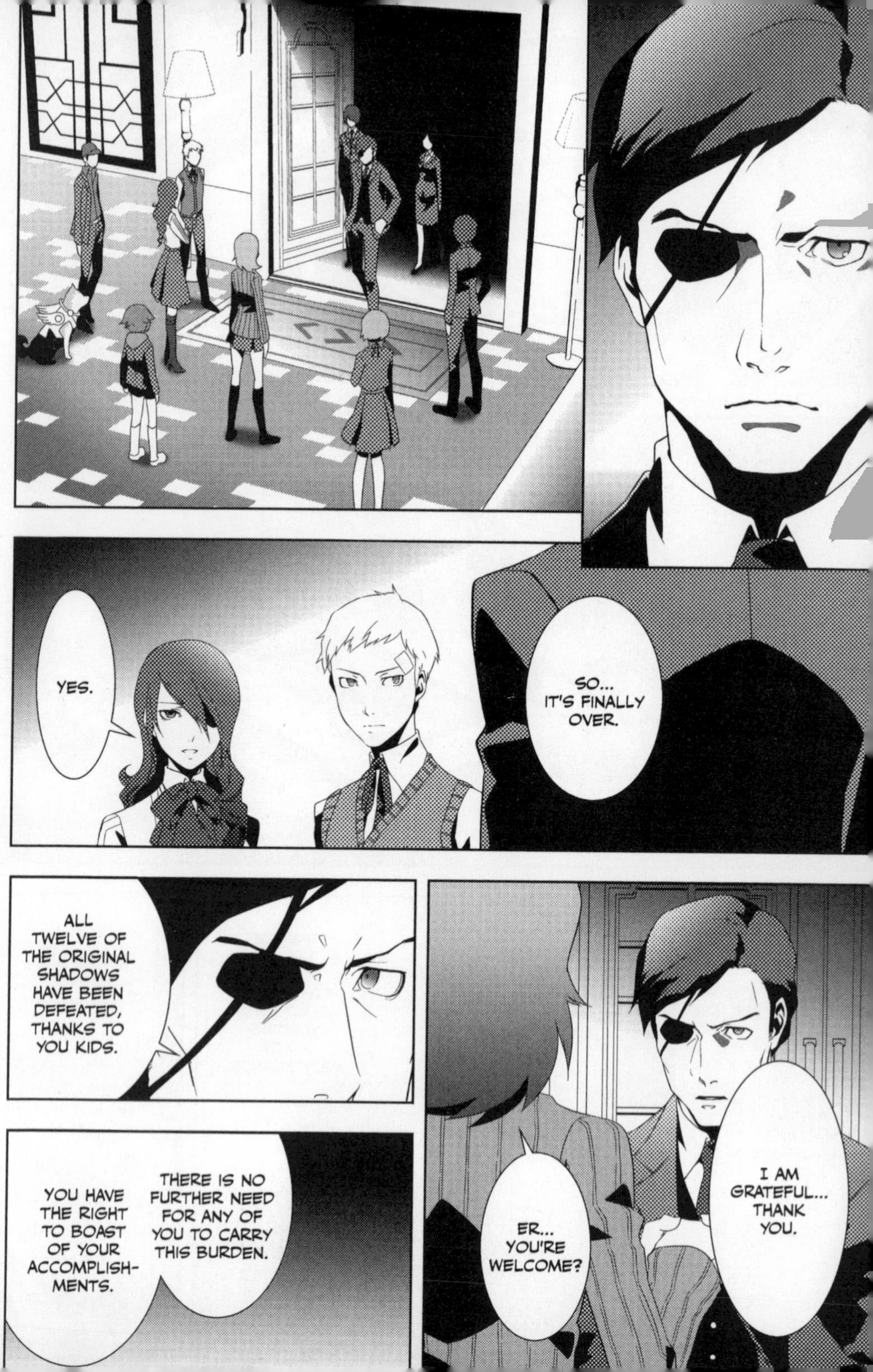
SO... IT'S FINALLY OVER.
YES.
I AM GRATEFUL... THANK YOU.
ER... YOU'RE WELCOME?
ALL TWELVE OF THE ORIGINAL SHADOWS HAVE BEEN DEFEATED, THANKS TO YOU KIDS.
THERE IS NO FURTHER NEED FOR ANY OF YOU TO CARRY THIS BURDEN.
YOU HAVE THE RIGHT TO BOAST OF YOUR ACCOMPLISH-MENTS.

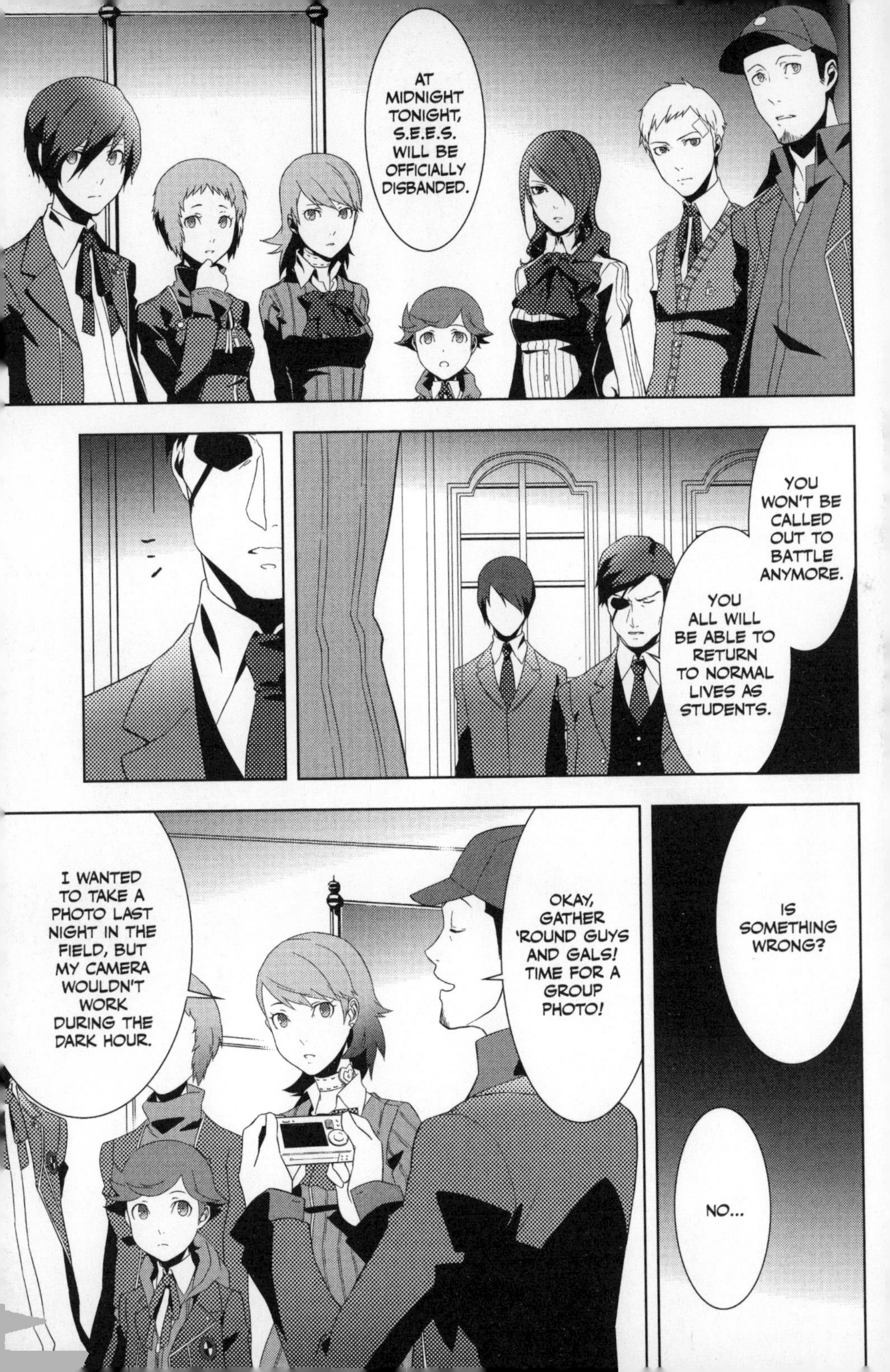
AT MIDNIGHT TONIGHT, S.E.E.S. WILL BE OFFICIALLY DISBANDED.
YOU WON'T BE CALLED OUT TO BATTLE ANYMORE.
YOU ALL WILL BE ABLE TO RETURN TO NORMAL LIVES AS STUDENTS.
IS SOMETHING WRONG?
NO...
OKAY, GATHER 'ROUND GUYS AND GALS! TIME FOR A GROUP PHOTO!
I WANTED TO TAKE A PHOTO LAST NIGHT IN THE FIELD, BUT MY CAMERA WOULDN'T WORK DURING THE DARK HOUR.

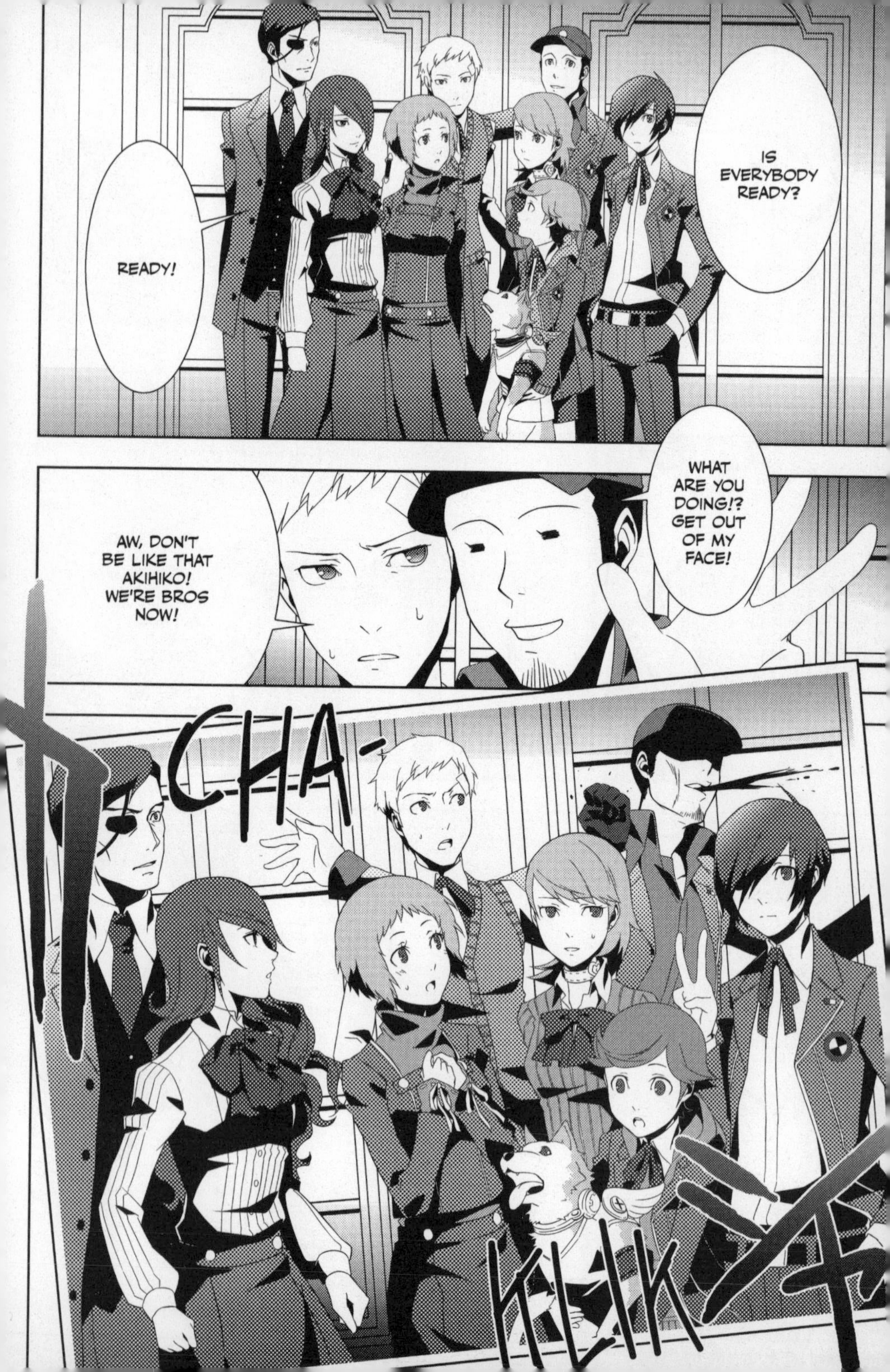
IS EVERYBODY READY?
READY!
WHAT ARE YOU DOING!? GET OUT OF MY FACE!
AW, DON'T BE LIKE THAT AKIHIKO! WE'RE BROS NOW!
CHA-
KLIK

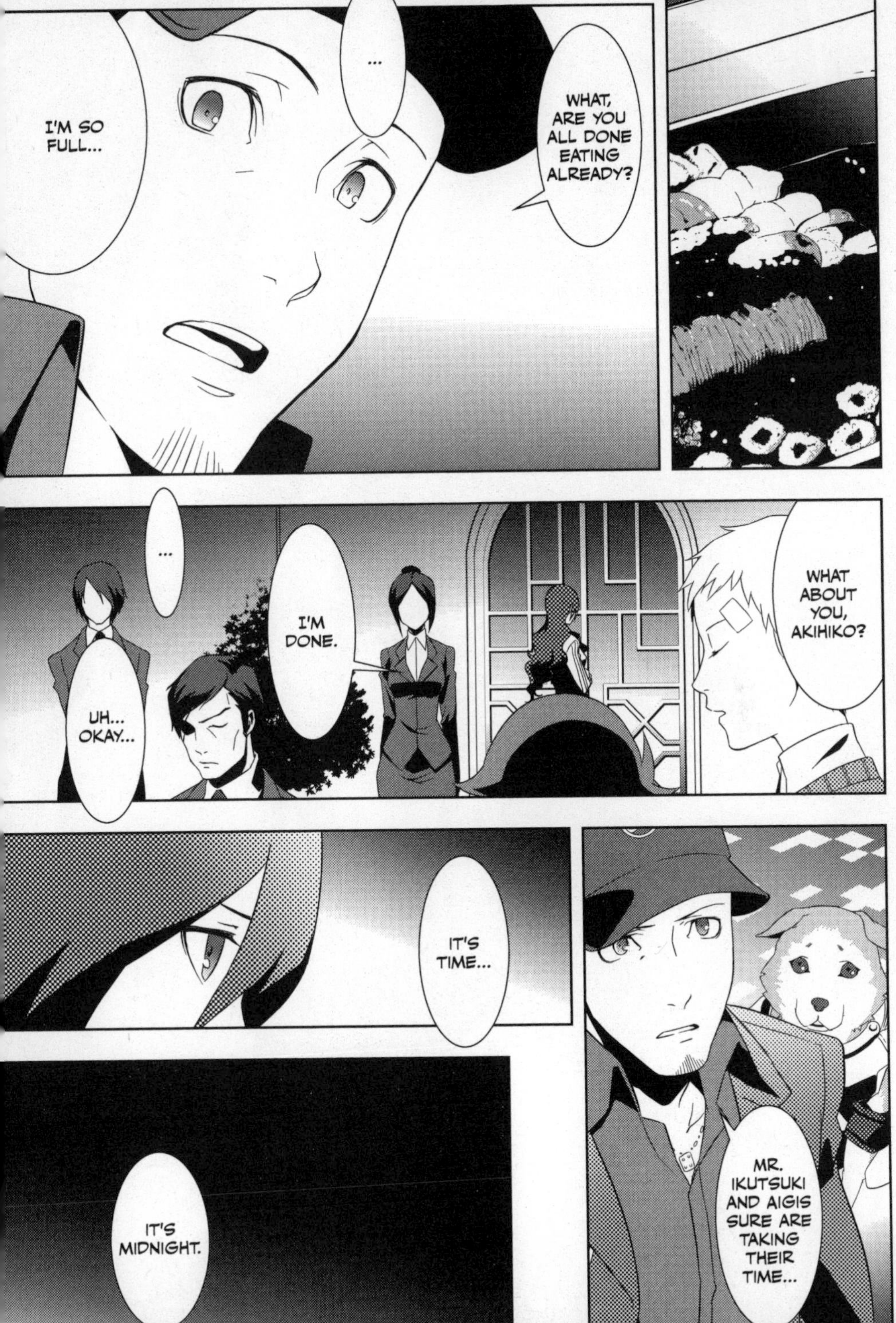
WHAT, ARE YOU ALL DONE EATING ALREADY?
...
I'M SO FULL...
WHAT ABOUT YOU, AKIHIKO?
I'M DONE.
...
UH... OKAY...
MR. IKUTSUKI AND AIGIS SURE ARE TAKING THEIR TIME...
IT'S TIME...
IT'S MIDNIGHT.

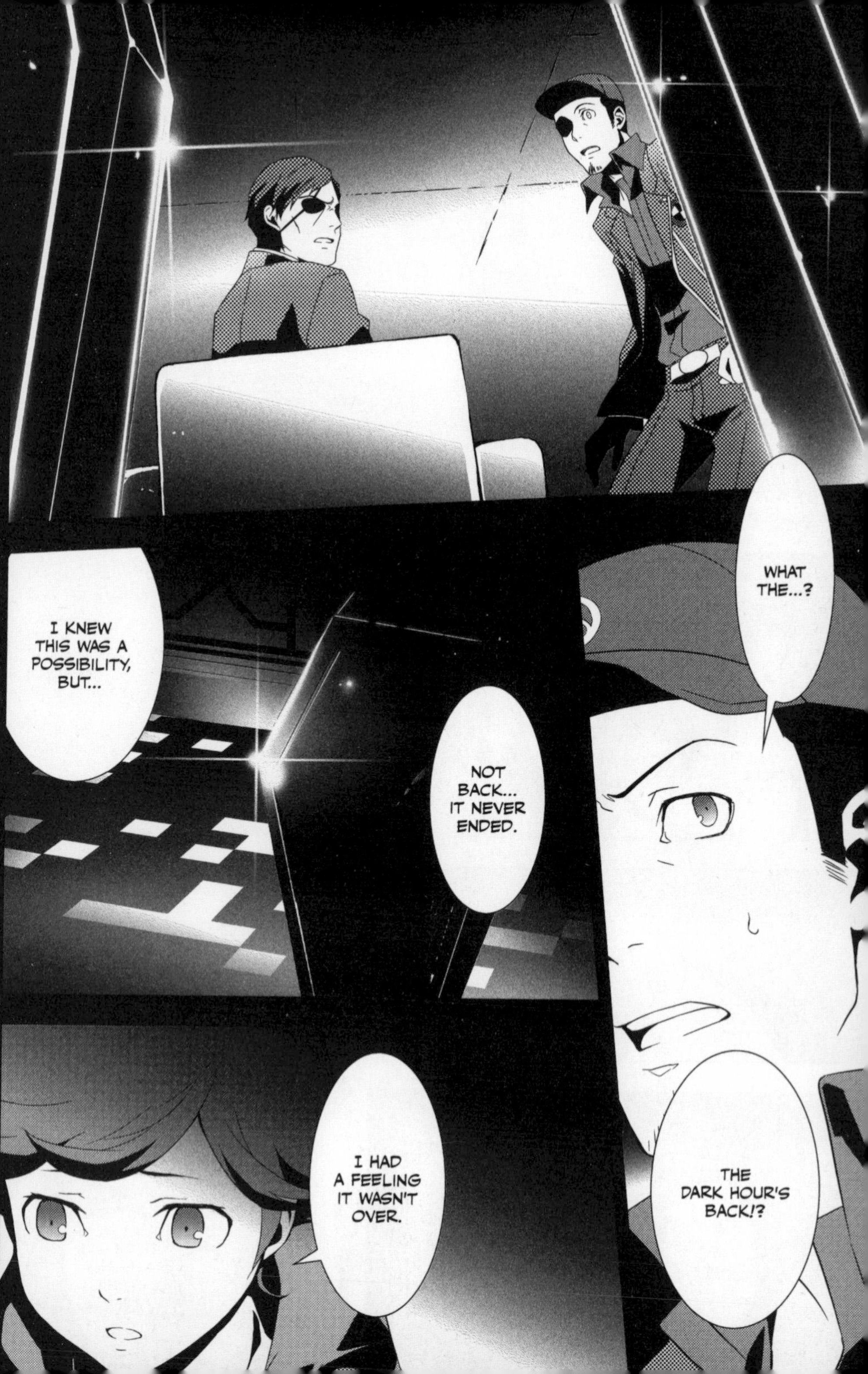
WHAT THE...?
THE DARK HOUR'S BACK!?
NOT BACK... IT NEVER ENDED.
I KNEW THIS WAS A POSSIBILITY, BUT...
I HAD A FEELING IT WASN'T OVER.

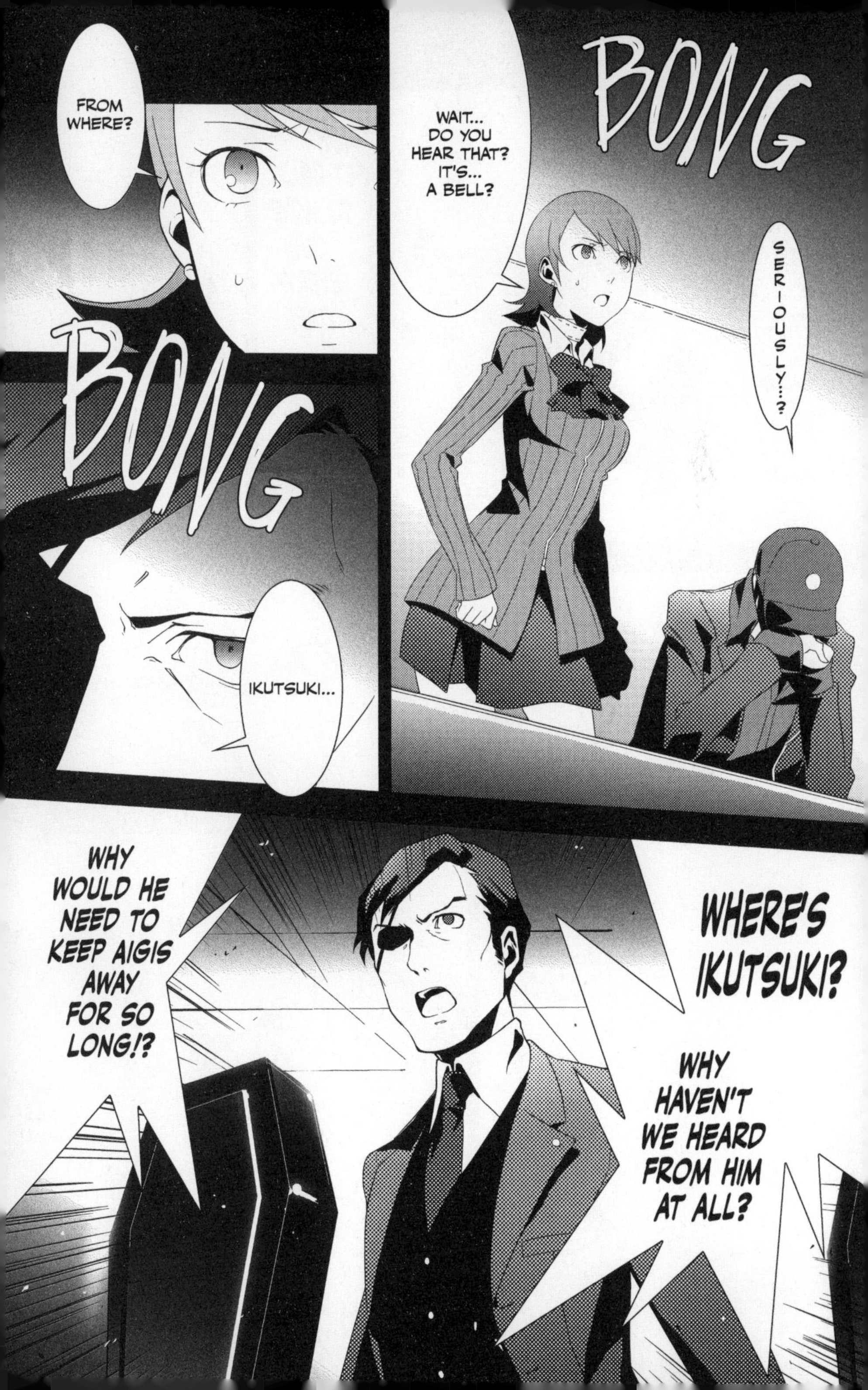
BONG
WAIT... DO YOU HEAR THAT? IT'S... A BELL?
SERIOUSLY...?
FROM WHERE?
BONG
IKUTSUKI...
WHERE'S IKUTSUKI?
WHY HAVEN'T WE HEARD FROM HIM AT ALL?
WHY WOULD HE NEED TO KEEP AIGIS AWAY FOR SO LONG!?

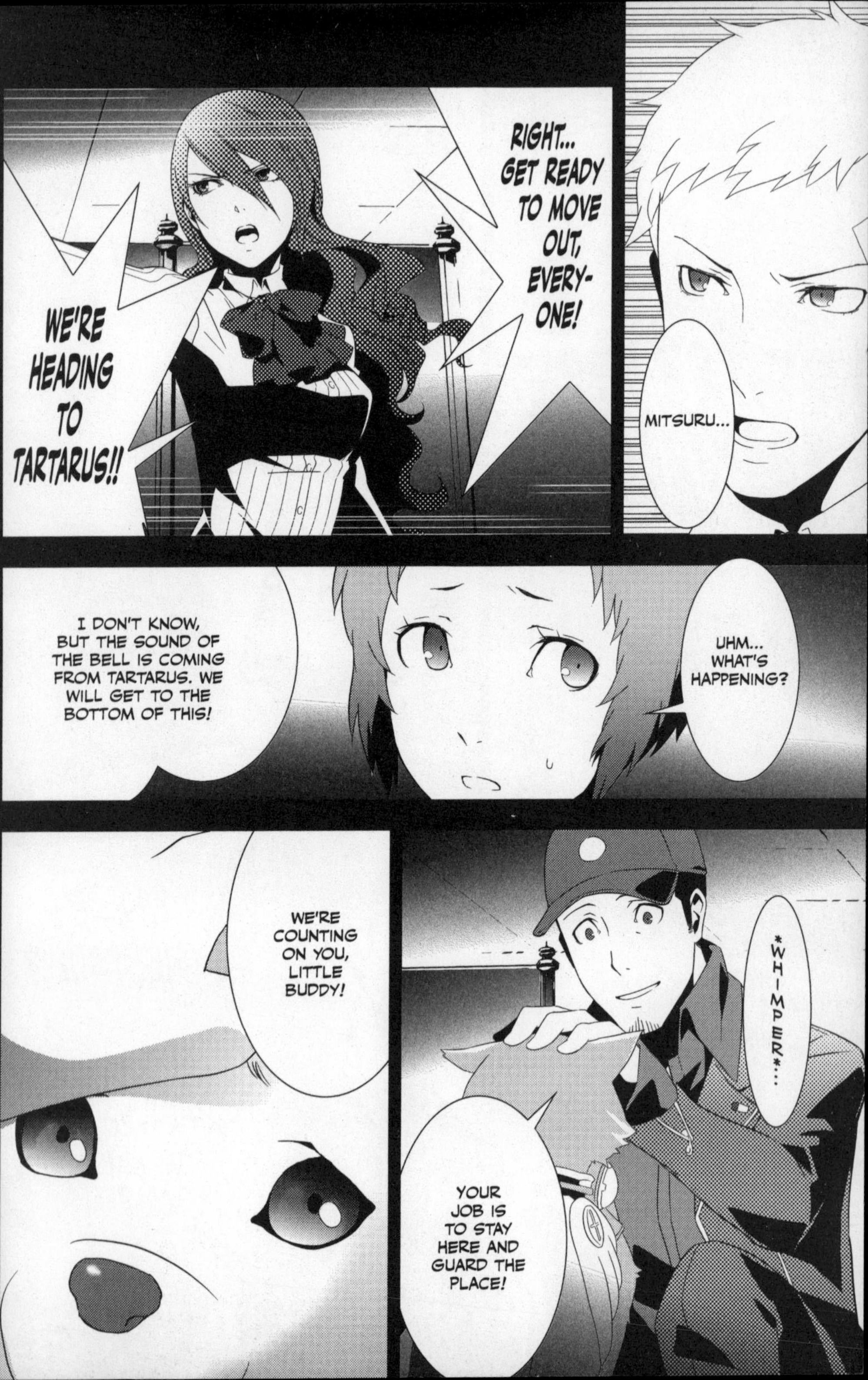
MITSURU...
RIGHT... GET READY TO MOVE OUT, EVERY-ONE!
WE'RE HEADING TO TARTARUS!!
UHM... WHAT'S HAPPENING?
I DON'T KNOW, BUT THE SOUND OF THE BELL IS COMING FROM TARTARUS. WE WILL GET TO THE BOTTOM OF THIS!
WHIMPER...
YOUR JOB IS TO STAY HERE AND GUARD THE PLACE!
WE'RE COUNTING ON YOU, LITTLE BUDDY!

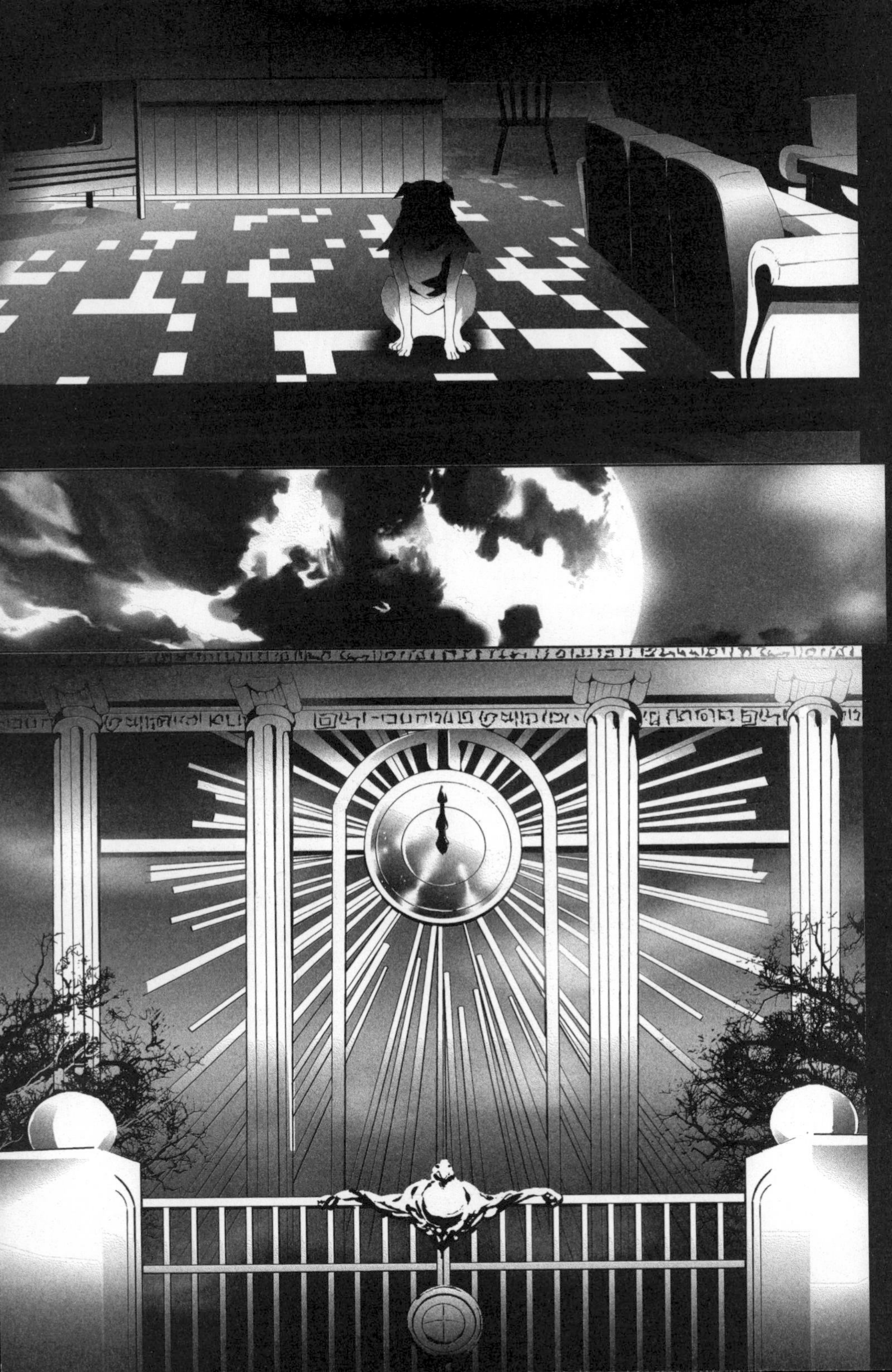

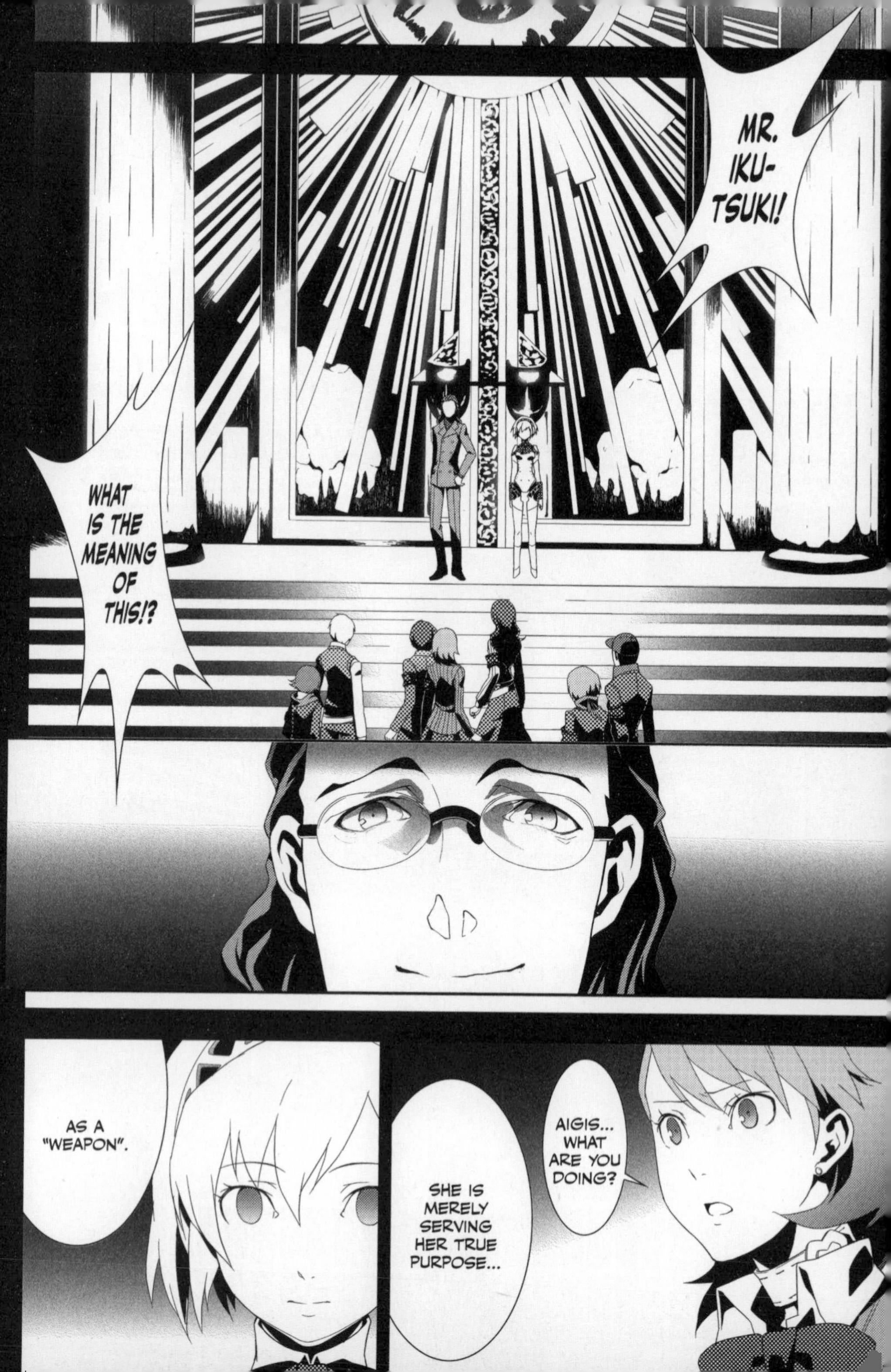
MR. IKU-TSUKI!
WHAT IS THE MEANING OF THIS!?
AIGIS... WHAT ARE YOU DOING?
SHE IS MERELY SERVING HER TRUE PURPOSE...
AS A "WEAPON".

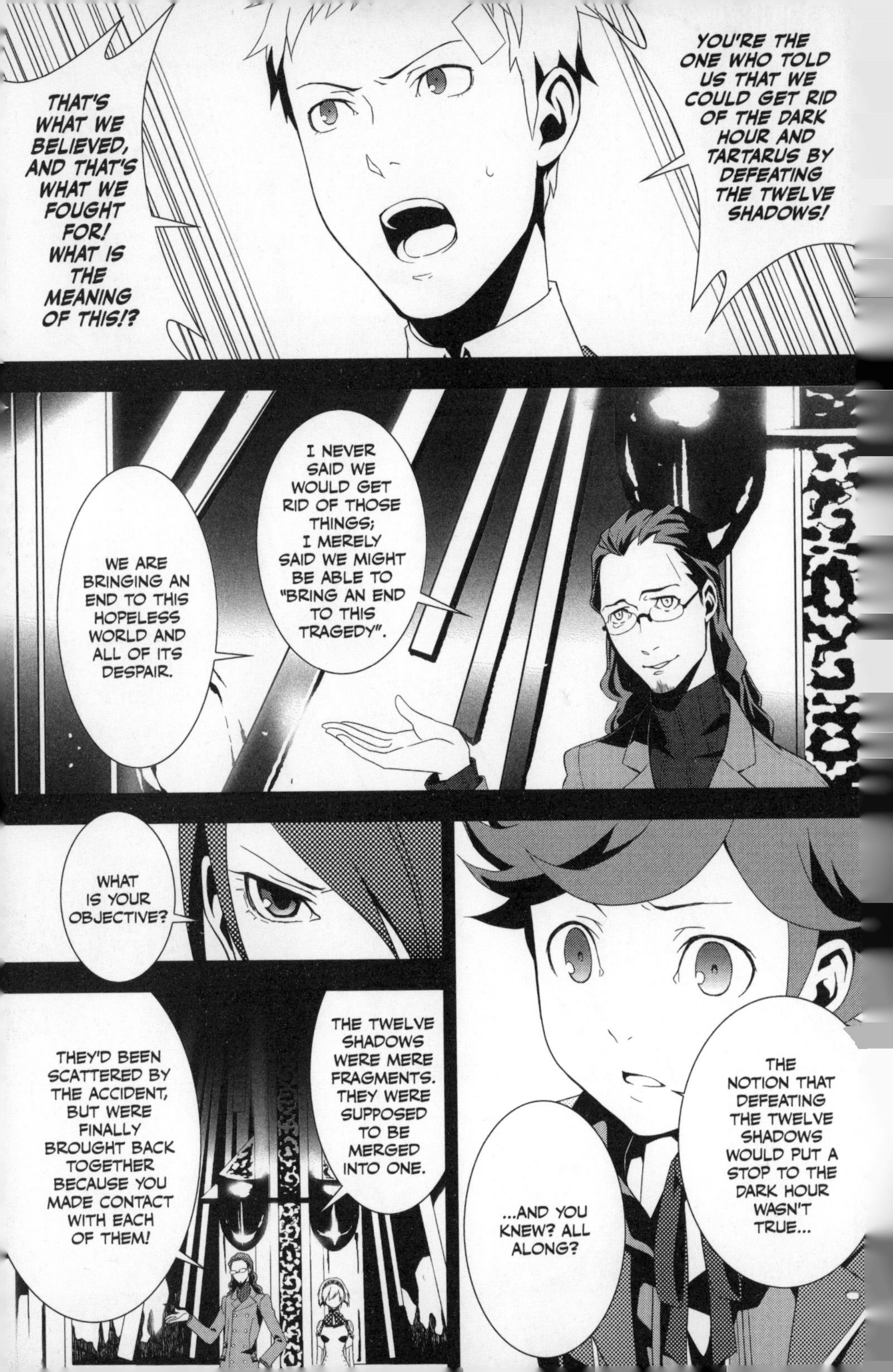
YOU'RE THE ONE WHO TOLD US THAT WE COULD GET RID OF THE DARK HOUR AND TARTARUS BY DEFEATING THE TWELVE SHADOWS!
THAT'S WHAT WE BELIEVED, AND THAT'S WHAT WE FOUGHT FOR! WHAT IS THE MEANING OF THIS!?
I NEVER SAID WE WOULD GET RID OF THOSE THINGS; I MERELY SAID WE MIGHT BE ABLE TO "BRING AN END TO THIS TRAGEDY".
WE ARE BRINGING AN END TO THIS HOPELESS WORLD AND ALL OF ITS DESPAIR.
THE NOTION THAT DEFEATING THE TWELVE SHADOWS WOULD PUT A STOP TO THE DARK HOUR WASN'T TRUE...
...AND YOU KNEW? ALL ALONG?
WHAT IS YOUR OBJECTIVE?
THE TWELVE SHADOWS WERE MERE FRAGMENTS. THEY WERE SUPPOSED TO BE MERGED INTO ONE.
THEY'D BEEN SCATTERED BY THE ACCIDENT, BUT WERE FINALLY BROUGHT BACK TOGETHER BECAUSE YOU MADE CONTACT WITH EACH OF THEM!

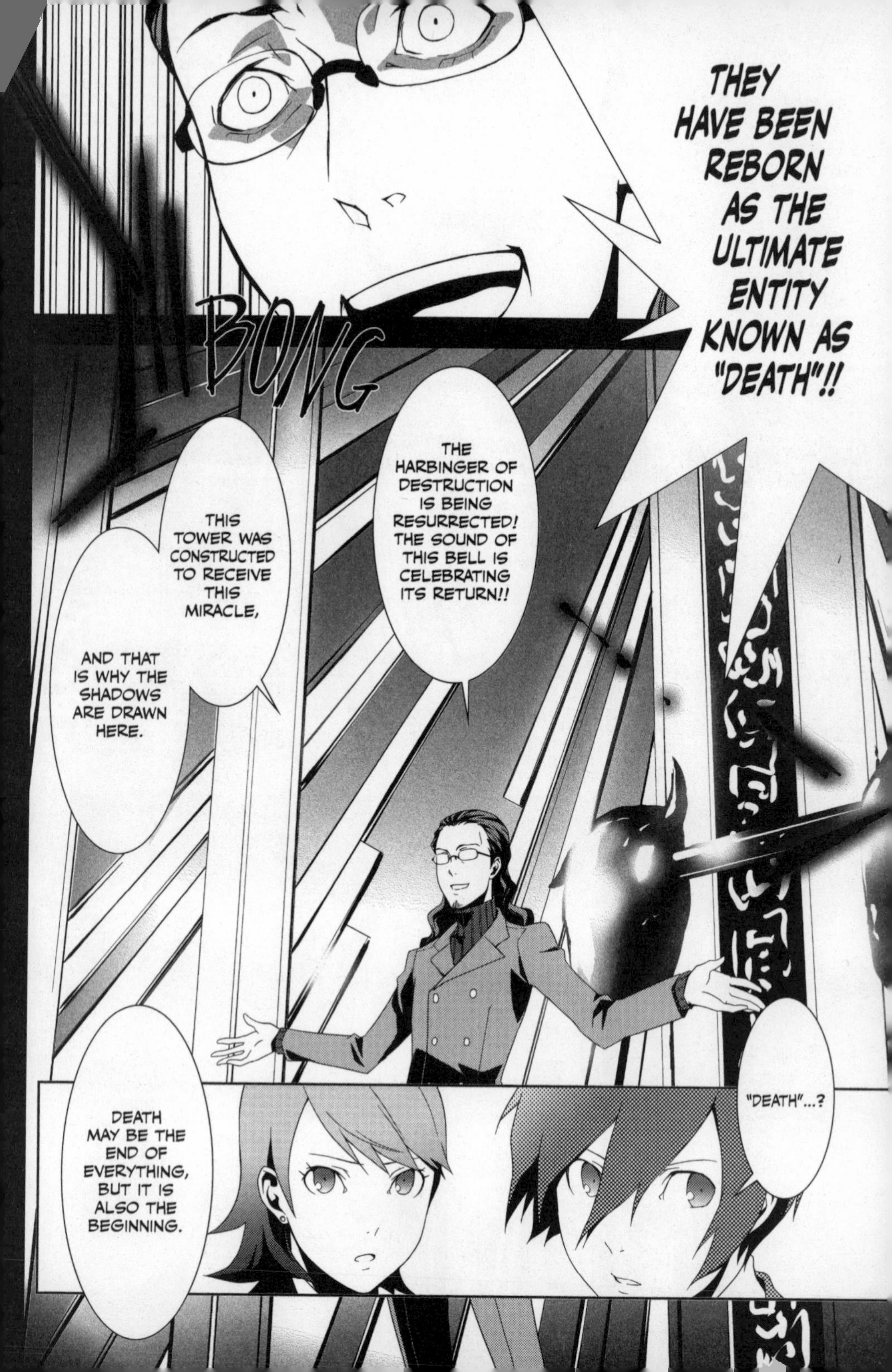
THEY HAVE BEEN REBORN AS THE ULTIMATE ENTITY KNOWN AS "DEATH"!!
BONG
THE HARBINGER OF DESTRUCTION IS BEING RESURRECTED! THE SOUND OF THIS BELL IS CELEBRATING ITS RETURN!!
THIS TOWER WAS CONSTRUCTED TO RECEIVE THIS MIRACLE,
AND THAT IS WHY THE SHADOWS ARE DRAWN HERE.
"DEATH"...?
DEATH MAY BE THE END OF EVERYTHING, BUT IT IS ALSO THE BEGINNING.

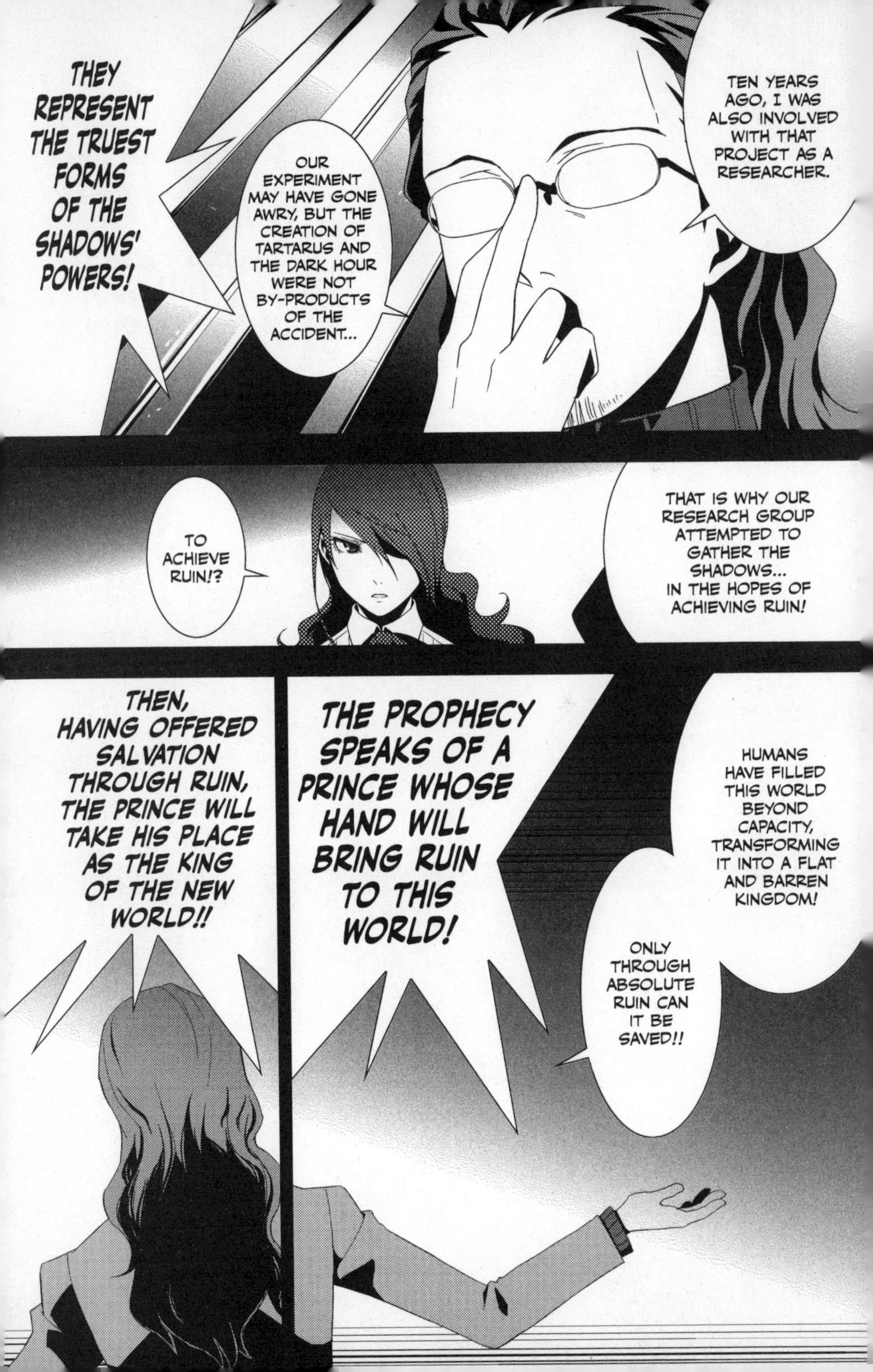
TEN YEARS AGO, I WAS ALSO INVOLVED WITH THAT PROJECT AS A RESEARCHER.
OUR EXPERIMENT MAY HAVE GONE AWRY, BUT THE CREATION OF TARTARUS AND THE DARK HOUR WERE NOT BY-PRODUCTS OF THE ACCIDENT...
THEY REPRESENT THE TRUEST FORMS OF THE SHADOWS' POWERS!
THAT IS WHY OUR RESEARCH GROUP ATTEMPTED TO GATHER THE SHADOWS... IN THE HOPES OF ACHIEVING RUIN!
TO ACHIEVE RUIN!?
HUMANS HAVE FILLED THIS WORLD BEYOND CAPACITY, TRANSFORMING IT INTO A FLAT AND BARREN KINGDOM!
ONLY THROUGH ABSOLUTE RUIN CAN IT BE SAVED!!
THE PROPHECY SPEAKS OF A PRINCE WHOSE HAND WILL BRING RUIN TO THIS WORLD!
THEN, HAVING OFFERED SALVATION THROUGH RUIN, THE PRINCE WILL TAKE HIS PLACE AS THE KING OF THE NEW WORLD!!

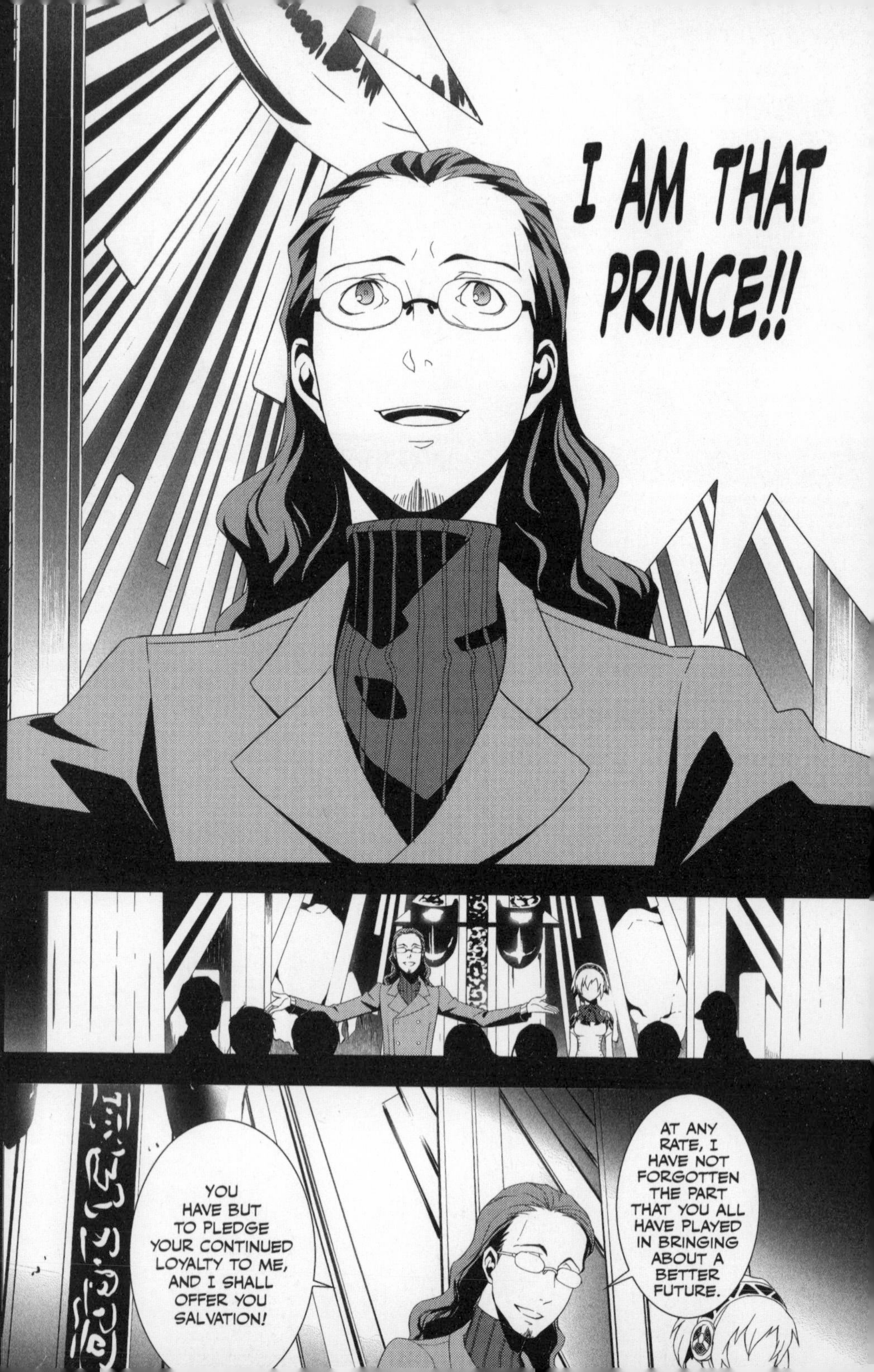
I AM THAT PRINCE!!
AT ANY RATE, I HAVE NOT FORGOTTEN THE PART THAT YOU ALL HAVE PLAYED IN BRINGING ABOUT A BETTER FUTURE.
YOU HAVE BUT TO PLEDGE YOUR CONTINUED LOYALTY TO ME, AND I SHALL OFFER YOU SALVATION!

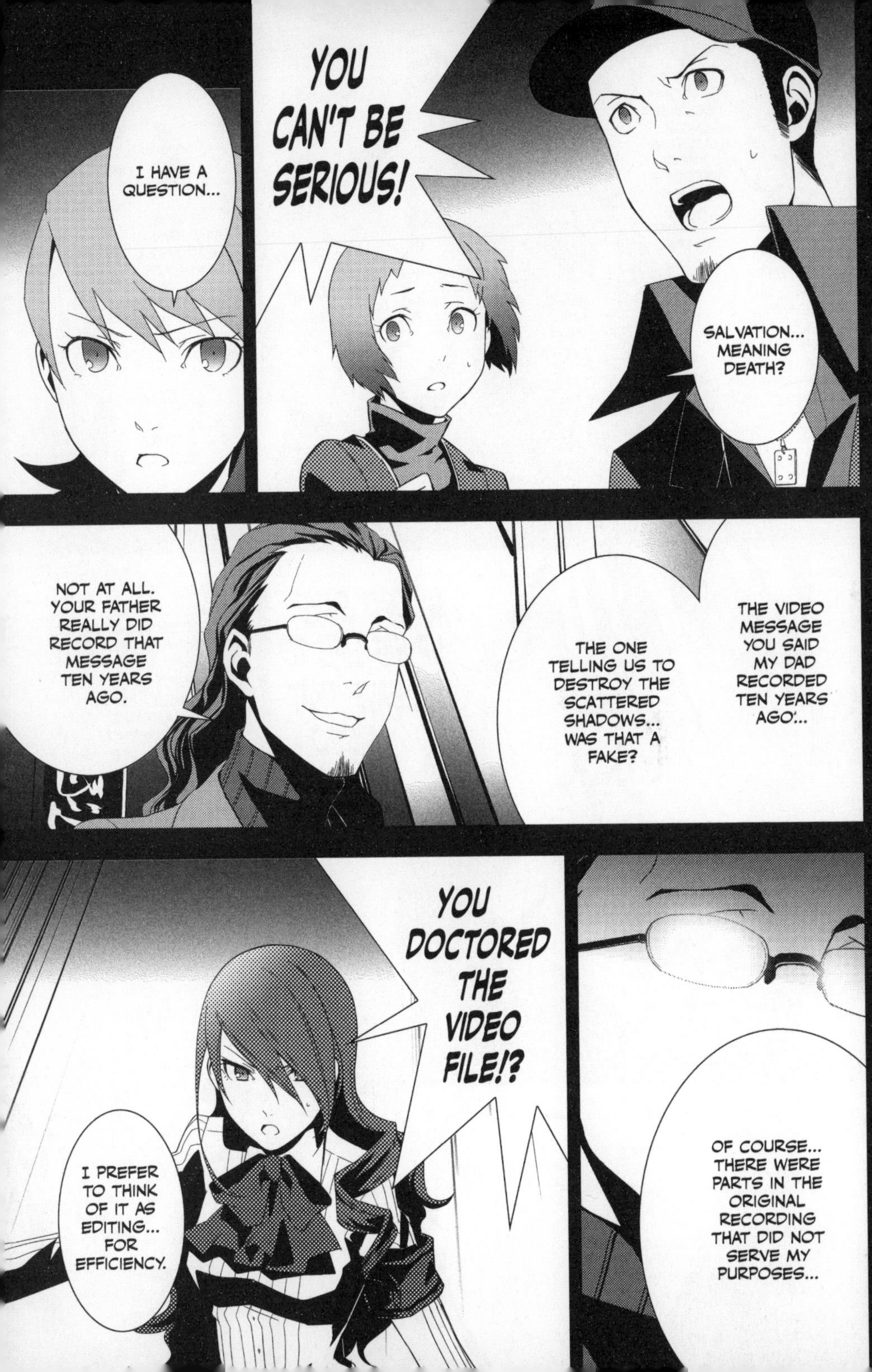
SALVATION... MEANING DEATH?
YOU CAN'T BE SERIOUS!
I HAVE A QUESTION...
THE VIDEO MESSAGE YOU SAID MY DAD RECORDED TEN YEARS AGO...
THE ONE TELLING US TO DESTROY THE SCATTERED SHADOWS... WAS THAT A FAKE?
NOT AT ALL. YOUR FATHER REALLY DID RECORD THAT MESSAGE TEN YEARS AGO.
OF COURSE... THERE WERE PARTS IN THE ORIGINAL RECORDING THAT DID NOT SERVE MY PURPOSES...
YOU DOCTORED THE VIDEO FILE!?
I PREFER TO THINK OF IT AS EDITING... FOR EFFICIENCY.

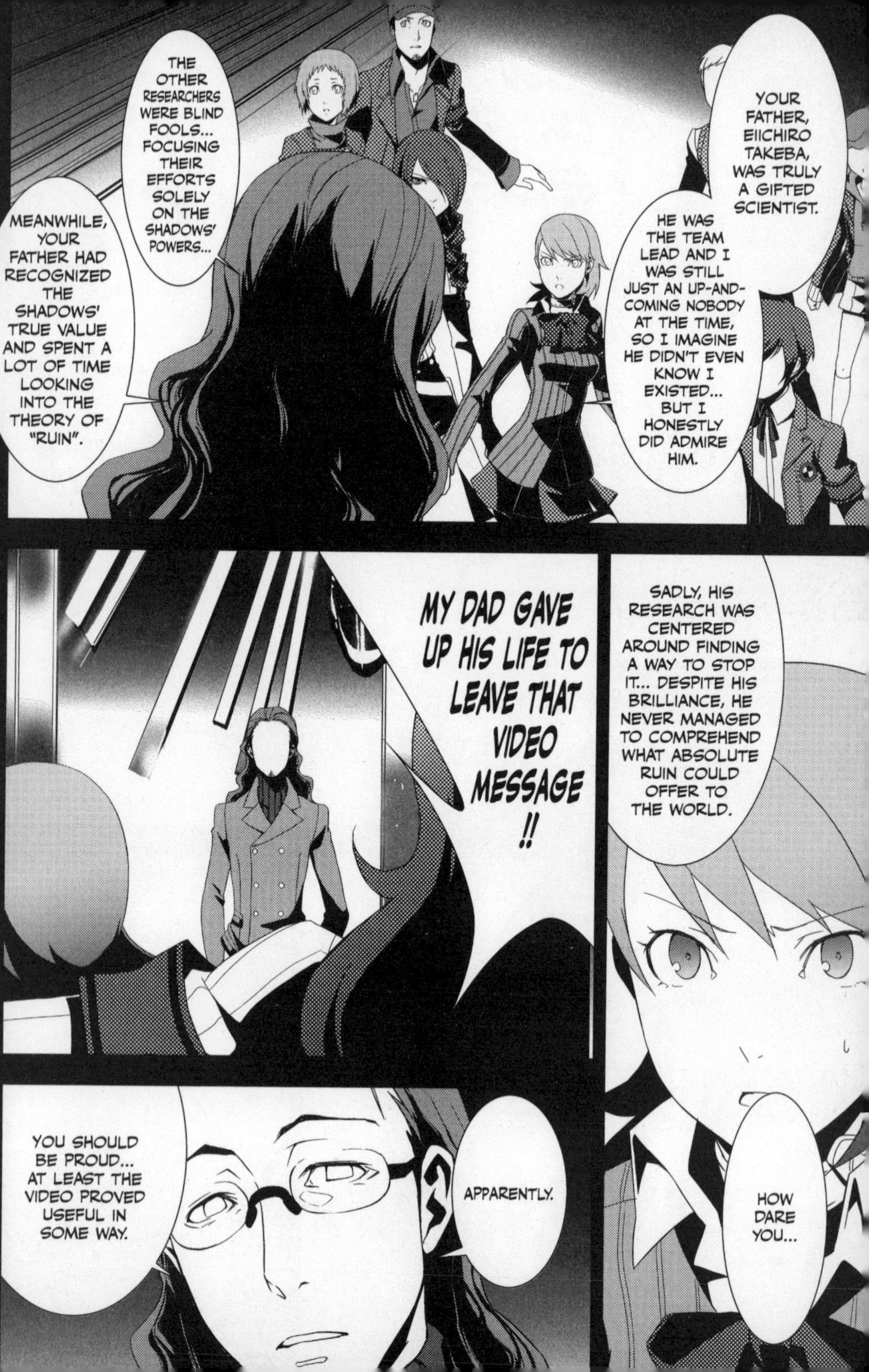
YOUR FATHER, EIICHIRO TAKEBA, WAS TRULY A GIFTED SCIENTIST.
HE WAS THE TEAM LEAD AND I WAS STILL JUST AN UP-AND-COMING NOBODY AT THE TIME, SO I IMAGINE HE DIDN'T EVEN KNOW I EXISTED... BUT I HONESTLY DID ADMIRE HIM.
THE OTHER RESEARCHERS WERE BLIND FOOLS... FOCUSING THEIR EFFORTS SOLELY ON THE SHADOWS' POWERS...
MEANWHILE, YOUR FATHER HAD RECOGNIZED THE SHADOWS' TRUE VALUE AND SPENT A LOT OF TIME LOOKING INTO THE THEORY OF "RUIN".
SADLY, HIS RESEARCH WAS CENTERED AROUND FINDING A WAY TO STOP IT... DESPITE HIS BRILLIANCE, HE NEVER MANAGED TO COMPREHEND WHAT ABSOLUTE RUIN COULD OFFER TO THE WORLD.
MY DAD GAVE UP HIS LIFE TO LEAVE THAT VIDEO MESSAGE !!
HOW DARE YOU...
APPARENTLY.
YOU SHOULD BE PROUD... AT LEAST THE VIDEO PROVED USEFUL IN SOME WAY.

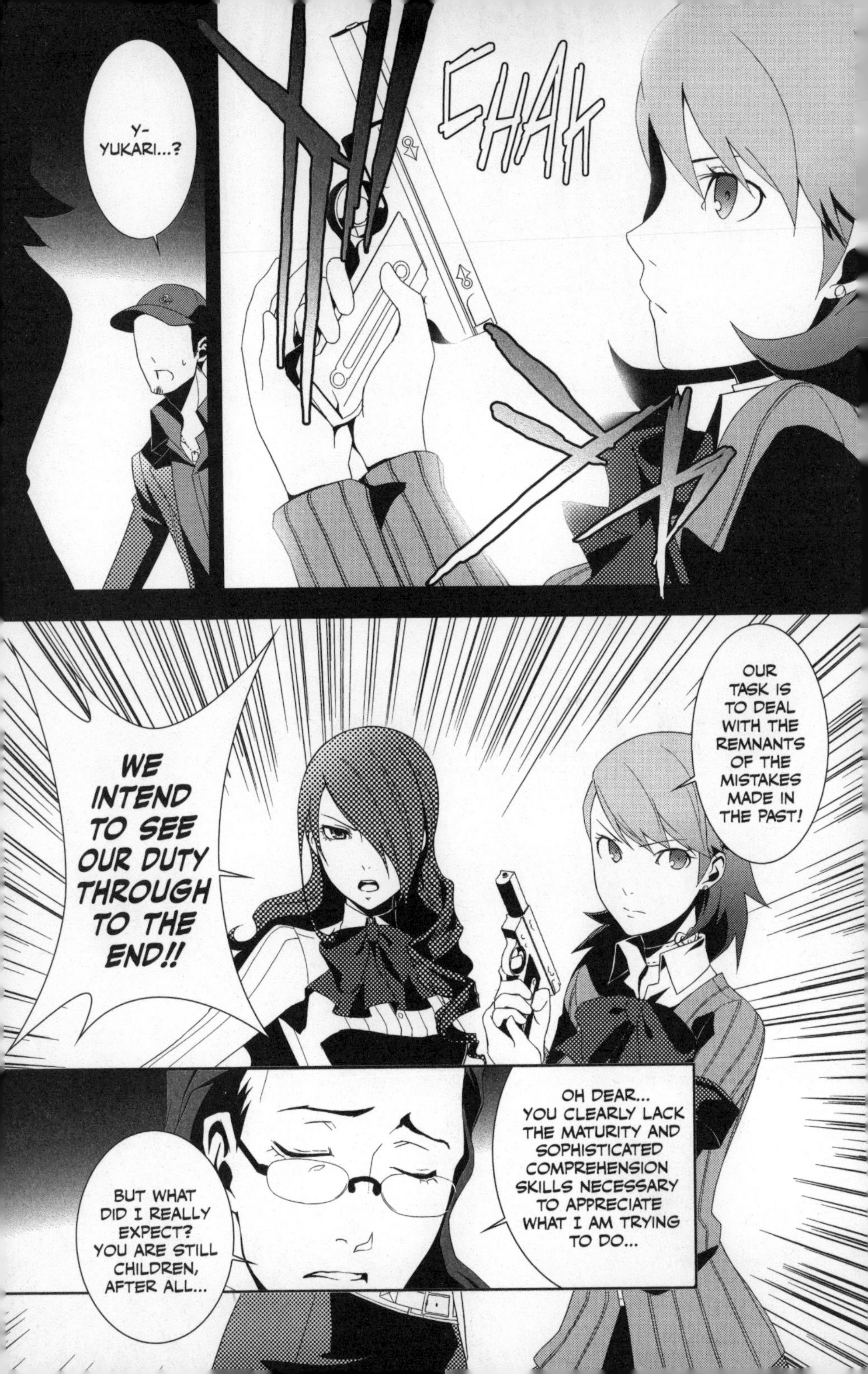
CHAK
Y- YUKARI...?
OUR TASK IS TO DEAL WITH THE REMNANTS OF THE MISTAKES MADE IN THE PAST!
WE INTEND TO SEE OUR DUTY THROUGH TO THE END!!
OH DEAR... YOU CLEARLY LACK THE MATURITY AND SOPHISTICATED COMPREHENSION SKILLS NECESSARY TO APPRECIATE WHAT I AM TRYING TO DO...
BUT WHAT DID I REALLY EXPECT? YOU ARE STILL CHILDREN, AFTER ALL...

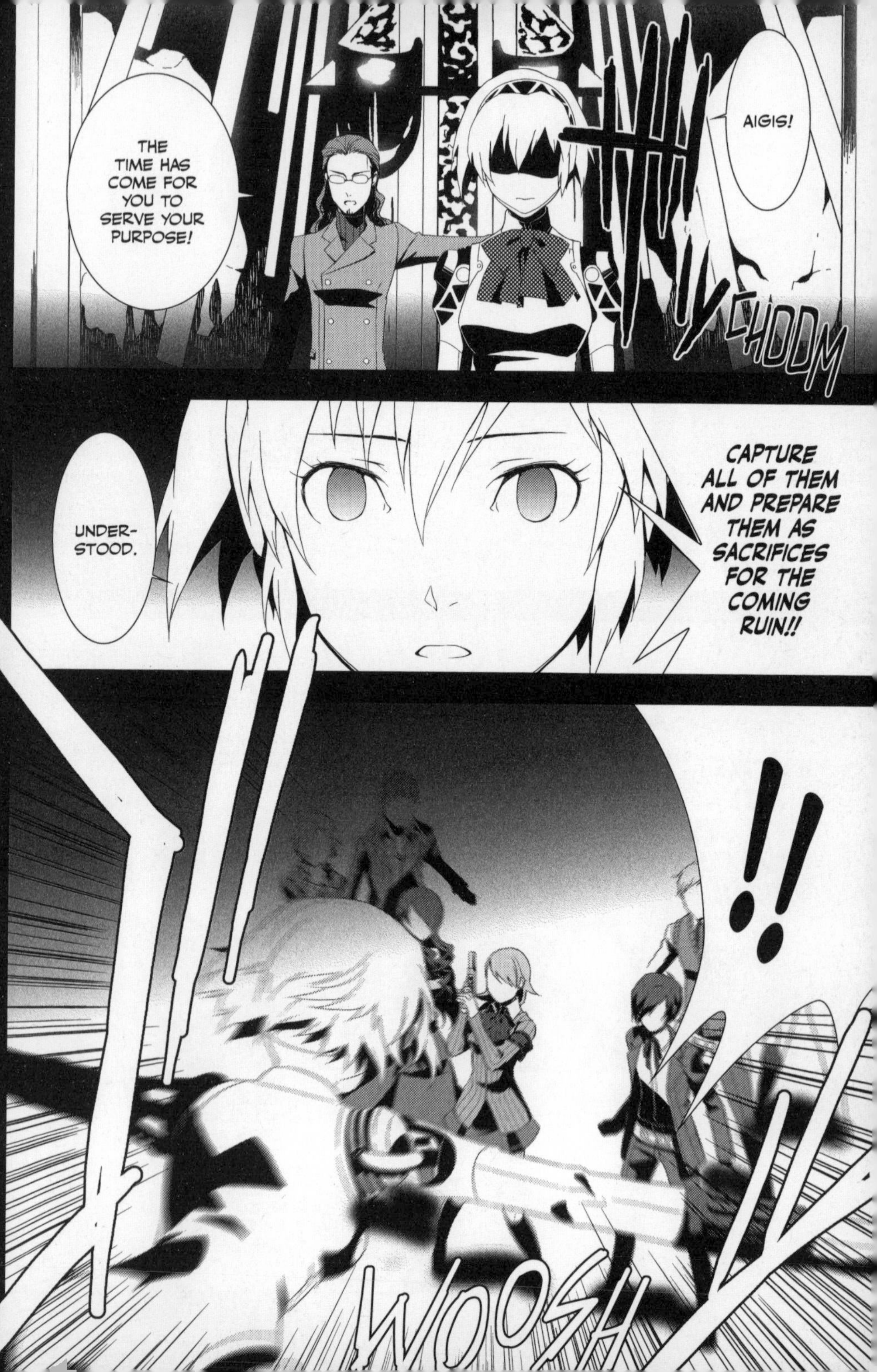
AIGIS!
THE TIME HAS COME FOR YOU TO SERVE YOUR PURPOSE!
CHOOM
CAPTURE ALL OF THEM AND PREPARE THEM AS SACRIFICES FOR THE COMING RUIN!!
UNDER-STOOD.
!!
WOOSH

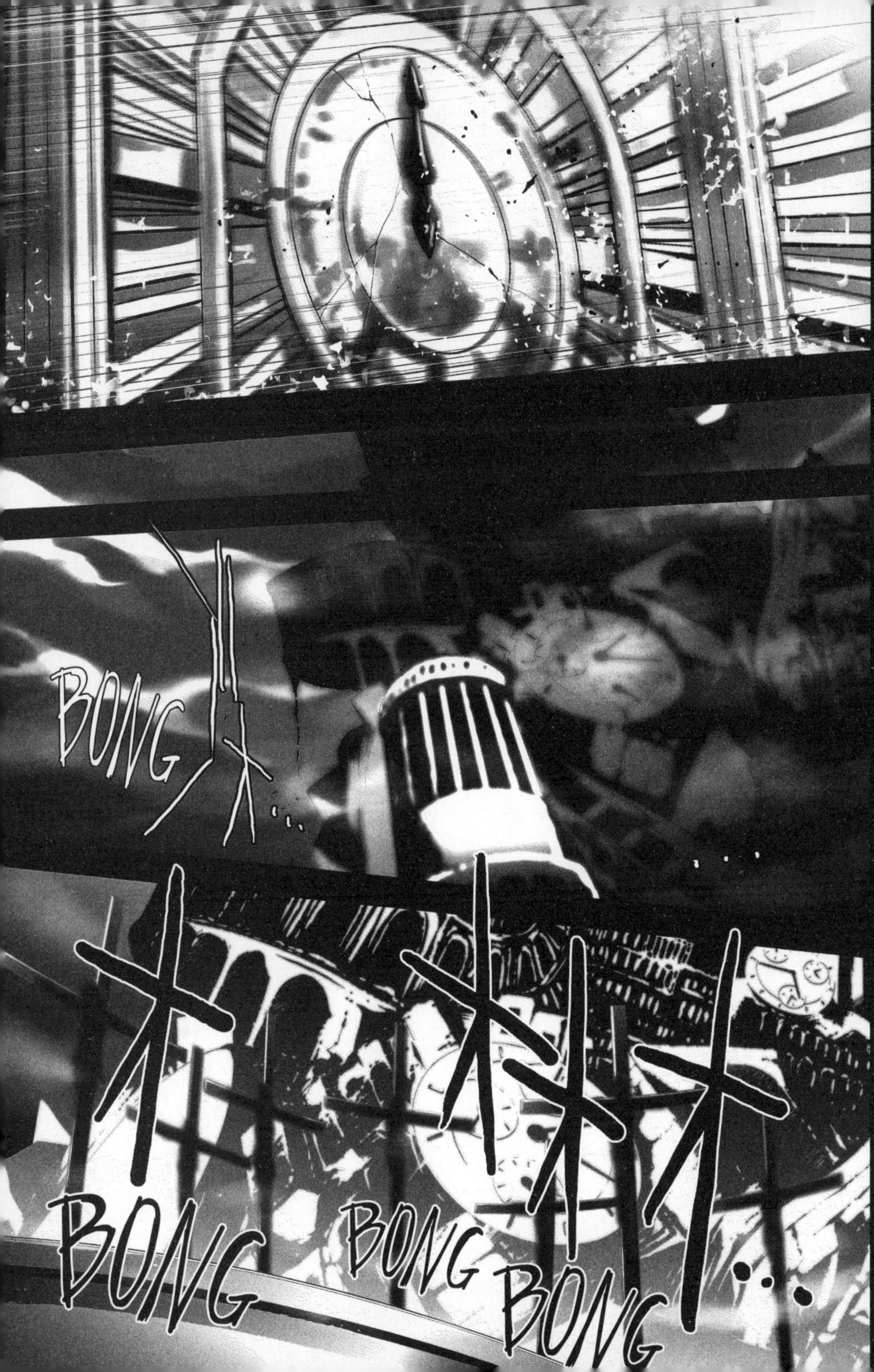
BONG
BONG
BONG
BONG

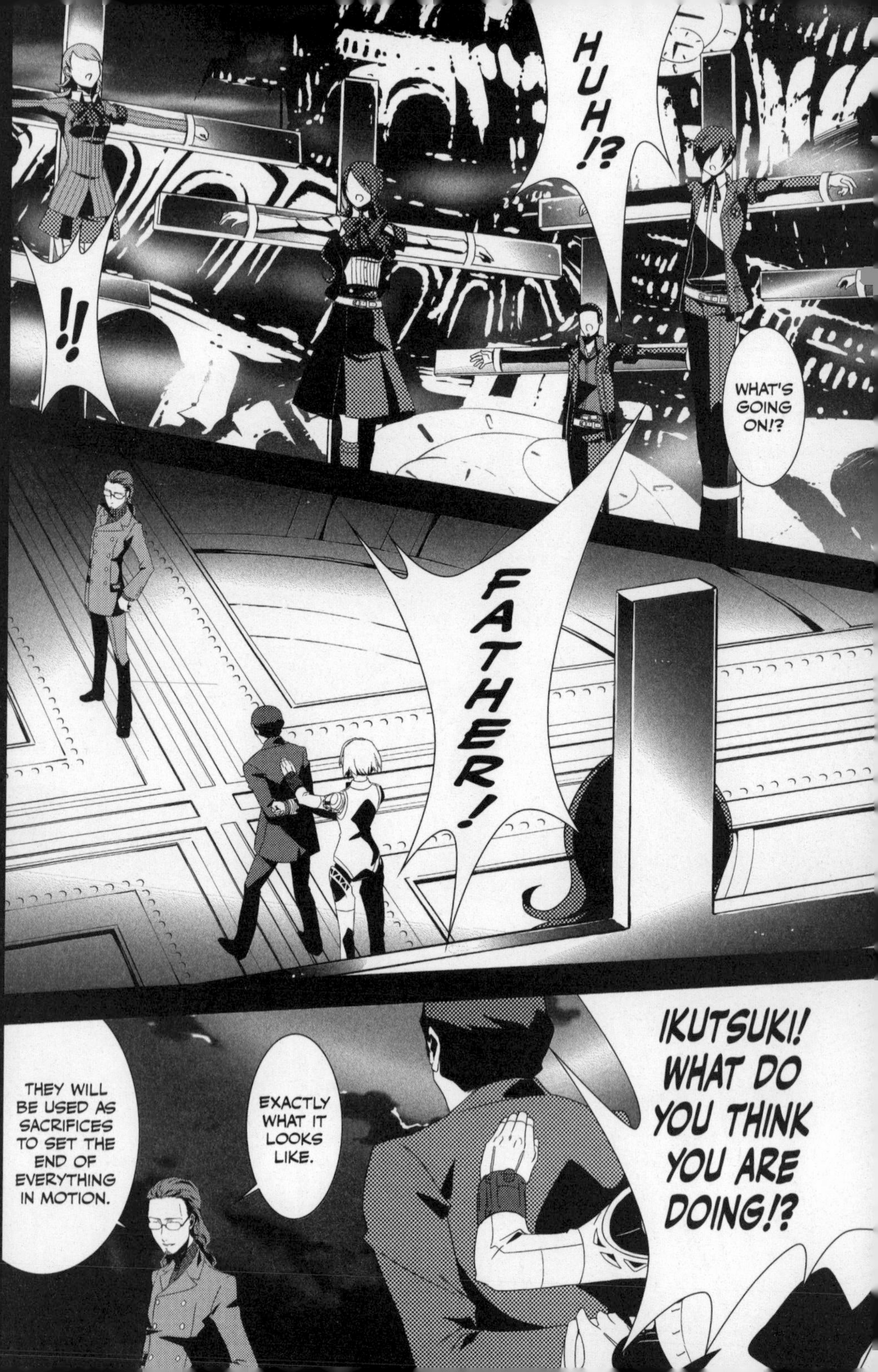
HUH!?
WHAT'S GOING ON!?
!!
FATHER!
IKUTSUKI! WHAT DO YOU THINK YOU ARE DOING!?
EXACTLY WHAT IT LOOKS LIKE.
THEY WILL BE USED AS SACRIFICES TO SET THE END OF EVERYTHING IN MOTION.

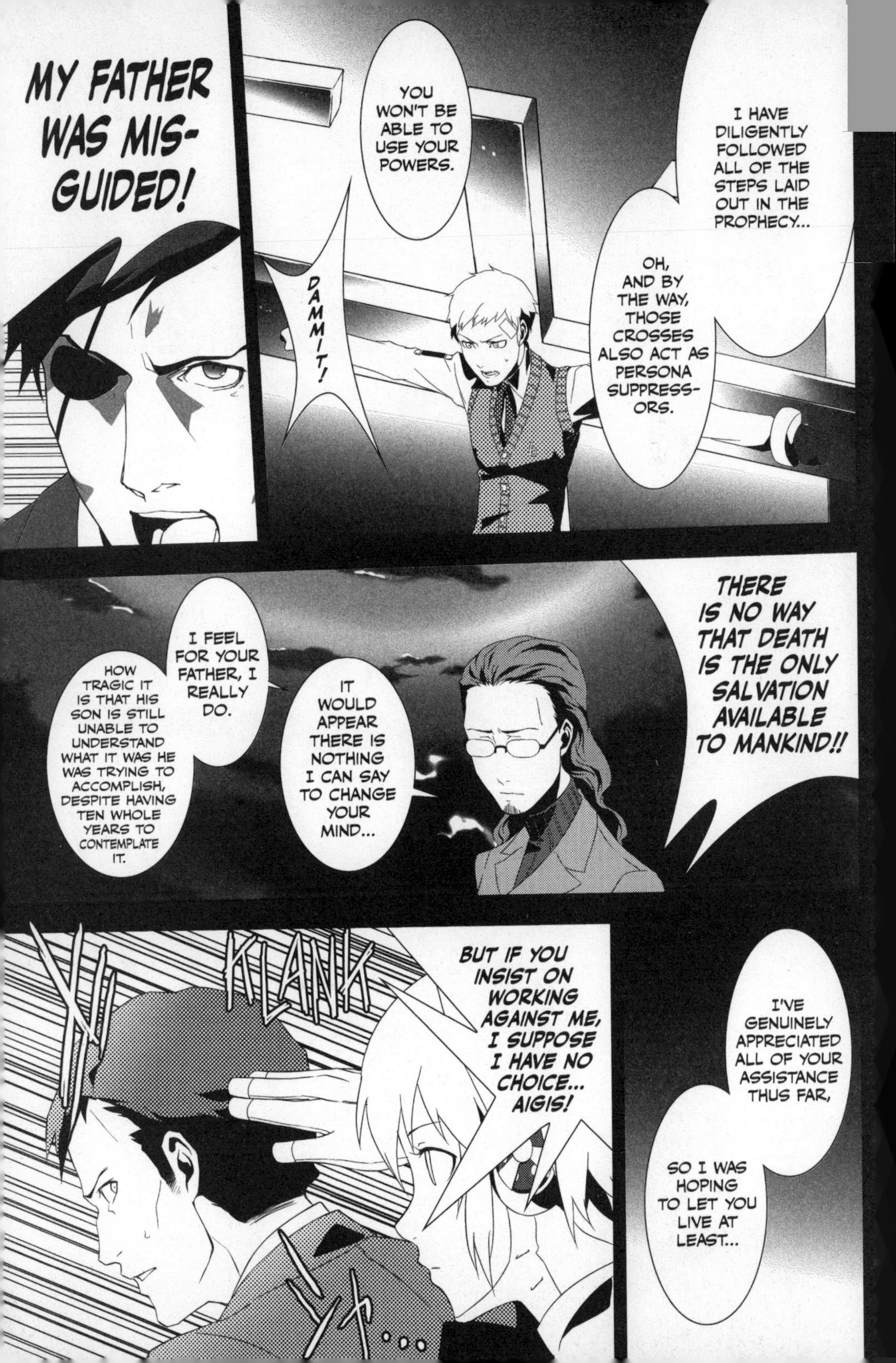
I HAVE DILIGENTLY FOLLOWED ALL OF THE STEPS LAID OUT IN THE PROPHECY...
OH, AND BY THE WAY, THOSE CROSSES ALSO ACT AS PERSONA SUPPRESS-ORS.
YOU WON'T BE ABLE TO USE YOUR POWERS.
DAMMIT!
MY FATHER WAS MIS-GUIDED!
THERE IS NO WAY THAT DEATH IS THE ONLY SALVATION AVAILABLE TO MANKIND!!
IT WOULD APPEAR THERE IS NOTHING I CAN SAY TO CHANGE YOUR MIND...
I FEEL FOR YOUR FATHER, I REALLY DO.
HOW TRAGIC IT IS THAT HIS SON IS STILL UNABLE TO UNDERSTAND WHAT IT WAS HE WAS TRYING TO ACCOMPLISH, DESPITE HAVING TEN WHOLE YEARS TO CONTEMPLATE IT.
I'VE GENUINELY APPRECIATED ALL OF YOUR ASSISTANCE THUS FAR,
SO I WAS HOPING TO LET YOU LIVE AT LEAST...
BUT IF YOU INSIST ON WORKING AGAINST ME, I SUPPOSE I HAVE NO CHOICE... AIGIS!
KLANK

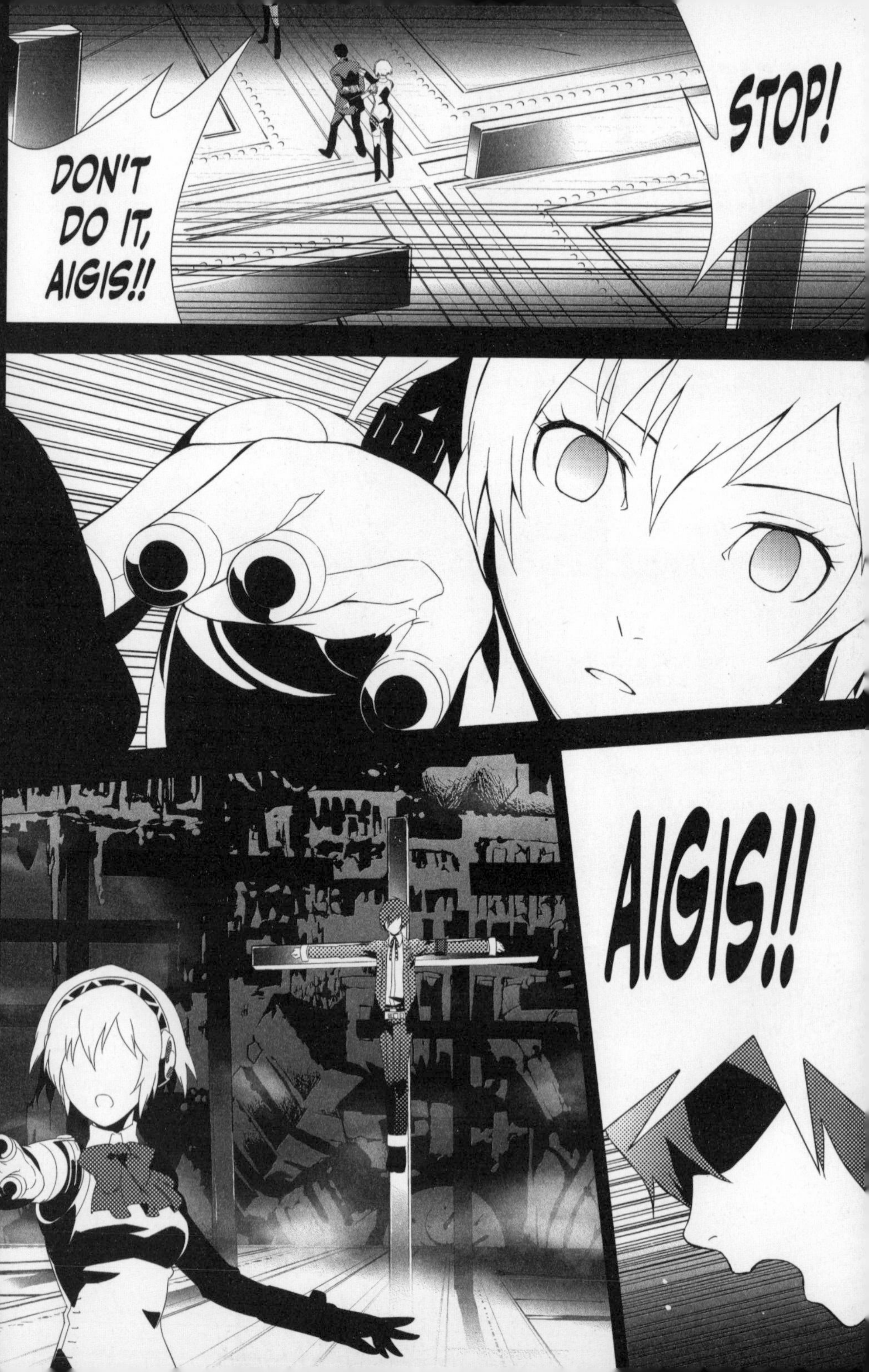
STOP!
DON'T DO IT, AIGIS!!
AIGIS!!

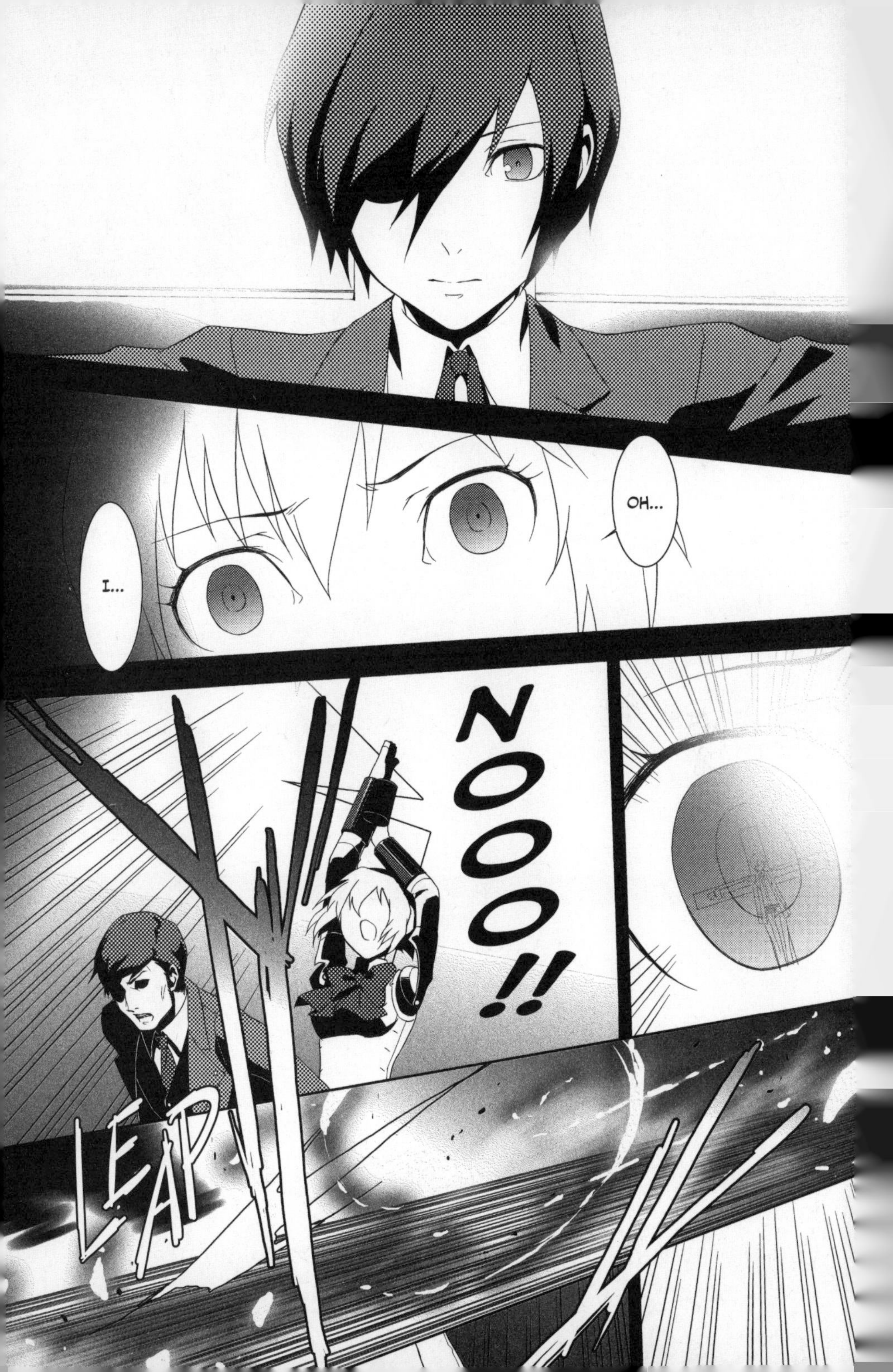
OH...
I...
NOOOO!!
LEAP

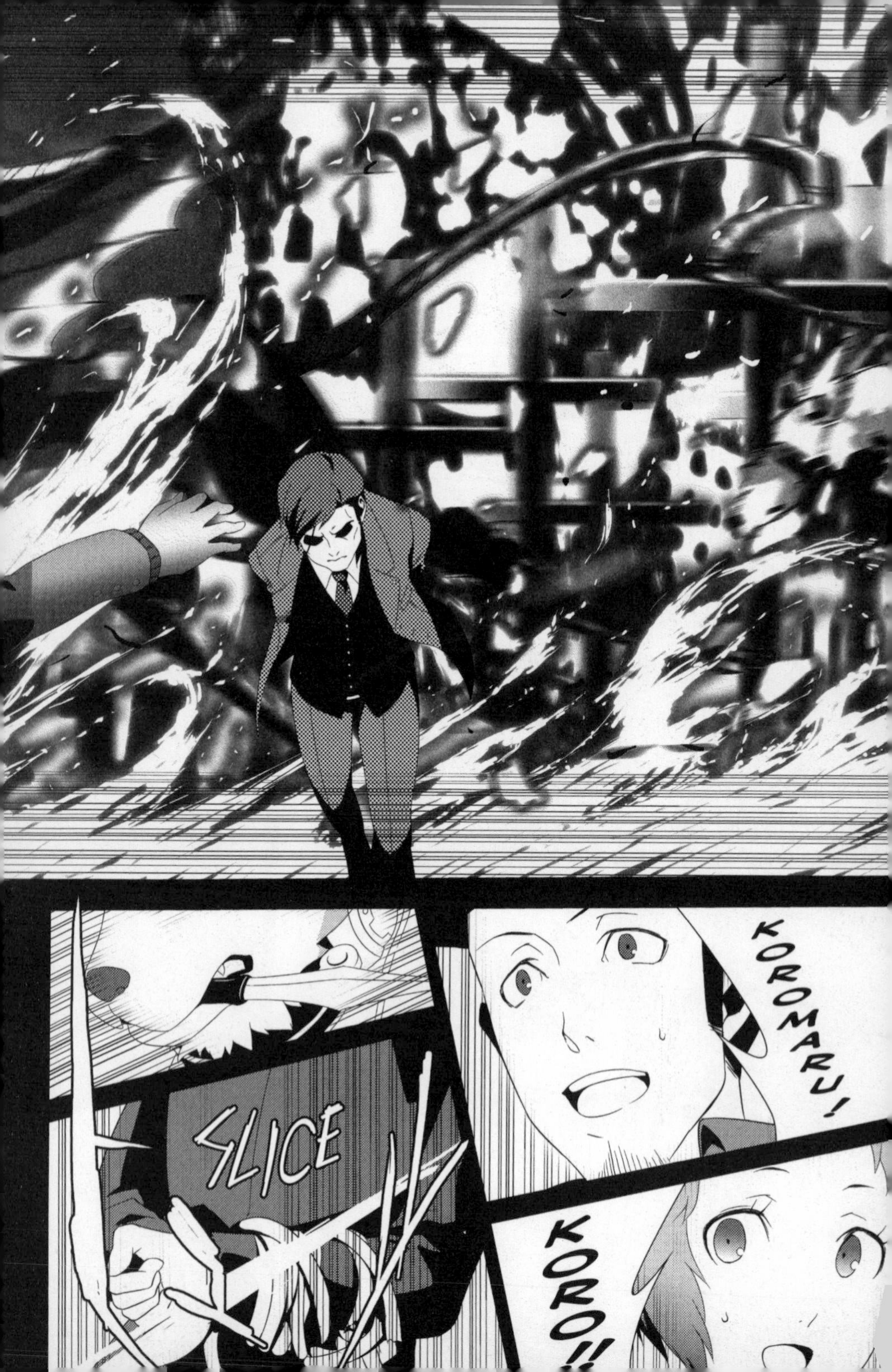
KOROMARU!
KORO!!
SLICE

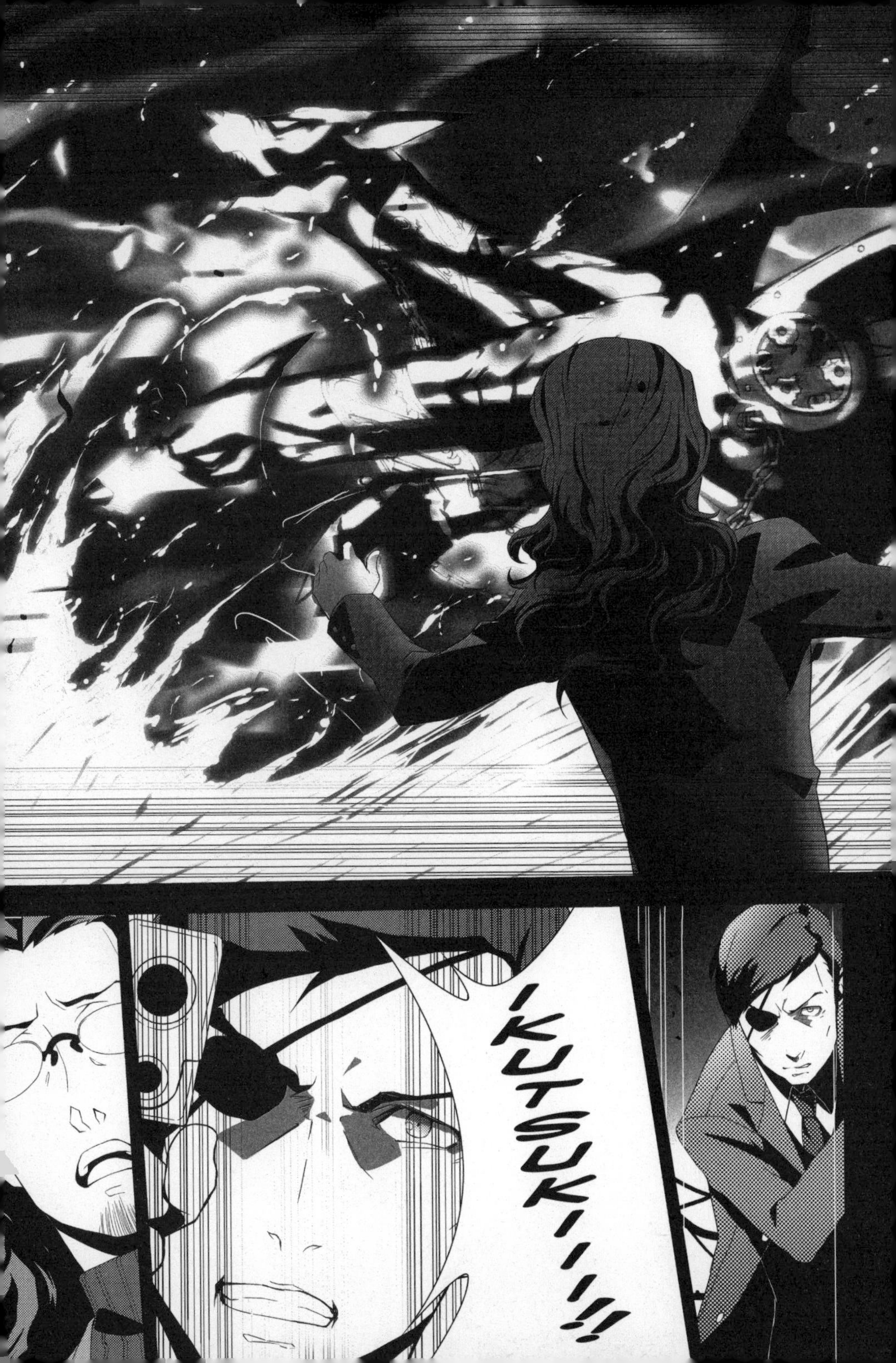
IKUTSUKI-!!!

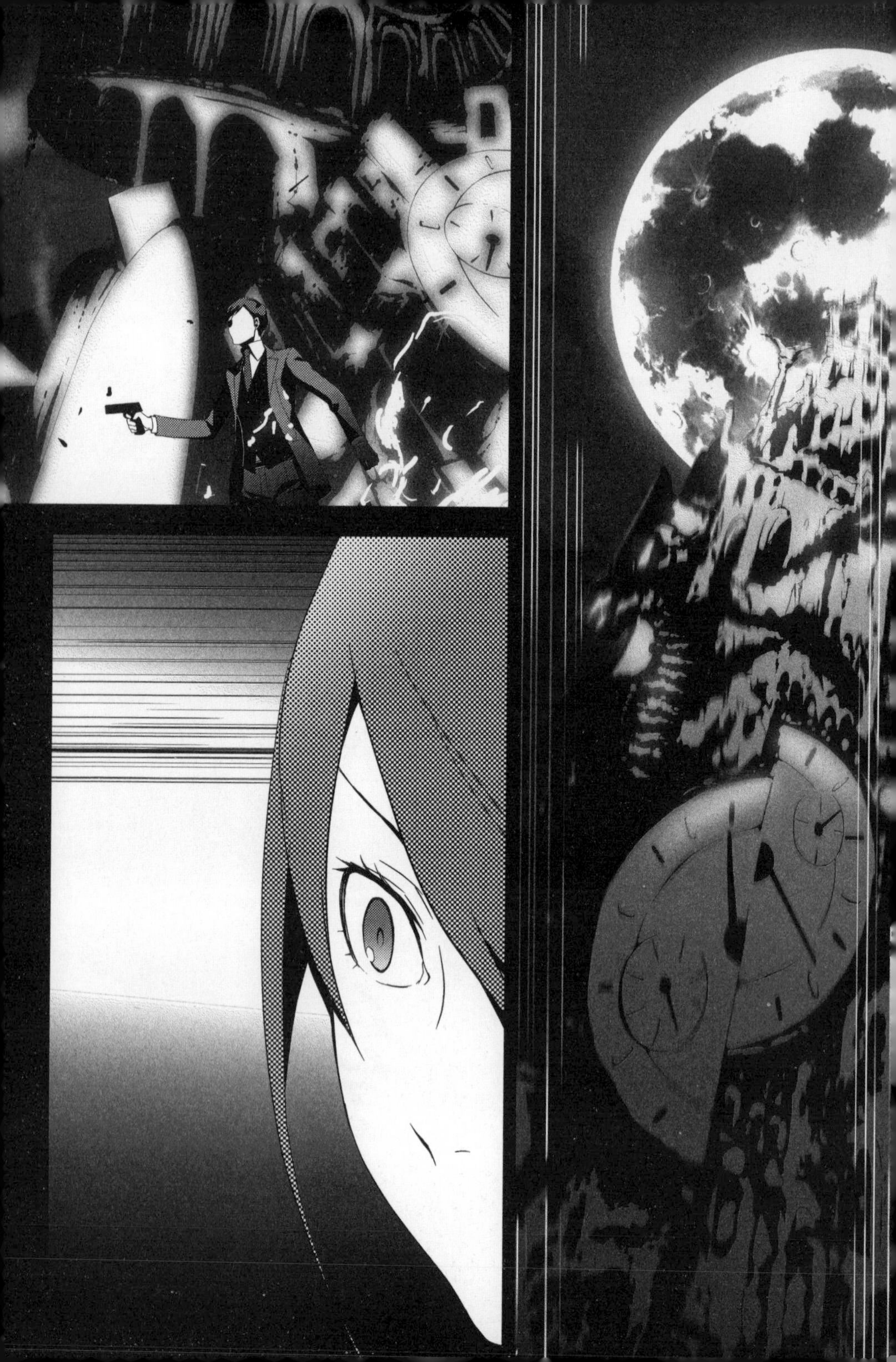

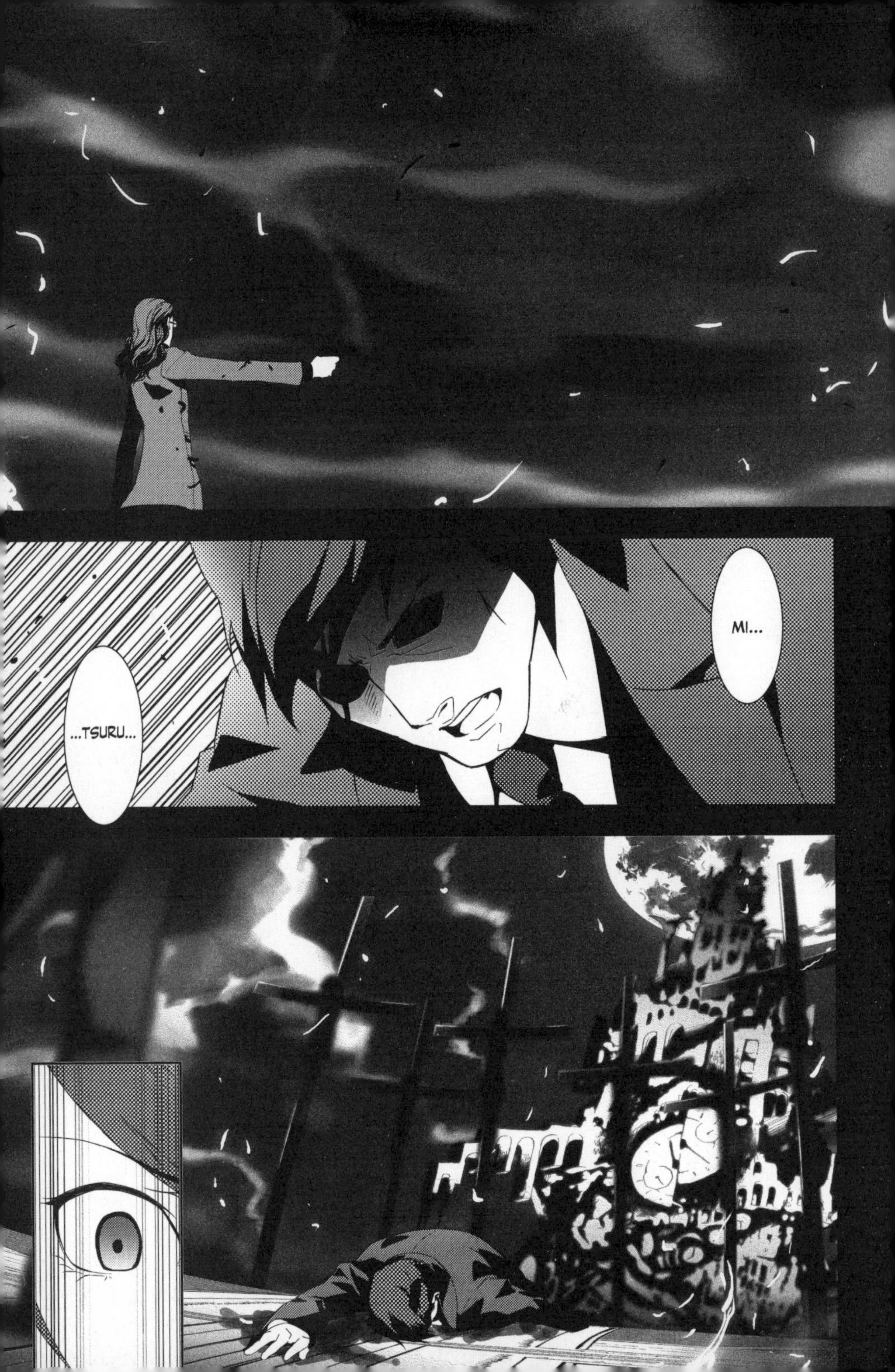
MI...
...TSURU...

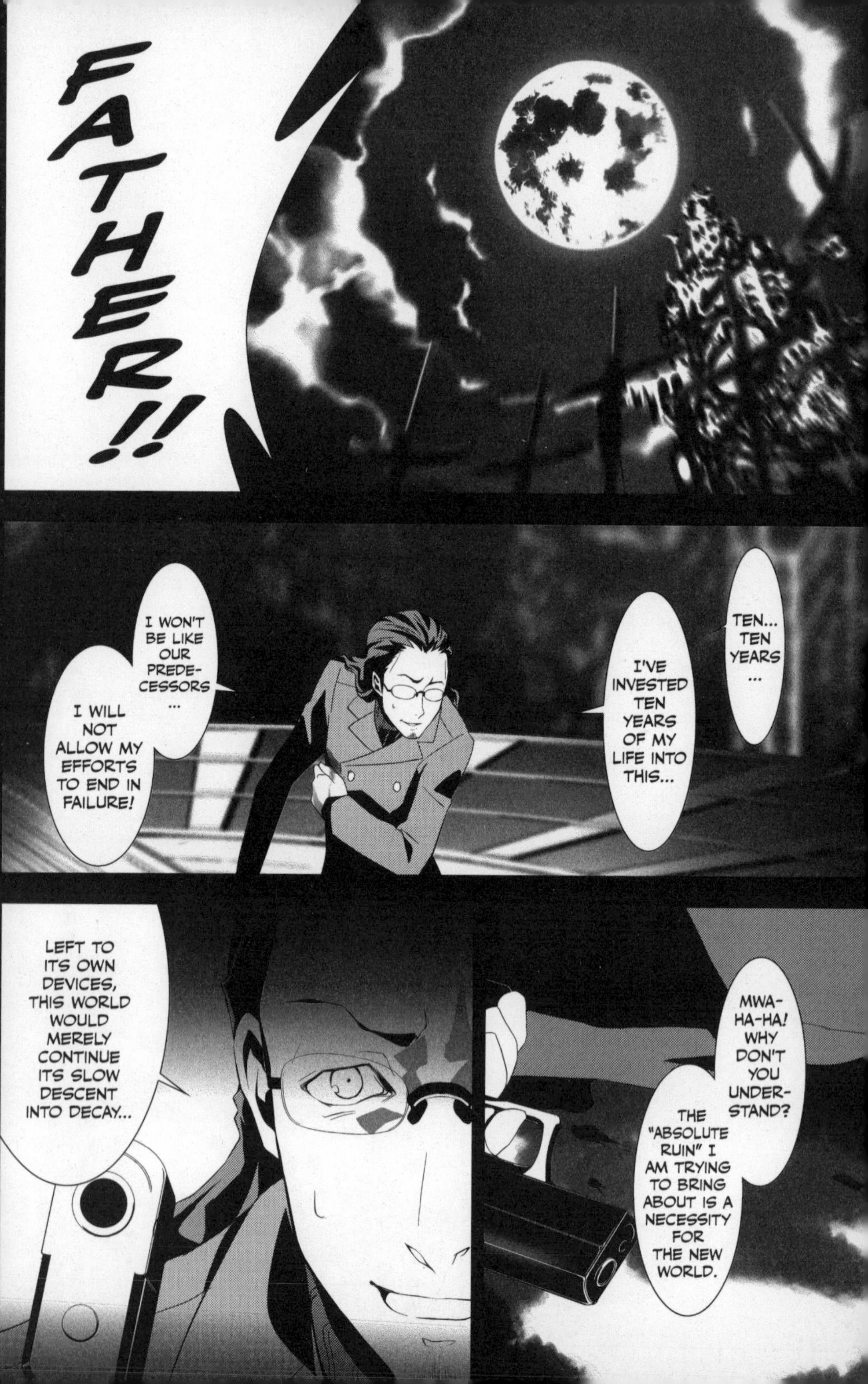
FATHER!!
TEN... TEN YEARS ...
I'VE INVESTED TEN YEARS OF MY LIFE INTO THIS...
I WON'T BE LIKE OUR PREDECESSORS ...
I WILL NOT ALLOW MY EFFORTS TO END IN FAILURE!
MWA-HA-HA! WHY DON'T YOU UNDERSTAND?
THE "ABSOLUTE RUIN" I AM TRYING TO BRING ABOUT IS A NECESSITY FOR THE NEW WORLD.
LEFT TO ITS OWN DEVICES, THIS WORLD WOULD MERELY CONTINUE ITS SLOW DESCENT INTO DECAY...

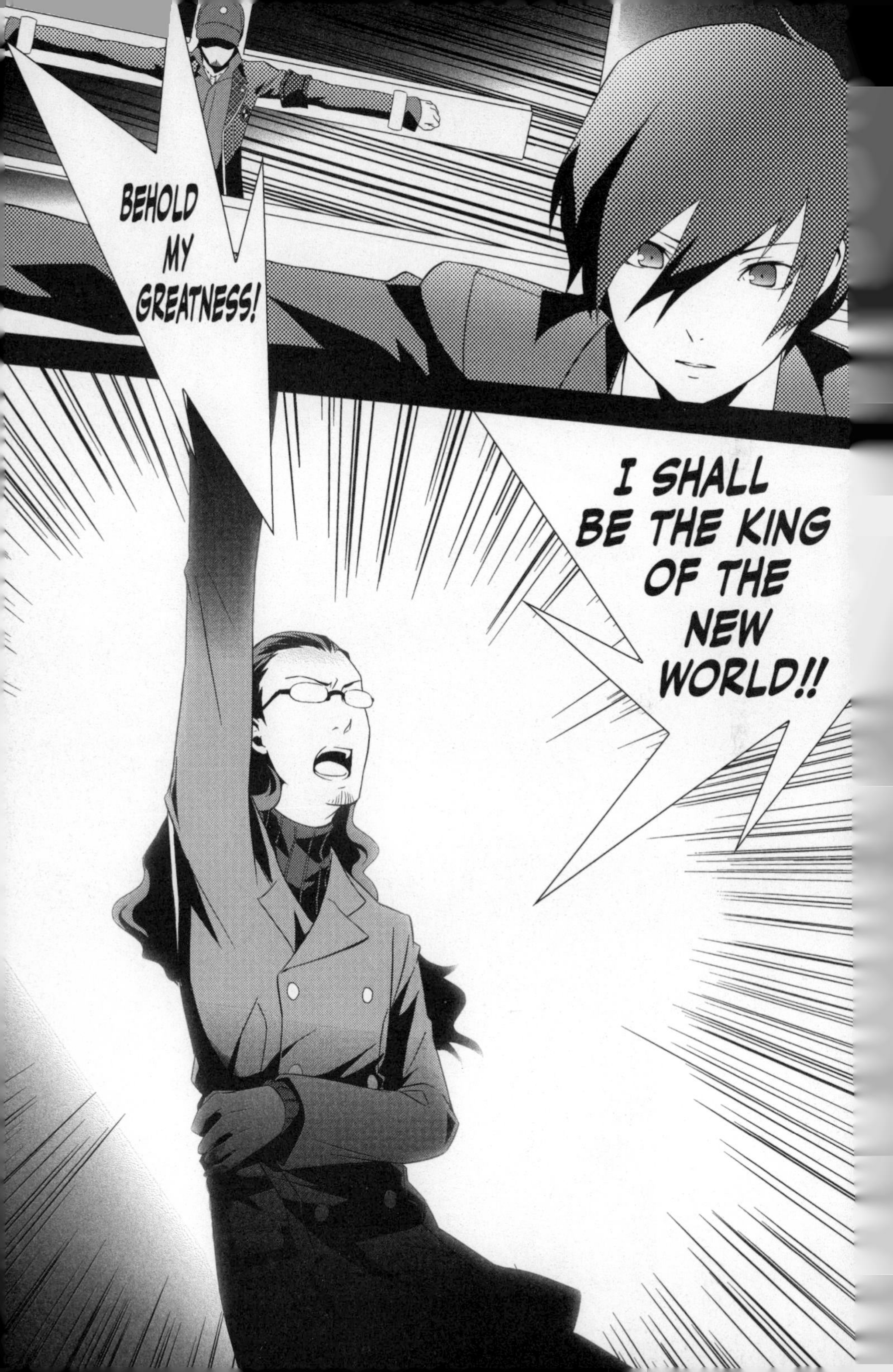
BEHOLD MY GREATNESS!
I SHALL BE THE KING OF THE NEW WORLD!!

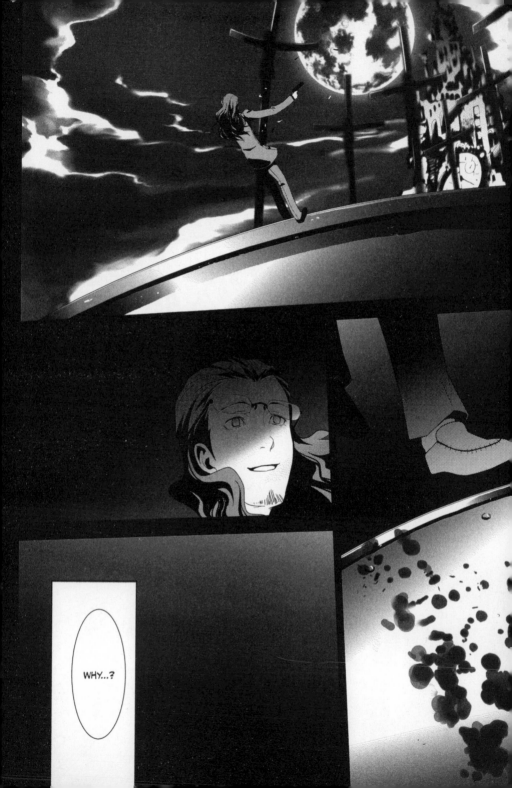

WHY...?

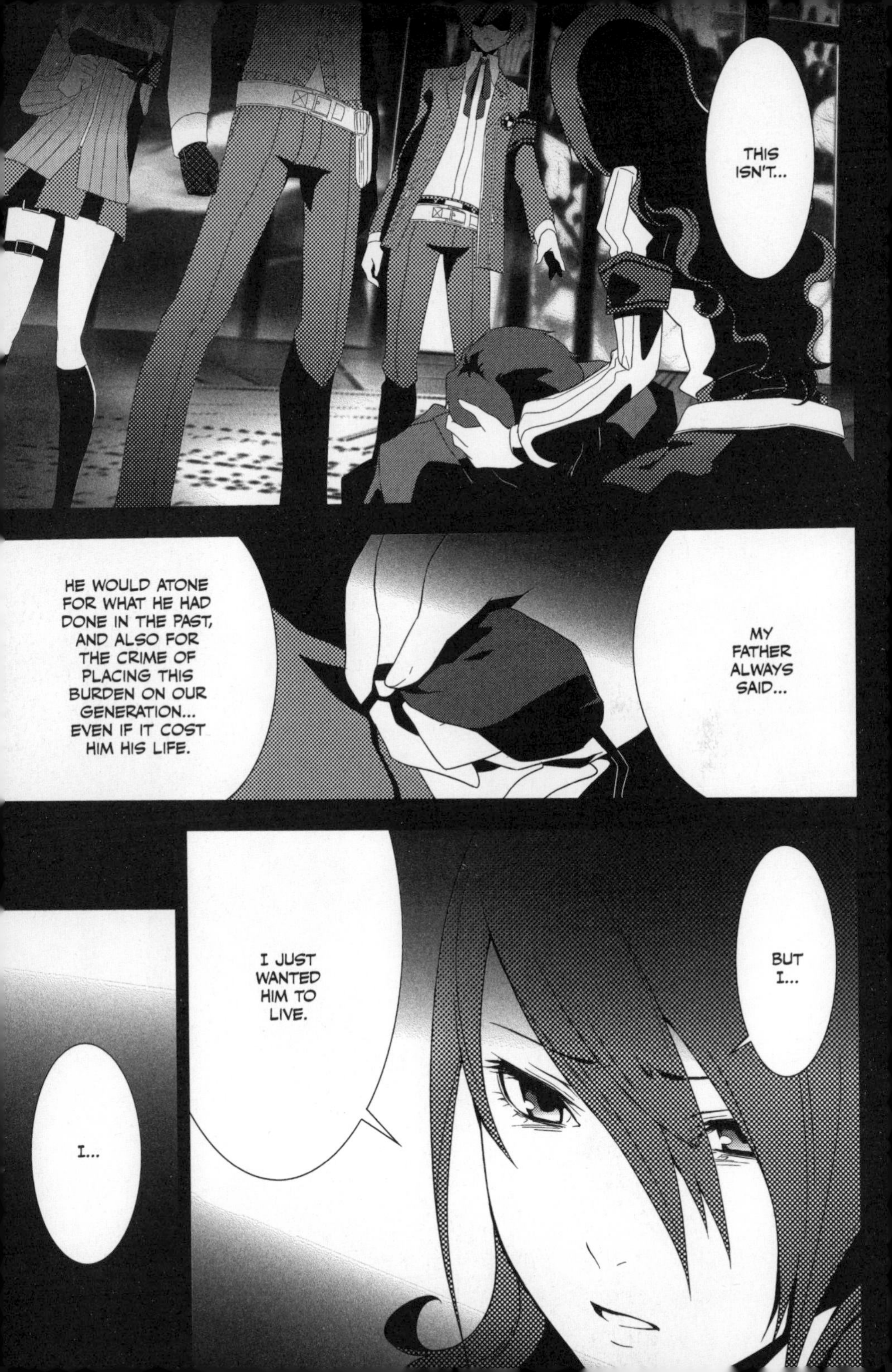
THIS ISN'T...
MY FATHER ALWAYS SAID...
HE WOULD ATONE FOR WHAT HE HAD DONE IN THE PAST, AND ALSO FOR THE CRIME OF PLACING THIS BURDEN ON OUR GENERATION... EVEN IF IT COST HIM HIS LIFE.
BUT I...
I JUST WANTED HIM TO LIVE.
I...

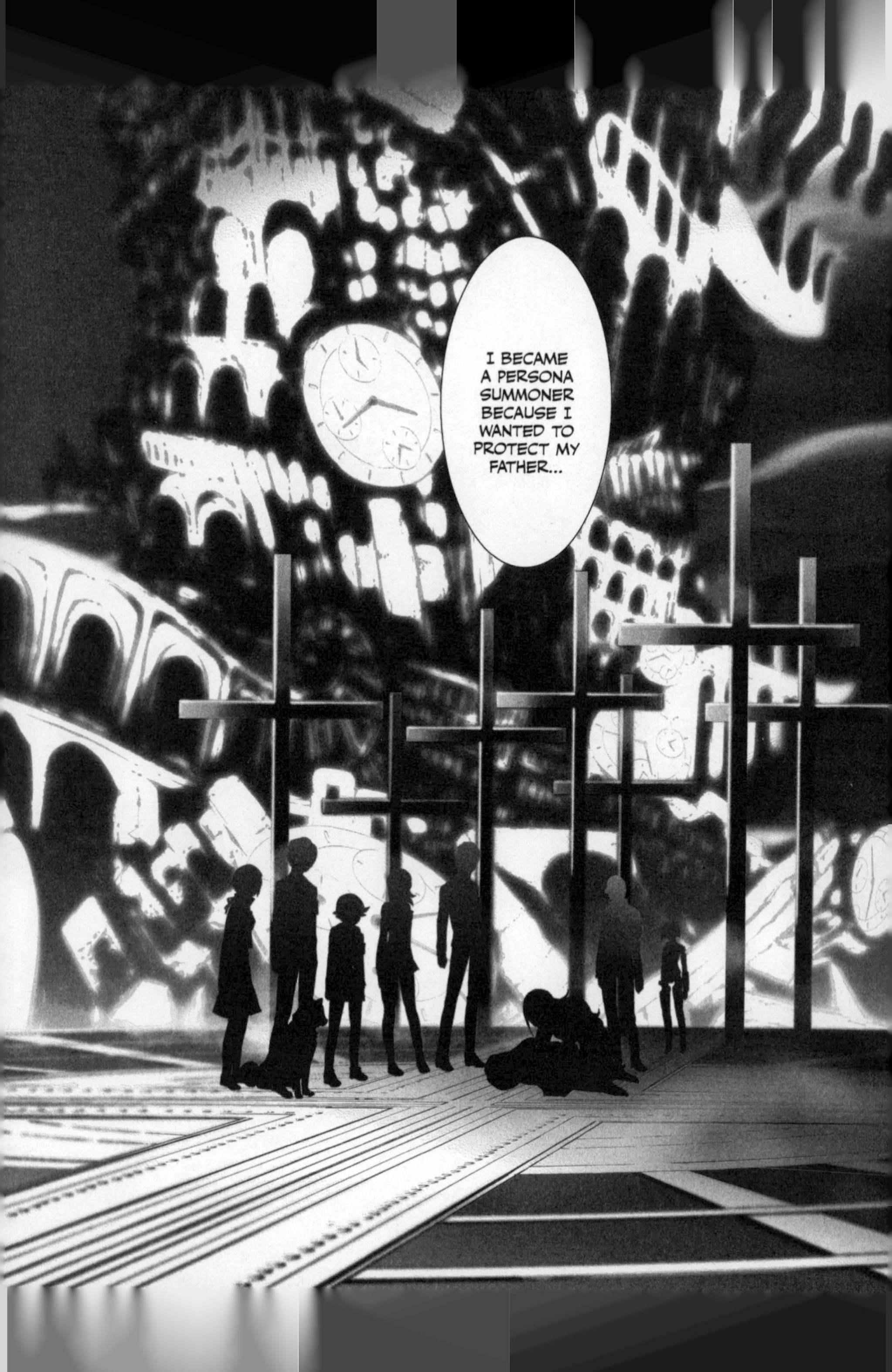
I BECAME A PERSONA SUMMONER BECAUSE I WANTED TO PROTECT MY FATHER...

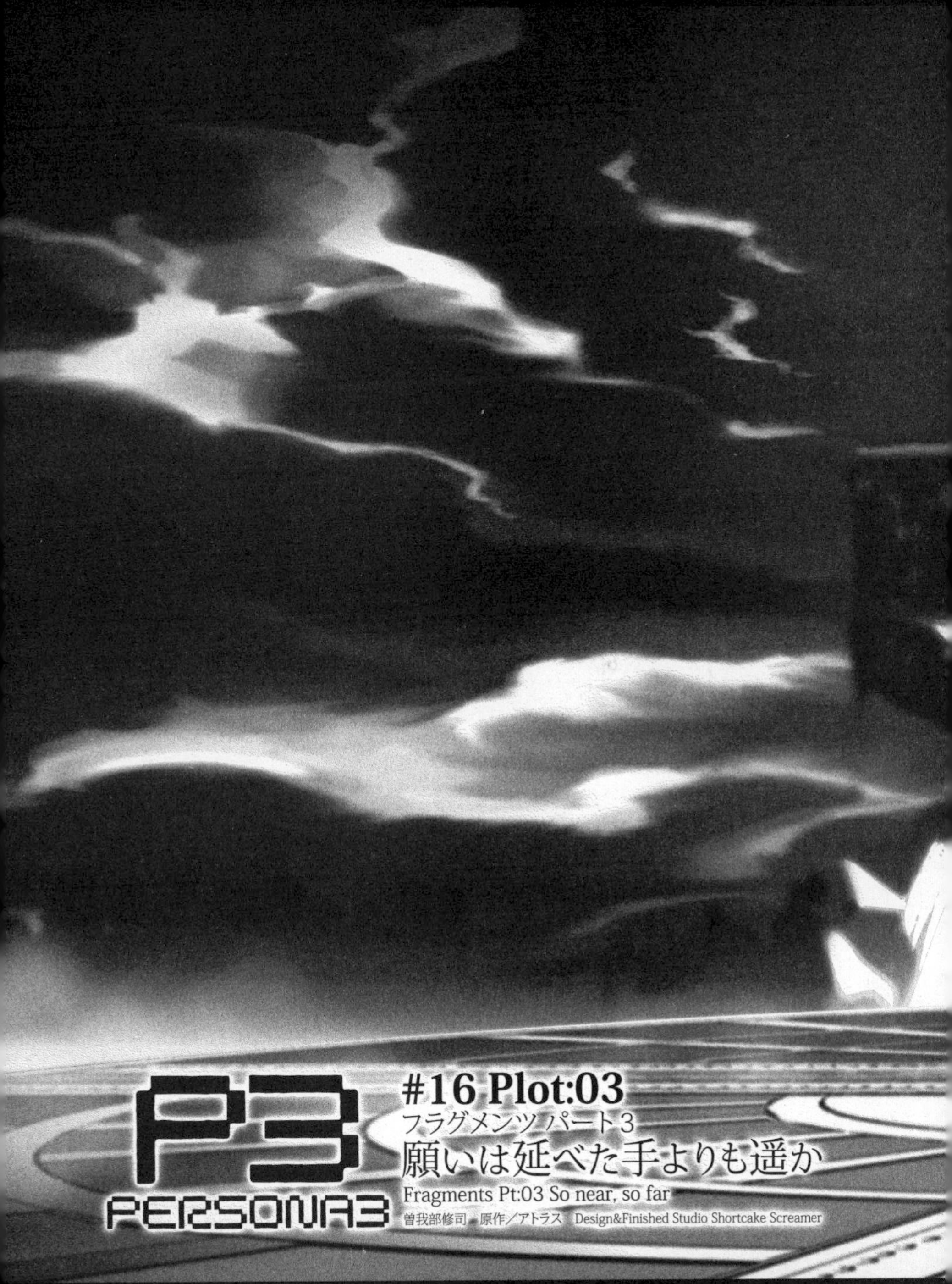
P3
PERSONA3
#16 Plot:03
フラグメンツ パート3
願いは延べた手よりも遥か
Fragments Pt:03 So near, so far
曽我部修司　原作／アトラス　Design&Finished Studio Shortcake Screamer

SPECIAL FEATURE 1
S.E.E.S. ACTIVITY REPORT

This not-so-special special feature is just an excuse for me to talk about stuff! I can hardly believe that my Persona 3 manga has already reached volume 4. I think we've covered about half of the storyline? I'm estimating that the story will last until volume 7 or 8, which should take about two more years. I wonder if the world will be playing "Persona 5" by then. That's a pretty exciting notion in and of itself. Consoles are great and all, but I wish they'd release some Persona games on portable devices as well. Maybe even an MMO! Could you imagine attending Gekkoukan High School as a student in "P3 Online"? I'd love to play a game like that.

Now that we've hit the midpoint of the story, I think it's safe to reveal some spoilers... though by "spoilers" I mean things that I had decided just before I first started working on this manga series.

1: I wanted to include as much of the main storyline as possible since this was an official manga. There was no way to know how long the project would last if I tried to include everything from Social Links to Tartarus, so I knew there'd be some restrictions. (When I initially laid out all of the content prior to starting the series, I was totally overwhelmed by the sheer volume of it all. I guess I shouldn't have expected any less from an RPG that could offer over 100 hours of gameplay!)

2: Since the manga series was getting its start quite a while after the game had been released, I would proceed on the premise that the readers of this manga were already familiar with the Persona world and the P3 characters. Since some of the characters don't get their official storyline debut until the latter half of the story, I wouldn't restrict myself too harshly in terms of chronology. Instead, I would take small opportunities to shine the spotlight on various characters.

3: While I wouldn't make any major changes to the events that took place in the game, I would inject the manga with touches of originality in the form of mini episodes and some dialogue, etc.

The above three points represent the main guidelines by which I crafted this manga.

The three characters who have yet to make an appearance will be doing so in later volumes. The success of this manga relies entirely on the support of fans like you, so I hope you will continue to enjoy reading the Persona 3 manga!

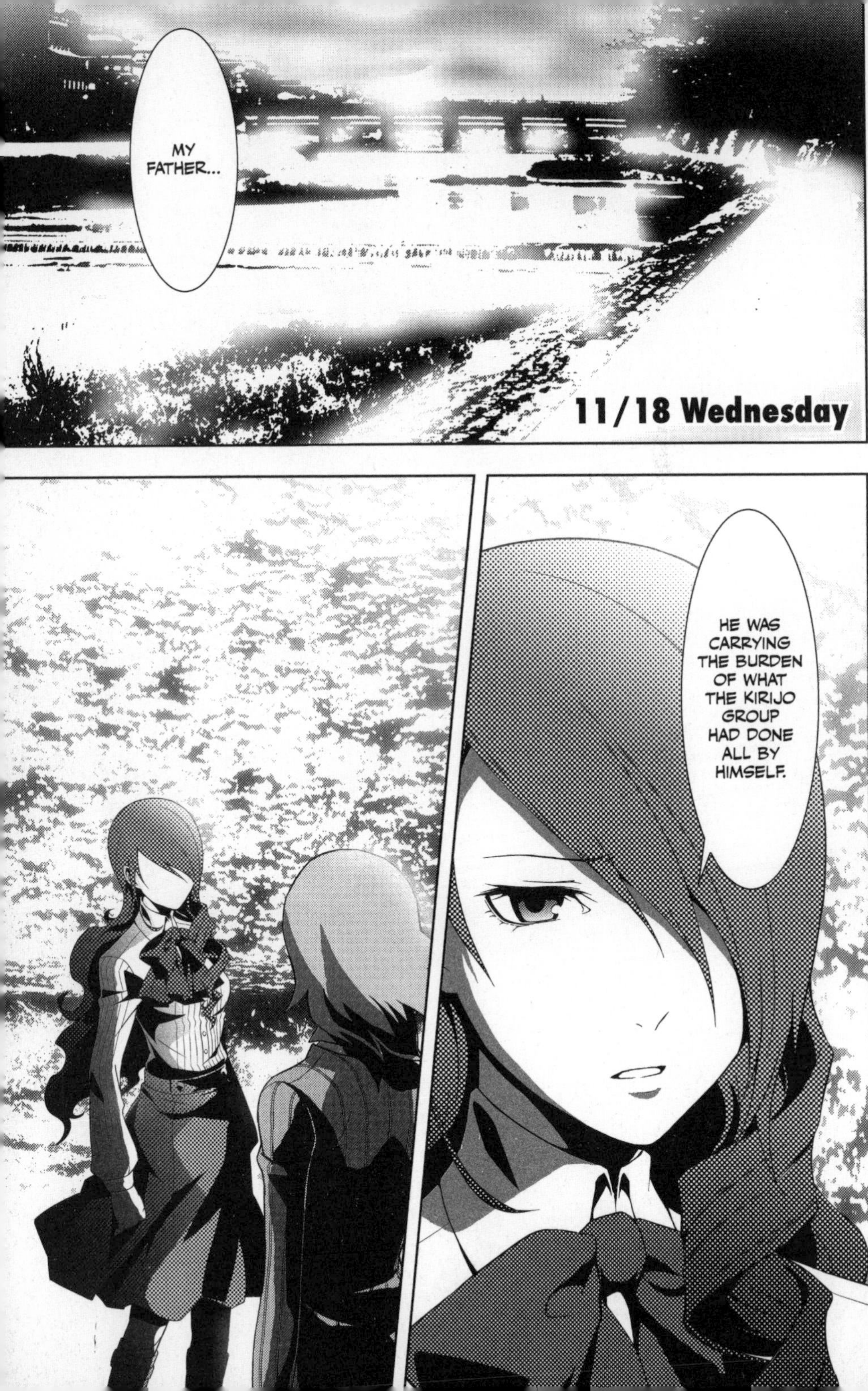
MY FATHER...
11/18 Wednesday
HE WAS CARRYING THE BURDEN OF WHAT THE KIRIJO GROUP HAD DONE ALL BY HIMSELF.

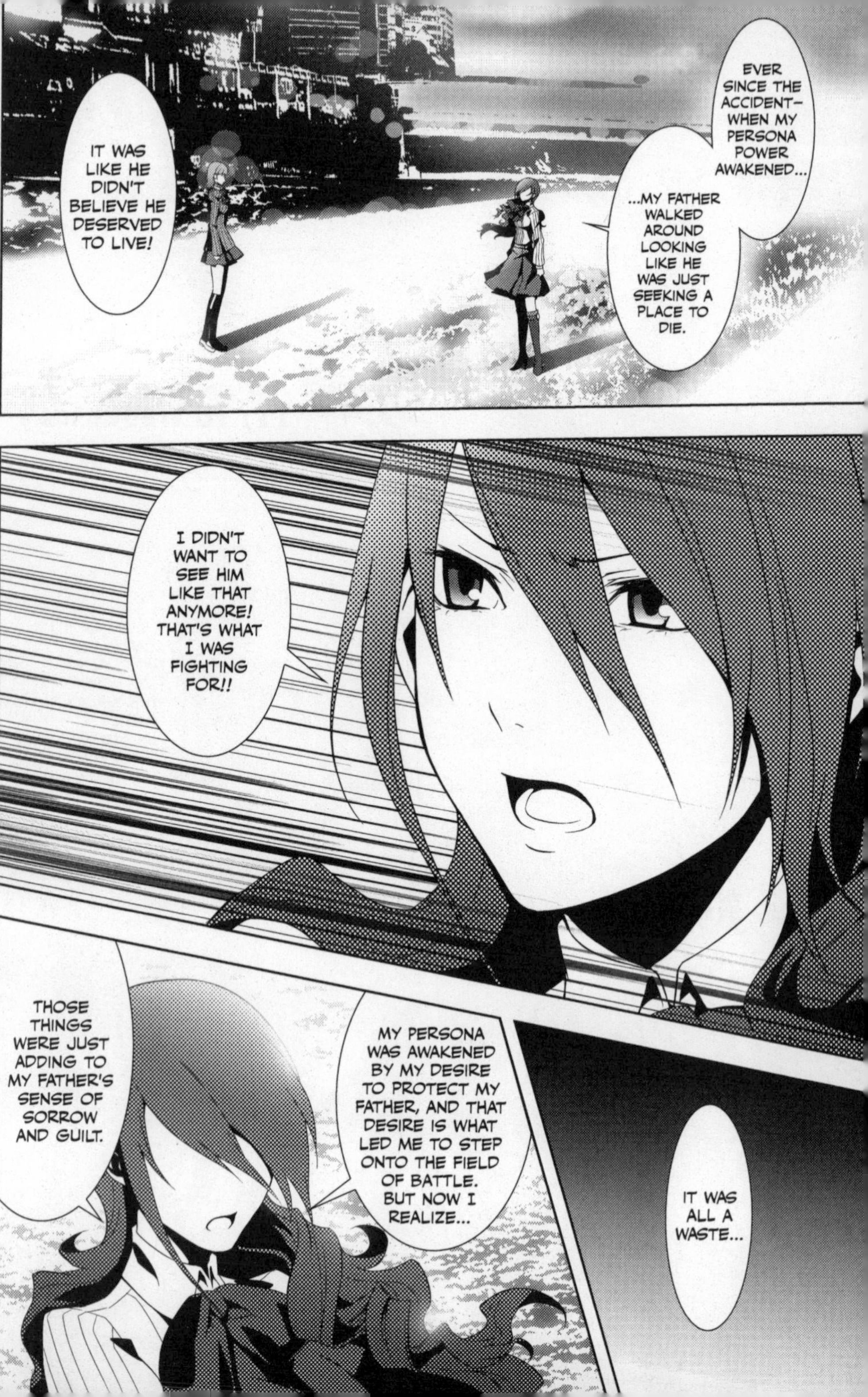
EVER SINCE THE ACCIDENT— WHEN MY PERSONA POWER AWAKENED...
...MY FATHER WALKED AROUND LOOKING LIKE HE WAS JUST SEEKING A PLACE TO DIE.
IT WAS LIKE HE DIDN'T BELIEVE HE DESERVED TO LIVE!
I DIDN'T WANT TO SEE HIM LIKE THAT ANYMORE! THAT'S WHAT I WAS FIGHTING FOR!!
IT WAS ALL A WASTE...
MY PERSONA WAS AWAKENED BY MY DESIRE TO PROTECT MY FATHER, AND THAT DESIRE IS WHAT LED ME TO STEP ONTO THE FIELD OF BATTLE. BUT NOW I REALIZE...
THOSE THINGS WERE JUST ADDING TO MY FATHER'S SENSE OF SORROW AND GUILT.

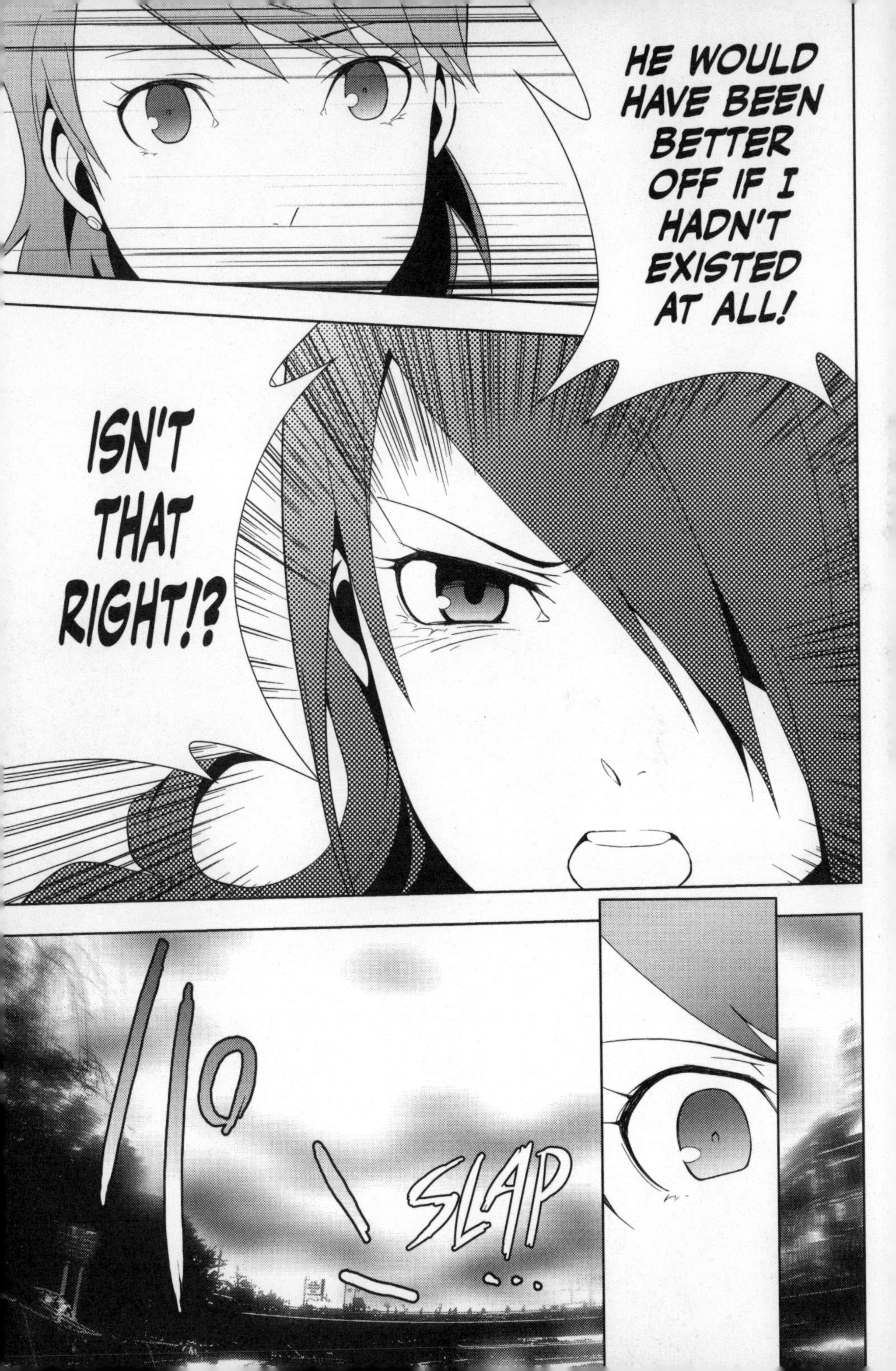
HE WOULD HAVE BEEN BETTER OFF IF I HADN'T EXISTED AT ALL!
ISN'T THAT RIGHT!?
...
SLAP

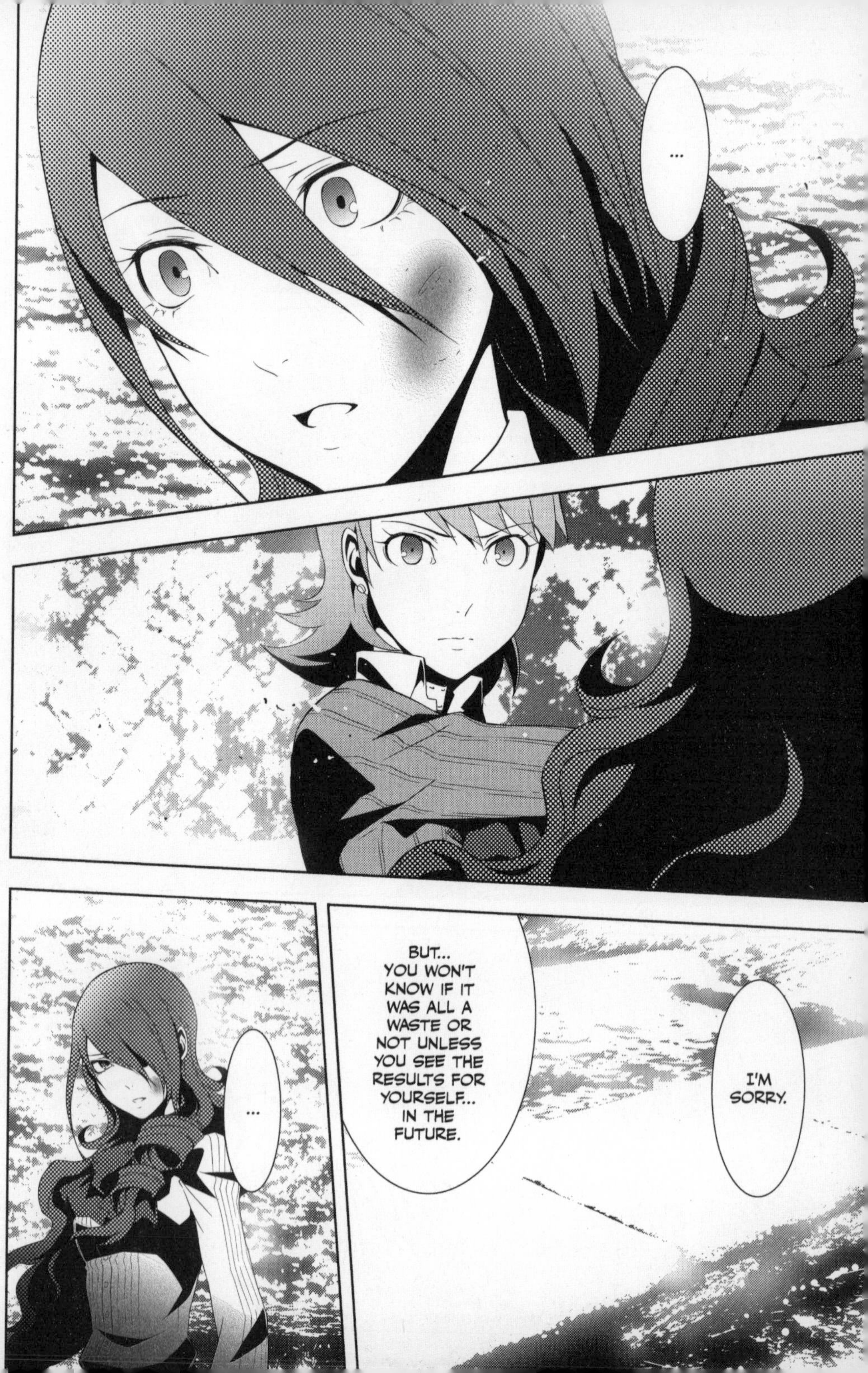
...
I'M SORRY.
BUT... YOU WON'T KNOW IF IT WAS ALL A WASTE OR NOT UNLESS YOU SEE THE RESULTS FOR YOURSELF... IN THE FUTURE.
...

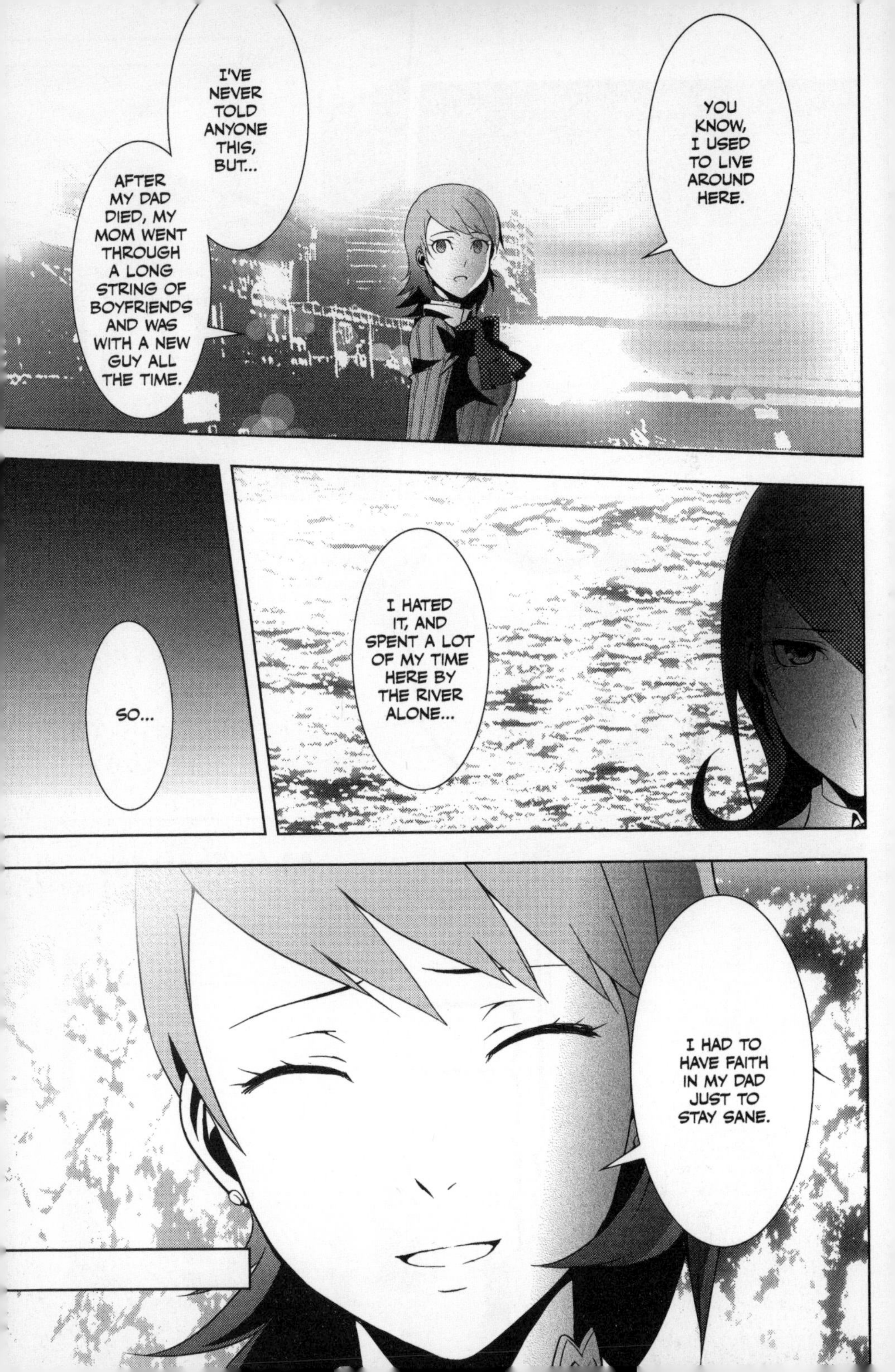
YOU KNOW, I USED TO LIVE AROUND HERE.
I'VE NEVER TOLD ANYONE THIS, BUT...
AFTER MY DAD DIED, MY MOM WENT THROUGH A LONG STRING OF BOYFRIENDS AND WAS WITH A NEW GUY ALL THE TIME.
I HATED IT, AND SPENT A LOT OF MY TIME HERE BY THE RIVER ALONE...
SO...
I HAD TO HAVE FAITH IN MY DAD JUST TO STAY SANE.

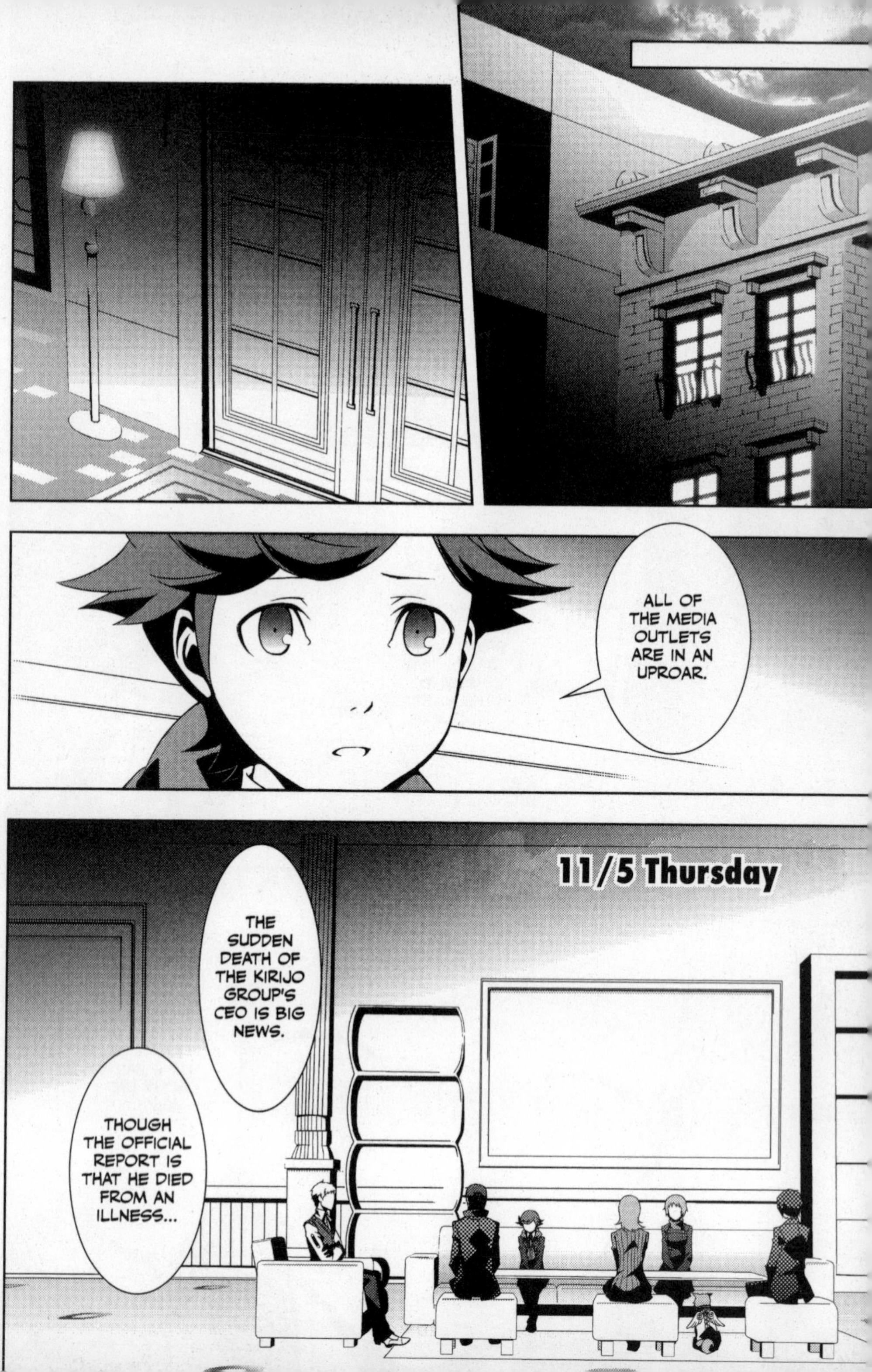
ALL OF THE MEDIA OUTLETS ARE IN AN UPROAR.
11/5 Thursday
THE SUDDEN DEATH OF THE KIRIJO GROUP'S CEO IS BIG NEWS.
THOUGH THE OFFICIAL REPORT IS THAT HE DIED FROM AN ILLNESS...

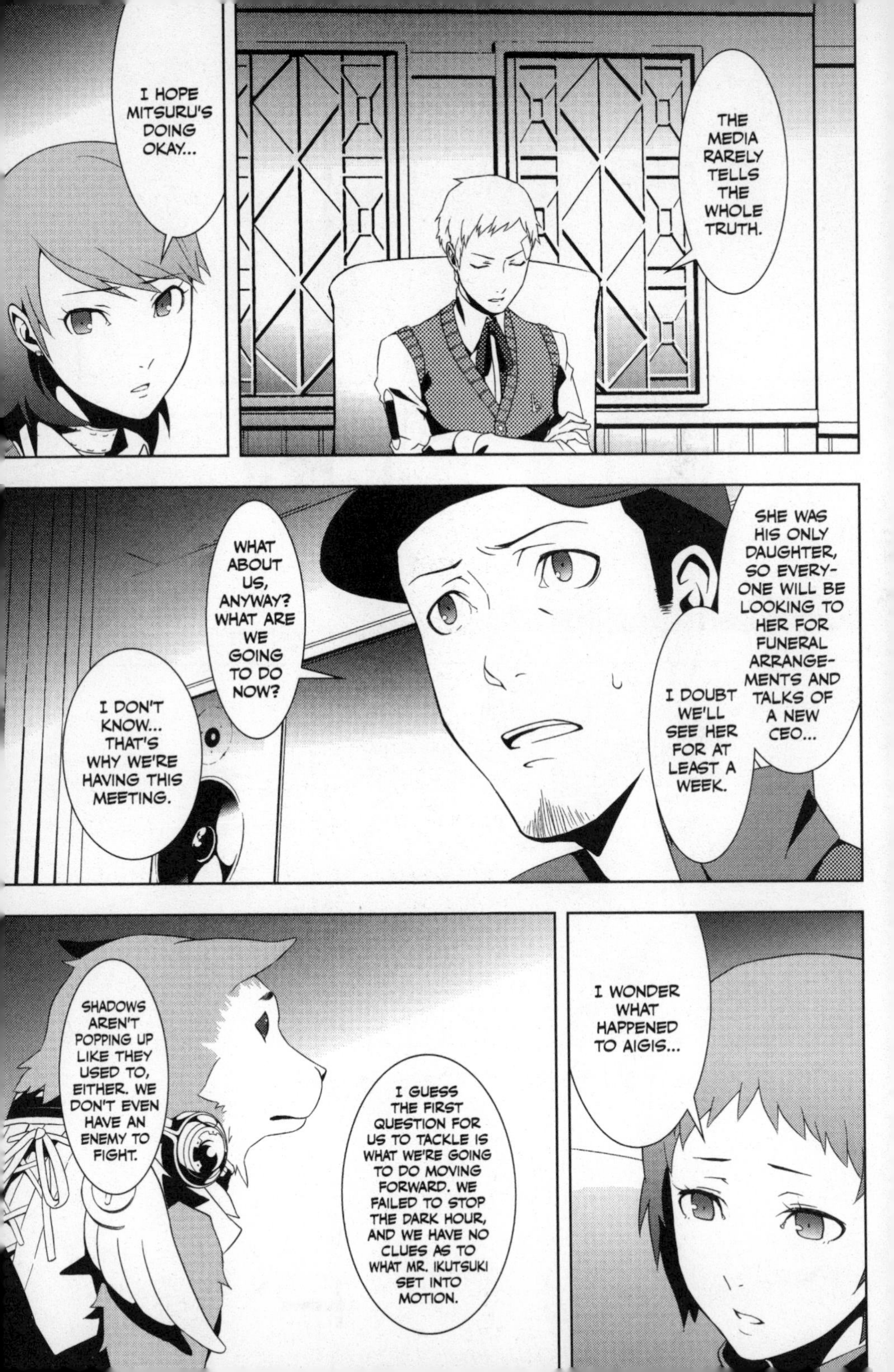
THE MEDIA RARELY TELLS THE WHOLE TRUTH.
I HOPE MITSURU'S DOING OKAY...
SHE WAS HIS ONLY DAUGHTER, SO EVERYONE WILL BE LOOKING TO HER FOR FUNERAL ARRANGEMENTS AND TALKS OF A NEW CEO...
I DOUBT WE'LL SEE HER FOR AT LEAST A WEEK.
WHAT ABOUT US, ANYWAY? WHAT ARE WE GOING TO DO NOW?
I DON'T KNOW... THAT'S WHY WE'RE HAVING THIS MEETING.
I WONDER WHAT HAPPENED TO AIGIS...
I GUESS THE FIRST QUESTION FOR US TO TACKLE IS WHAT WE'RE GOING TO DO MOVING FORWARD. WE FAILED TO STOP THE DARK HOUR, AND WE HAVE NO CLUES AS TO WHAT MR. IKUTSUKI SET INTO MOTION.
SHADOWS AREN'T POPPING UP LIKE THEY USED TO, EITHER. WE DON'T EVEN HAVE AN ENEMY TO FIGHT.

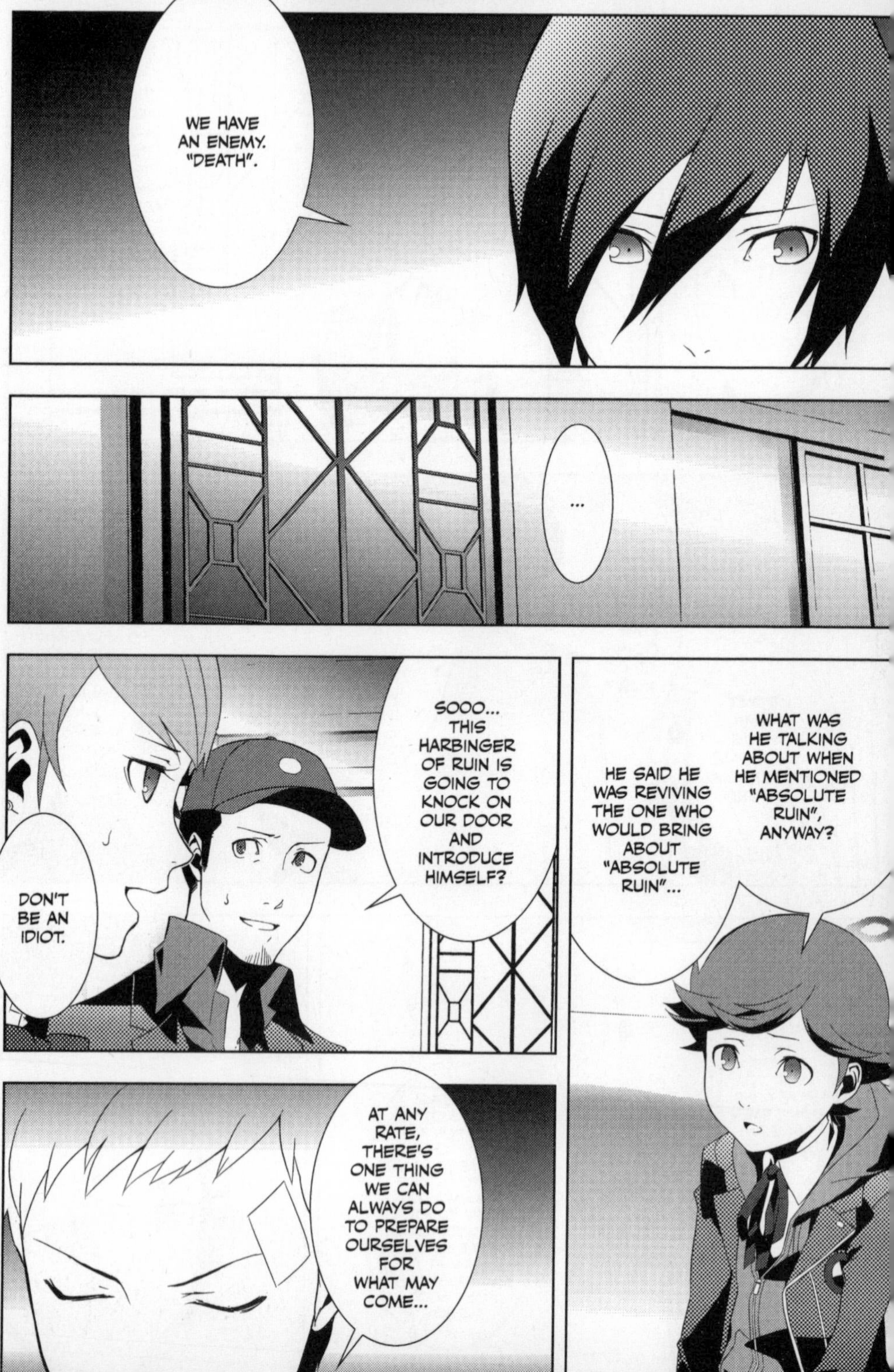

WE HAVE AN ENEMY. "DEATH".
...
WHAT WAS HE TALKING ABOUT WHEN HE MENTIONED "ABSOLUTE RUIN", ANYWAY?
HE SAID HE WAS REVIVING THE ONE WHO WOULD BRING ABOUT "ABSOLUTE RUIN"...
SOOO... THIS HARBINGER OF RUIN IS GOING TO KNOCK ON OUR DOOR AND INTRODUCE HIMSELF?
DON'T BE AN IDIOT.
AT ANY RATE, THERE'S ONE THING WE CAN ALWAYS DO TO PREPARE OURSELVES FOR WHAT MAY COME...

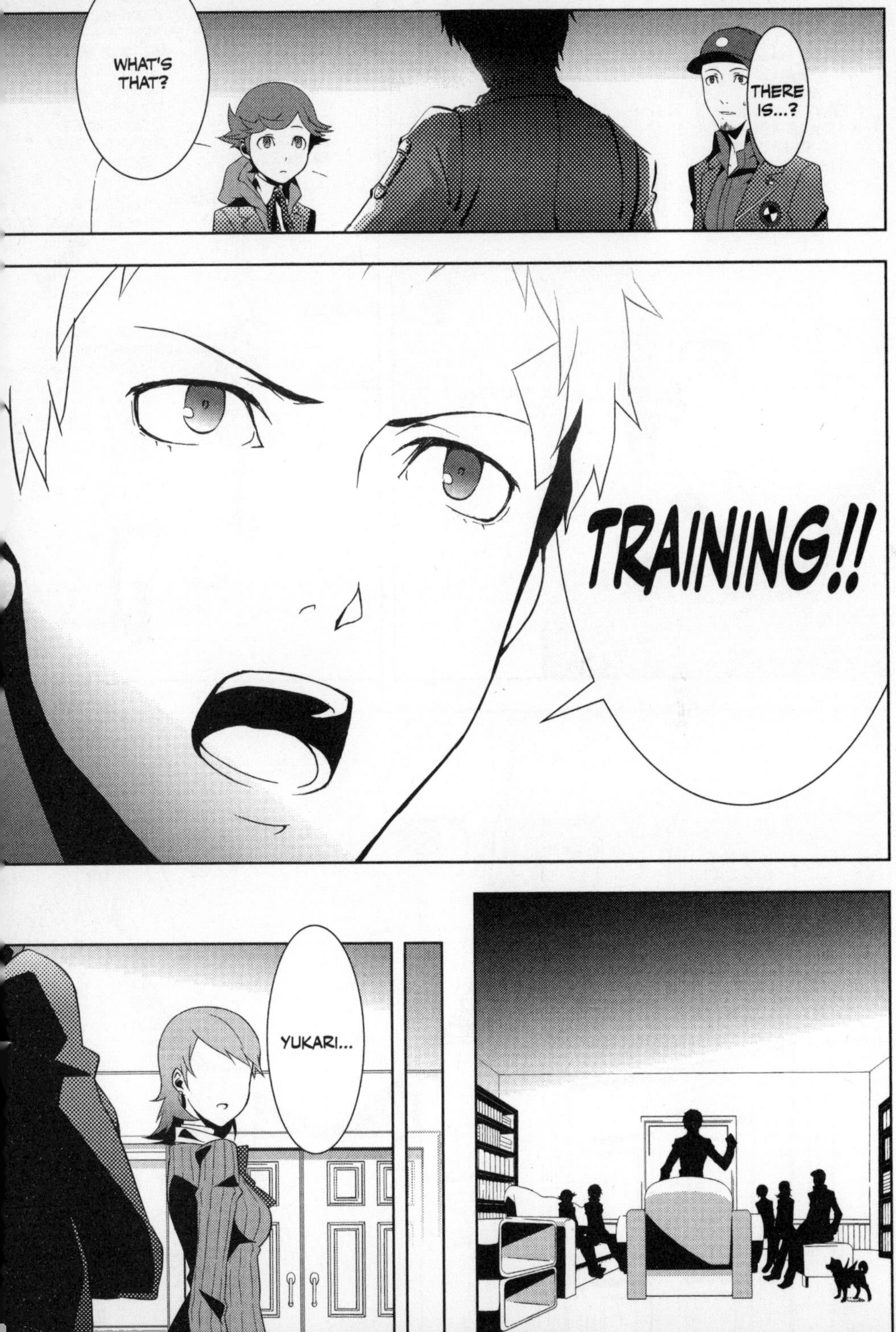
THERE IS...?
WHAT'S THAT?
TRAINING!!
YUKARI...

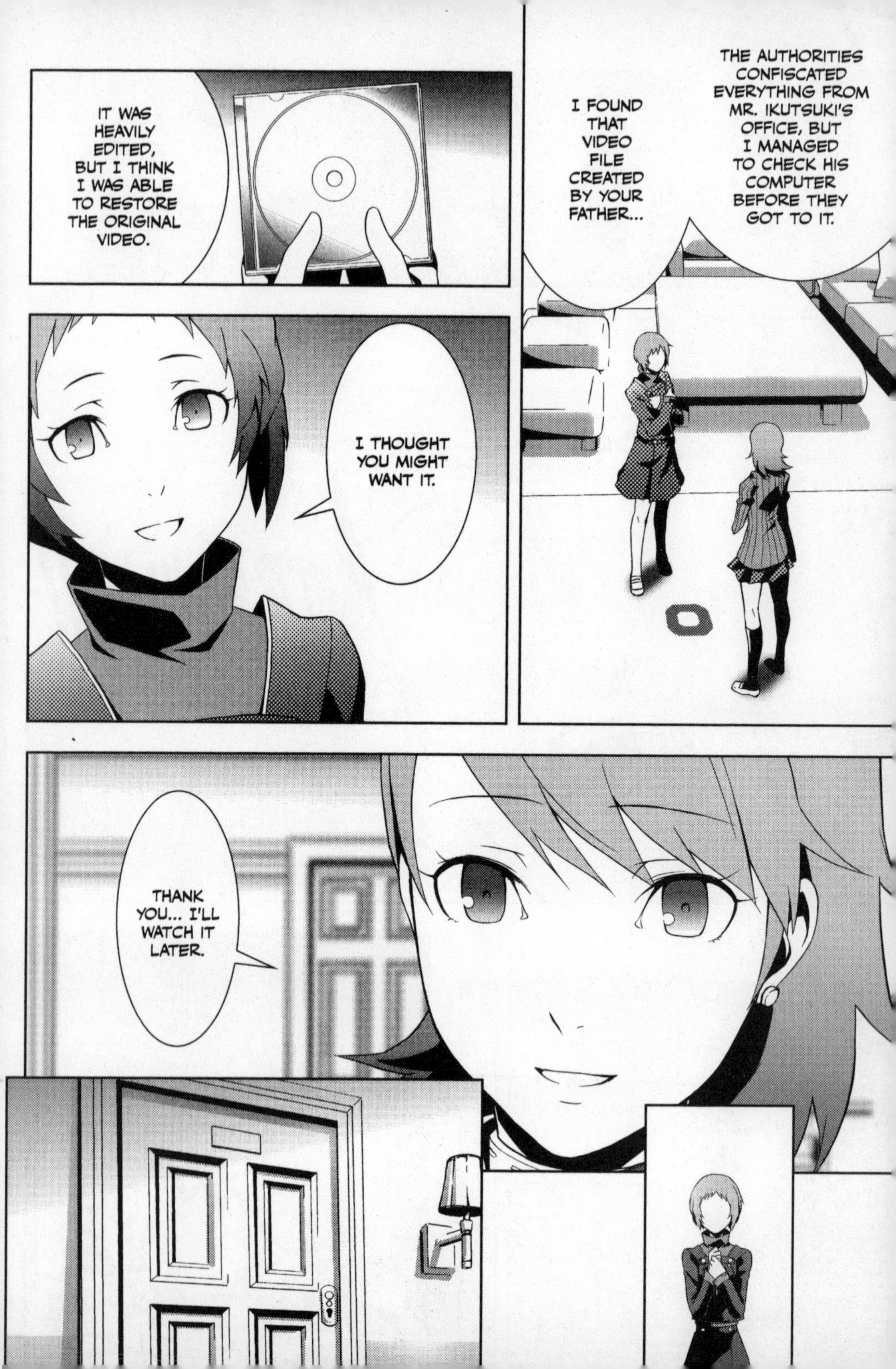
THE AUTHORITIES CONFISCATED EVERYTHING FROM MR. IKUTSUKI'S OFFICE, BUT I MANAGED TO CHECK HIS COMPUTER BEFORE THEY GOT TO IT.
I FOUND THAT VIDEO FILE CREATED BY YOUR FATHER...
IT WAS HEAVILY EDITED, BUT I THINK I WAS ABLE TO RESTORE THE ORIGINAL VIDEO.
I THOUGHT YOU MIGHT WANT IT.
THANK YOU... I'LL WATCH IT LATER.

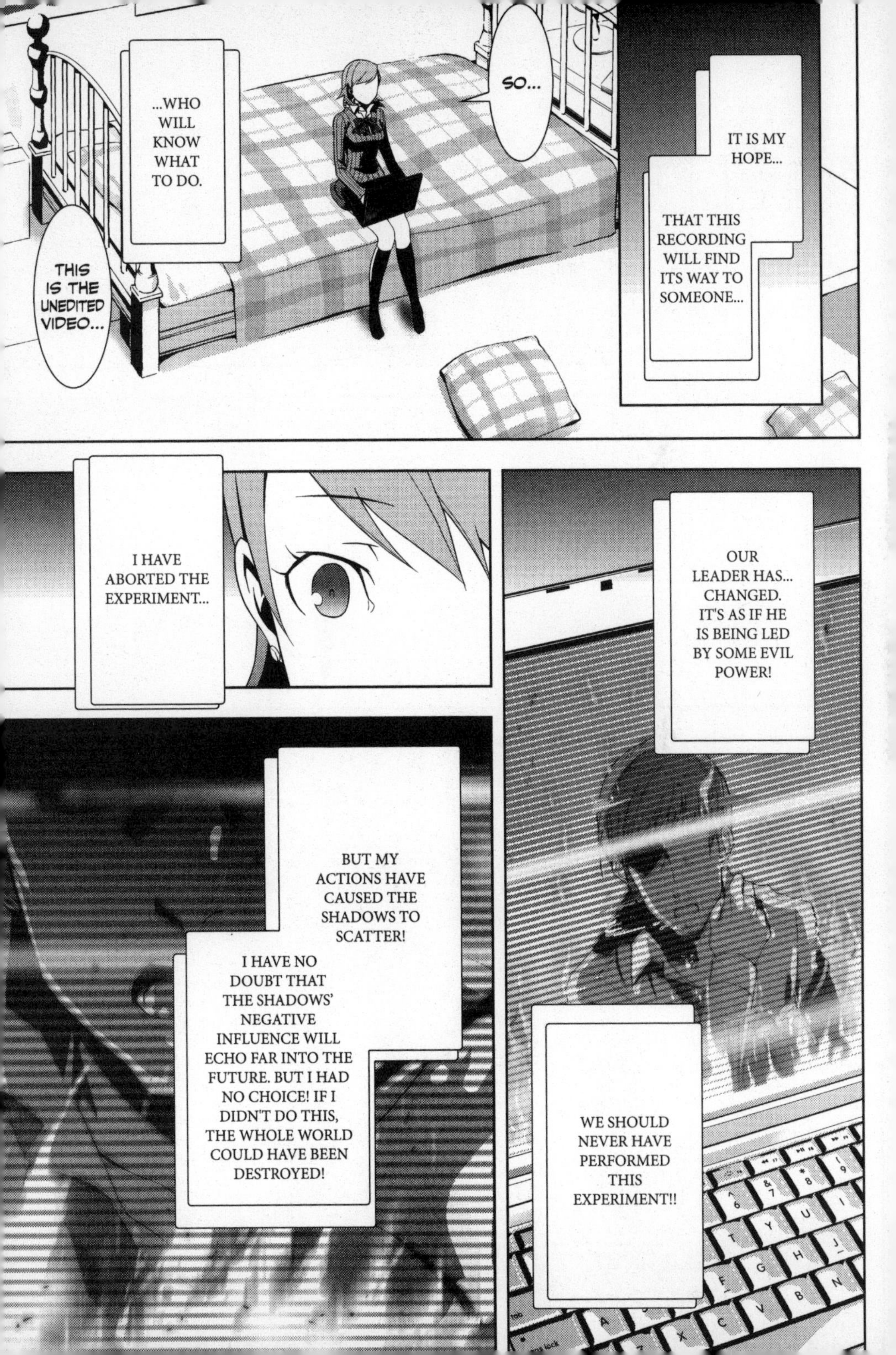
IT IS MY HOPE...
THAT THIS RECORDING WILL FIND ITS WAY TO SOMEONE...
...WHO WILL KNOW WHAT TO DO.
SO...
THIS IS THE UNEDITED VIDEO...
OUR LEADER HAS... CHANGED. IT'S AS IF HE IS BEING LED BY SOME EVIL POWER!
WE SHOULD NEVER HAVE PERFORMED THIS EXPERIMENT!!
I HAVE ABORTED THE EXPERIMENT...
BUT MY ACTIONS HAVE CAUSED THE SHADOWS TO SCATTER!
I HAVE NO DOUBT THAT THE SHADOWS' NEGATIVE INFLUENCE WILL ECHO FAR INTO THE FUTURE. BUT I HAD NO CHOICE! IF I DIDN'T DO THIS, THE WHOLE WORLD COULD HAVE BEEN DESTROYED!

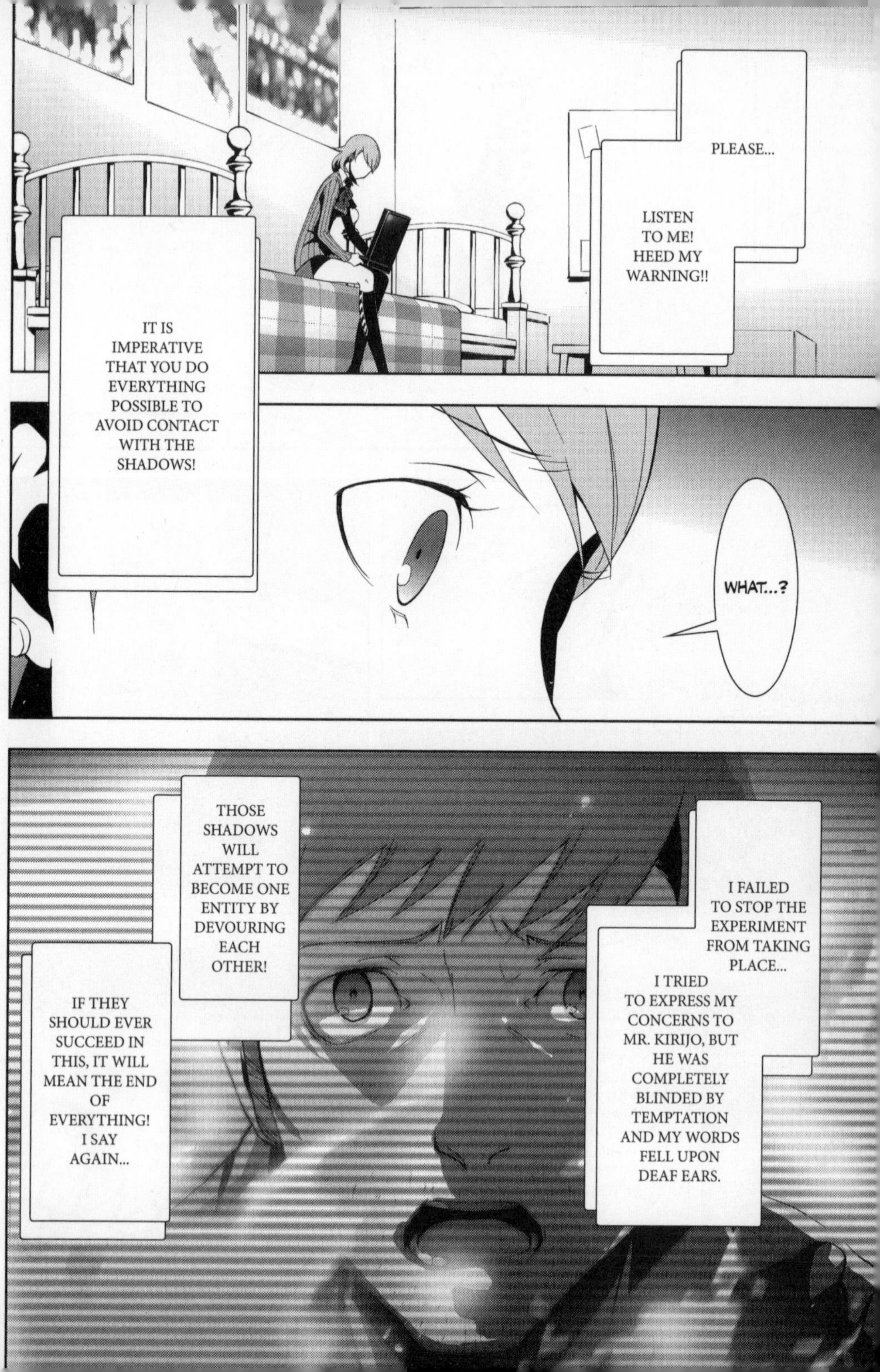
PLEASE...
LISTEN TO ME! HEED MY WARNING!!
IT IS IMPERATIVE THAT YOU DO EVERYTHING POSSIBLE TO AVOID CONTACT WITH THE SHADOWS!
WHAT...?
I FAILED TO STOP THE EXPERIMENT FROM TAKING PLACE...
I TRIED TO EXPRESS MY CONCERNS TO MR. KIRIJO, BUT HE WAS COMPLETELY BLINDED BY TEMPTATION AND MY WORDS FELL UPON DEAF EARS.
THOSE SHADOWS WILL ATTEMPT TO BECOME ONE ENTITY BY DEVOURING EACH OTHER!
IF THEY SHOULD EVER SUCCEED IN THIS, IT WILL MEAN THE END OF EVERYTHING! I SAY AGAIN...

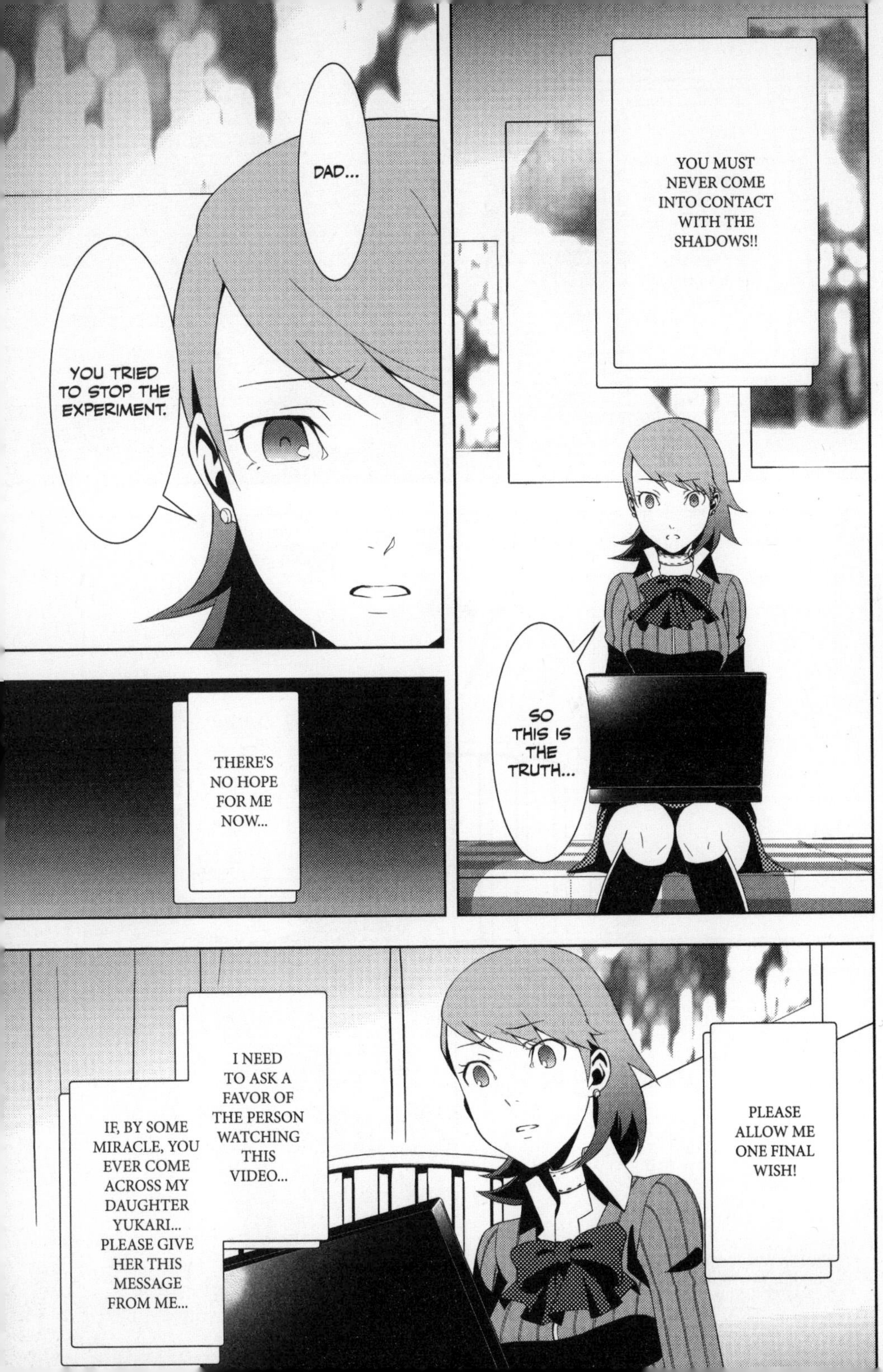
YOU MUST NEVER COME INTO CONTACT WITH THE SHADOWS!!
SO THIS IS THE TRUTH...
DAD...
YOU TRIED TO STOP THE EXPERIMENT.
THERE'S NO HOPE FOR ME NOW...
PLEASE ALLOW ME ONE FINAL WISH!
I NEED TO ASK A FAVOR OF THE PERSON WATCHING THIS VIDEO...
IF, BY SOME MIRACLE, YOU EVER COME ACROSS MY DAUGHTER YUKARI... PLEASE GIVE HER THIS MESSAGE FROM ME...

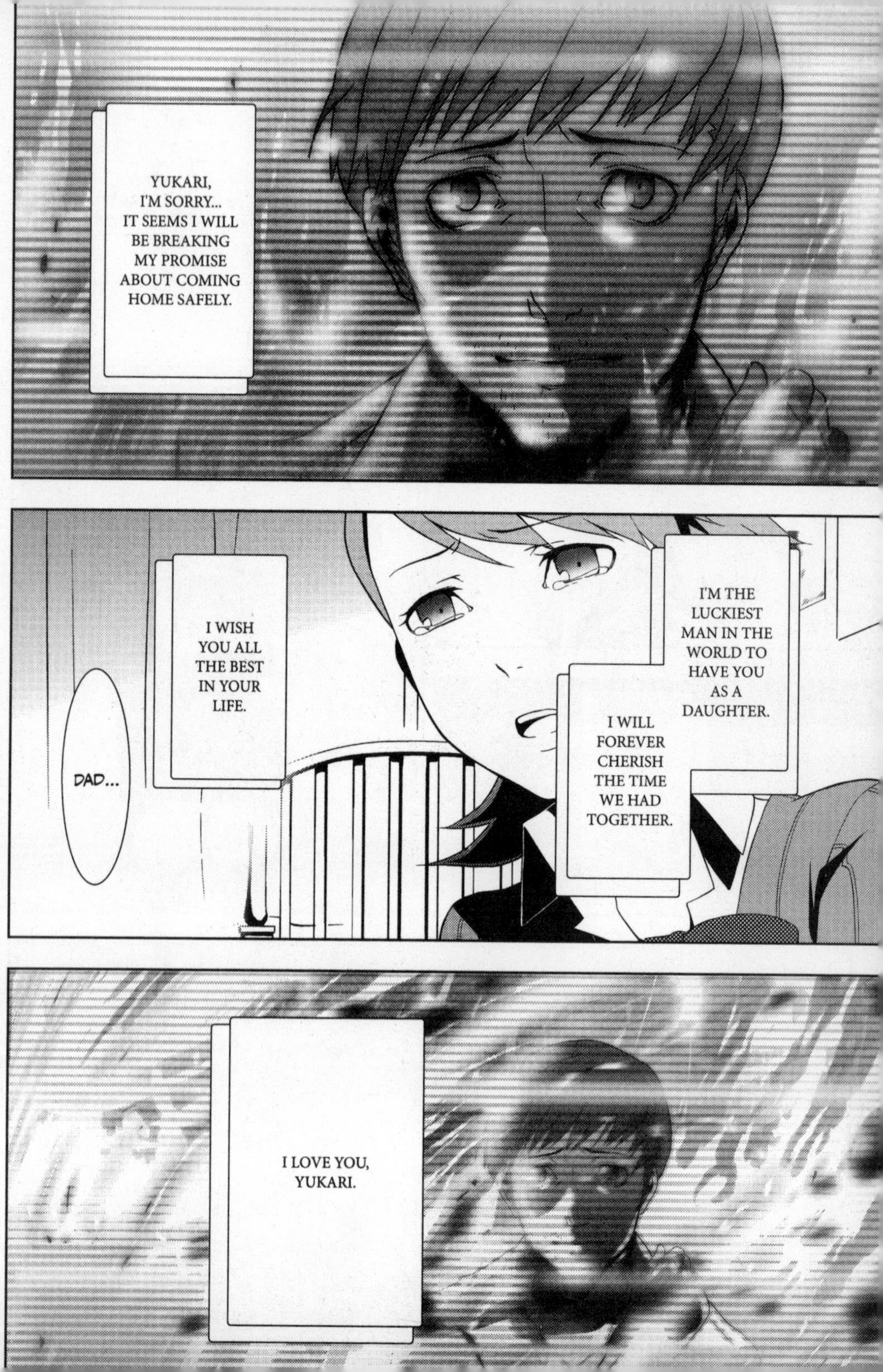
YUKARI, I'M SORRY... IT SEEMS I WILL BE BREAKING MY PROMISE ABOUT COMING HOME SAFELY.
I'M THE LUCKIEST MAN IN THE WORLD TO HAVE YOU AS A DAUGHTER.
I WILL FOREVER CHERISH THE TIME WE HAD TOGETHER.
I WISH YOU ALL THE BEST IN YOUR LIFE.
DAD...
I LOVE YOU, YUKARI.

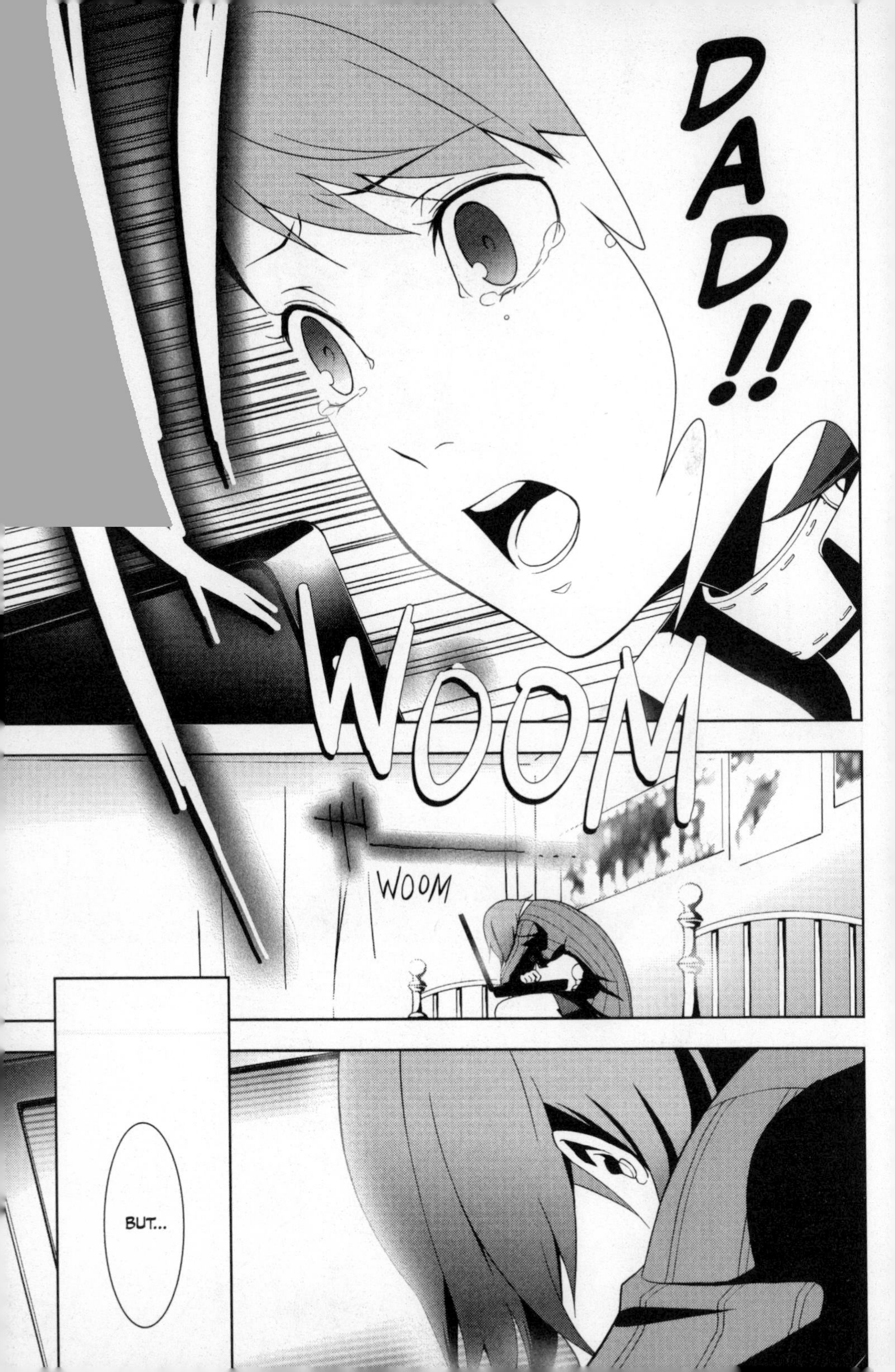
DAD!!
WOOM
WOOM
BUT...

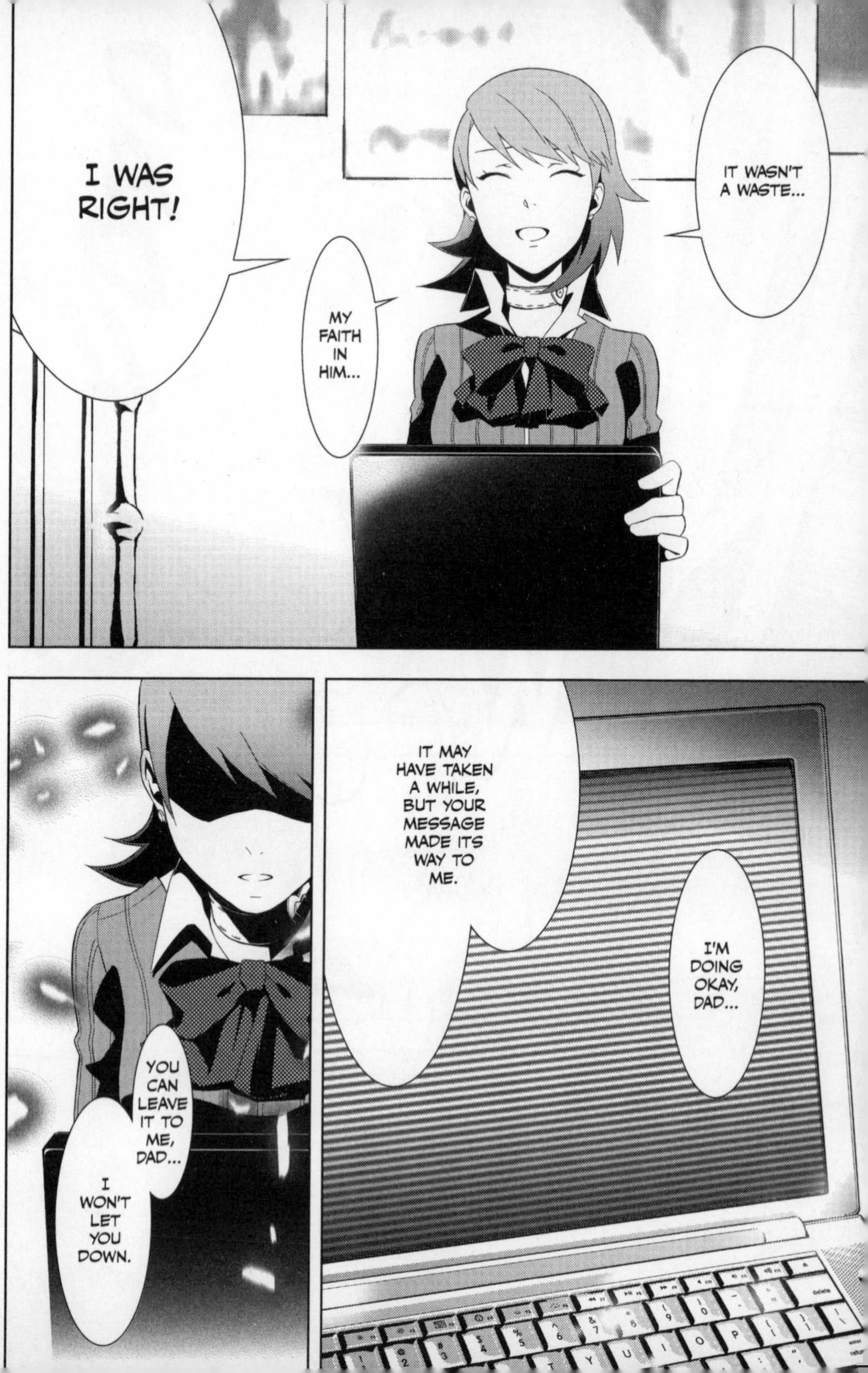
IT WASN'T A WASTE...
MY FAITH IN HIM...
I WAS RIGHT!
IT MAY HAVE TAKEN A WHILE, BUT YOUR MESSAGE MADE ITS WAY TO ME.
I'M DOING OKAY, DAD...
YOU CAN LEAVE IT TO ME, DAD...
I WON'T LET YOU DOWN.

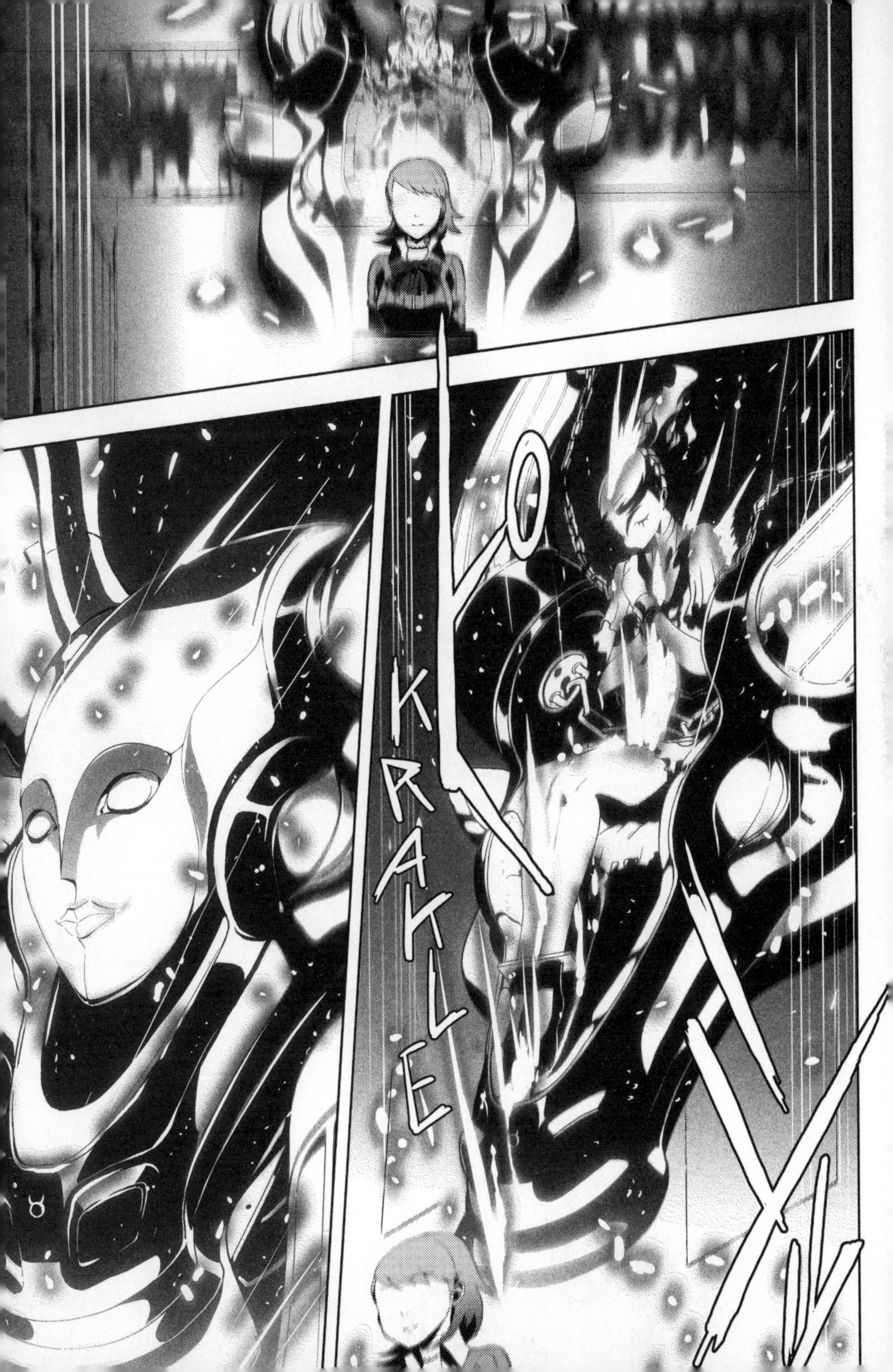
KRAKLE

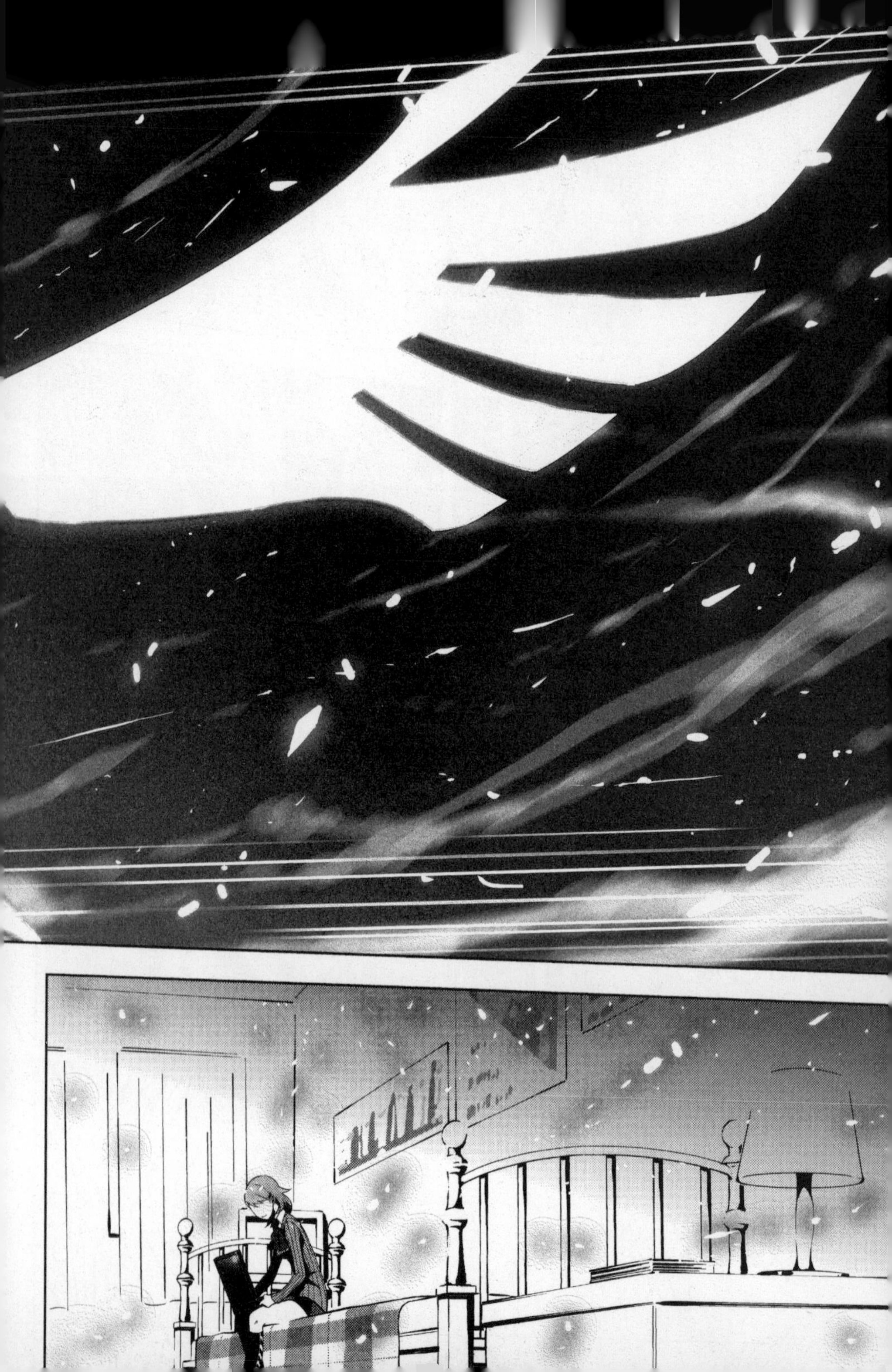

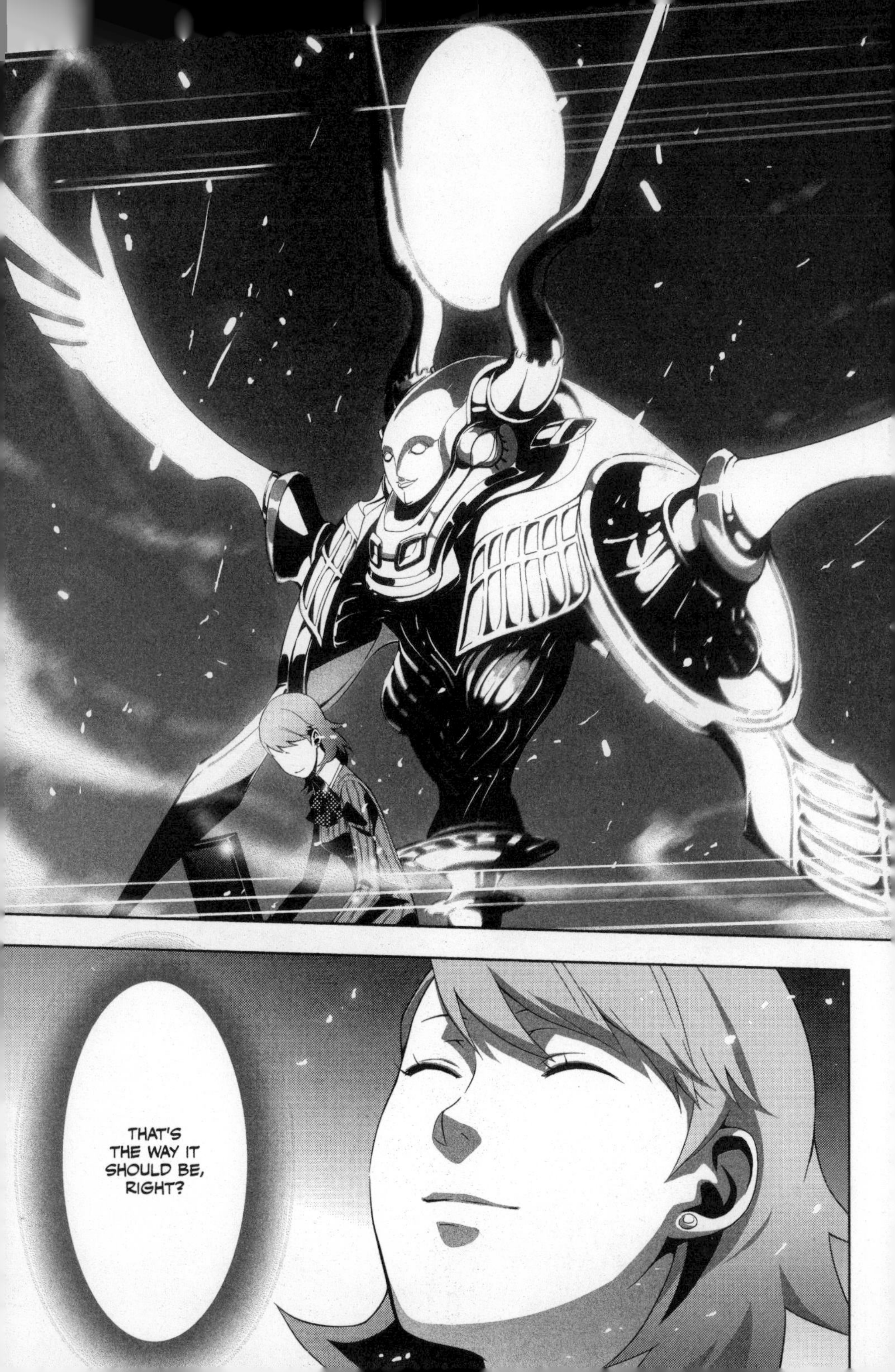
THAT'S THE WAY IT SHOULD BE, RIGHT?

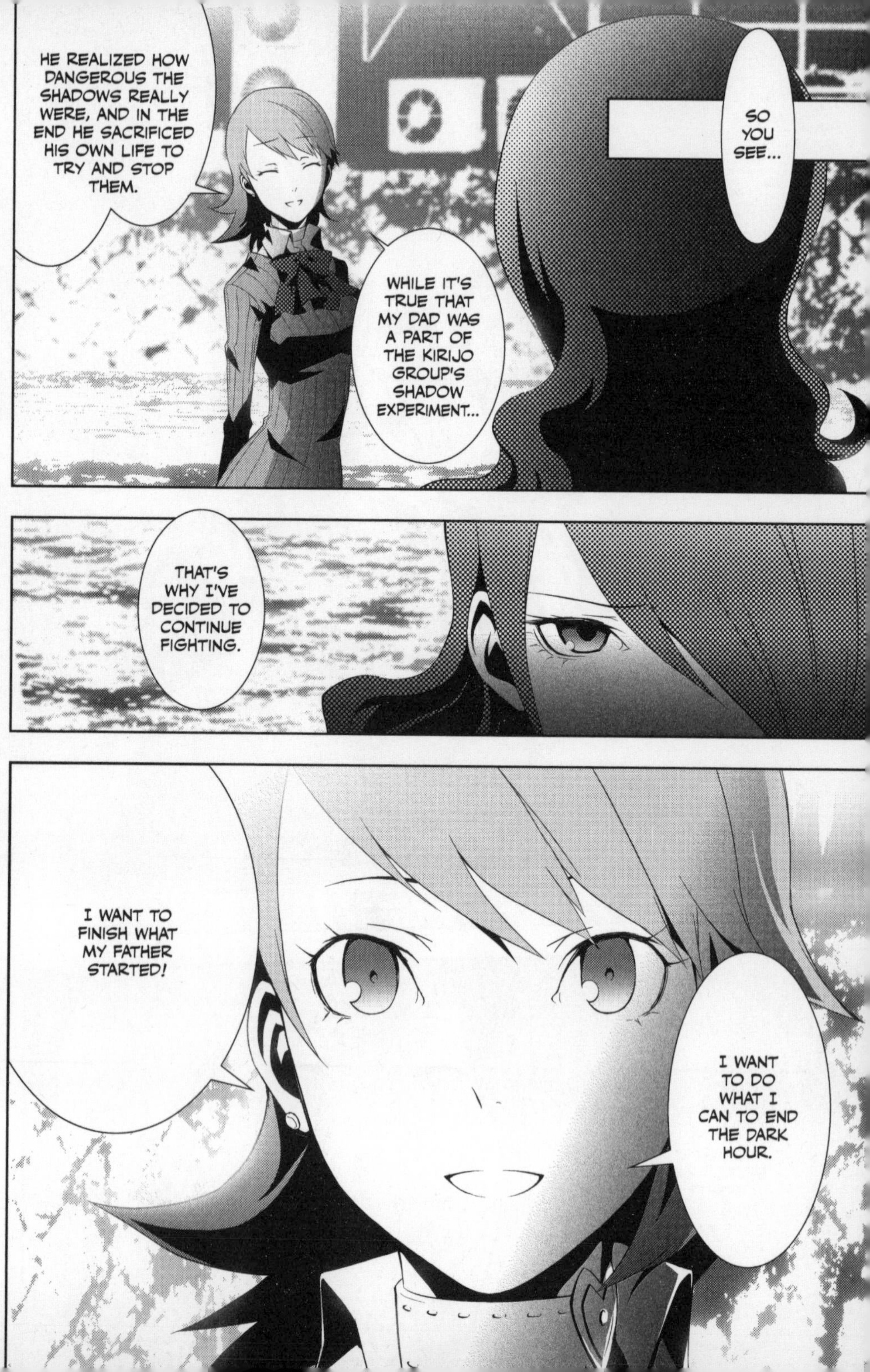
SO YOU SEE...
WHILE IT'S TRUE THAT MY DAD WAS A PART OF THE KIRIJO GROUP'S SHADOW EXPERIMENT...
HE REALIZED HOW DANGEROUS THE SHADOWS REALLY WERE, AND IN THE END HE SACRIFICED HIS OWN LIFE TO TRY AND STOP THEM.
THAT'S WHY I'VE DECIDED TO CONTINUE FIGHTING.
I WANT TO DO WHAT I CAN TO END THE DARK HOUR.
I WANT TO FINISH WHAT MY FATHER STARTED!

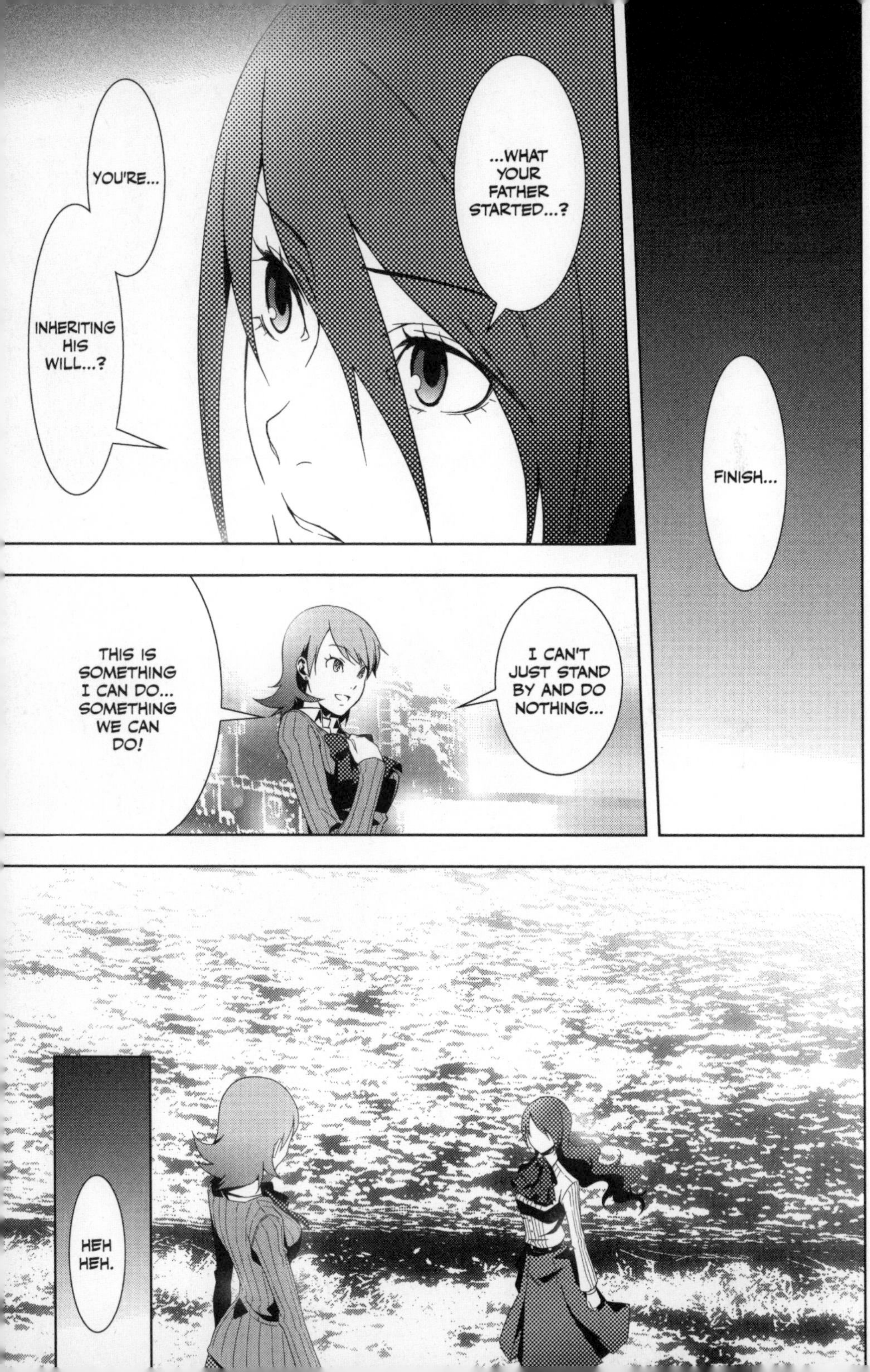
FINISH...
...WHAT YOUR FATHER STARTED...?
YOU'RE...
INHERITING HIS WILL...?
I CAN'T JUST STAND BY AND DO NOTHING...
THIS IS SOMETHING I CAN DO... SOMETHING WE CAN DO!
HEH HEH.

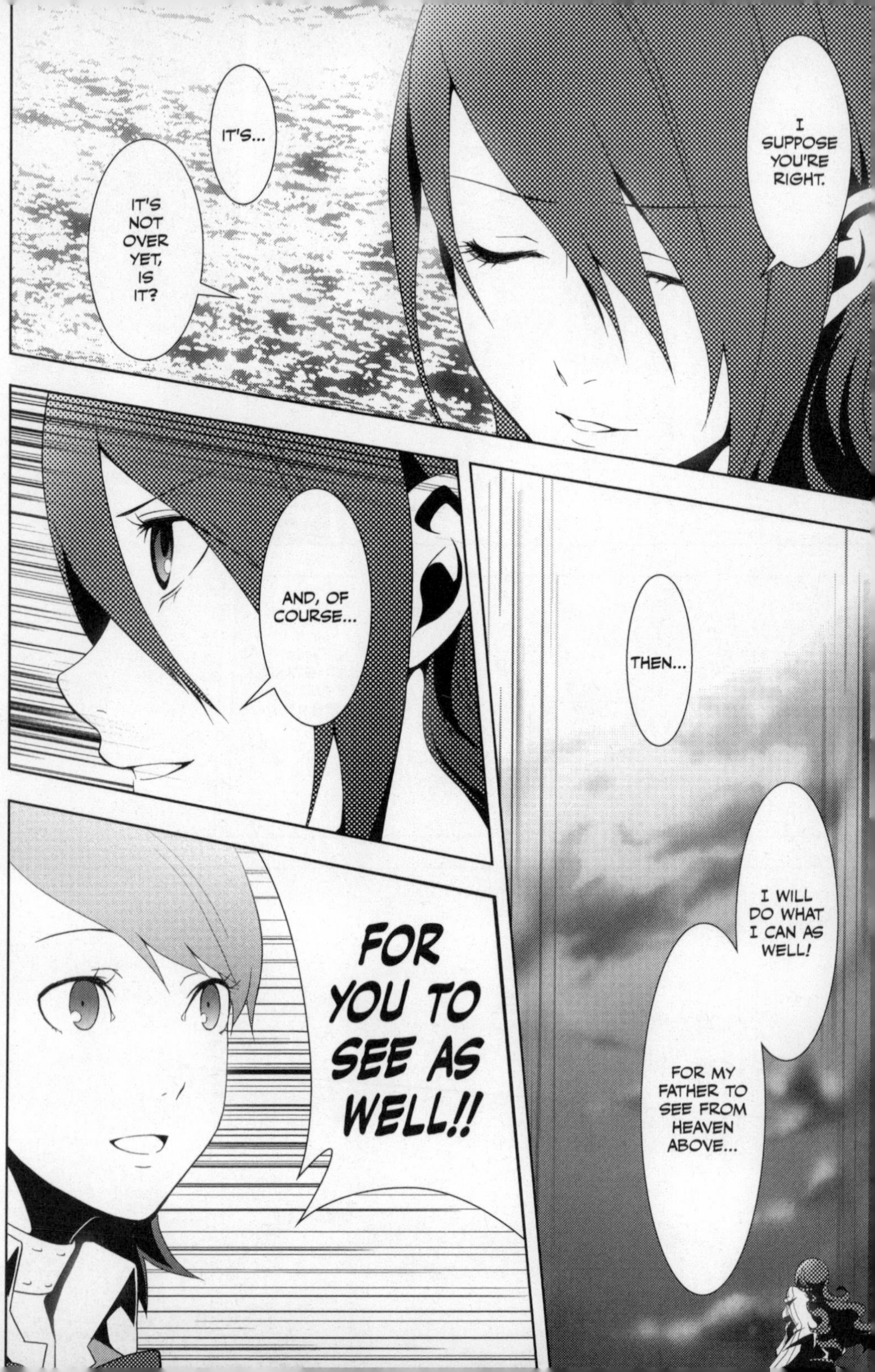
I SUPPOSE YOU'RE RIGHT.
IT'S...
IT'S NOT OVER YET, IS IT?
THEN...
I WILL DO WHAT I CAN AS WELL!
FOR MY FATHER TO SEE FROM HEAVEN ABOVE...
AND, OF COURSE...
FOR YOU TO SEE AS WELL!!

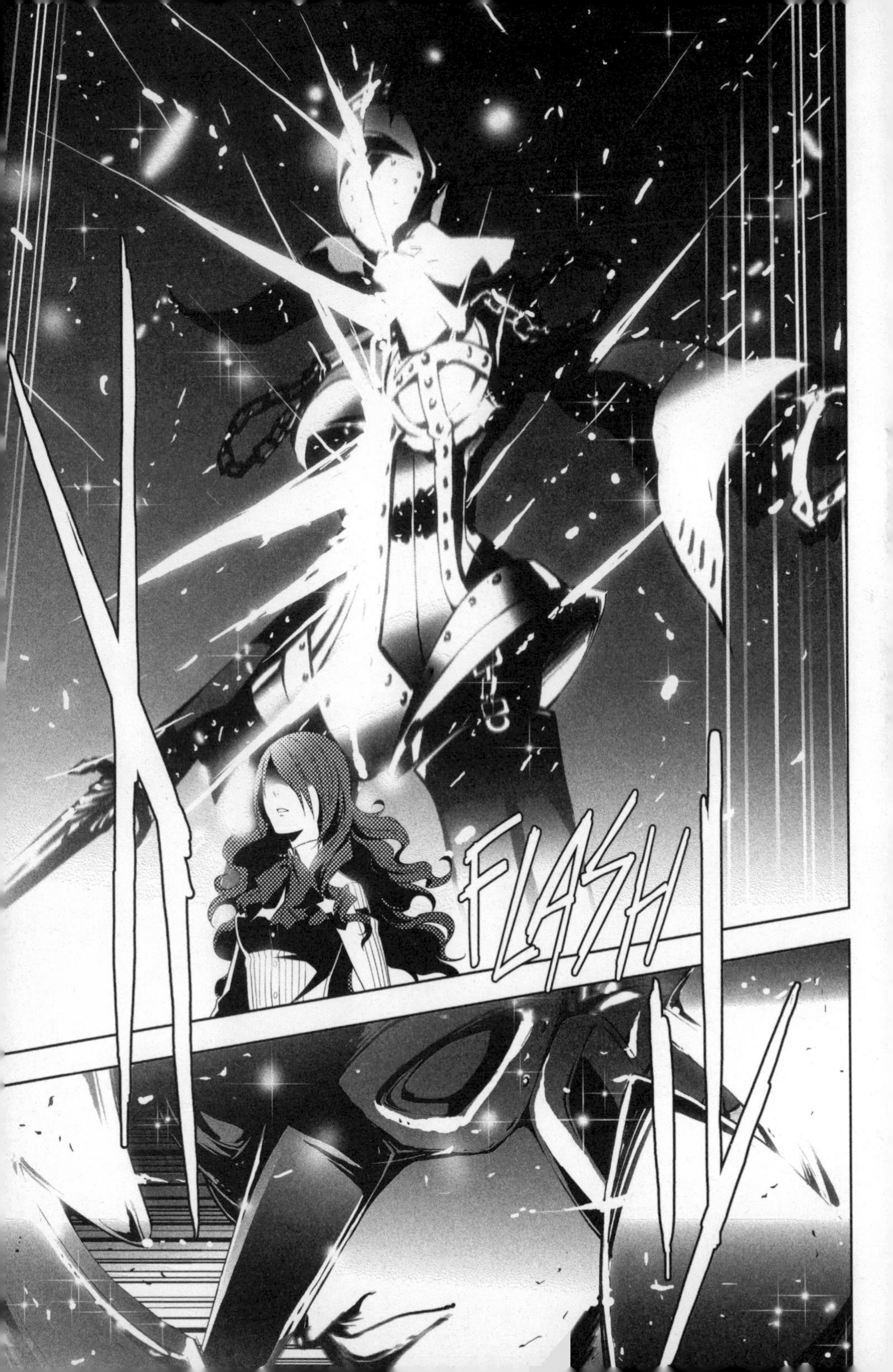
FLASH

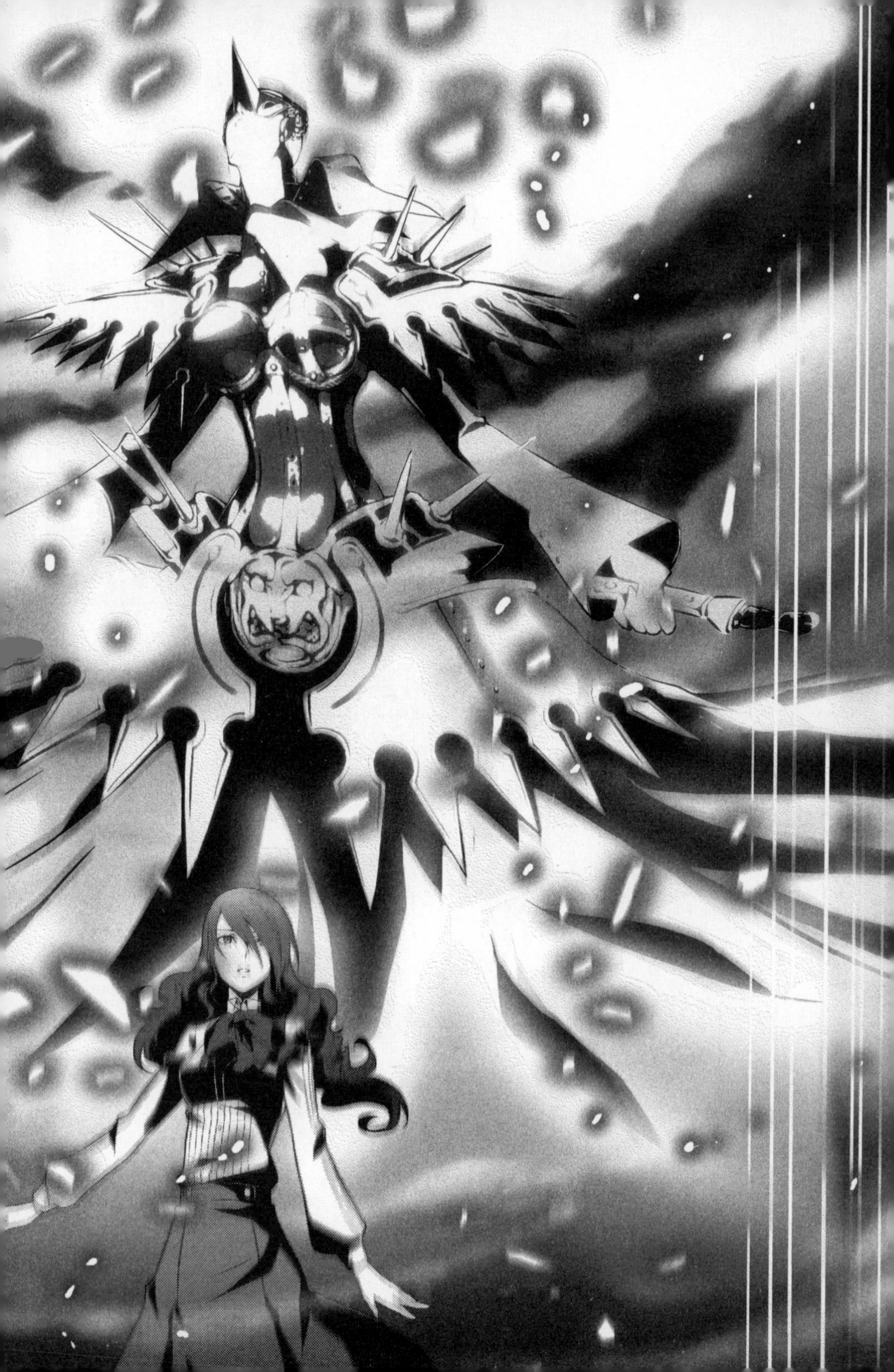

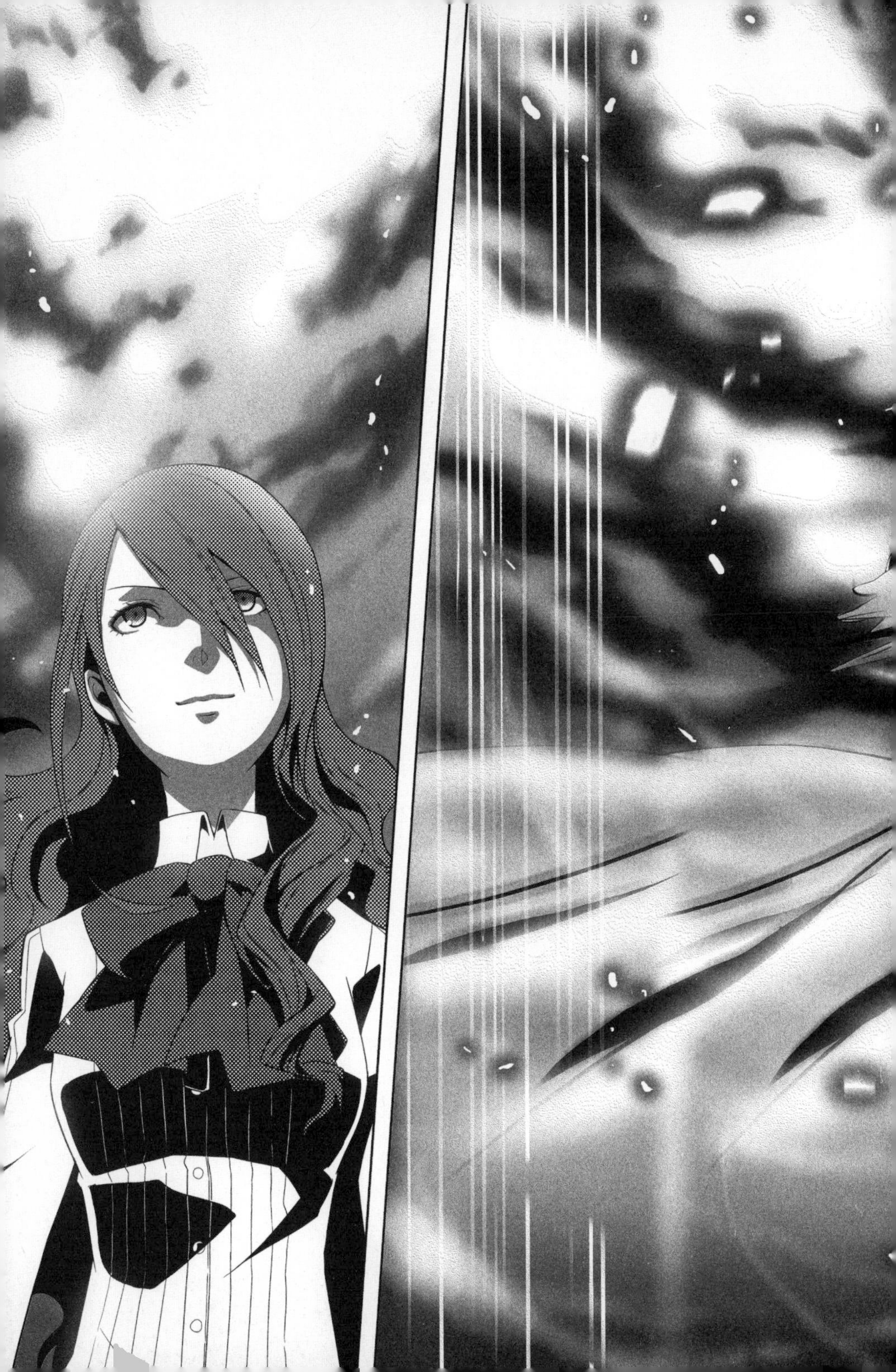

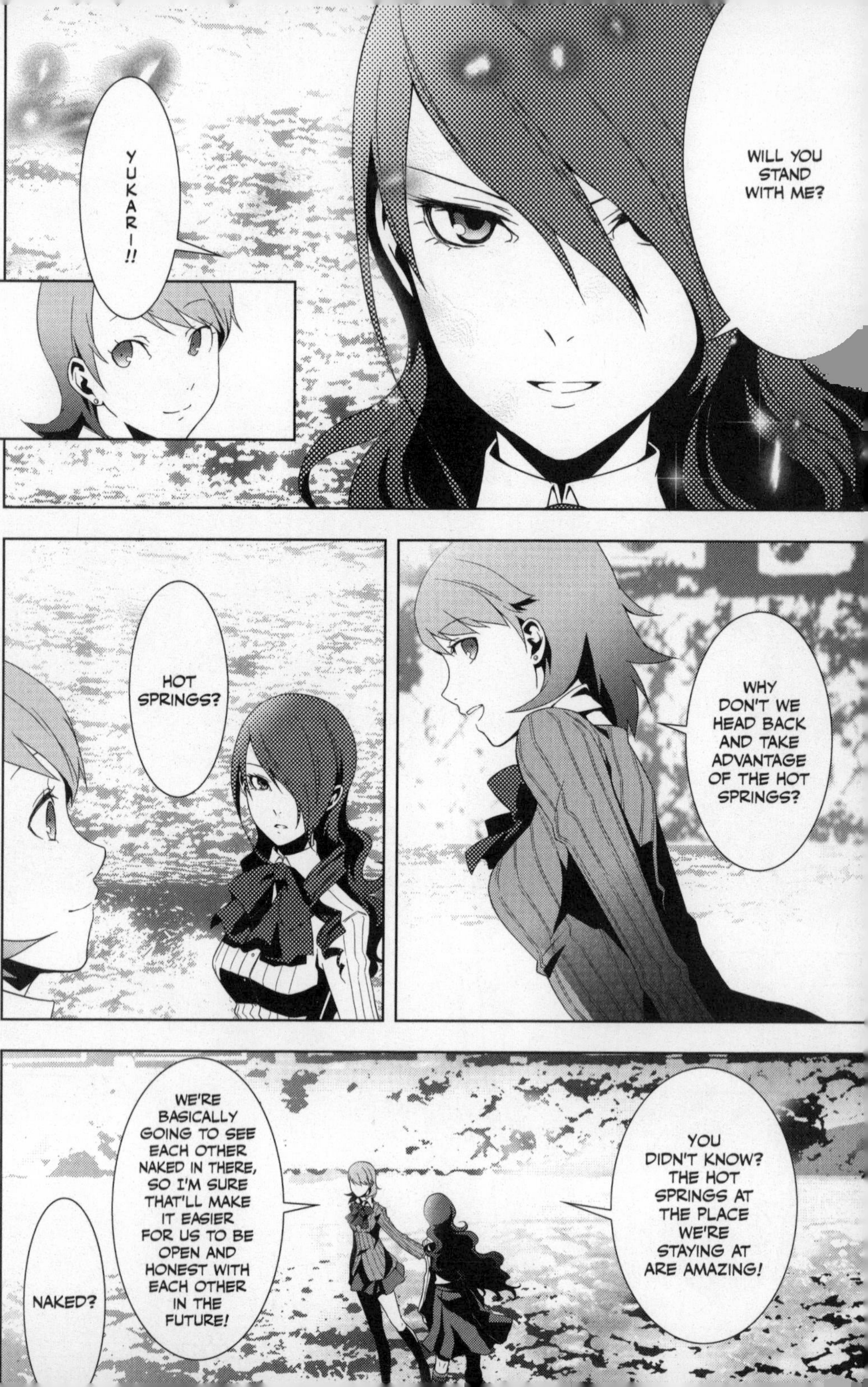
WILL YOU STAND WITH ME?
YUKARI!!
WHY DON'T WE HEAD BACK AND TAKE ADVANTAGE OF THE HOT SPRINGS?
HOT SPRINGS?
YOU DIDN'T KNOW? THE HOT SPRINGS AT THE PLACE WE'RE STAYING AT ARE AMAZING!
WE'RE BASICALLY GOING TO SEE EACH OTHER NAKED IN THERE, SO I'M SURE THAT'LL MAKE IT EASIER FOR US TO BE OPEN AND HONEST WITH EACH OTHER IN THE FUTURE!
NAKED?

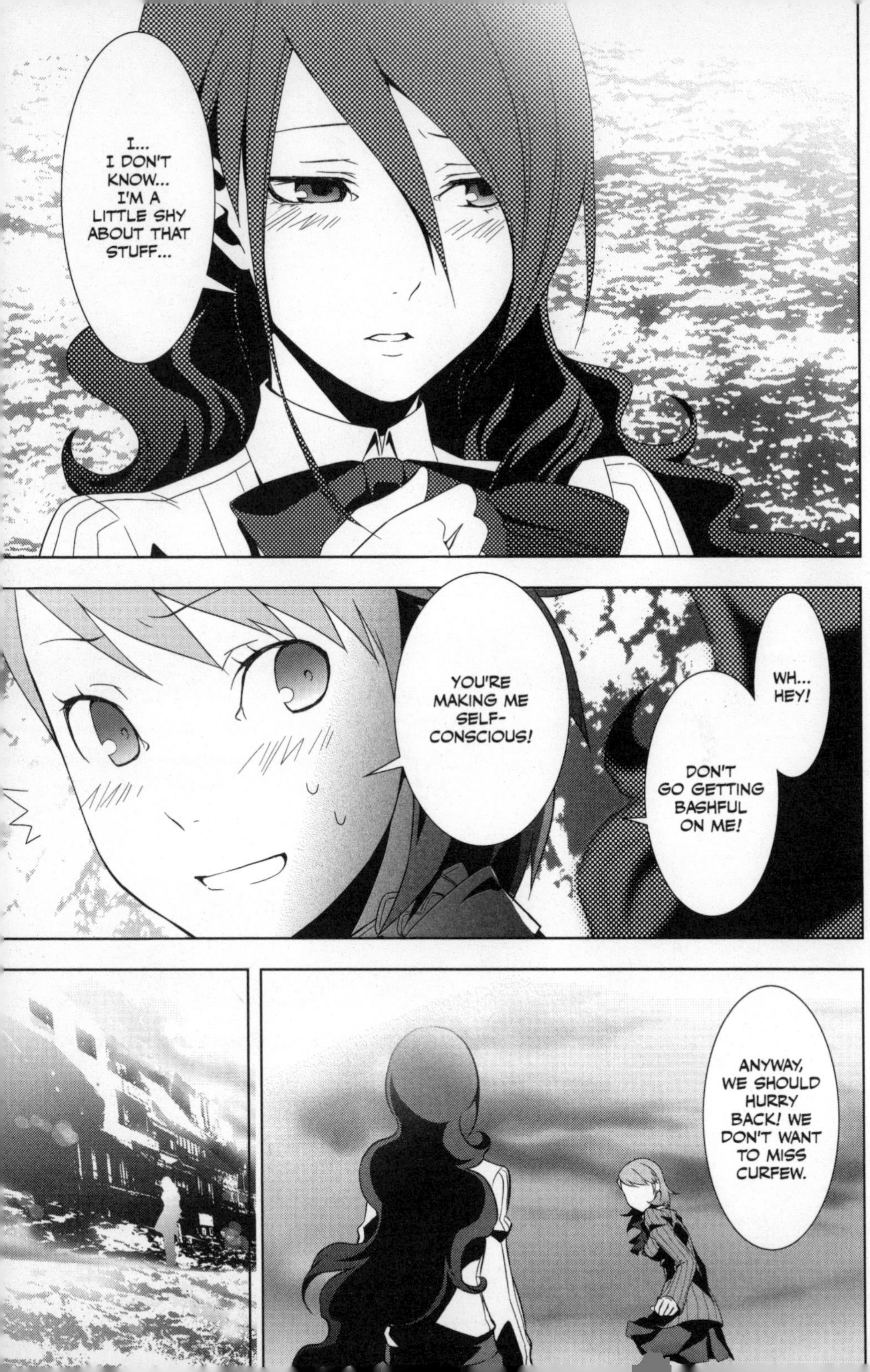
I... I DON'T KNOW... I'M A LITTLE SHY ABOUT THAT STUFF...
WH... HEY!
DON'T GO GETTING BASHFUL ON ME!
YOU'RE MAKING ME SELF-CONSCIOUS!
ANYWAY, WE SHOULD HURRY BACK! WE DON'T WANT TO MISS CURFEW.

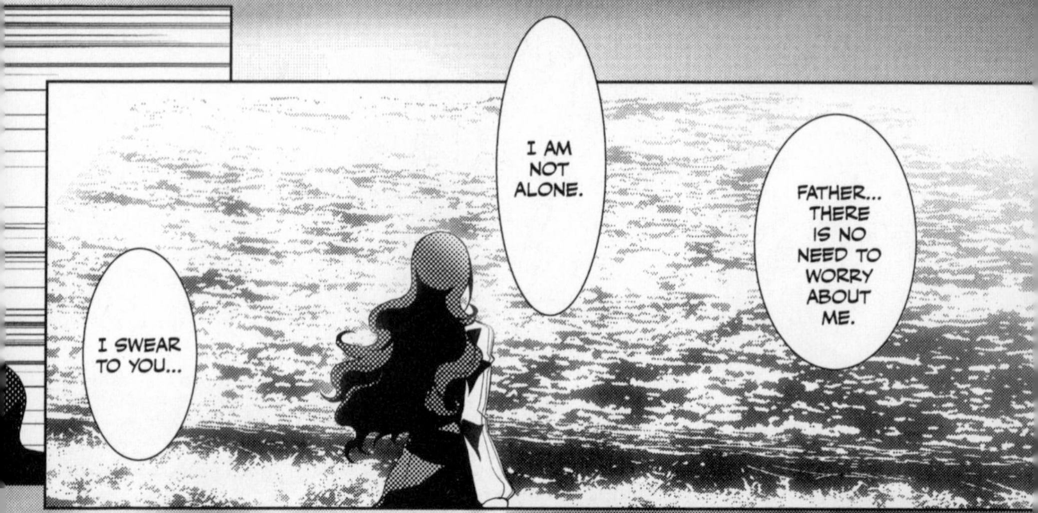
FATHER... THERE IS NO NEED TO WORRY ABOUT ME.
I AM NOT ALONE.
I SWEAR TO YOU...

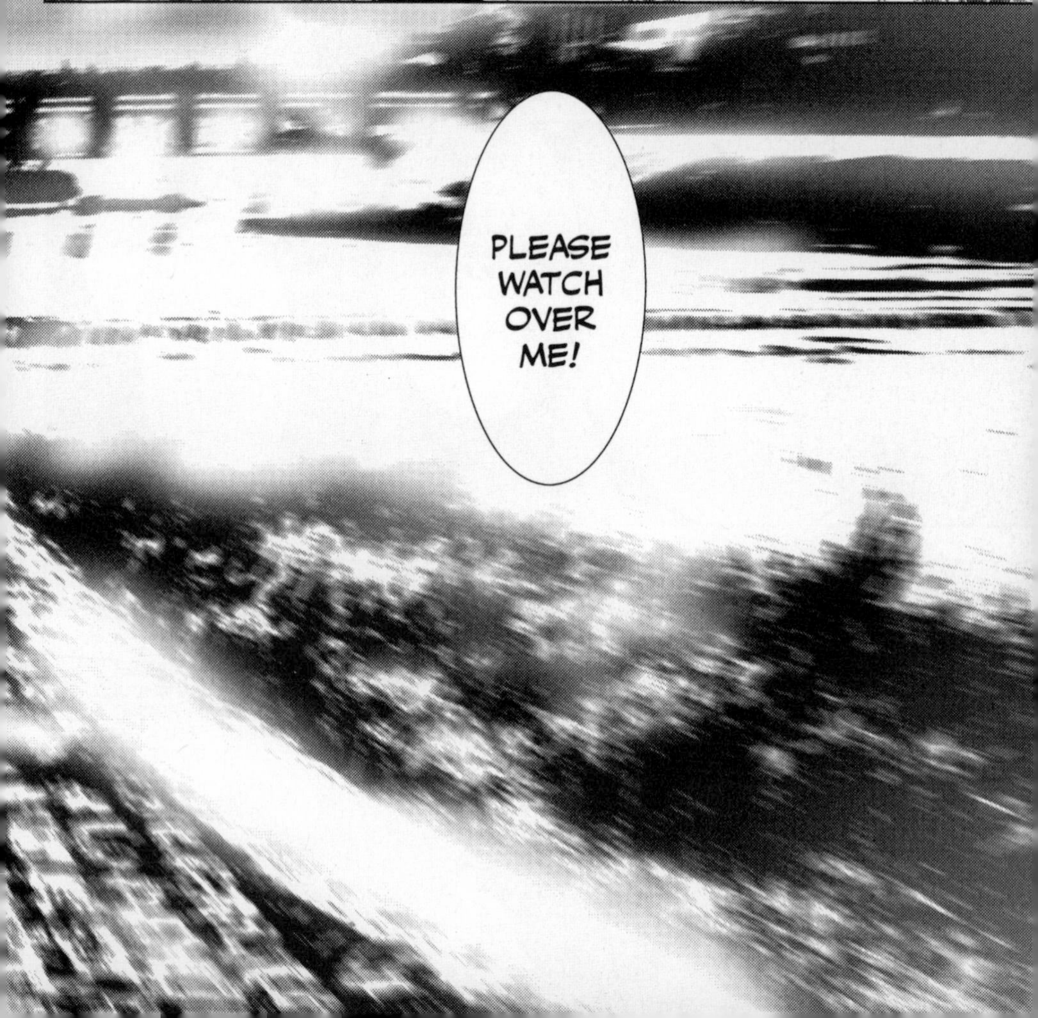
PLEASE WATCH OVER ME!

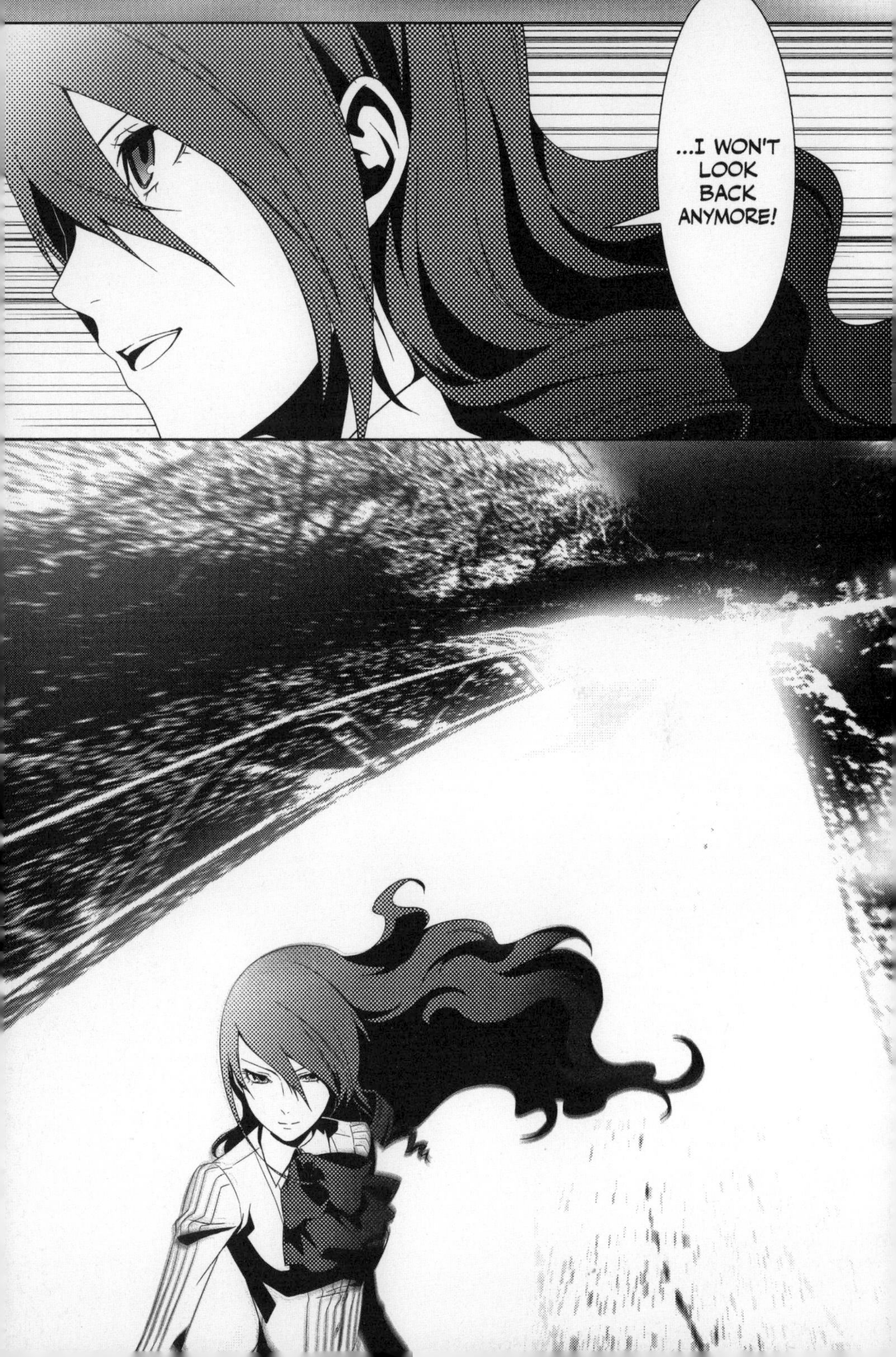
...I WON'T LOOK BACK ANYMORE!

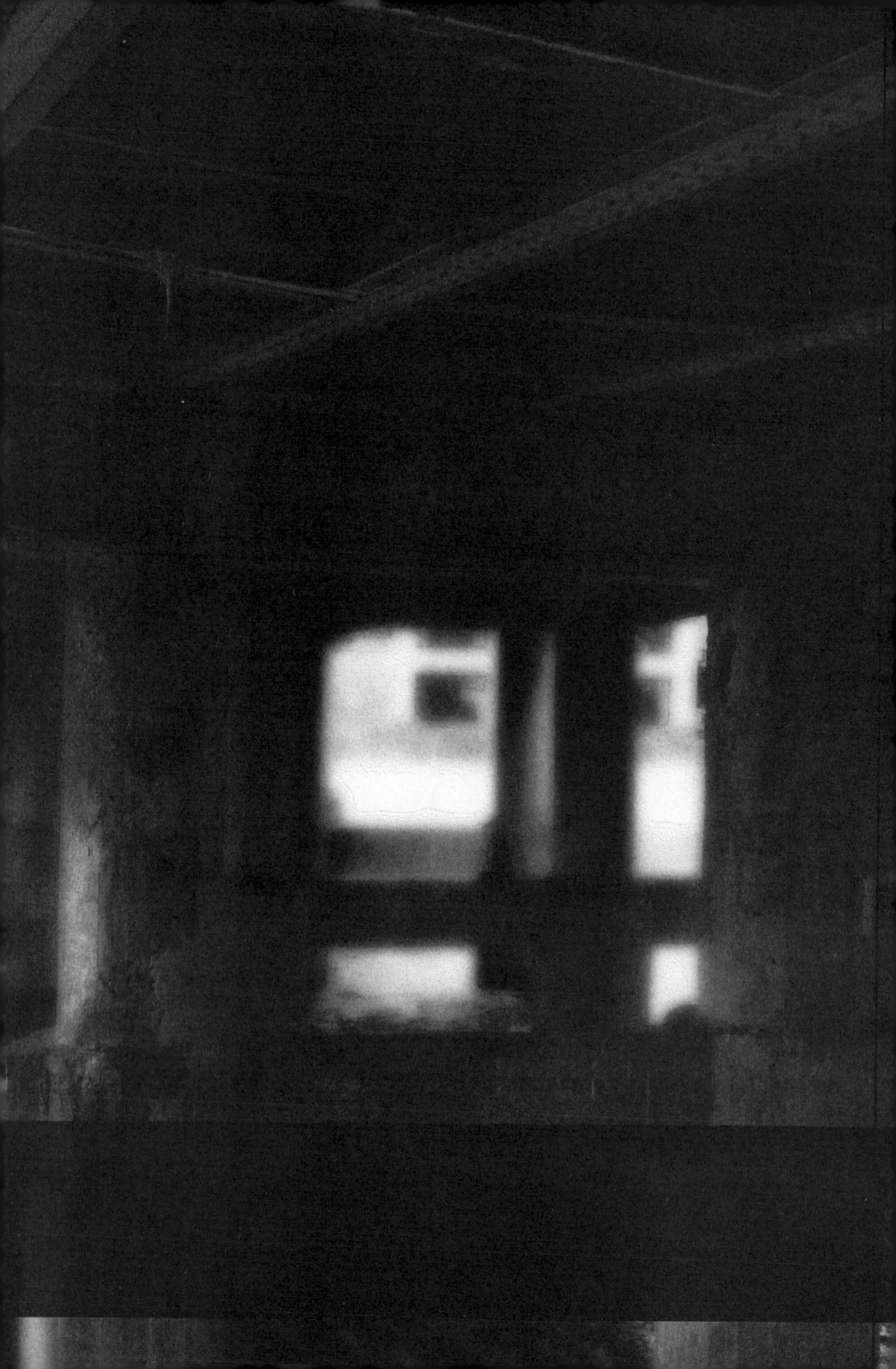

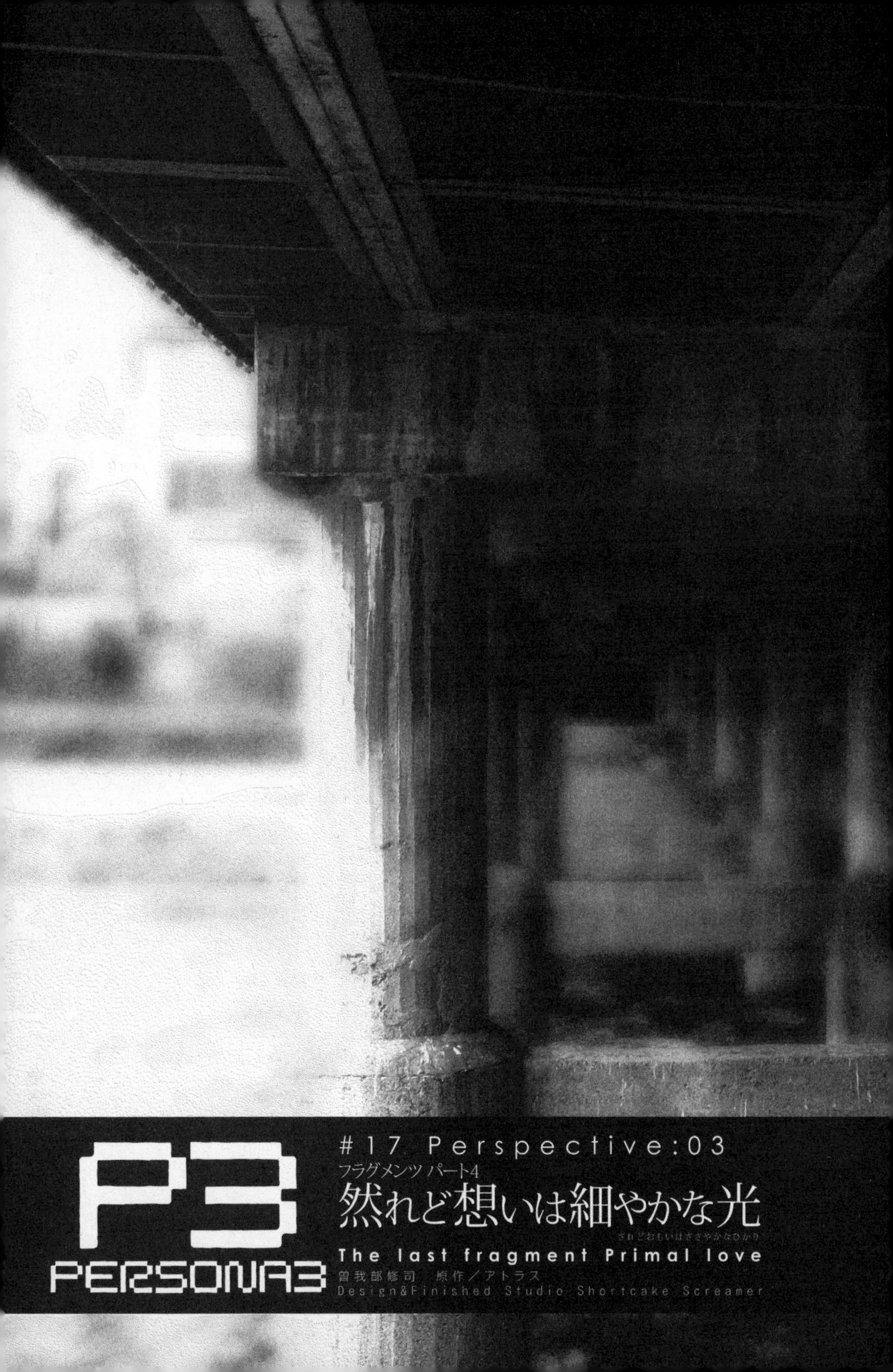

P3
PERSONA3

#17 Perspective:03

フラグメンツ パート4

然れど想いは細やかな光

されどおもいはささやかなひかり

The last fragment Primal love

曽我部修司　原作／アトラス
Design&Finished Studio Shortcake Screamer

SPECIAL FEATURE 2
S.E.E.S. ACTIVITY REPORT

I changed up the format for the cover a bit this time. Since this is a "P3" manga, I decided I wanted to set things up in groups of three whenever possible. One example of what I mean is to have the volumes share a cover format in sets of three.

The previous cover style had a lot of stuff going on and filled the entire surface of the cover, to the point where the characters almost had a hard time standing out. For this set of three covers, I wanted to go with a much simpler approach... but as you might expect, I started feeling uncertain about it, like I was skimping on the cover content too much. So I ended up adding little bits here and there anyway. I'm so weak.

The concept for the covers of volumes 1, 2, and 3 was "Hop step jump", featuring transitions in the backgrounds. I think you'll see the transitions if you compare the three volumes side by side. I'll be making the next three covers (volumes 4, 5, and 6) distinct yet similar as well, so I hope you look forward to checking those out.

Despite my zeal over the covers, a part of me does wonder if any of my readers are geeky enough to be examining the covers so closely... so a great big thank you to those who do take the time to notice my cover art.

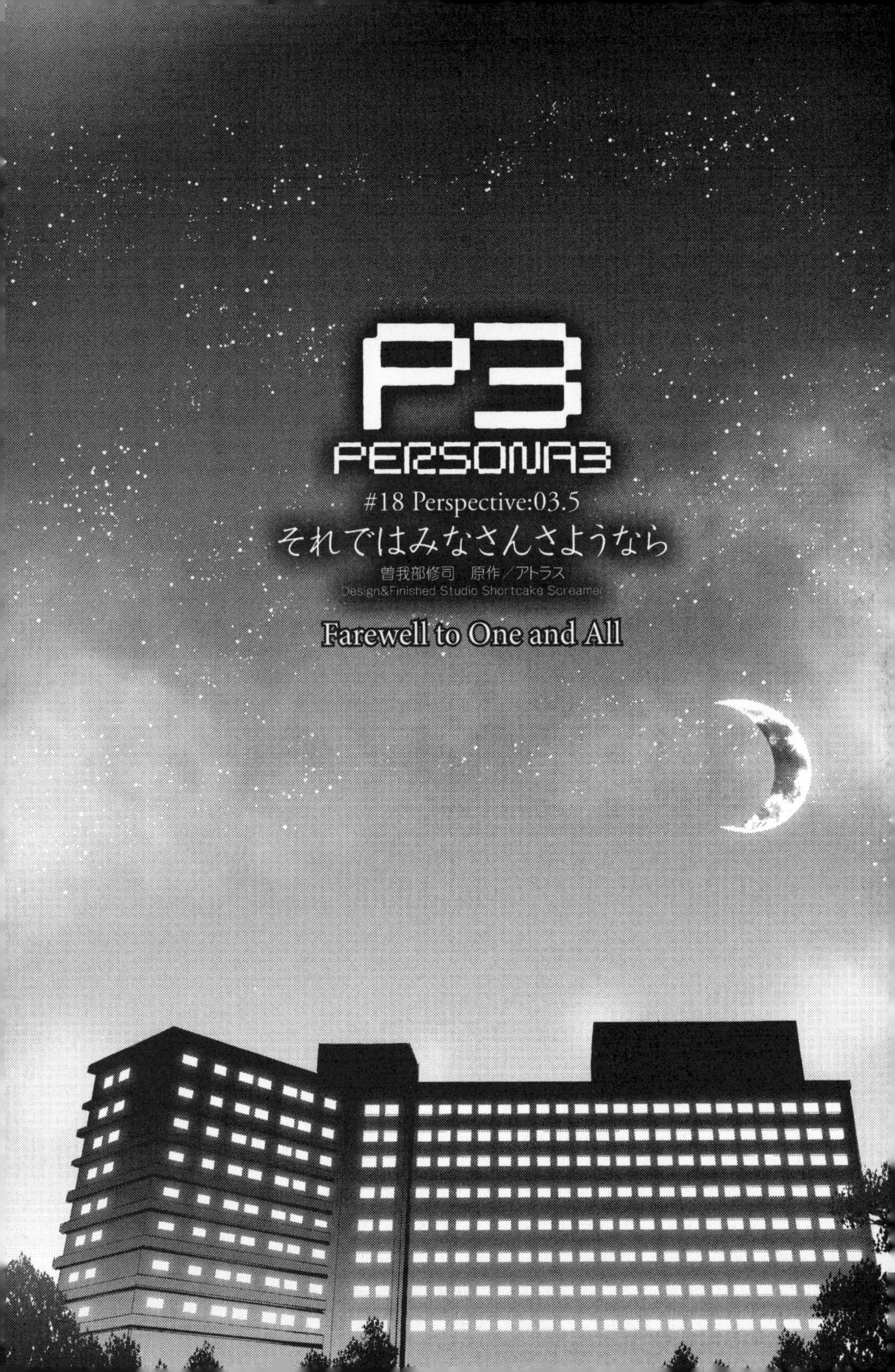
P3
PERSONA3
#18 Perspective:03.5
それではみなさんさようなら
曽我部修司　原作／アトラス
Design&Finished Studio Shortcake Screamer
Farewell to One and All

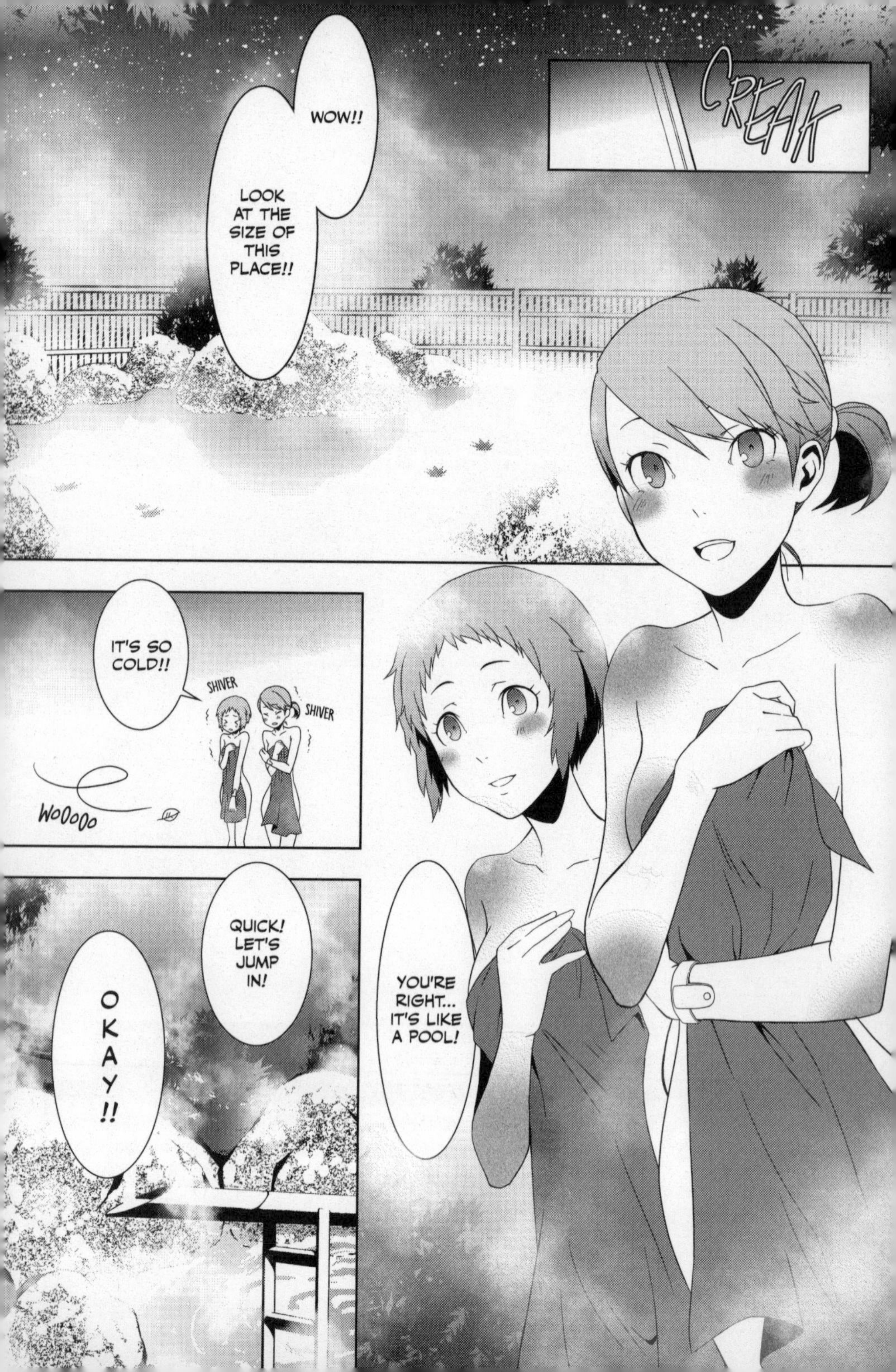
CREAK
WOW!!
LOOK AT THE SIZE OF THIS PLACE!!
YOU'RE RIGHT... IT'S LIKE A POOL!
IT'S SO COLD!!
SHIVER
SHIVER
WOOOOO
QUICK! LET'S JUMP IN!
OKAY!!

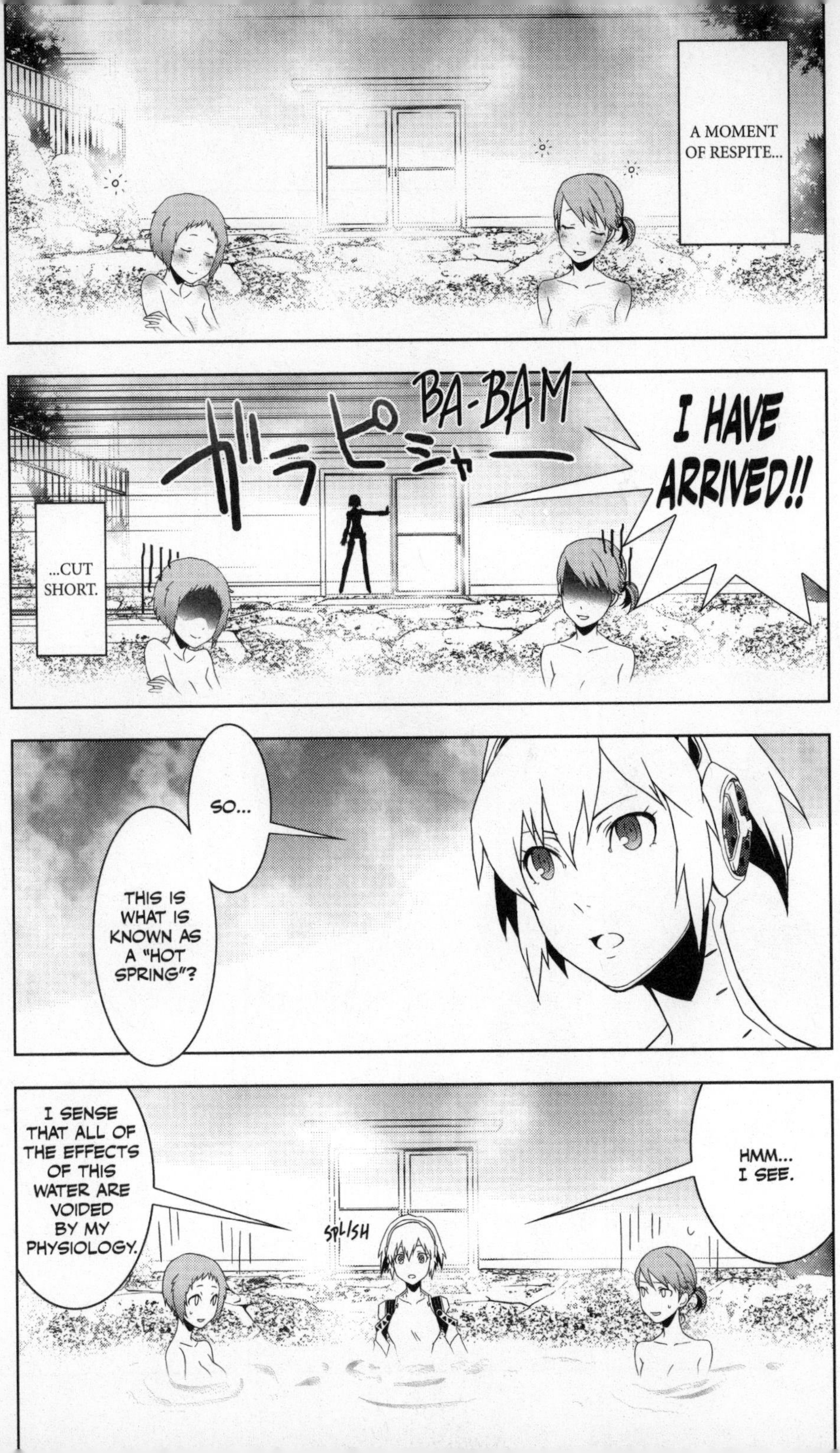
A MOMENT OF RESPITE...
BA-BAM
ガラピシャー
I HAVE ARRIVED!!
...CUT SHORT.
SO...
THIS IS WHAT IS KNOWN AS A "HOT SPRING"?
HMM... I SEE.
SPLISH
I SENSE THAT ALL OF THE EFFECTS OF THIS WATER ARE VOIDED BY MY PHYSIOLOGY.

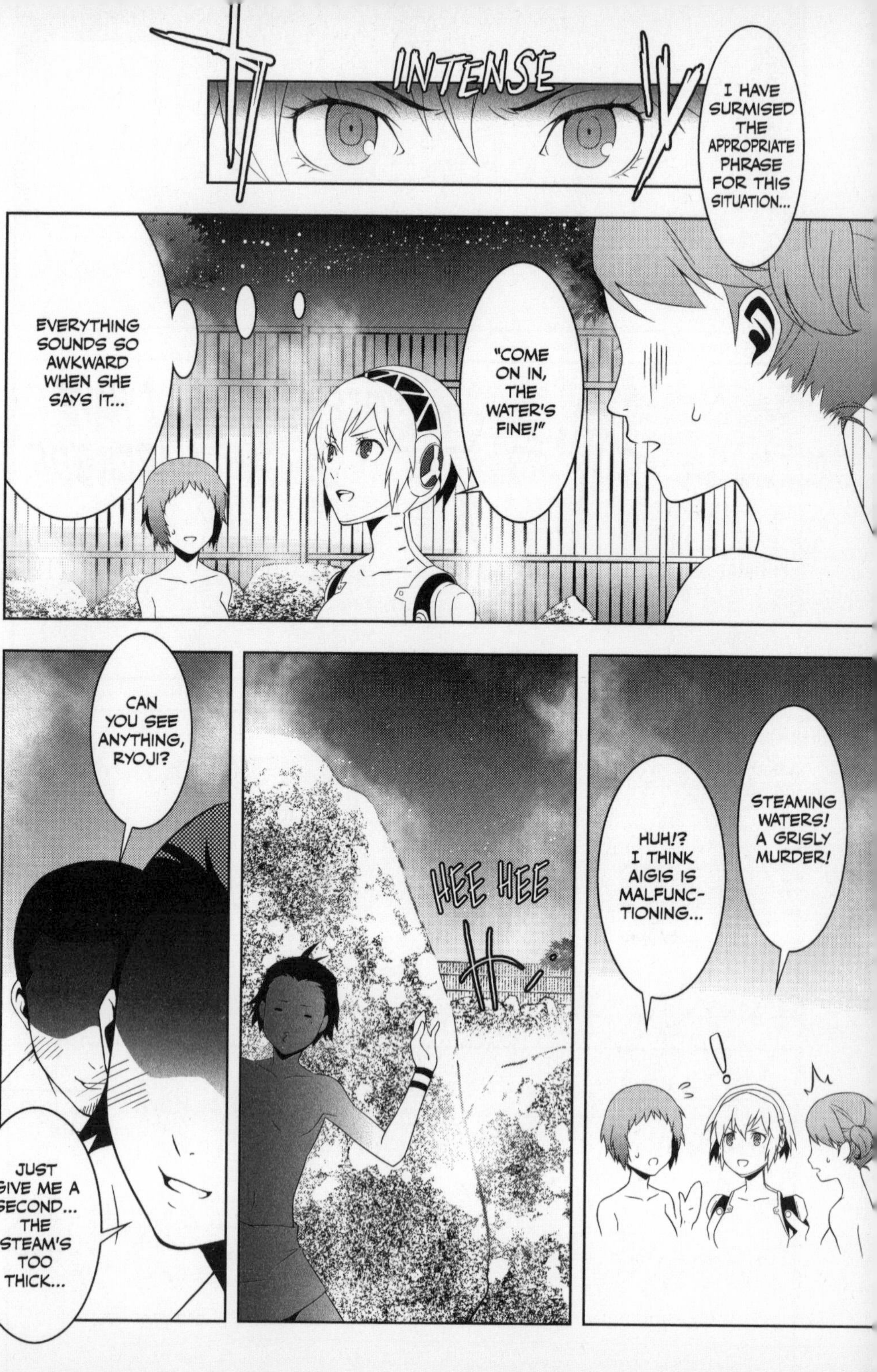
I HAVE SURMISED THE APPROPRIATE PHRASE FOR THIS SITUATION...
INTENSE
"COME ON IN, THE WATER'S FINE!"
EVERYTHING SOUNDS SO AWKWARD WHEN SHE SAYS IT...
STEAMING WATERS! A GRISLY MURDER!
HUH!? I THINK AIGIS IS MALFUNC-TIONING...
!
HEE HEE
CAN YOU SEE ANYTHING, RYOJI?
JUST GIVE ME A SECOND... THE STEAM'S TOO THICK...

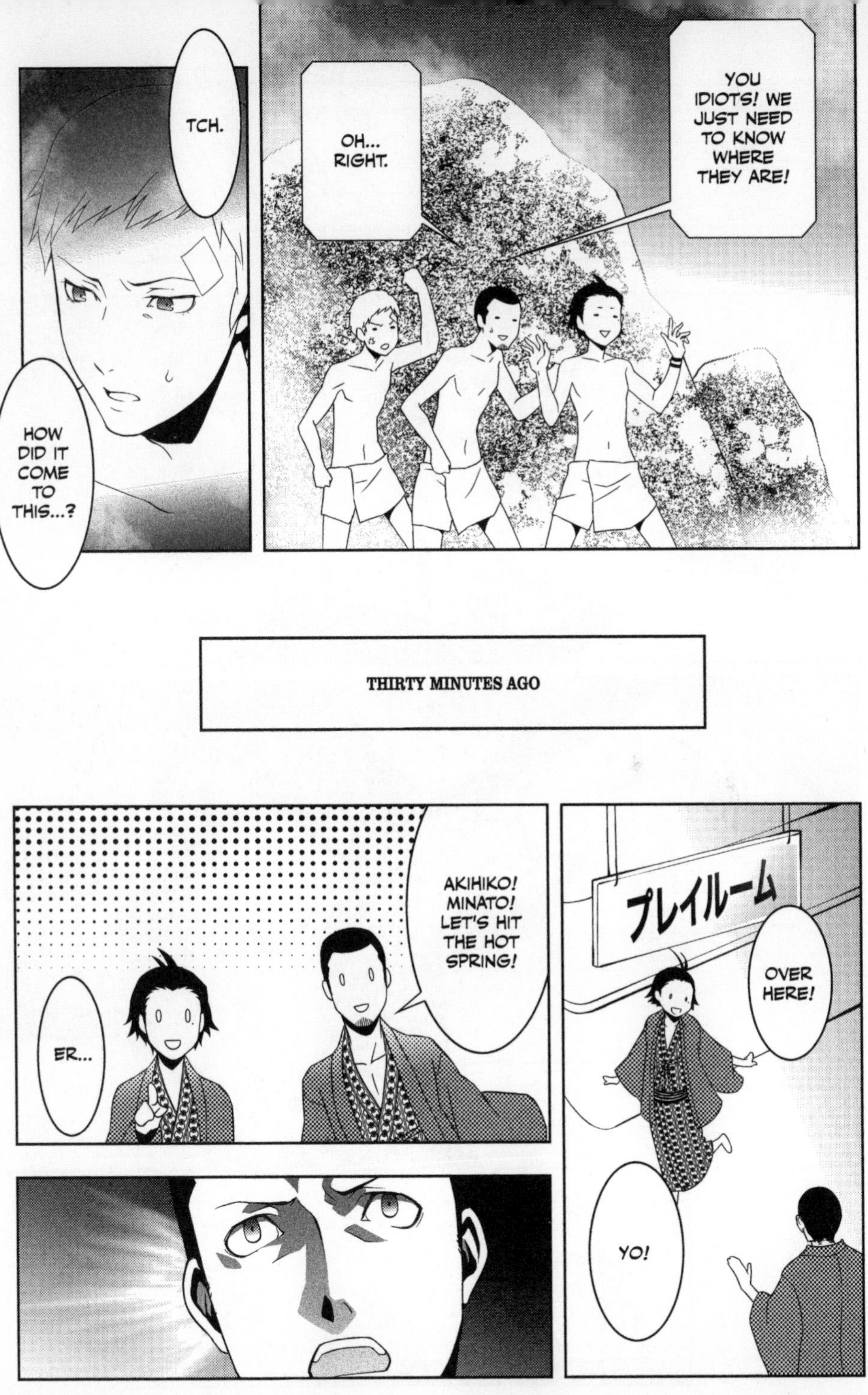
YOU IDIOTS! WE JUST NEED TO KNOW WHERE THEY ARE!
OH... RIGHT.
TCH.
HOW DID IT COME TO THIS...?
THIRTY MINUTES AGO
プレイルーム
OVER HERE!
YO!
AKIHIKO! MINATO! LET'S HIT THE HOT SPRING!
ER...

ZIIIP
PING PONG PING PONG

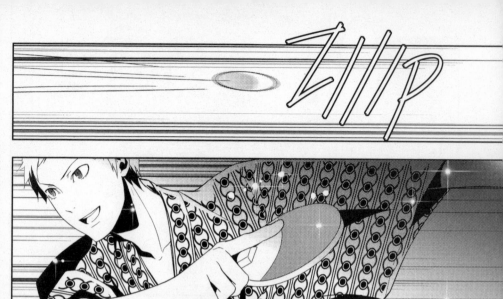

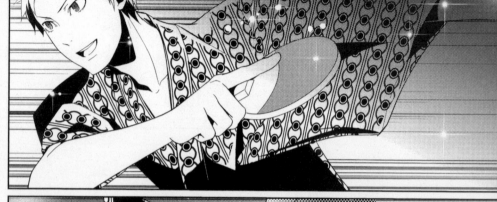

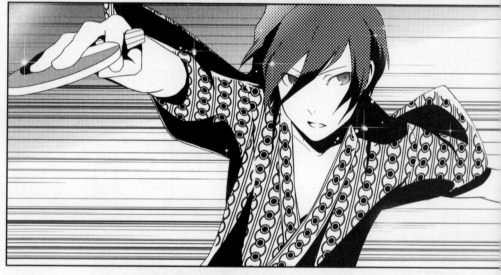

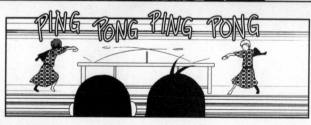

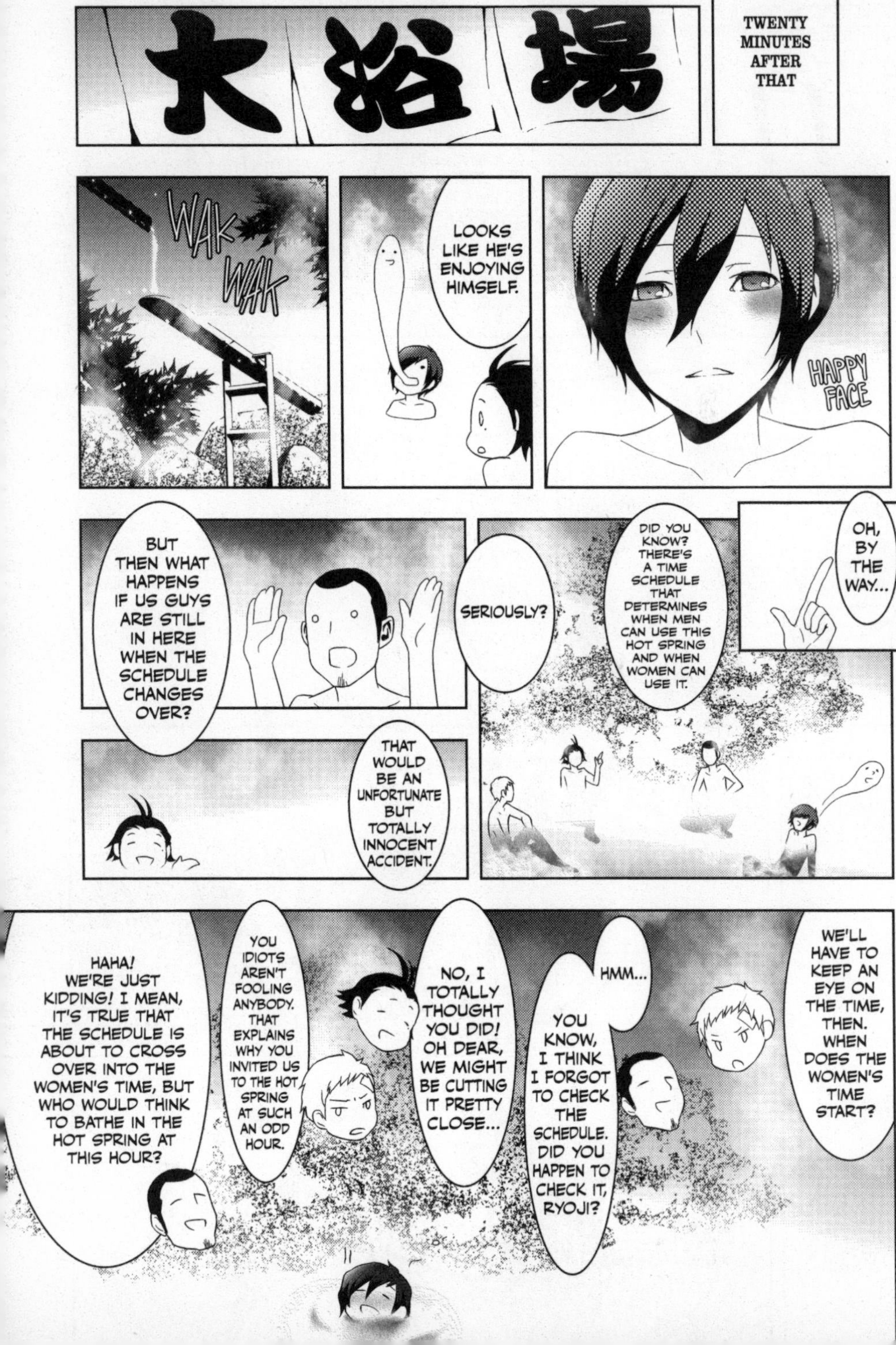
TWENTY MINUTES AFTER THAT
大浴場
HAPPY FACE
LOOKS LIKE HE'S ENJOYING HIMSELF.
WAK WAK
OH, BY THE WAY...
DID YOU KNOW? THERE'S A TIME SCHEDULE THAT DETERMINES WHEN MEN CAN USE THIS HOT SPRING AND WHEN WOMEN CAN USE IT.
SERIOUSLY?
BUT THEN WHAT HAPPENS IF US GUYS ARE STILL IN HERE WHEN THE SCHEDULE CHANGES OVER?
THAT WOULD BE AN UNFORTUNATE BUT TOTALLY INNOCENT ACCIDENT.
WE'LL HAVE TO KEEP AN EYE ON THE TIME, THEN. WHEN DOES THE WOMEN'S TIME START?
HMM...
YOU KNOW, I THINK I FORGOT TO CHECK THE SCHEDULE. DID YOU HAPPEN TO CHECK IT, RYOJI?
NO, I TOTALLY THOUGHT YOU DID! OH DEAR, WE MIGHT BE CUTTING IT PRETTY CLOSE...
YOU IDIOTS AREN'T FOOLING ANYBODY. THAT EXPLAINS WHY YOU INVITED US TO THE HOT SPRING AT SUCH AN ODD HOUR.
HAHA! WE'RE JUST KIDDING! I MEAN, IT'S TRUE THAT THE SCHEDULE IS ABOUT TO CROSS OVER INTO THE WOMEN'S TIME, BUT WHO WOULD THINK TO BATHE IN THE HOT SPRING AT THIS HOUR?

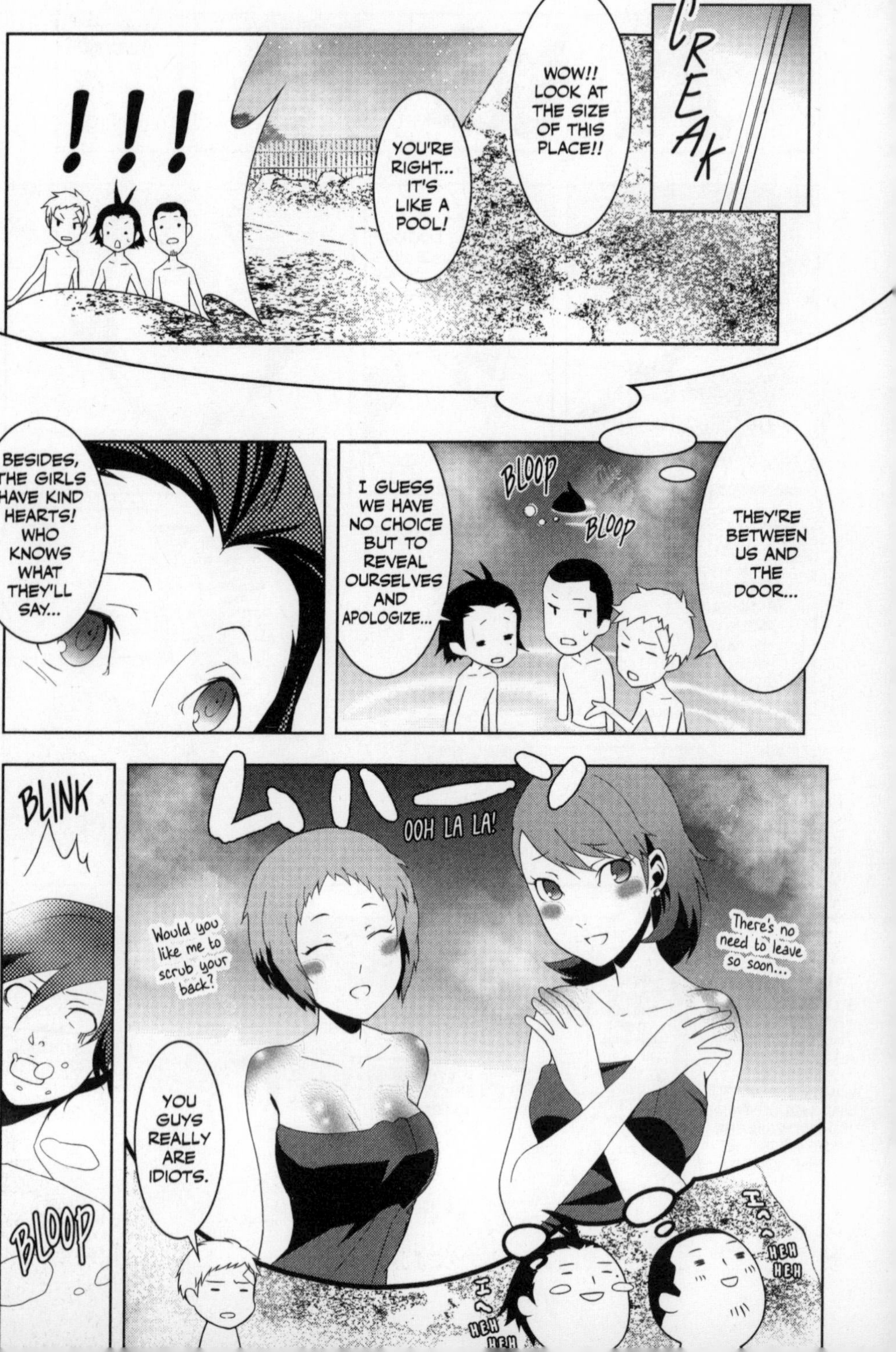
CREAK
WOW!! LOOK AT THE SIZE OF THIS PLACE!!
YOU'RE RIGHT... IT'S LIKE A POOL!
!!!
THEY'RE BETWEEN US AND THE DOOR...
BLOOP
BLOOP
I GUESS WE HAVE NO CHOICE BUT TO REVEAL OURSELVES AND APOLOGIZE...
BESIDES, THE GIRLS HAVE KIND HEARTS! WHO KNOWS WHAT THEY'LL SAY...
ムハー
OOH LA LA!
There's no need to leave so soon...
Would you like me to scrub your back?
HEH HEH
YOU GUYS REALLY ARE IDIOTS.
HEH HEH
BLINK
BLOOP

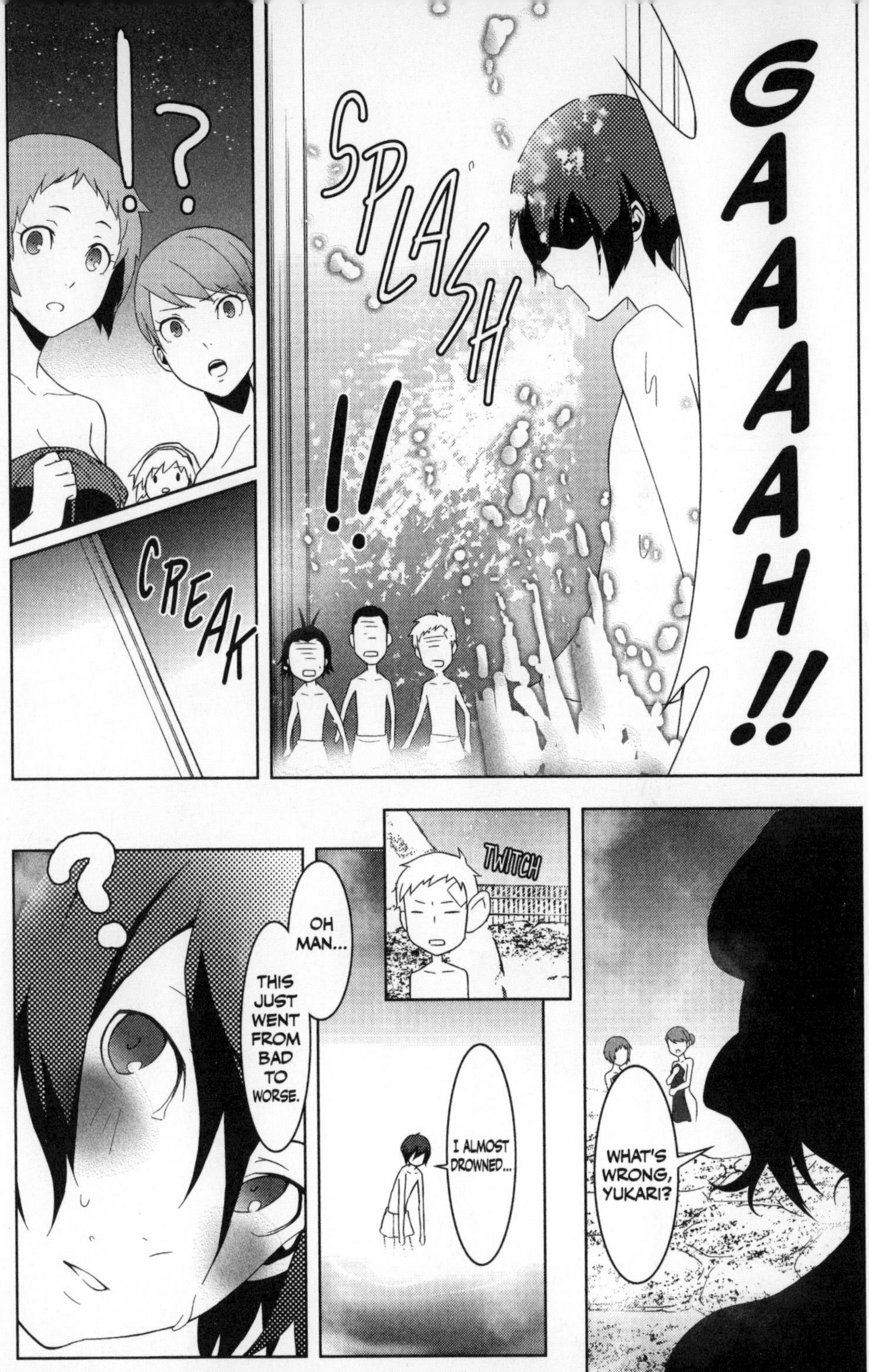
GAAAAH!!
SPLASH!!
!?
CREAK
WHAT'S WRONG, YUKARI?
TWITCH
OH MAN... THIS JUST WENT FROM BAD TO WORSE.
I ALMOST DROWNED...
?

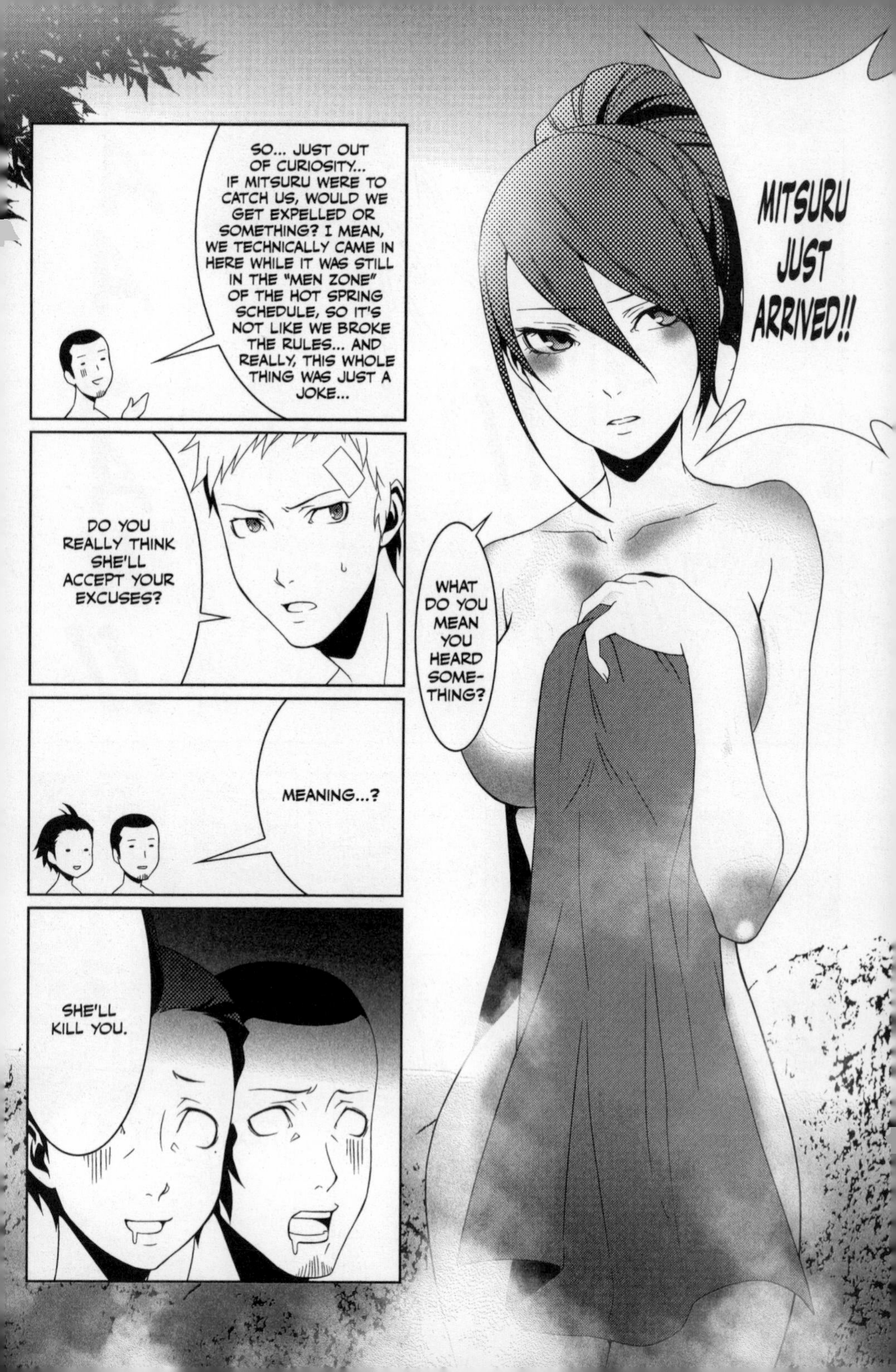
MITSURU JUST ARRIVED!!
WHAT DO YOU MEAN YOU HEARD SOMETHING?
SO... JUST OUT OF CURIOSITY... IF MITSURU WERE TO CATCH US, WOULD WE GET EXPELLED OR SOMETHING? I MEAN, WE TECHNICALLY CAME IN HERE WHILE IT WAS STILL IN THE "MEN ZONE" OF THE HOT SPRING SCHEDULE, SO IT'S NOT LIKE WE BROKE THE RULES... AND REALLY, THIS WHOLE THING WAS JUST A JOKE...
DO YOU REALLY THINK SHE'LL ACCEPT YOUR EXCUSES?
MEANING...?
SHE'LL KILL YOU.

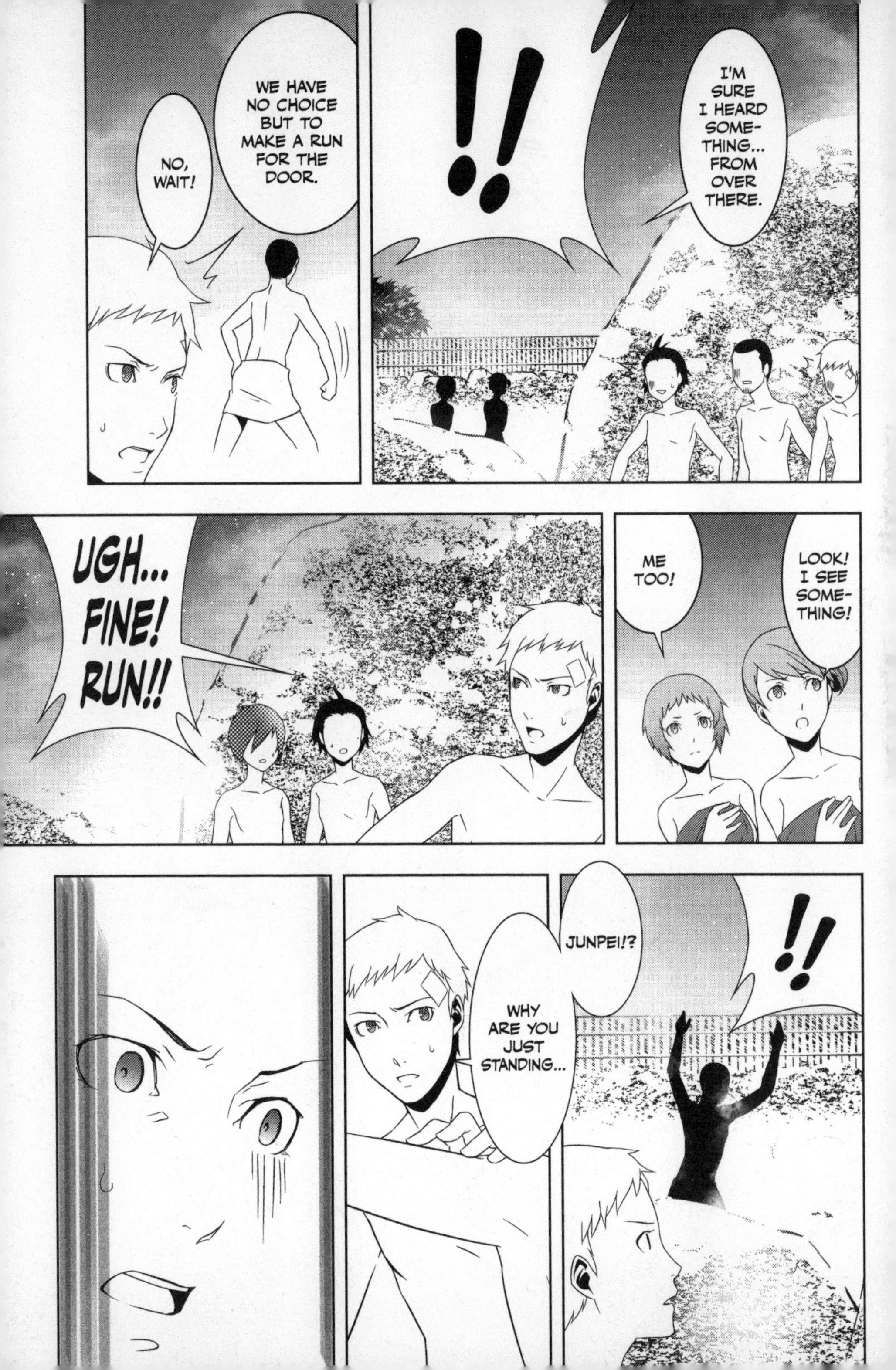
I'M SURE I HEARD SOMETHING... FROM OVER THERE.
!!
WE HAVE NO CHOICE BUT TO MAKE A RUN FOR THE DOOR.
NO, WAIT!
LOOK! I SEE SOMETHING!
ME TOO!
UGH... FINE! RUN!!
!!
JUNPEI!?
WHY ARE YOU JUST STANDING...

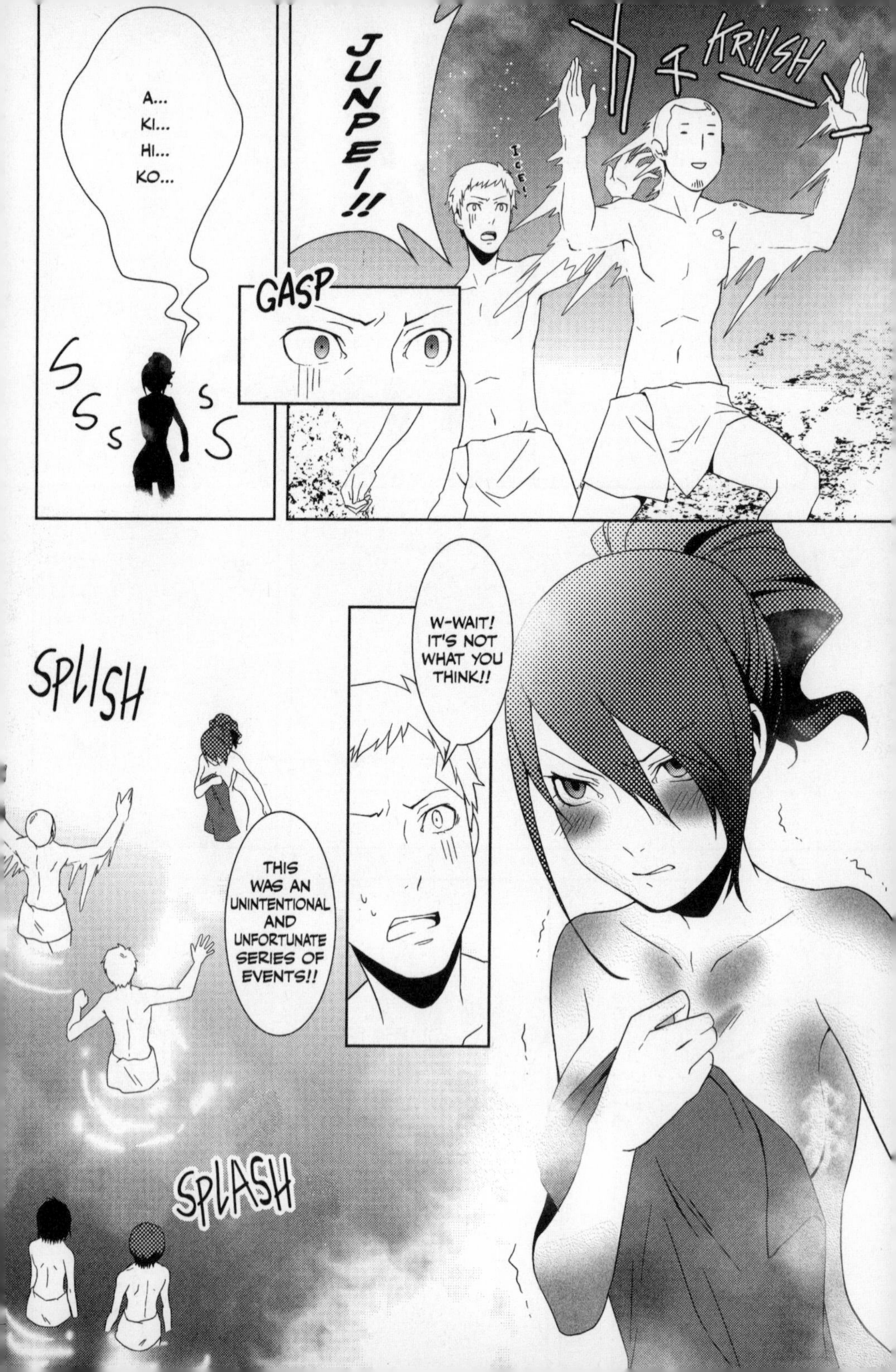

KRIISH
JUNPEI!!
ICE!
GASP
A... KI... HI... KO...
SSSS
W-WAIT! IT'S NOT WHAT YOU THINK!!
THIS WAS AN UNINTENTIONAL AND UNFORTUNATE SERIES OF EVENTS!!
SPLISH
SPLASH

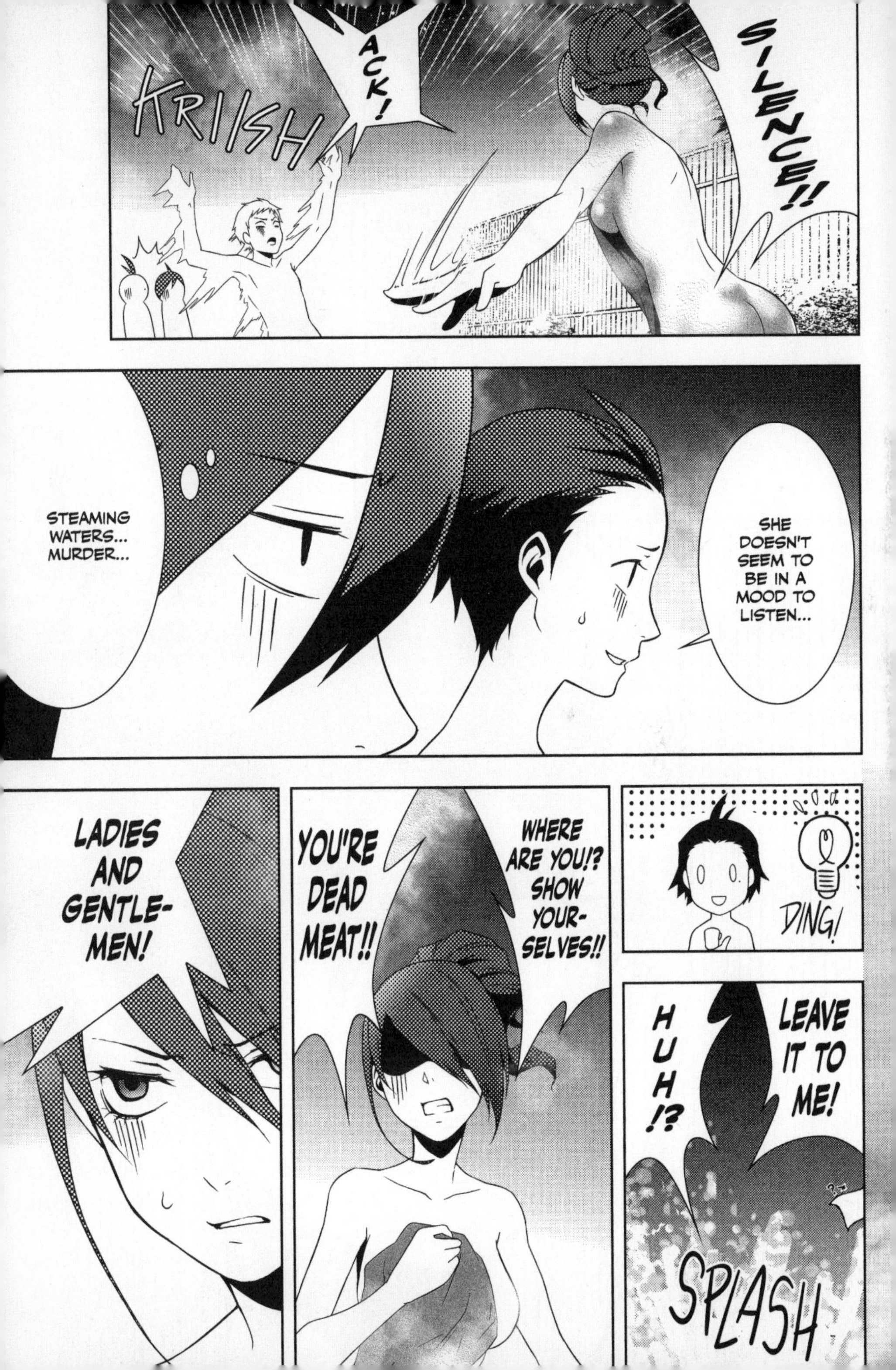

SILENCE!!
ACK!
KRIISH
SHE DOESN'T SEEM TO BE IN A MOOD TO LISTEN...
STEAMING WATERS... MURDER...
DING!
LEAVE IT TO ME!
HUH!?
SPLASH
WHERE ARE YOU!? SHOW YOUR-SELVES!!
YOU'RE DEAD MEAT!!
LADIES AND GENTLE-MEN!

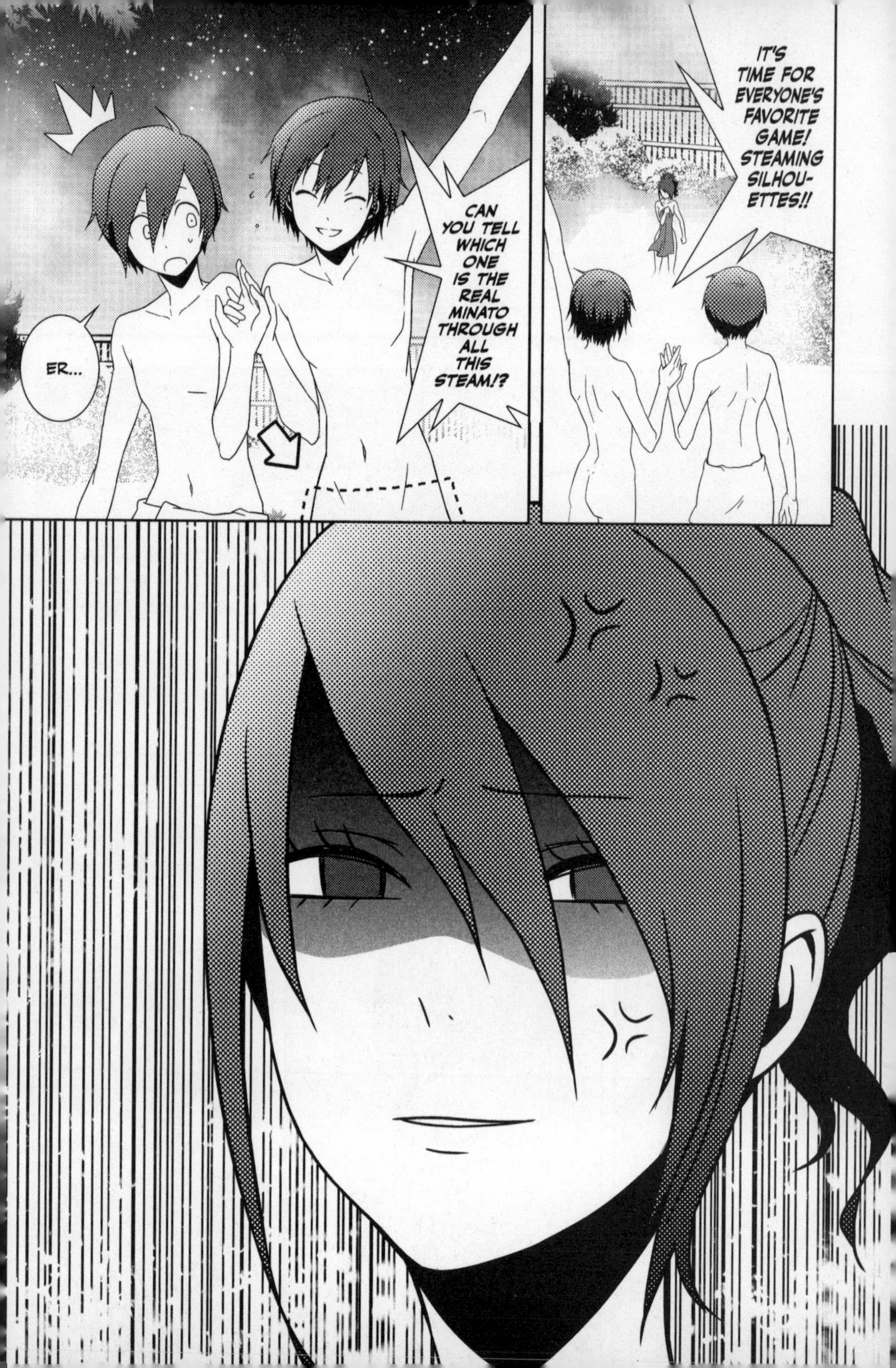
IT'S TIME FOR EVERYONE'S FAVORITE GAME! STEAMING SILHOU-ETTES!!
CAN YOU TELL WHICH ONE IS THE REAL MINATO THROUGH ALL THIS STEAM!?
ER...

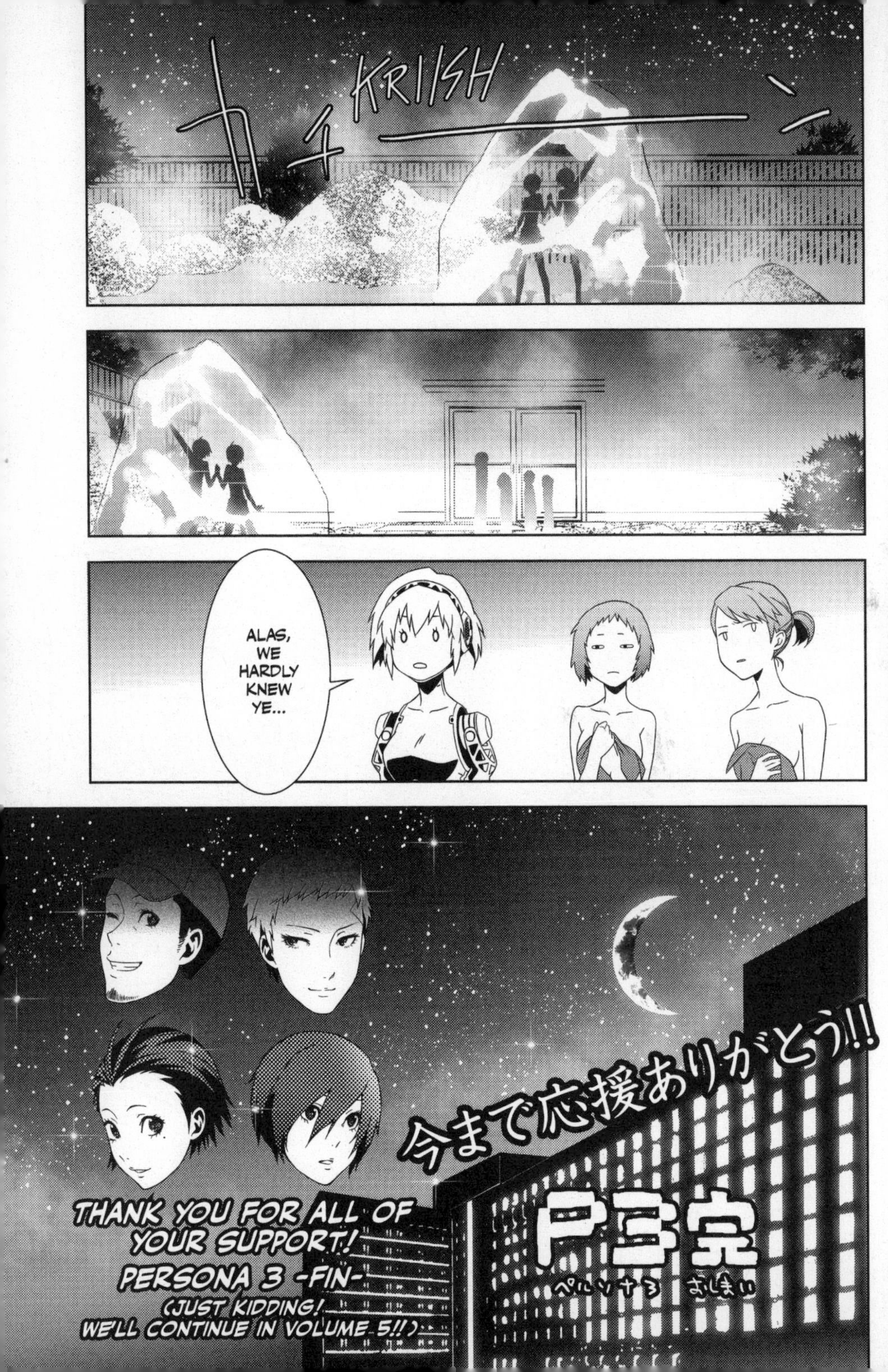
KRIISH
ALAS, WE HARDLY KNEW YE...
今まで応援ありがとう!!
P3完
ペルソナ3 おしまい
THANK YOU FOR ALL OF YOUR SUPPORT!
PERSONA 3 -FIN-
(JUST KIDDING! WE'LL CONTINUE IN VOLUME 5!!)

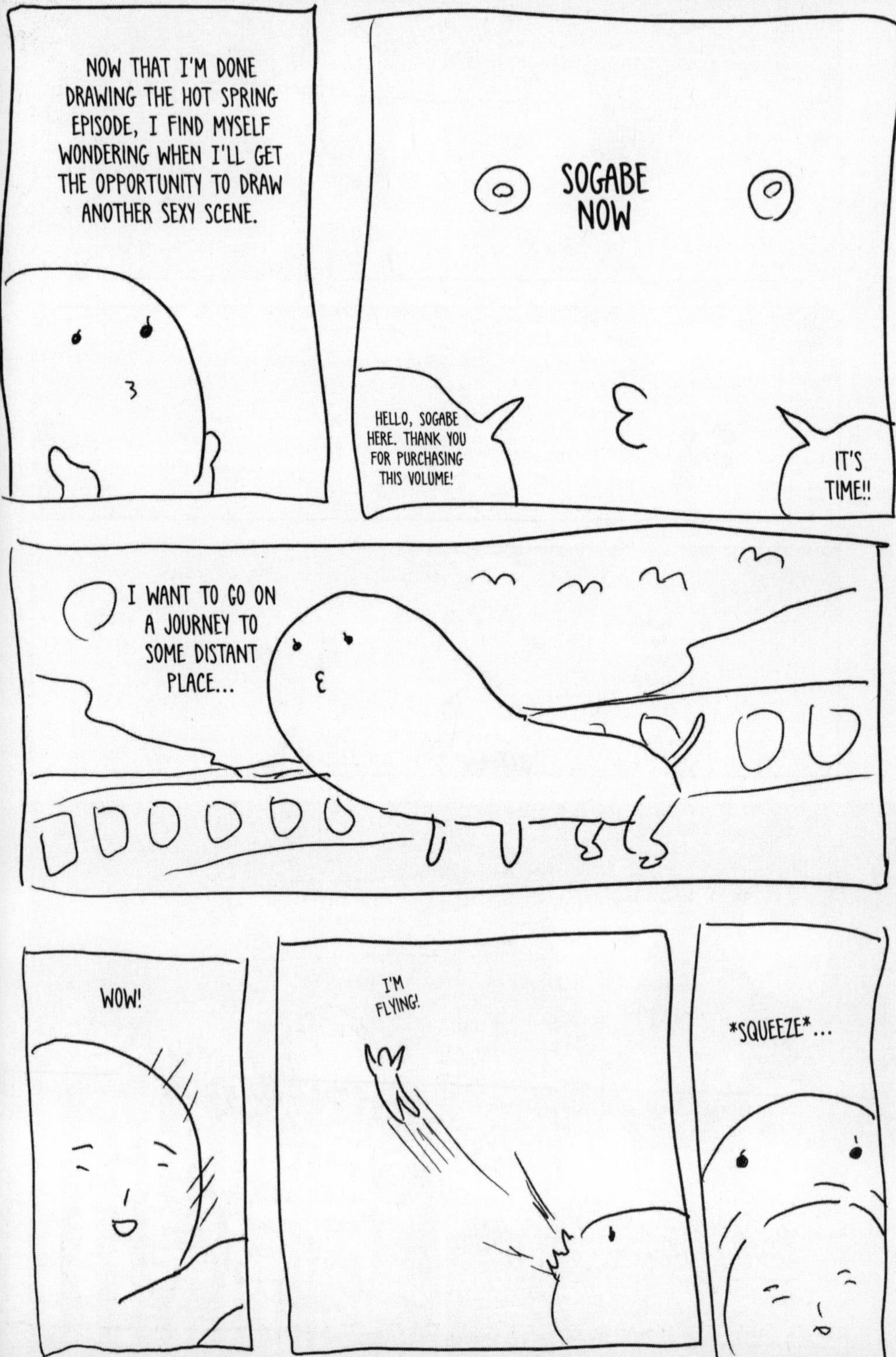
SOGABE NOW
HELLO, SOGABE HERE. THANK YOU FOR PURCHASING THIS VOLUME!
IT'S TIME!!
NOW THAT I'M DONE DRAWING THE HOT SPRING EPISODE, I FIND MYSELF WONDERING WHEN I'LL GET THE OPPORTUNITY TO DRAW ANOTHER SEXY SCENE.
I WANT TO GO ON A JOURNEY TO SOME DISTANT PLACE...
SQUEEZE...
I'M FLYING!
WOW!

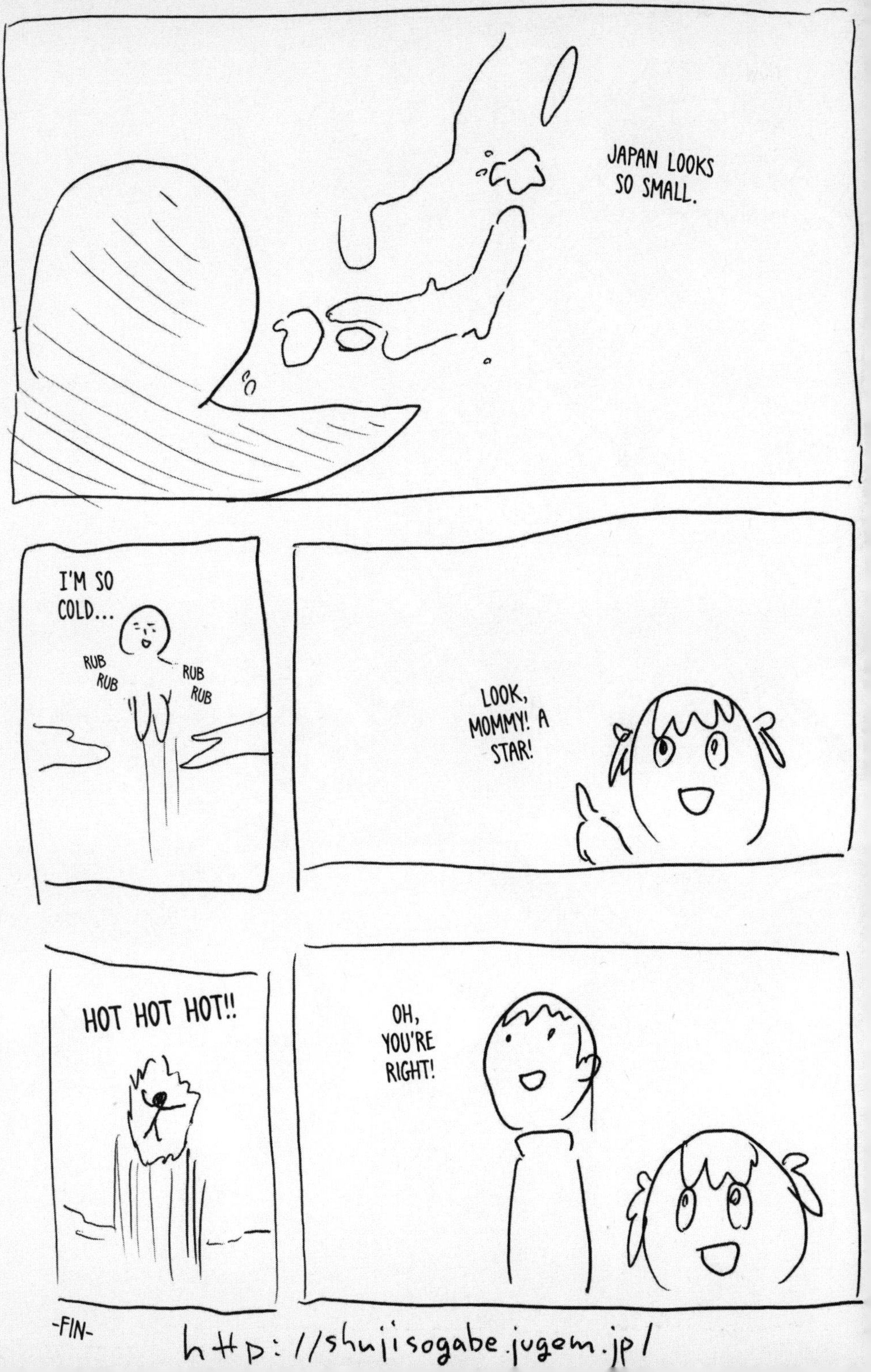
JAPAN LOOKS SO SMALL.
LOOK, MOMMY! A STAR!
I'M SO COLD...
RUB RUB
RUB RUB
OH, YOU'RE RIGHT!
HOT HOT HOT!!

-FIN-

http://shujisogabe.jugem.jp/

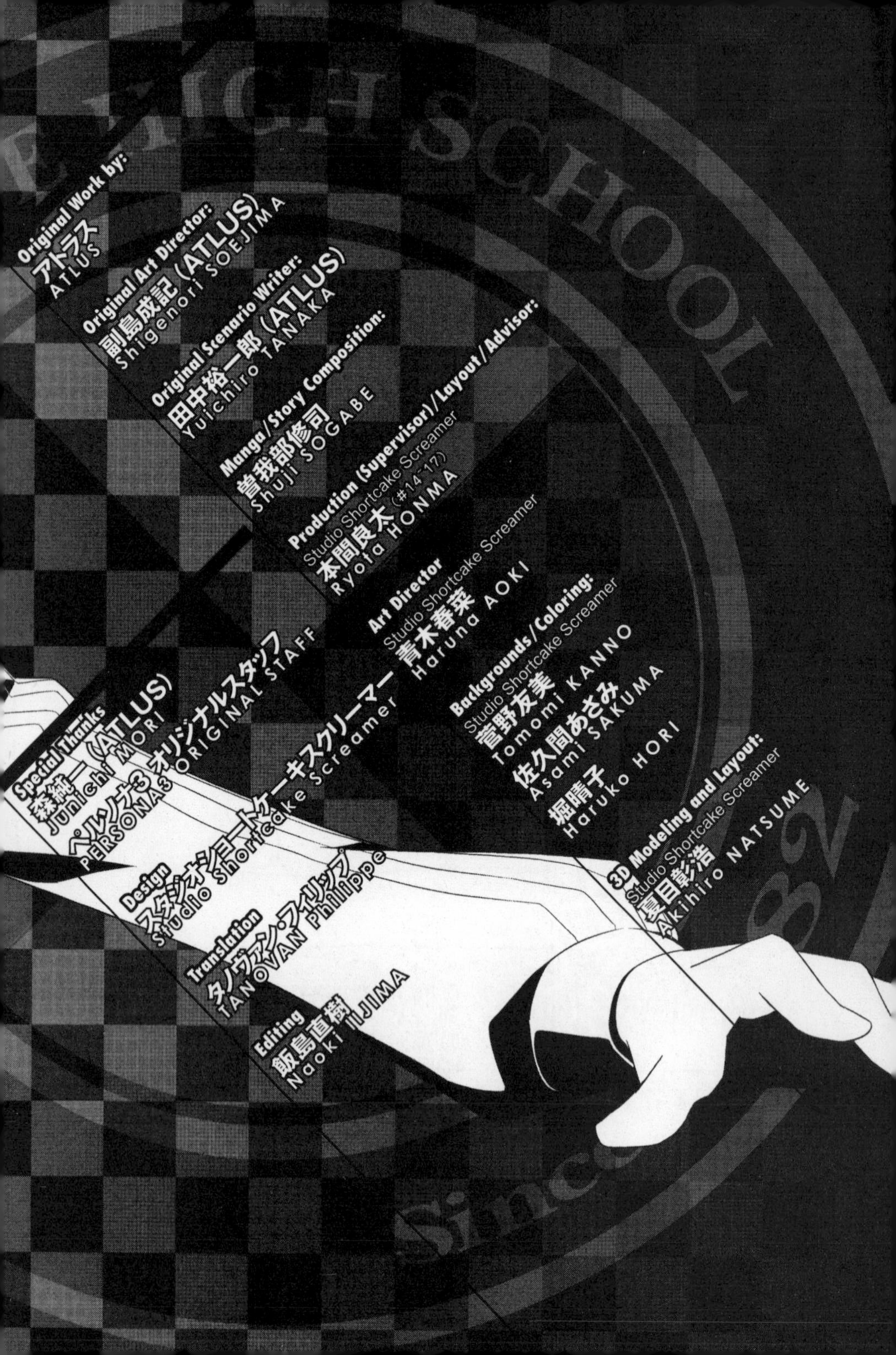

Original Work by:
アトラス
ATLUS
Original Art Director:
副島成記（ATLUS）
Shigenori SOEJIMA
Original Scenario Writer:
田中裕一郎（ATLUS）
Yuichiro TANAKA
Manga/Story Composition:
曽我部修司
Shuji SOGABE
Production (Supervisor)/Layout/Advisor:
Studio Shortcake Screamer
本間良太（#14~17）
Ryota HONMA
Art Director
Studio Shortcake Screamer
青木春菜
Haruna AOKI
Backgrounds/Coloring:
Studio Shortcake Screamer
菅野友美
Tomomi KANNO
佐久間あさみ
Asami SAKUMA
堀晴子
Haruko HORI
3D Modeling and Layout:
Studio Shortcake Screamer
夏目彰浩
Akihiro NATSUME
Special Thanks
森純一（ATLUS）
Junichi MORI
ペルソナ3オリジナルスタッフ
PERSONA3 ORIGINAL STAFF
Design
スタジオショートケーキスクリーマー
Studio Shortcake Screamer
Translation
タノヴァン・フィリップ
TANOVAN Philippe
Editing
飯島直樹
Naoki IIJIMA